ARTIFICIAL INTELLIGENCE AND INTERNATIONAL ECONOMIC LAW

Artificial intelligence (AI) technologies are transforming economies, societies, and geopolitics. Enabled by the exponential increase of data that is collected, transmitted, and processed transnationally, these changes have important implications for international economic law (IEL). This volume examines the dynamic interplay between AI and IEL by addressing an array of critical new questions, including: How to conceptualize, categorize, and analyze AI for purposes of IEL? How is AI affecting established concepts and rubrics of IEL? Is there a need to reconfigure IEL, and if so, how? Contributors also respond to other cross-cutting issues, including digital inequality, data protection, algorithms and ethics, the regulation of AI-use cases (autonomous vehicles), and systemic shifts in e-commerce (digital trade) and industrial production (fourth industrial revolution).

Shin-yi Peng is Distinguished Professor of Law at National Tsing Hua University. She specializes in international trade law, with a focus on trade in services, digital trade and increasingly data governance. She is a former Commissioner of the National Communications Commission of Taiwan and has served as Vice President of the Society of International Economic Law. Professor Peng is also a member of the Indicative List of Panelists for resolving WTO disputes. She tweets @pengshinyi.

Ching-Fu Lin is Associate Professor at National Tsing Hua University, where he teaches artificial intelligence law and policy, international law and global governance, and law and technology. He tweets @ChingFuLin.

Thomas Streinz is Adjunct Professor of Law and Executive Director, Guarini Global Law & Tech at New York University School of Law. He co-convenes the Guarini Colloquium: Regulating Global Digital Corporations and co-teaches a course on Global Data Law. His research encompasses global digital governance, global law and technology, and the regulation of the global data economy. He tweets @t_streinz.

This title is also available as Open Access on Cambridge Core with funding support by the Erasmus+ Programme of the European Union.

Artificial Intelligence and International Economic Law

DISRUPTION, REGULATION, AND RECONFIGURATION

Edited by

SHIN-YI PENG

National Tsing Hua University

CHING-FU LIN

National Tsing Hua University

THOMAS STREINZ

New York University School of Law

CAMBRIDGE
UNIVERSITY PRESS

CAMBRIDGE
UNIVERSITY PRESS

University Printing House, Cambridge CB2 8BS, United Kingdom

One Liberty Plaza, 20th Floor, New York, NY 10006, USA

477 Williamstown Road, Port Melbourne, VIC 3207, Australia

314–321, 3rd Floor, Plot 3, Splendor Forum, Jasola District Centre, New Delhi – 110025, India

103 Penang Road, #05–06/07, Visioncrest Commercial, Singapore 238467

Cambridge University Press is part of the University of Cambridge.

It furthers the University's mission by disseminating knowledge in the pursuit of education, learning, and research at the highest international levels of excellence.

www.cambridge.org
Information on this title: www.cambridge.org/9781108844932
DOI: 10.1017/9781108954006

Published with the support of the Erasmus+ Program me of the European Union

When citing this work, please include a reference to the DOI 10.1017/9781108954006

First published 2021

A catalogue record for this publication is available from the British Library.

ISBN 978-1-108-84493-2 Hardback

Contents

Figures

Contributors

Yi-Shyuan Chiang LLM candidate at the National Tsing Hua University Institute of Law for Science and Technology

Dan Ciuriak Director and Principal, Ciuriak Consulting Inc. (Ottawa); Senior Fellow with the Centre for International Governance Innovation (Waterloo); Fellow-in-Residence with the CD Howe Institute (Toronto); Distinguished Fellow with the Asia Pacific Foundation of Canada (Vancouver)

Rachel R. Du Master of Advanced Studies in International Law and Economics (MILE), World Trade Institute, University of Bern

Yuka Fukunaga Professor, Waseda University

Henry Gao Associate Professor of Law, Singapore Management University

Alan Hervé Professor and Jean Monnet Chair, Sciences Po Rennes

Aik Hoe Lim Director, Trade and Environment Division, World Trade Organization

Ching-Fu Lin Associate Professor of Law, National Tsing Hua University

Bryan Mercurio Simon FS Li Professor of Law, Chinese University of Hong Kong

Neha Mishra Lecturer, ANU College of Law, Australian National University

Shin-yi Peng Distinguished Professor of Law, National Tsing Hua University

Vlada Rodionova Associate, Ciuriak Consulting Inc.

Gregory Shaffer Chancellor's Professor of Law, University of California, Irvine

Kelly K. Shang Fellow, World Trade Institute, University of Bern

Thomas Streinz Adjunct Professor of Law and Executive Director, Guarini Global Law & Tech, New York University School of Law

Lisa Toohey Professor of Law and Deputy Head (Research) at Newcastle Law School, University of Newcastle, Australia

Rolf H. Weber Professor for International Business and Economic Law, Faculty of Law, University of Zurich; Practicing Attorney-at-Law, Zurich

Jane K. Winn Professor of Law, University of Washington School of Law

Ronald Yu Research Associate, Chinese University of Hong Kong

Raphael Zingg Assistant Professor, Waseda University, Institute for Advanced Study, Tokyo; Research Affiliate at the ETH Zurich, Center for Law and Economics

Frederike Zufall Senior Research Fellow, Max Planck Institute for Research on Collective Goods, Bonn, Germany; Adjunct Researcher, Waseda Institute for Advanced Study, Tokyo

Preface

The chapters assembled in this volume were written on machines distributed across four continents by humans who have devoted a significant part of their professional lives to studying and practicing international economic law.

Most authors met in person in Taipei in the fall of 2019 for the Society of International Economic Law's (SIEL's) Asian International Economic Law Network (AIELN) sixth biennial conference, *International Trade Regime for the Data-Driven Economy: How Will Artificial Intelligence Transform International Economic Law?*, organized by the Institute of Law for Science and Technology at National Tsing Hua University (NTHU). The editors and contributors are grateful to the chairs, discussants, and participants on various panels for their inputs, which fueled the momentum for our collective endeavor. The programmatic theme of the conference animated our discussions then and laid the groundwork for the framing of this book. Our insights were further developed and refined through scholarly debates and discussions and are now the joint product of twenty-one authors.

We thank the many humans who made this event, and by extension this volume, possible. We would like to express our gratitude to the anonymous reviewers of the book proposal for all their critical comments on the book as a whole, as well as on individual chapters. We thank Sally Evans-Darby for her careful editing of the final manuscript. We would also like to acknowledge a number of promising graduate students at NTHU – thanks go to Sharu Luo for his excellent editorial work as well as I-Ching Chen, Yen-Chieh Lin, and Tzu-Yin Hsu for their coordinative assistance.

This collaborative project received generous financial and technical support from SIEL and AIELN, Taiwan's Ministry of Science and Technology, the Research Center for Humanities and Social Sciences at NTHU, and the Jean Monnet Network – Trade & Investment in Services Associates (TIISA), co-funded by the Erasmus+ Programme of the European Union. We are particularly thankful to TIISA Director Jane Drake-Brockman and other steering committee members who have been generous in sharing their expertise, and for the funding from the Erasmus+ Programme of the European Union that makes this book freely available online under a Creative Commons Open Access license. Last but not least, we are indebted to Matt Gallaway, Cameron Daddis, and the rest of the team at Cambridge University Press for their invaluable guidance and support throughout the publication process.

This book was finalized while countries around the world were still confronting a global public health crisis caused by the COVID-19 pandemic. Many came to rely on digital services as an infrastructure for social interaction and professional endeavors, including academic and educational work. The pandemic seems to have precipitated a further shift toward digital technologies and artificial intelligence. It is our hope that this book will contribute to an informed discussion about the relevance of and implications for international economic law beyond the pandemic.

1

Artificial Intelligence and International Economic Law

A Research and Policy Agenda

Shin-yi Peng, Ching-Fu Lin, and Thomas Streinz

I INTRODUCTION

By approaching the complex set of phenomena the term "artificial intelligence" (AI) encapsulates from the vantage point of international economic law (IEL), we aim to advance the discourse surrounding the ways in which the development and use of AI transform economies, societies, and (geo)politics. We raise what we regard as important but also daunting questions regarding how IEL might, for better or worse, shape these developments – while being transformed itself in the process, both substantively and practically.

These questions include foundational clarifications about the nature, scope, and transformative potential of AI. In this context, it is essential to distinguish not only between different kinds of AI – ultimately an underspecified umbrella term – but also between what already exists, what is yet to come, and what might only materialize in the distant future (if ever). Moreover, even within (relatively) clearly defined forms or fields of existing AI, there is considerable variation in the methods and technologies used. For these reasons, the traditional lawyerly task of "defining AI" is caught between the Scylla of variety and specificity and the Charybdis of vagueness and expansiveness, which may jeopardize (if not eliminate) practical usefulness. In other words, while it is certainly possible to define AI as a field of inquiry or as an umbrella term for algorithms and robots with certain functionalities, comprehensive legal analysis requires a careful dissection of AI's constitutive parts and its applications. AI technologies constitute complex socio-technical systems involving humans, machines, algorithms, and data, and their deployment raises legal questions across a wide range of domains, including but not limited to data protection and privacy law, antidiscrimination law, intellectual property law, and tort law.

As the chapters in this volume illustrate, IEL speaks to various aspects of AI development, deployment, and use, as well as their corresponding regulation. In this chapter, we introduce three cross-cutting themes that illustrate the relationship between AI and IEL: disruption, regulation, and reconfiguration.

We begin by exploring the theme of continuity and *disruption*: we trace contemporary AI's foundational ideas back to the 1950s and explain how a combination of exponential growth in datafication and computing power enabled a certain AI technology – machine learning (ML) via "deep" neural networks (deep learning) – to advance in largely unexpected, and hence sometimes disruptive, ways since the mid-2000s. Contemporary ML's dependence on large datasets is but one illustration of how AI is generally intertwined with the digital transformation of the economy. While some of these transformations contribute to long standing goals of IEL, others stretch and potentially disrupt certain assumptions, under which IEL has developed since the creation of the General Agreement on Tariffs and Trade (GATT) in 1947 and the founding of the World Trade Organization (WTO) in 1995.

We then turn to the important theme of AI *regulation*, or indeed the absence thereof. The deployment of digital technologies, including AI-powered applications, has effects that can themselves be understood as regulatory in nature, as they enable certain activities (but not others), shape and condition human behavior, and expand and (re)allocate wealth and resources. They may also empower or diminish people. Growing concerns about the adverse impact of AI technology, especially with regard to patterns of inequality, exclusion, and outright discrimination, have led to a plethora of initiatives that seek to regulate AI technology through often overlapping but ultimately rather vague value sets (often emphasizing human-centered design and fundamental principles of ethics). These initiatives aspire to have a transformative effect on the technological development and societal deployment of AI, which is fundamentally driven by the academic-industrial complex and in significant part regulated by various, often transnational, standard-setting bodies. Governments have only slowly begun to confront AI-enabled transformations through legislative and regulatory action, with the European Union (EU) emerging as the most aggressive AI regulator. IEL provides a (meta)regulatory framework that aspires to govern these regulatory initiatives. Yet IEL's traditional focus on state-led regulation and its preference for multilateralism pose particular challenges in this regard.

All of these developments raise the question of IEL's ongoing and future *reconfiguration*. Several traditional domains of IEL, especially its multilateral trade dispute settlement system and the largely bilateral albeit widespread web of investor–state dispute settlement mechanisms, have been under pressure to reform and adapt. Major geopolitical shifts, most notably the rise of China, have called into question the WTO's relevance, as well as its capacity to sustain a quasi-universal multilateral trading system and prevent the "decoupling" of major trading blocs. The digital transformation of the global economy, which is in significant part influenced by the development and deployment of AI, adds further pressure to reconfigure the procedural, substantive, and enforcement aspects of IEL. Ultimately, AI technologies could be deployed to reconfigure the practice of IEL itself. Along these lines, we assess the extent to which IEL has already been reconfigured and explore the need for further reconfiguration.

In the following, we expand on the three themes of disruption, regulation, and reconfiguration that permeate the volume. Ultimately, this book seeks to engineer a broader discourse around AI and IEL as a field of scholarly inquiry and technologically informed legal practice. To this end, we conclude this introduction by bringing the contributions we assembled in this volume into conversation with one another and identify topics that warrant further research.

II THE (RE)EMERGENCE OF ARTIFICIAL INTELLIGENCE AND THE TRANSFORMATION OF THE GLOBAL ECONOMY

AI is often grouped together with other "disruptive" technologies, as Clayton Christensen's influential theory of innovation has entered the mainstream.[1] In this section, we explore the theme of disruption with regard to AI along three dimensions: first, we show how, *technologically*, the emergence of contemporary AI demonstrates remarkable continuity with ideas from the 1950s that only came to fruition after the 2000s because of exponential increases in computing power and the availability of large datasets. Second, we explain how, *economically*, AI, in combination with other digital technologies, is gradually but significantly transforming the global economy. Third, we show how these transformations lead to *legal* disruptions of longstanding assumptions and conceptualizations on which IEL has come to rely. This trifecta of AI-related technological, economic, and legal change is not a force of nature but is, rather, the result of human ingenuity in pursuit of innovation, efficiency, and profit maximization.[2]

A *Artificial Intelligence's Technological Development*

As we noted earlier, the term "artificial intelligence" is difficult to neatly define for legal purposes.[3] The term is being used in various interdisciplinary research communities encompassing computer and data science, philosophy and ethics, as well as the study of human and machine minds by psychology, cognitive science, and neuroscience. Even within computer science, definitions and related aspirations for AI differ.[4] The term's invention is usually credited to John McCarthy and his

1 CM Christensen, *The Innovator's Dilemma: When New Technologies Cause Great Firms to Fail* (Boston, Harvard Business School Press, 1997). For a sharp critique of the use of the term in the tech discourse see A Daub, "The Disruption Con: Why Big Tech's Favourite Buzzword Is Nonsense" (*The Guardian*, 24 September 2020), https://perma.cc/92VM-WM58.

2 This is not to say that these are the only objectives that could or should be pursued; see, for example, the innovation-skeptical account by L Vinsel and AL Russell, *The Innovation Delusion: How Our Obsession with the New Has Disrupted the Work That Matters Most* (New York, Currency, 2020).

3 See also the chapter by Mercurio and Yu in this volume (Chapter 7), which uses the definition adopted by the World Intellectual Property Organization (WIPO).

4 "Artificial Intelligence and Life in 2030: One Hundred Year Study on Artificial Intelligence – Report of the 2015 Study Panel" (2016), https://ai100.stanford.edu, at 12 (claiming that the "lack of a precise,

collaborators, who convened the legendary 1956 workshop at Dartmouth to investigate "the conjecture that every aspect of learning or any other feature of intelligence can in principle be so precisely described that a machine can be made to simulate it."[5] This definition still encapsulates the field of AI research today.[6] It also identified human intelligence as the relevant benchmark against which developments of artificial or machine intelligence are to be assessed. One well-known, albeit reductive, instantiation of this idea is the Turing test.[7] Inversely, the AI effect denotes the phenomenon that once machines have mastered a task that used to be accomplished exclusively by humans, the task itself is no longer deemed to require "intelligence."[8] Another paradox is that what is easy for humans is often hard for machines.[9] Increasingly, however, human intelligence is being displaced as the relevant benchmark for what counts as "intelligence."[10]

In any case, humans are not merely a baseline by which to assess advances in AI. They also make decisions about how AI is developed and deployed at every point along the way. Mentioning this fact may seem trite, but it appears to be necessary in light of the frequent confusion between the (limited) autonomy of AI applications on the one hand and the essential roles that (largely) autonomous humans play in AI development and deployment on the other. This includes the human labor-intensive tasks of data preparation and model selection and training.[11]

AI development is a complex process, with humans, machines, algorithms, and data serving as its key components (see Figure 1.1). AI problem domains range from perception, reasoning, knowledge-generation, and planning to communication. The AI paradigms invoked to tackle these challenges include logic- and knowledge-based modeling (where human rationales and expertise are turned into code), statistical methods (including traditional probabilistic methods, now encompassed by "data science"), and subsymbolic systems that venture toward distributed and evolutionary AI.[12]

The most important AI technology today is deep learning, a machine learning technique based on neural networks of several ("deep") layers (hence "deep"

universally accepted definition of AI probably has helped the field to grow, blossom, and advance at an ever-accelerating pace").

5 J McCarthy et al., "A Proposal for the Dartmouth Summer Research Project on Artificial Intelligence" (31 May 1955), reprinted in (2006) 27 *AI Magazine* 12, at 12.

6 An excellent introduction to contemporary AI and its history is provided by M Mitchell, *Artificial Intelligence: A Guide for Thinking Humans* (London, Picador, 2019).

7 AP Saygin et al., "Turing Test: 50 Years Later" (2000) 10 *Minds and Machines* 463.

8 D Hofstadter, *Gödel, Escher, Bach: An Eternal Golden Braid* (New York, Basic Books, 1979), at 609 (allegedly misquoting Larry Tesler, who said: "Intelligence is whatever *machines* haven't done yet," with emphasis added to highlight the divergence).

9 M Minsky, *The Society of Mind* (New York, Simon and Schuster, 1986), at 29.

10 S Dick, "Artificial Intelligence" (2019) 1.1 *Harvard Data Science Review*.

11 D Lehr and P Ohm, "Playing with the Data: What Legal Scholars Should Learn About Machine Learning" (2017) 51 *UC Davis Law Review* 653.

12 See the helpful visualization in F Corea, *An Introduction to Data: Everything You Need to Know About AI, Big Data and Data Science* (Cham, Springer, 2019), at 26.

learning).[13] The basic idea behind this kind of ML dates back to the 1960s: deep neural networks simulate the processes through which neurons in the human brain make determinations about the world. It is ultimately a process of pattern recognition on the basis of large datasets. Initial enthusiasm for the idea dissipated, as alternative routes of AI development seemed more promising until the 1990s. It was only after sufficiently large datasets became available after the 2000s and the computing power necessary to compute these amounts of data was readily available that deep learning finally took off. Achievements that had been presumed to be out of reach in the near future became possible within surprisingly short timeframes.

AlphaGo's stunning success against one of the world's leading Go players, Lee Sedol, was enabled by deep learning, which trained the algorithms toward maximizing win probability and produced a nonhuman move that stunned Go experts.[14] Its later iteration, AlphaZero, was trained entirely by playing against itself and mastered the games of Go, chess, and shogi.[15] In addition, the prospect of autonomous driving vehicles has attracted significant attention. The Defense Advanced Research Projects Agency (DARPA), the US defense research organization also responsible for funding the Internet's foundational technology, launched its "Grand Challenge" for self-driving vehicles in 2004. The goal was to travel 150 miles through the Mojave Desert but no car reached the finish line, with the furthest advancing vehicle getting stuck after traversing less than eight miles. One year later, this marker was surpassed by all but one of the twenty-three finalists, and five cars completed the full distance of 132 miles. Suddenly, the prospect of (more or less) autonomous vehicles seemed to become a more near-term possibility – with implications for both AI regulation and IEL.[16]

The remarkable progress made by AI technology over the course of the last two decades notwithstanding, contemporary AI technology's significant limitations must not be ignored. In this regard, one can distinguish between tasks that AI is not able to perform at all and tasks that AI is supposedly able to do but that are executed poorly and with adverse effects, potentially causing harm to humans. The latter is an issue that we will address further later when we discuss the relevance of IEL to AI regulation, including AI regulation meant to guard against AI-caused harms. The former deserves clarification at this point: AI remains far from what has been termed "artificial general intelligence" (AGI); that is, the ability to perform the human-like functions of reasoning, knowledge-generation, and planning *generally*.

[13] I Goodfellow et al., *Deep Learning* (Cambridge, MA, MIT Press, 2016); TJ Sejnowski, *The Deep Learning Revolution* (Cambridge, MA, MIT Press, 2018).

[14] Contrast IBM's "Deep Blue" victory against chess world champion Gary Kasparov in 1998, which symbolizes the achievements of AI in the pre-deep learning era but also indicates its limitations: the machine had to use its vast resources to analyze human-played matches in real time to calculate the best move.

[15] David Silver et al., "A General Reinforcement Learning Algorithm That Masters Chess, Shogi, and Go Through Self-Play" (2018) 362 *Science* 1140.

[16] See the chapters in this volume by Peng (Chapter 6) and Lin (Chapter 12).

Contemporary AI remains largely limited to *discrete tasks* for which the algorithms have been trained with large datasets. Nondiscrete tasks, or tasks for which no reliable datasets exist, are beyond the ambit of contemporary AI technology. Companies that claim otherwise are often in the business of selling AI snake oil.[17] These limitations notwithstanding, the impact of AI technology on the global economy, to which we next turn, is already tangible and is likely to increase over the course of the next decade.

B *Artificial Intelligence and the Digital Transformation of the Global Economy*

As we have seen, the resurgence of AI and its transformative potential are intertwined with other technological developments in the global economy, most notably digitalization, computation, and interconnectedness, the latter of which is made possible by the Internet. AI relies on these foundational technologies of the digital era and coexists in synergy with other advanced digital technologies. For these reasons, our volume does not address AI in isolation but, rather, considers AI in the context of other transformative digital technologies, most notably "big data," cloud computing, the Internet of Things (IoT), and new forms of robotics.

Big data is often used quasi-synonymously with AI, but it is worth distinguishing between the two concepts to understand their respective impact on the global economy. Big data denotes the generation and analysis of datasets whose quantity surpasses human comprehension – only through machine-provided computing power can the available data be "mined" and insight gleaned from it.[18] However, the fact that because of its large quantity, big data cannot be analyzed by humans without help from machines in itself does not justify its designation as a form of (human-comparable) "intelligence." It is only when data analysis resorts to ML methods through which the algorithms themselves detect those patterns that justify a certain conclusion or prediction that it is appropriate to refer to AI. Contemporary data science teaches the statistical foundations of data analytics (including Bayesian networks) but increasingly includes and trends toward the use of ML to glean insights from data. Both technologies are dependent on large quantities of data, thereby transforming data into an important yet contested resource in the AI economy.[19]

The data on which both big data analytics and AI rely flow through the interconnected networks that constitute the Internet. Cloud computing builds on this

[17] A Narayanan, "How to Recognize AI Snake Oil" (Arthur Miller lecture on science and ethics, Massachusetts Institute of Technology, 18 November 2019), www.cs.princeton.edu/~arvindn/talks.

[18] V Mayer-Schönberger and K Cukier, *Big Data: A Revolution That Will Transform How We Live, Work, and Think* (London, John Murray, 2014).

[19] See the chapter in this volume on regulating data as a resource under IEL by Streinz (Chapter 9); see also Zufall and Zingg's chapter (Chapter 11) on data portability as a way to reallocate data.

underlying infrastructure and makes data storage and processing capabilities available at a distance ("infrastructure as a service," or IaaS). AI development is increasingly reliant on and in symbiosis with cloud computing. As part of their "platform as a service" (PaaS) business, cloud providers offer virtual AI development environments that integrate access to large datasets and libraries of algorithms. AI-enabled services, for example the translation of text or the transcription of audio recordings, can be offered on a cloud basis ("software as a service," or SaaS).[20]

Another evolution of the Internet – the IoT – also has AI-related implications. IoT denotes the Internet-enabled connectivity installed in objects (things) that previously did not possess the capability to interconnect and communicate with other objects or, indeed, humans. The Internet-enabled fridge is the stereotypical example, and a wide range of household items are expected to become equipped with internetworking ability. However, the IoT extends far beyond the household and features important industry applications as it enables interconnected machines (e.g., for farming) to operate in sync. Complex systems of this kind may rely on AI for management. Moreover, the interconnected objects that constitute the IoT are also often equipped with sensors used for data gathering, thereby expanding the volumes of data on which contemporary AI/ML relies. To the extent that IoT devices feature sufficient computing power, they may also be used to (re)train AI algorithms with local data in a decentralized fashion, thereby reducing the reliance on (centralized) cloud computing.

It is a mistake to believe that AI or other digital technologies occupy a virtual space detached from the physical world. To the contrary, all digital technologies are in various ways reliant on and intertwined with the physical world – for example, through the data centers where the data is stored, as well as the subsea cables through which most transnational Internet traffic flows.[21] AI-enabled services can be delivered online, including transnationally. But AI can also enable physical objects to perform certain functions locally.[22] These configurations are often called "robots": while public imagination remains captivated by human-like (humanoid) robots that seek to combine a human appearance with human-like capabilities, most robots are industrial machines that look nothing like humans. They play an increasingly important role in manufacturing, ushering in new forms of automation and mechanization that may affect developmental models and global supply chain calculations, especially in light of additive manufacturing (3D printing).[23] These

20 C Yoo and J-F Blanchette (eds), *Regulating the Cloud: Policy for Computing Infrastructure* (Cambridge, MA, MIT Press, 2015).

21 N Starosielski, *The Undersea Network* (Durham, NC, Duke University Press, 2015). ML may be used to optimize these systems: M Ionescu et al., "Design Optimisation of Power-Efficient Submarine Line through Machine Learning" (24 February 2020), arXiv:2002.11037.

22 For a discussion of the legal implications see R Calo, "Robotics and the Lessons of Cyberlaw" (2015) 103 *California Law Review* 513; I Cofone, "Servers and Waiters: What Matters in the Law of A.I." (2018) 21 *Stanford Technology Law Review* 167.

23 For a discussion of various use cases see LE Murr, "Frontiers of 3D Printing/Additive Manufacturing: From Human Organs to Aircraft Fabrication" (2016) 32 *Journal of Materials Science & Technology* 987.

changes have inversely correlated implications for trade in goods and trade in services as production at home and service delivery abroad become more feasible, with complex ramifications for the future of workers.[24] All of these digital technology-enabled transformations taken together are sometimes described as the "Fourth Industrial Revolution," or "Industry 4.0."[25] By comparing and contrasting the digital transformation with prior industrial revolutions that were enabled by the steam engine, electricity, and the computer, the infrastructural relevance of digital technologies in general, and AI in particular, to economic development becomes apparent.[26] While various types of AI applications will transform different sectors in different ways, the generalizable feature of AI is its ability to create *insights* through ML on the basis of large datasets. At least since the information economy revolution, it has become obvious that asymmetric control over information is critical to comparative economic advantage. AI's ability to generate information based on existing digitalized information has become an essential infrastructure for all businesses, not just the financial sector, which seems to have recognized this transformation early on.[27] Dan Ciuriak has described this transformation as the shift from a knowledge-based economy to a data-driven economy.[28] AI is a central feature of the data-driven economy because of its ability to create more data, information, and knowledge from existing data. AI's reliance on data also means that existing literature on the digital transformation before current AI technology took off and its implications for IEL remains relevant but must be reassessed against the backdrop of a reality in which AI interacts with various advanced digital technologies.

C *Disrupting Established Assumptions of International Economic Law*

The technological development of AI, as well as the economic transformation it enabled and reinforced, pose distinct challenges for IEL. In this book, we focus primarily on international trade law.[29] The multilateral international economic order has been operating under the auspices of the WTO since 1995. Its

24 R Baldwin, *The Globotics Upheaval: Globalisation, Robotics and the Future of Work* (Oxford, Oxford University Press, 2019).

25 The term was coined by World Economic Forum founder Klaus Schwab; the chapters by Lim (Chapter 5) and Toohey (Chapter 17) in this volume use the concept for their analysis.

26 The leading AI researcher Andrew Ng compared AI to electricity: "Just as electricity transformed almost everything 100 years ago, today I actually have a hard time thinking of an industry that I don't think AI will transform in the next several years." S Lynch, "Andrew Ng: Why AI Is the New Electricity" (*Stanford Business*, 11 March 2017), https://perma.cc/FVA3-W2GA.

27 J Truby, R Brown, and A Dahdal, "Banking on AI: Mandating a Proactive Approach to AI Regulation in the Financial Sector" (2020) 14 *Law and Financial Markets Review* 110 (discussing regulatory challenges).

28 D Ciuriak, "Economic Rents and the Counters of Conflict in the Data-Driven Economy" (2020) CIGI Paper No. 245.

29 As with AI, there is no universally accepted definition of IEL but trade is generally recognized as the core domain of the field. Compare S Charnowitz, "The Field of International Economic Law" (2014) 17 *Journal of International Economic Law* 607.

substantive rules can be traced back to the GATT of 1947, which ushered in a series of tariff liberalizations, followed by agreements that increasingly focused on regulatory matters.[30] With the founding of the WTO, the General Agreement on Trade in Services (GATS) and the agreement on Trade-Related Aspects of Intellectual Property Rights (TRIPS) expanded the scope of international trade law beyond trade in goods. At the same time, the creation of the GATS led to a bifurcation of the international trade regime into trade in goods and trade in services. The distinction is significant, because countries retained more control over services liberalization under the GATS's complex system of positive lists (indicating market access) and negative lists (indicating persistent limitations).[31] The goods/services distinction,[32] however, is increasingly difficult to align with economic reality and may lead to arbitrary results.[33] Moreover, AI-enabled services, even if they are clearly services, may escape the established GATS classification of services or lead to interpretive contests regarding the question of whether a previously analog service is not being performed digitally and should be treated according to the same liberalization commitment the WTO member initially made.[34]

The goods/services distinction and the expansion of AI-enabled services are not the only ways in which assumptions IEL has come to rely on are being upended by transformations in the global economy brought about by AI. Another example concerns the complex incentive structures international intellectual property (IP) law seeks to construct in pursuit of the TRIPS agreement's twin objectives of promoting technological innovation and the transfer and dissemination of technology.[35] The question of whether underlying assumptions about human agency still hold arises, as owners of AI technology have suggested that the AI itself should be designated as "inventor."[36]

Ultimately, foundational conceptual underpinnings of IEL may be disrupted. IEL is often understood to be fundamentally about "trade," the cross-border exchange of goods and services, and "investment," the long-term commitment

30 Ciuriak and Rodionova (Chapter 4 in this volume) take the agreement on technical barriers to trade (TBT) and the agreement on sanitary and phytosanitary measures (SPS) as a baseline to assess the regulatory challenge that AI poses for IEL. Lim (Chapter 5) and Peng (Chapter 6) discuss TBT in more detail.

31 P Low and A Mattoo, "Is There a Better Way? Alternative Approaches to Liberalization under GATS," in P Sauve and RM Stern (eds), *GATS 2000: New Direction in Services Trade Liberalization* (Washington D.C., Brookings Institution, 2000), at 449.

32 S-Y Peng, "A New Trade Regime for the Servitization of Manufacturing: Rethinking the Goods-Services Dichotomy" (2020) 54(5) *Journal of World Trade* 699.

33 See the discussion by Weber (Chapter 3) and Peng (Chapter 6) in this volume.

34 For a brief discussion of the potential and limits of technological neutrality to resolve such conflicts, see Streinz's Chapter 9 in this volume.

35 TRIPS, art 7. On the increasing depth and breadth of intellectual property rights, see S Frankel, "It's Raining Carrots: The Trajectory of Increased Intellectual Property Protection," in G Ghidini et al. (eds), *Kritika: Essays on Intellectual Property Vol. 2* (Cheltenham, Edward Elgar, 2017), at 224.

36 See Mercurio and Yu's Chapter 7 in this volume.

of resources by businesses in host states. The use of inherently multijurisdictional infrastructures for global AI development and deployment may render the notion that this kind of economic activity constitutes "trade" analytically unhelpful or politically unpersuasive.[37] Similarly, digital businesses may operate transnationally without the need to commit resources to a local presence or local means of production akin to conventional "investments." Accordingly, how to conceptualize, categorize, and measure the different transnational commercial interactions in the AI economy remains a major challenge for IEL at this point.

As the next section will discuss, the need for and complexity of AI regulation and the privatization of AI governance pose further challenges for IEL, which has been traditionally geared toward constraining governmental regulation.

III ARTIFICIAL INTELLIGENCE REGULATION AND THE RELEVANCE OF INTERNATIONAL ECONOMIC LAW

AI technologies present new challenges to existing regulatory framework and may require the creation of new regulatory infrastructures. Policymakers must balance different and sometimes competing legitimate public policy objectives, such as fair competition, nondiscrimination, privacy, and security,[38] while avoiding regulatory overreach that may inhibit socially beneficial innovations. Governments around the world are contemplating various forms of AI regulation, ranging from "AI ethics" over transparency requirements for public and private algorithmic decision-making to outright bans of certain AI use cases (such as governmental use of facial recognition technology). At the same time, governments are frantically racing to develop national AI strategies to develop their digital economies. AI technologies trigger and channel political and economic pressures, as evidenced by intensive lobbying and engagement in different governance venues for and against various regulatory choices, including who and what will be regulated, for what purpose, by whom, and how.

Through this volume, we seek to inject IEL into these conversations with two objectives in mind: one is to explore how extant IEL frames these different regulatory initiatives. Which limits do WTO law and the disciplines contained in preferential trade agreements impose on AI regulators? How is IEL shaping different forms of AI regulation and with what outcomes? The other goal is to reflect on IEL's suitability and adaptability to generate societally beneficial outcomes in the context

37 See Fukunaga's Chapter 8 (questioning whether digital trade disputes are trade disputes).

38 In this regard, Art. 198 of the EU-UK Trade and Cooperation Agreement (TCA) represents an example of creating an inclusive list of legitimate objectives. It reaffirms the Parties' right to regulate to achieve legitimate policy objectives, "such as the protection of public health, social services, public education, safety, the environment including climate change, public morals, social or consumer protection, privacy and data protection, or the promotion and protection of cultural diversity."

of AI regulation with a view toward IEL's ongoing reconfiguration and a potential need for further change.

AI is multifaceted and complex and the global regulatory landscape reflects this to a certain extent. Global AI governance is in flux and gradually and iteratively being shaped and reshaped.

The proliferation of relatively vague "AI principles" in past years established an initial pathway regarding how to further develop societal norms surrounding AI development, deployment, use, and governance. These "AI principles" present a first vision for the relationship between general AI governance (including through ethics and standards) and governmental AI regulation.[39] Although it remains to be seen what approaches will eventually materialize, some common approaches can be identified from existing national policies.[40] Increasingly, proposals for more forceful governmental AI regulation are emerging, with the EU asserting and promoting itself as a pioneering AI regulator.[41] Various global standard-setting bodies are engaged in their own initiatives to standardize and thereby address certain regulatory aspects of AI governance.

To untangle the complex and dynamic relationship between AI and IEL, we suggest three analytical prisms that shed light on different yet related aspects of AI regulation, as presented in Figure 1.1.

The first prism differentiates between different *domains* of AI regulation (economic, social, and administrative) and asks for what purpose and under what framing AI regulation is being pursued. The choices of whether or not to regulate AI, how to regulate AI, and whom should be regulated are closely related to the balancing of innovation effects and the interpretation of existing economic, social, and administrative regulation.[42]

The second prism disintegrates AI into its constitutive *components* – hardware, algorithms, and data – and asks how each of them is being regulated by domestic and international law as well as industry standards within the framework that IEL provides. While hardware and algorithms are important elements and increasingly subject to trade disputes, our focus in this volume is on "data regulation as AI regulation."

39 See the contributions in MD Dubber, F Pasquale, and S Das (eds), *The Oxford Handbook of Ethics of AI* (Oxford, Oxford University Press, 2020).

40 J Fjeld et al., "Principled Artificial Intelligence: Mapping Consensus in Ethical and Rights-Based Approaches to Principles for AI" (2020) Berkman Klein Center for Internet & Society, https://dash.harvard.edu/handle/1/42160420.

41 The EU White Paper on AI left key concepts such as "high risk" and "robustness and accuracy" undefined. See European Commission, "White Paper on Artificial Intelligence: A European Approach to Excellence and Trust" COM (2020) 65 final. Contrast the European Commission's proposal for a regulation laying down harmonized rules on artificial intelligence (Artificial Intelligence Act) COM(2021) 206.

42 E Balleisen et al., *Government and Market: Toward a New Theory of Regulation* (Cambridge, Cambridge University Press, 2010), at 93–94. See also OECD, "Regulatory Reform and Innovation," www.oecd.org/sti/inno/2102514.pdf.

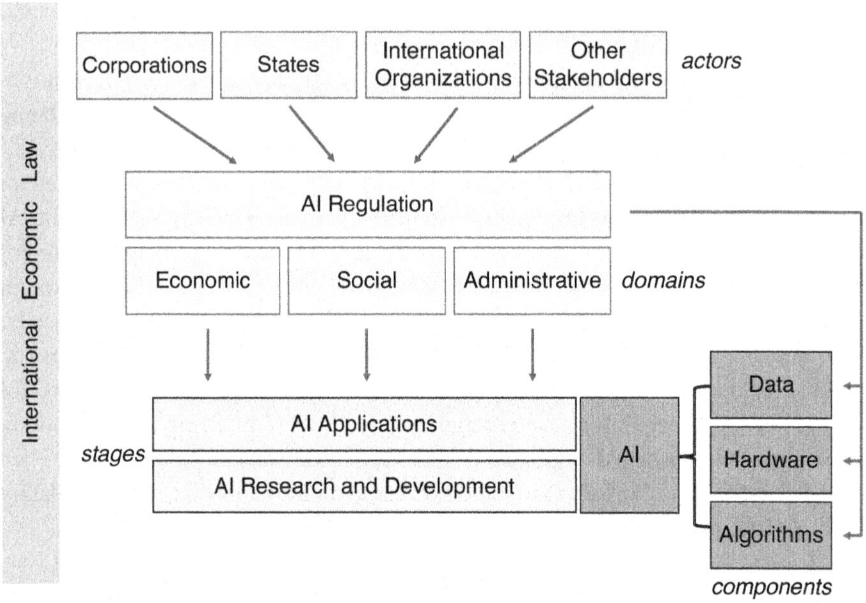

FIGURE 1.1 Artificial intelligence regulation in the context of international economic law

The third prism identifies different *actors* engaged in AI regulation including corporations, states, international organizations, and other stakeholders to assess the relative relevance or irrelevance of IEL for their regulatory interventions.

As becomes clear from this kind of analysis, the regulatory target is never "AI" in the abstract. AI regulation is about the creation of a regulatory framework that matches the complexity and distributed nature of AI research, development, and deployment and is commensurate with their economic, social, and administrative impact. This requires different regulatory interventions by different stakeholders in different domains aimed at different aspects of AI at different *stages* of AI development, deployment, and use.

A *Artificial Intelligence Regulation Across Domains*

A three-fold typology of regulation, as shown in Figure 1.1, can illustrate possible linkages between AI regulation and IEL across three overlapping but still analytically distinguishable domains: economic, social, and administrative AI regulation. Each of these advances a certain framing of AI regulation around concepts such as innovation, harm, and accountability and intersects with IEL in different ways.

The first type of AI regulation is designed to pursue economic-oriented objectives. Labeled by the OECD as "economic regulation," this type of regulation is primarily related to innovation and is often intended to improve the market efficiency of goods and services. It can include, among other matters, technical standards/conformity assessments, competition law, and IP rights.[43] The data-driven economy has led to winner-takes-all dynamics under which certain companies have acquired monopoly status and infrastructural importance.[44] Anticompetitive behavior enabled by the overwhelming dominance of a few players in digital markets has become the main regulatory target of competition authorities in more and more jurisdictions.[45] In a similar vein, a more subtle example of economic regulation is AI's uneasy fit with the existing IP regime.[46] Moreover, the WTO, as a system ostensibly dedicated to open, fair, and undistorted trade, embraces principles of nondiscrimination. Many of the WTO agreements are designed to secure "fair trade" conditions. Governments' turn to economic regulation raises the question of whether this kind of AI regulation may create new ambiguities in WTO law. In other words, are conventional trade rules adequate for governing the policies that governments pursue to spur AI innovation?[47]

A second group of AI regulations is shaped by noneconomic objectives, which are often designed to protect society at large or certain groups within a society. Although this kind of "social" regulation is not entirely distinguishable from "economic" regulation, such rationales may include AI regulation of privacy, security, discrimination, or other concerns. In this context, the winner-takes-all nature of the platform economy exacerbates the need to strike a balance between trade efficiency and other policy objectives. Several chapters in this book address the question of how IEL can help reduce imbalances of digital markets. One of the challenges facing the WTO e-commerce talks is the allegation that the proposed rules for digital trade will benefit large companies at the expense of small businesses. Civil society groups have been pressing for development-focused digital industrialization, indicating the need to ensure the universal benefits of the digital economy and to close the digital divide.[48] The exceptions to the general trade disciplines provided by WTO law allow members to use domestic measures to promote non-trade values. But are the existing exceptions to trade rules overinclusive or underinclusive with respect to AI applications, in general and in particular with regard to data ethics and public moral issues surrounding automated driving systems?[49]

A third domain of AI regulation is "administrative regulation," which governs the practical functioning of both public and private sectors, and therefore can function

43 OECD, "Examples of AI National Policies" (2020), www.oecd.org/sti/examples-of-ai-national-policies.pdf.

44 See Shaffer's Chapter 2.

45 The EU has launched competition law proceedings against major US tech companies. In fall 2020, the US Department of Justice sued Google for violating antitrust laws; see DOJ press release of 20 October 2020, justive.gov (https://perma.cc/7RQV-QS72). See also Weber's Chapter 3.

46 See Mercurio and Yu's Chapter 7.

47 See Shang and Du's Chapter 14, discussing limits to AI subsidies.

48 See Shaffer's Chapter 2.

49 See Mishra's Chapter 13 and Lin's Chapter 12.

as a means of setting up the conditions for technological advance.[50] This can include AI regulation that safeguards accountability, transparency/explainability, and human control of technology. How can IEL promote mechanisms to ensure that accountability for the impacts of AI applications is appropriately distributed? Can IEL incorporate transparency requirements that AI systems be designed and implemented to allow for oversight?[51] Perhaps the most basic yet heavily contested example in this regard is the improvement of transparency to ensure public access and oversight over algorithms, their application, and the underlying datasets.[52]

B *Data Regulation as Artificial Intelligence Regulation*

Another important angle is the examination of specific aspects of AI to determine whether AI-specific regulation is necessary or feasible given the breadth and range of data-driven technologies. Such legal and policy analysis needs to take account of technological developments. AI-specific regulation only makes sense when the regulatory objectives are closely connected to AI technologies. In other words, AI-specific regulation should be framed in a way that allows the "new" legal issues to be addressed in an AI-specific way by taking account of the "AI system lifecycle" and its "enabling ecosystem."[53]

Indeed, some regulatory initiatives avoid the "AI" moniker altogether and distinguish instead between regulation of "algorithmic systems" (whether entirely human coded or, in part, self-trained) and regulation of "data."[54] Algorithms are increasingly subject to novel protections in instruments of IEL to guard against mandatory source code disclosure.[55] At the same time, and in contrast to the dominant discourse in IEL, a lot of algorithmic development is being conducted by academia and industry using "open-source" licenses under which algorithms are freely available. This is not true to the same extent for data and hardware, despite various "open data" and "open hardware" initiatives. Indeed, specialized AI hardware, in particular microprocessors optimized for ML, is becoming increasingly important. In this domain, the USA retains a comparative advantage over China and has imposed export

50 OECD, note 44 above.

51 OECD, note 45 above, at 27.

52 M Kaminski, "Understanding Transparency in Algorithmic Accountability," in W Barfield (ed), *The Cambridge Handbook of the Law of Algorithms* (Cambridge, Cambridge University Press, 2020), at 121. See also Weber's Chapter 3.

53 LB Moses, "How to Think about Law, Regulation and Technology: Problems with Technology as a Regulatory Target" (2013) 5(1) *Law, Innovation and Technology* 1.

54 One example of this approach is the Opinion of the German Data Ethics Commission (22 January 2020), www.bmjv.de (https://perma.cc/6YZW-YYX3).

55 See K Irion, "AI Regulation in the European Union and Trade Law: How Can Accountability of AI and a High Level of Consumer Protection Prevail over a Trade Discipline on Source Code?" (23 January 2021), https://ssrn.com/abstract=3786567.

restrictions to retain this leverage in the ongoing trade conflict between the two AI superpowers.[56]

Our focus in this volume is on "data governance" as "AI governance." AI-specific regulation may create additional requirements for data quality, transparency, and accountability.[57] Such requirements would complement existing data protection laws such as the EU's General Data Protection Regulation (GDPR). Data laws regulate a decisive input factor of contemporary AI technology that is fundamentally data-driven because of its reliance on ML algorithms.[58] Therefore, a broader perspective – data regulations as AI regulation – is adopted in this book to explore the interaction between AI and data governance. Why is data governance critical for AI and ML?[59] How can a balance be struck between data protection and data-driven innovations, including AI?[60] Addressing the topic of datafication as a technological trend, modern life, especially in the context of AI, has become dependent on computerized data.[61] AI, robotics, 3D printing, blockchain, and the IoT are converging into "digitally connected networks of production, communication and consumption."[62] The tension between the emerging regulatory interventions in AI and the existing international trade and investment rules, therefore, can be understood along the dimensions of data control and data mobility.[63]

C *Privatization of Artificial Intelligence Regulation*

One important issue for AI regulation is that there are many actors at play, developing norms of varying quality, precision, and significance that could potentially shape the regulatory framework. Considering the rapid pace of AI developments, a regulatory framework that is sufficiently flexible to keep up with technological innovation and business developments is a significant challenge.

Many AI principles have been created through collaborative, multistakeholder efforts, with a wide breadth of experts involved. Relevant stakeholders have been included in pursuit of a normative consensus surrounding the governance of AI technologies. Stakeholders hail from many different public and private sector

[56] D Ernst, "Competing Artificial Intelligence Chips: China's Challenge amid Technology War" (26 March 2020), CIGI Special Report, www.cigionline.org/publications/competing-artificial-intelligence-chips-chinas-challenge-amid-technology-war. See also Winn and Chiang's Chapter 16 on the AI rivalry between China and the USA.

[57] See Article 10 of the European Commission's proposal for a regulation laying down harmonized rules on artificial intelligence (Artificial Intelligence Act) COM(2021) 206 (creating data governance and management requirements for high-risk AI systems, focusing on training, validation, and testing data).

[58] See on the GDPR as a form of AI regulation P Nemitz, "Constitutional Democracy and Technology in the Age of Artificial Intelligence" (2013) 376(2133) *Philosophical Transactions of the Royal Society* A.

[59] See in particular Zufall and Zingg's Chapter 11.

[60] See Hervé's Chapter 10.

[61] See Weber's Chapter 3.

[62] See Lim's Chapter 5.

[63] See Streinz's Chapter 9.

entities and include individuals directly or indirectly involved with the AI system lifecycle, which may encompass governments, industry, technology developers, data providers, academic communities, civil society, and trade unions, as well as other entities.[64] Initiatives such as codes of conduct, voluntary standards, and best practices are meant to guide AI actors through the AI lifecycle, including monitoring, assessing, and addressing the harmful effects of AI applications.[65] These initiatives aspire to have a transformative effect on the technological development and societal deployment of AI, which is fundamentally driven by the academic-industrial complex and is in significant part regulated by various, often transnational, standard-setting bodies. Governments have only slowly begun to confront AI-enabled transformations through legislative and regulatory action, with the EU emerging as the most aggressive AI regulator. IEL provides a (meta) regulatory framework, which aspires to govern these regulatory initiatives. IEL's traditional focus on state-led regulation and its preference for multilateralism poses particular challenges in this regard.

The widespread embrace of multistakeholder AI governance raises pivotal questions concerning AI norm development. Human rights advocates have lamented the lack of attention toward established commitments under international human rights law in the discourse on law and technology.[66] Some nongovernmental organizations (NGOs) have left multistakeholder initiatives on AI governance out of concern over corporate capture and lack of change.[67] AI governance was initially dominated by "AI ethics" because of a widespread belief that such frameworks were best suited to govern the emerging technology.[68] Governments initially embraced such initiatives but then ventured toward more traditional forms of regulation. The EU is contemplating comprehensive AI regulation more akin to the regulation common in other regulated industries (such as chemicals or pharmaceuticals).

For these reasons, the question of the appropriate role of government in regulating AI is resurfacing. The industry-led voluntary standards for autonomous vehicles, as an example, demonstrate that the development of disruptive innovation inherently involves changes in governance frameworks and calls for new governance approaches that break the boundaries of existing trade disciplines.[69] The WTO needs to respond to the predominantly decentralized nature of data governance, including market-driven or self-regulatory alternatives to data-related

64 OECD, note 43 above, at 56.

65 WA Kaal and EPM Vermeulen, "How to Regulate Disruptive Innovation: From Facts to Data" (2017) 57 *Jurimetrics Journal* 169.

66 See generally MK Land and JD Aaronson, "Human Rights and Technology: New Challenges for Justice and Accountability" (2020) 16 *Annual Review of Law and Social Science* 223.

67 Khari Johnson, "Access Now Resigns from Partnership on AI Due to Lack of Change Among Tech Companies" (*Venturebeat*, 14 October 2020), https://venturebeat.com/2020/10/14/access-now-resigns-from-partnership-on-ai-due-to-lack-of-change-among-tech-companies.

68 J Cowls and L Floridi, "Prolegomena to a White Paper on an Ethical Framework for a Good AI Society" (2018).

69 See Peng's Chapter 6.

measures.[70] However, if governments reassert themselves as AI regulators,[71] the WTO may be in more familiar territory in terms of the relevant actors, but still faces considerable conceptual challenges.

IV ARTIFICIAL INTELLIGENCE AND THE RECONFIGURATION OF INTERNATIONAL ECONOMIC LAW

IEL may need to reconfigure itself to remain relevant, but there is no consensus that the venues that produce and administer IEL – such as the WTO – are the optimal forum for states and nonstate actors to deliberate over AI governance. The study of trade law architecture after the Fourth Industrial Revolution demonstrates that there is potential to use emergent technologies, including AI, to transform the functions and operations of the WTO, and to reconfigure its management of trade.[72] Indeed, there are several reasons why the WTO is probably not the best forum for global AI governance and should hence not be the only or dominant one. For example, a central, preliminary question is whether special or additional dispute settlement rules and procedures should be incorporated into the international trade regime to handle digital trade disputes,[73] when a particular AI-related domestic regulation constitutes a violation of a right or obligation provided for in an international agreement. At the same time, one may never identify an ideal, uncontested forum. From an organizational capacity perspective, it certainly makes sense to leverage the WTO and its existing networks of actors, agreements, and institutions to engage with AI technologies and applications, because the economic implications are obvious. Beyond the WTO, bilateral, regional, and plurilateral endeavors aim to reconfigure IEL to keep abreast of the changing faces of the AI economy.

Apart from the ongoing plurilateral negotiation on e-commerce at the WTO,[74] at the multilateral level there have been limited (if any) endeavors in response to the challenges brought about by the gradual embrace of AI technologies. At the mini-lateral level, there have been increasing negotiations among various WTO members, leading to a variety of dynamic interactions and innovative arrangements that have engineered an incipient reconfiguration of IEL. A growing number of free trade agreements (FTAs) incorporate new rules to discipline government regulations on cross-border data flows, privacy and personal data, competition, and source code.[75]

70 See Mishra's Chapter 13.

71 See F Pasquale, *New Laws of Robotics: Defending Human Expertise in the Age of AI* (Cambridge, MA, Harvard University Press, 2020), who, inter alia, calls for licensing requirements for certain AI applications.

72 See Toohey's Chapter 17.

73 See Fukunaga's Chapter 8 for a discussion on dispute settlement issues under the prospective e-commerce agreement.

74 See Gao's Chapter 15 for an overview of the joint statement initiative.

75 See M Burri and R Polanco, "Digital Trade Provisions in Preferential Trade Agreements: Introducing a New Dataset" (2020) 23 *Journal of International Economic Law* 187 (observing that new digital trade provisions in FTAs have increased in both length and scope).

For instance, both the Comprehensive and Progressive Agreement for Trans-Pacific Partnership (CPTPP) and the United States-Mexico-Canada Agreement (USMCA) incorporate provisions that facilitate the "free flow" of data.[76] Such reconfiguration tends to focus on the imminent challenges of data regulation but has not traversed the extra mile to address broader AI governance issues. Some argue for new approaches to be developed at the WTO level, so as to provide foundational data regulation principles to address the regulatory challenges of cross-border data flows.[77] Others contend that "free flow" of data is not an absolute principle and should not be readily embraced as the "gold standard" for digital trade.[78] The tension between various economic, political, social, and even ideological underpinnings among WTO members regarding their approaches to addressing data and AI regulation will shape the form and substance of IEL's future reconfiguration.

Specifically, the emerging geopolitical, geoeconomics, and geotechnological power struggle between the USA and China may have a lasting impact on the future reconfiguration of IEL in relation to AI. The "free flow" of data enhances efficiency and welfare but it also facilitates economic processes that exacerbate inequality. Attempts to regulate data flows will likely be divergent and contested, which creates a need for broadly enough defined international frameworks.[79] The Comprehensive Economic and Trade Agreement's (CETA's) reference to international standards of data protection in the context of e-commerce, which can be seen as part of its regulatory approach to the AI economy, could be a promising first step.[80] Japan's G20 Data Free Flow with Trust (DFFT) initiative, embraced by the World Economic Forum, is another attempt to reconcile the competing interests under a common framework.[81]

The Digital Economy Partnership Agreement (DEPA) between Chile, New Zealand, and Singapore presents an innovative reconfiguration – and remodulation – of IEL for the AI economy.[82] Recognizing that the line between trade and nontrade is blurring, DEPA takes a much broader perspective to AI and the digital economy and covers a wide range of issues.[83] DEPA not only strengthens obligations in now conventional "digital trade" provisions – such as the nonimposition of custom duties on electronic transmissions, nondiscriminatory treatment, promotion and facilitation of e-commerce, rules on data flows, paperless trading, electronic

76 See T Streinz, "Digital Megaregulation Uncontested? TPP's Model for the Global Digital Economy," in B Kingsbury et al. (eds), *Megaregulation Contested: Global Economic Ordering After TPP* (Oxford, Oxford University Press, 2019), ch. 14.

77 See Weber's Chapter 3.

78 See Gao's Chapter 15.

79 See Shaffer's Chapter 2.

80 CETA, Article 16.4.

81 World Economic Forum, "Data Free Flow with Trust: Paths towards Free and Trusted Data Flows" (May 2020), www.weforum.org (https://perma.cc/KYR7-AZAM).

82 Signed in June 2020, www.mfat.govt.nz (https://perma.cc/U23E-URUS).

83 Per DEPA, Article 1.1 the agreement encompasses all measures that "affect trade in the digital economy." Notably, DEPA avoids the term "digital trade" altogether.

authentication, and data localization – but also includes new rules for algorithms, digital inclusion, financial technology (FinTech), and AI-related ethical and governance frameworks.[84] A crucial institutional design that may greatly expand DEPA's normative impact is that it is open to all other nonmembers to join as new members or agree upon and use any of the modules as building blocks to update existing FTAs and relevant domestic policies. DEPA's "modular" approach to regional cooperation – dividing the agreement into "modules" covering rights and obligations under different digital economy issue areas – marks a deviation from the WTO's single undertaking approach that "comprehensive" FTAs have replicated.

In addition to DEPA, a few other WTO members have concluded new agreements on the broader theme of the digital economy to expand upon and deepen their cooperation under existing FTAs, continuing the trend toward nonmultilateral agreements. For instance, the Australia-Singapore Digital Economy Agreement (ASDEA) was signed in August 2020 to update and replace the e-commerce chapter of the Singapore-Australia Free Trade Agreement (SAFTA) previously signed in 2003. Like DEPA, ASDEA "moves away from the increasingly antiquated, unhelpfully narrow notion of 'e-commerce' in international trade negotiation,"[85] and offers much broader coverage of emerging issues of technological and regulatory cooperation. Cross-border data flows, personal data protection, IP and algorithms, FinTech and RegTech, digital standards, and access to government data are addressed, albeit with significant variation in terms of specificity. Through ASDEA, Australia and Singapore aim to expand their normative influence globally, "signaling vital directions for the WTO negotiations on . . . e-commerce."[86]

The parties to DEPA and ASDEA – Australia, Chile, New Zealand, and Singapore – are also parties to CPTPP, whose "electronic commerce" chapter was significantly shaped by the USA before it abandoned the initial TPP after the election of Donald J. Trump as president. However, even under his presidency and despite the withdrawal from the TPP, the USA has inserted essentially the same model into further agreements, including the United States-Japan Digital Trade Agreement (USJDTA), which was concluded between two of the most digitally advanced economies in October 2019.[87] Similar to ASDEA, the USJDTA includes rules on digital products, cross-border data flows (prohibiting data localization measures), cybersecurity, protection of proprietary computer source code and algorithms, cryptography, and access to government data. DEPA, ASDEA, and USJDTA demonstrate certain WTO members' ambition to play a leading role in global rule-making for the AI economy. Their shared endorsement of the "free flow" of data is in

84 DEPA, Articles 8.1 and 8.2; DEPA, Module 11.

85 J Drake-Brockman, "Australia-Singapore Digital Trade Agreement: Setting New Benchmarks in Trade Governance" (Institute for International Trade, University of Adelaide, 24 August 2020), https://perma.cc/3FLA-WEPE.

86 Ibid.

87 Signed on 7 October 2019. Text available at www.ustr.gov (https://perma.cc/UUA9-7NUD).

tension with the EU's GDPR, which restricts the cross-border transfers of personal data.[88] Future multilateral rules would need to account for these systemic differences, for example by differentiating between different kinds of data flows.

Treaty creation and change are not the only ways through which IEL is being reconfigured. Contestation in committees and litigation through dispute settlement procedures will test the application of existing IEL disciplines to new technologies, business models, and regulatory approaches. The continued reinterpretation of IEL may gradually clarify boundaries under existing disciplines but may also reveal, conversely, where new rules are needed. Growing pressure for change – in whatever form – is in tension with IEL's commitments to stability, predictability, and legal certainty, which have been widely regarded as vital for trade-enabled economic growth. Whether rules that purport to address challenges arising from fast-developing digital technologies and associated fast-scaling business models can or should aspire to the same levels of evenhanded generality as their predecessors or whether more flexible, differentiated, and granular rules are needed is an important question for IEL's future development.

The use of digital technologies for the implementation of IEL has so far been mainly explored for automation and electronic communication ("paperless trade") in the context of customs procedures under the rubric of "trade facilitation." Aligning with the text-as-data approach and moving toward the data-driven future of IEL,[89] digital technologies could lead to a more radical reconfiguration of IEL if the regulatory force of computer code is being deployed more widely as a complement to or substitute for traditional IEL rule-making.[90] Recognizing that the human-made law is not the only way to make and enforce trade rules or to settle disputes opens up a research agenda that integrates IEL into broader debates around law and technology and the relationship between "human law" and "computer law."[91] The use of AI technologies to support IEL creation and implementation may be especially warranted when the quantity or complexity of economic interactions exceeds human comprehension.[92] Considering this possibility is not an endorsement of the questionable idea of replacing human lawyers with robots. Instead of framing the debate as one about replacing human with artificial intelligence, one ought to explore the potential and purpose of human "intelligence augmentation" (IA).[93] On this basis, one could ask fundamental questions about the need for further reconfiguration of IEL: How should IEL adapt and reorient as

88 S Yakovleva and K Irion, "Pitching trade against privacy: Reconciling EU governance of personal data flows with external trade" (2020) 10 *International Data Privacy Law* 201.

89 See W Alschner et al., "The Data-Driven Future of International Economic Law" (2017) 20(2) *Journal of International Economic Law* 217–231.

90 J Mohen and A Roberts, "Cracking the Code: Rulemaking for Humans and Machines" (2020), OECD Working Papers on Public Governance, No. 42, https://doi.org/10.1787/3afe6ba5-en.

91 See Mireille Hildebrandt's project COHUBICOL on "computational law" (www.cohubicol.com).

92 See further Toohey's Chapter 17.

93 Pasquale, note 72 above.

a framework with relevance in this AI era? What are the key elements to be incorporated into a new vision for IEL? And finally, how should a reconfigured IEL shape the future direction of the global AI economy?

V GENERATING INTERNATIONAL ECONOMIC LAW AND ARTIFICIAL INTELLIGENCE DISCOURSE IN THIS VOLUME AND GOING FORWARD

Given the broad array of issues that are raised when AI and IEL intersect, this volume is not comprehensive in nature. And yet, we hope to provide more than a snapshot of the interplay between AI and IEL in the early 2020s. In the following, we outline the various contributions and their relationships to one another before turning to questions we could not address in this volume but hope to tackle going forward.

The first three chapters address systemic shifts in the global economic order and argue for carefully crafted responses: What readjustments are needed in an increasingly data-driven economy with pervasive deployment of AI capabilities? According to Gregory Shaffer, trade law needs to adjust "with modesty and resilience," while Rolf H. Weber calls for rule-making on the basis of regulatory principles such as transparency, accountability, safety, and robustness.[94] Dan Ciuriak and Vlada Rodionova's chapter discusses the rites of passage of AI as it enters the trading system and the need to revisit the established dichotomy between legitimate risk regulation and unjustifiable protectionism under which international trade law has operated so far.[95]

The subsequent part brings together chapters that focus on certain instruments that form part of the WTO law acquis and its application and further development with regard to AI: Aik Hoe Lim hails the toolkit provided by the Technical Barriers to Trade (TBT) Agreement as a mechanism to avoid unnecessary regulatory diversity and reduce trade costs as the global economy transition toward "Industry 4.0."[96] Shin-yi Peng strikes a different tone when she calls for the modernization of the TBT Agreement to reflect current standardization trends in the context of autonomous vehicles.[97] Bryan Mercurio and Ronald Yu discuss how international IP law, specifically the WTO's agreement on TRIPS, might need to be readjusted to account for shifts along the human–machine frontier in terms of the generation of outputs that have to date been protected and incentivized by various forms of IP.[98] Finally, Yuka Fukunaga discusses how future conflicts regarding compliance with such new rules could be resolved through WTO-provided dispute settlement procedures and

94 See Shaffer's Chapter 2 and Weber's Chapter 3.
95 See Ciuriak and Rodionova's Chapter 4.
96 See Lim's Chapter 5.
97 See Peng's Chapter 6.
98 See Mercurio and Yu's Chapter 7.

exposes the extent to which such conflicts deviate from conventional trade disputes.[99]

The two ensuing parts explore the relevance of IEL to AI regulation: Chapters 9 to 11 focus on governmental data regulation as a form of AI regulation, while Chapters 12 to 14 address a broader array of regulatory efforts, ranging from standard-setting to ethics and the limits IEL imposes on such initiatives. Thomas Streinz conceptualizes data as a resource for the AI economy, concentrated in Chinese and US big tech companies, and surveys governmental efforts to redistribute data by way of data localization, open data initiatives, and mandatory data-sharing. Such efforts run into limits in extant IEL, which favors data mobility and entrenches data control.[100] Alan Hervé analyzes the EU's model of data (protection) regulation in contrast with the US model and explores the extent to which these different dispositions can be accommodated in IEL.[101] Frederike Zufall and Raphael Zingg focus on one particular intervention the EU has pioneered, namely data portability for personal and nonpersonal data, to redistribute economically valuable data for AI development, and discuss whether this approach could or should be globalized, including through IEL instruments.[102]

Ching-Fu Lin explores the complex ethical questions raised by algorithmic design and divergent cultural, demographic, and value-driven factors, which may lead to heterogeneous regulation that is subject to challenges under existing IEL.[103] In a similar vein, Neha Mishra discusses the trend toward data/AI ethics and explores whether their trade-restrictive impact is defensible under the GATS.[104] Turning to governments, Kelly K. Shang and Rachel R. Du analyze the compatibility of government-mandated data-sharing mechanisms and governmental sanctions against countries that use AI technology to undermine fundamental rights or national security.[105]

The concluding part contains three thought-provoking pieces about the future of the international economic order. Henry Gao assesses the prospects of creating a dedicated instrument addressing electronic commerce and digital trade under the shelter of the WTO in the form of the Joint Statement Initiative (JSI), with particular attention accorded to China.[106] Jane K. Winn and Yi-Shyuan Chiang explore the emerging competition between the USA and China for control over global knowledge infrastructures.[107] While most of this volume has been concerned with the ways in which IEL might respond to AI and the transformation of the global

99 See Fukunaga's Chapter 8.
100 See Streinz's Chapter 9.
101 See Hervé's Chapter 10.
102 See Zufall and Zingg's Chapter 11.
103 See Lin's Chapter 12.
104 See Mishra's Chapter 13.
105 See Shang and Du's Chapter 14.
106 See Gao's Chapter 15.
107 See Winn and Chiang's Chapter 16.

PART I

Systemic Shifts in the Global Economic Order

2

Trade Law in a Data-Driven Economy

The Need for Modesty and Resilience

*Gregory Shaffer**

Data, it is said, is the new oil. Treated as a raw material, once processed, once refined, it fuels the new economy. But unlike oil, data is not only nondepletable, it is also constantly generated and exponentially growing. Unlike oil, data exhaust from transactions is not waste but recycled for further use. And unlike oil, data is nonrivalrous as it can be exploited by multiple users. Despite the differences, the metaphor is powerful not only because data fuels the new economy, but also because data is *extracted* (in this case not only from land but from humans), and because data is protected and traded through law as a new form of *property*. The value of data vastly surpasses that of oil as measured by the capitalization of the world's largest firms.[1] The only question for companies is how to gather, store, analyze, and deploy data ever more efficiently since data can significantly reduce transaction and production costs. This chapter examines the social challenges posed by such an economy, their implications for trade law, the current trade negotiating context, and a way forward that can both enhance trade and regulatory efficacy. Section I sets the stage regarding law as a "channeling" tool in the digital economy. Section II examines eight critical challenges. Section III presents the negotiating context in which major powers advance different governance models. Section IV provides a governance framework for moving forward in light of the challenges, a framework that is modest and that foregrounds the importance of building

* This chapter is adapted from a keynote presentation at a conference organized by the Asian International Economic Law Network (AIELN) in Taipei, titled "International Trade Regime for the Data-Driven Economy: How Will Artificial Intelligence Transform International Economic Law?". I thank Anne van Aaken, Mira Burri, Jacob Cogan, Monica Hakimi, Alex Huneeus, Christopher Leslie, participants at a workshop at the University of California, Irvine, and participants at the AIELN conference for their comments and questions.

1 Seven of the eight most valuable listed firms in 2019 profit critically from data: Microsoft, Apple, Amazon, Alphabet (parent of Google), Facebook, Alibaba, and Tencent (parent of WeChat). The eighth is Berkshire Hathaway, a holding company whose largest holding is Apple. We pay for the "free" services of Google, Facebook, Alibaba, and WeChat by exchanging access to us and our data. WeChat, owned by Tencent, is the largest social network in China. Facebook envies it in terms of the range of services that WeChat (the "everything app") offers. N Statt and S Liao, "Facebook Wants to Be WeChat" (*The Verge*, 8 March 2019), https://perma.cc/PBW5-V5QV.

resilience and engaging in problem solving, learning, and adaptation. Section V concludes.

I THE DATA-DRIVEN ECONOMY AND LAW

The data-driven economy refers to the collection, aggregation, organization, analysis, exchange, and exploitation of digital information, whether for use in production (such as in "smart manufacturing" and "smart agriculture"), the sale of goods and services (such as through electronic commerce), the provision of services (such as through online platforms like Uber), or trade in data itself (whether for advertising, solicitation, or assessment, such as for credit ratings).[2] The data-driven economy is fueled by the data generated from connected devices, which is then used to innovate, produce, operate, and sell responsive machines, goods, and services.[3] McKinsey estimates that the value of global data flows surpassed that of trade in goods as early as 2014.[4]

Technology has been and is being developed through the exponential rise in computing power, storage, and bandwidth to exploit data. 5G wireless technology expands capacity, enhances the speed of information flows, reduces latency for near-real-time communication, and transforms scalability for new services. Data-trained artificial intelligence (AI) industrializes learning, which increases productivity, reduces costs, and improves logistical services, facilitating trade.[5] Microchips enable

[2] OECD, "Exploring Data-Driven Innovation as a New Source of Growth: Mapping the Policy Issues Raised by 'Big Data'" (2013), https://perma.cc/QX38-5LT8 (noting data products, data-intensive products, data-driven research and development, data-driven processes, data-driven marketing, and data-driven organization across sectors); A Kusiak, "Smart Manufacturing" (2018) 56 *International Journal of Production Research* 508–517 ("Smart manufacturing is an emerging form of production integrating manufacturing assets of today and tomorrow with sensors, computing platforms, communication technology, control, simulation, data intensive modelling and predictive engineering"); S Wolfert et al., "Big Data in Smart Farming: A Review" (2017) 153 *Agricultural System* 69, at 69–80 ("New technologies such as the Internet of Things and Cloud Computing are expected to leverage this development and introduce more robots and artificial intelligence in farming. This is encompassed by the phenomenon of Big Data, massive volumes of data with a wide variety that can be captured, analysed and used for decision-making"). For different definitions of digital trade that vary in their expansiveness, see J Meltzer, "Governing Digital Trade" (2019) 18 *World Trade Review* 23, at 33 (including those of the World Trade Organization (WTO) Work Program on Electronic Commerce and the U.S. International Trade Commission). Ciuriak and Ptashkina break down digital trade into five modes: D Ciuriak and M Ptashkina, "The Digital Transformation and the Transformation of International Trade" (2018), https://perma.cc/M2SS-4SJN.

[3] D Ciuriak, "The Economics of Data: Implications for the Data-Driven Economy," in *Data Governance in the Digital Age: Special Report* (2018), at 12.

[4] McKinsey Global Institute, "The Internet of Things: Mapping the Value Beyond the Hype" (2015), https://perma.cc/PZ2A-EF7B; J Manyika and M Chui, "By 2025, Internet of Things Applications Could Have U.S. 11 Trillion Impact" (*Fortune*, 22 July 2015), https://perma.cc/93VS-UNC9.

[5] D Ciuriak, "Digital Trade: Is Data Treaty-Ready?" (2018) CIGI Papers No. 162. AI can reduce transport, storage, and logistics costs by optimizing production and route planning and reducing uncertainty of delivery times. It can facilitate localized manufacturing through 3D printing. These costs represent a major share in overall trade costs, and therefore their reduction can have a large

powerful computers at our fingertips, generating new data to be processed. "Smart" manufacturing self-automates, trumpeted in Germany as "Industry 4.0" and in the United States as the "Industrial Internet." Linking big data, cloud computing, wireless sensor networks, and automated analytic tools with industrial equipment, it makes manufacturing more efficient, more precise, and more responsive.[6] Daily life – from driverless cars to heart monitors and security locks – revolutionize through the so-called Internet of Things.[7]

Many if not most commentators on trade and technology are technological optimists since, in basic economic theory, "technological progress by definition shifts out the production possibilities frontier" and thus enhances aggregate social welfare.[8] Basic trade law and economics casebooks deploy parables that compare trade with technology with a moral that countries should embrace the social welfare benefits of trade.[9] Even Dani Rodrik, a leading critic of the trade regime for having liberalized too far, has argued that technology is more benign than trade in its distributional effects.[10]

If one is a technology optimist, then our task is less daunting: law should incentivize technology's development and use. Ronald Gilson, writing from Stanford in the nerve center of Silicon Valley, famously called lawyers "transaction cost engineers."[11] It is lawyers who grease the wheels and driverless cars of

impact on trade flows. WTO, "World Trade Report 2018: The Future of World Trade: How Digital Technologies Are Transforming Global Commerce" (2018), https://perma.cc/A98E-N28P, at 8.

6 McKinsey Global Institute, "The Age of Analytics: Competing in a Data-Driven World" (2016), https://perma.cc/CK95-VY4H. The characteristics of data-driven smart manufacturing include: (i) the enabling of "customer-centric product development by exploiting user data"; (ii) the enabling of smart production planning by exploiting task data; (iii) the enabling of precise control by exploiting data from the manufacturing process; (iv) the enabling of manufacturing process monitoring through exploiting real-time data; and (v) the enabling of proactive maintenance and quality control by exploiting historical and real-time data. F Tao et al., "Data-Driven Smart Manufacturing" (2018) 48 *Journal of Manufacturing Systems* 157, at 161.

7 The Internet of Things equips everyday objects, such as thermostats, refrigerators, and coffee machines, with identifying, sensing, networking, and processing capabilities that allow them to communicate with other devices via the Internet to achieve their objectives. See WTO, note 5 above, at 7.

8 A Korinek and J Stiglitz, "Artificial Intelligence and Its Implications for Income Distribution and Unemployment" (2017) NBER Working Paper 24174, at 21.

9 In the parable, an entrepreneur declares that they have found a way to transform wheat into cars, thereby significantly lowering the cost of production, decreasing the cost of cars for consumers, and increasing standards of living. A competitor, however, discovers that the purported production facilities are in fact empty and that the lower-cost production comes from trading domestic-produced wheat for foreign-produced cars, leading to a public outcry. JHB Pauwelyn et al., *International Trade Law* (New York, Wolters Kluwer, 2016), at 12–13; and J Ingram, *International Economics* (New York, John Wiley, 1983) .

10 D Rodrik, *The Globalization Paradox: Democracy and the Future of Trade Law* (New York, W.W. Norton & Company, 2011), at 59–60.

11 R Gilson, "Lawyers as Transaction Cost Engineers," in P Newman (ed), *The New Palgrave Dictionary of Economics and the Law* (New York, Stockton Press, 1998), at 509. Compare K Pistor, *The Code of Capital: How the Law Creates Wealth and Inequality* (Oxford, Princeton University Press, 2019), at

innovation – the creative disruptor of not just commerce but our life worlds. It is law and lawyers that construct the intangibles of the data-driven economy, such that its potential as energy is released.[12] Because AI systems require huge quantities of updated data to "train" themselves and continuously learn, improve, and refine their output, the data-driven economy relies on the free flow of data across borders generated from digitized societies.[13] Predictions made through AI improve with more data, driving its demand. For economic globalization, the "free flow of data" becomes the "fifth freedom" alongside the free movement of goods, services, capital, and labor – the "four freedoms" of the European Union's internal market.[14]

The great contract scholars and rule-of-law theorists stressed law's channeling function.[15] For the technological optimist, lawyers' role is to free up data flows so as to release pent-up energy for a leap in efficiency, facilitating the making of responsive, just-in-time products adapted to individual and group desires and needs. The challenge of trade law scholars then is to combat constraints on data flows such as data localization requirements that are proliferating,[16] and new digital taxes,[17] constituting a new protectionism impeding progress in the digitalized world. The challenge is to press for interoperative standards to ensure frictionless flow across borders and combat fragmentation. The dream is a world where small- and medium-sized enterprises (SMEs) – the Jeffersonian democrats of the marketplace – can compete on a fair footing with the multinational behemoths.[18] The goal is a terrain where developing country entrepreneurs can better participate and compete

158–182 (chapter 7 on lawyers as "The Masters of the Code," servicing capital's needs); and A Chander, "How Law Made Silicon Valley" (2014) 63 *Emory Law Journal* 639.

12 Compare W Hurst, *Law and the Conditions of Freedom in the 19th Century United States* (Madison, WI, University of Wisconsin Press, 1956), at 3 (chapter 1 titles law as "The Release of Energy").

13 D Barton et al., "Artificial Intelligence: Implications for China" (2017), https://perma.cc/98Q5-CGUA, at 7; D Ciuriak, "The Knowledge-Based and Data-Driven Economy: Quantifying the Impacts of Trade Agreements" (2017) CIGI Papers No. 156, at 5.

14 Ciuriak, note 5 above, at 9.

15 L Fuller, "Consideration and Form" (1941) 41 *Columbia Law Review* 799, at 801 (on legal form's "channeling function"); K Llewellyn, "The Normative, the Legal, and the Law Jobs: The Problem of Juristic Method" (1940) 49 *Yale Law Journal* 1355, at 1376–1383 ("The function includes, to repeat, not only the channeling of overt behavior but the channeling of expectations, norms and claims"); HLA Hart, *The Concept of Law* (Oxford, Oxford University Press, 1961) (law as "facilitative"); S Shapiro, *Legality*, (Cambridge, MA, Harvard University Press, 2013) (law as "planning," or plan-like norms, that help guide and coordinate action).

16 A Chander and U Lê, "Data Nationalism" (2015) 64 *Emory Law Journal* 677, at 679.

17 G Hufbauer and Z Lu, "The European Union's Proposed Digital Services Tax: A De Facto Tariff" (2018), https://perma.cc/S9TA-U45A, at 2. The imposition of digital taxes has become a new subject of trade disputes. Office of the United States Trade Representative, Docket No. USTR-2019-0009, Initiation of a Section 301 Investigation of France's Digital Services Tax (2019); PA Glicklich and H Martin, "Not Whether But When and How: U.S. Response to Unilateral Digital Taxation" (*Bloomberg Tax*, 30 October 2019), https://perma.cc/W6R3-B898.

18 WTO, note 5 above, at 9 ("The potential decline in trade costs can disproportionately benefit MSMEs and firms from developing countries"); and at 39, 69 (digitalization "leads to a substantial decrease in the cost of entry, making it easier for firms to produce, promote and distribute media products"); J Meltzer, "A WTO Reform Agenda: Data Flows and International Regulatory Cooperation" (2019),

because deficiencies of physical infrastructure matter less in a world of handheld computers and digitalized communications and services.[19] The vision is a world of affordable products tailored for individual wants produced in an environmentally sustainable way.[20] With advances such as 3D printing, we conceivably could live in a more localized society that would, in the words of Richard Baldwin in his book *The Globotics Upheaval*, "make for a better society."[21] Trade lawyers' role, from this vantage, is to release the potential of microchips, circuits, and smart machines through the free flow of data. If only government representatives could see policy from the individual consumer's perspective and understand the utilitarian benefits of global markets, the neoclassical trade theorist posits, the world would be more prosperous, more free, and more peaceful.

But if one is not a technology optimist, if one is a pragmatist who believes that there are tradeoffs, if one finds that technology may be unstoppable but there remain choices for governing it, if one is concerned about not just pathologies but also pathogens that law can channel, then what channel should governments choose? In a world of uncertainty, of speculation, amidst the fog of transnational distrust, insecurity, and rivalry, governments face a daunting task.

II THE CHALLENGES POSED

Let us consider eight risks that the technological tsunami of AI could unleash, which are both distinct and interrelated. They are the rise of social inequality and "winner-takes-all" industries, social control through surveillance, risks to democracy, national security threats, economic vulnerability and systemic risk, premature deindustrialization implicating development, geopolitical conflict, and threats to personal privacy and dignity. Although technological change offers great societal benefits, it also raises new regulatory challenges for which responses vary depending on societal contexts and preferences. There is thus reason for pause before concluding ambitious trade agreements that free data flows, at least without significant

https://perma.cc/S6NG-97J9, at 4 ("e-commerce provides a potentially significant opportunity to increase small business participation in international trade").

19 Meltzer, note 18 above, at 9, 11.

20 WTO, note 5 above, at 32 ("Additive manufacturing is expected to lead to a shift towards more digital and localized supply chains and lower energy use, resource demands and related CO2 emissions over the product life cycle"); M Gebler et al., "A Global Sustainability Perspective on 3D Printing Technologies" (2014) 74 *Energy Policy* 158. Additive manufacturing, for example, should reduce wasteful excess production because of its focus on efficiency and just-in-time production. However, maintaining massive amounts of data in the cloud and analyzing it through AI also require large amounts of energy that may come with significant environmental costs. N Jones, "The Information Factories: Data Centres Are Chewing Up Vast Amounts of Energy" (2018) 561 *Nature* 163, at 163–166.

21 R Baldwin, *The Globotics Upheaval: Globalization, Robotics, and the Future of Work* (Oxford, Oxford University Press, 2019), at 261. See also V Mayer-Schonberger and T Ramge, *Reinventing Capitalism in the Age of Big Data* (New York, Basic Books, 2018), at 14 ("Even rich data markets won't be perfect; but pragmatically, they will be far superior to what we have today"); P Barwise, "Nine Reasons Why Tech Markets Are Winner-Take-All" (*Think*, 10 July 2018), https://perma.cc/BU2P-5M82.

safeguards. This section examines each of these challenges before the next sections address future trade governance options.

First, the data-driven economy could spur growing inequality in multiple ways, raising social conflict. On the one hand, because of network effects, increasing returns of scale and scope, and the dynamic of first-mover advantage, the data-driven economy increasingly gives rise to winner-takes-all – or winner-takes-most – companies, such as Amazon for e-commerce, Google for search engines, and Facebook for social networking.[22] Companies proficiently using AI can serve additional customers globally at little marginal cost at the same time as they enhance quality, enabling the owner of this form of capital to capture unprecedented rents.[23] Unlike traditional industries, scale can be increased without the costs of "mass" because data is weightless; its storage is in the cloud. It thus entails near-zero marginal production costs. From this vantage, the trumpeting of e-commerce in terms of how it will benefit SMEs could be a utopian fantasy.

A data-driven economy not only enables economic behemoths to monopolize but also enables them to engage in price discrimination so that they price at what each individual consumer is willing to pay. One of the staple arguments for the benefit of markets in neoclassical economics – that of "consumer surplus" – is thus extracted from individuals since companies have the ability to predict what exactly each consumer is willing to pay and charge that amount.[24] In addition, AI permits companies to engage in cartel-like behavior through reactive, tit-for-tat responses to coordinate prices, once more to extract rents.[25] As winner-takes-most companies reap monopoly, oligopoly, and collusive rents, inequality proliferates (including between high- and low-skilled workers). The trade regime is already under considerable stress; simply removing trade barriers to data flows could contribute to social conflict within countries unless growing inequality is addressed.

Second, companies and governments gather data through surveillance that can exploit and shape us. The algorithms they use to process our data enable them to know our future and predict what we want and when we want it better than ourselves. Our wired world creates opportunities for enhanced state control through harnessing social pressure, epitomized by the development of "social credit" systems

22 D Autor et al., "Concentrating on the Fall of the Labor Share" (2017) 107 *American Economic Review* 180, at 184.

23 Ciuriak and Ptashkina, note 2 above, at 9.

24 Consumer surplus represents the difference between the maximum price a consumer is willing to pay and the actual price they pay based on market prices. There are benefits to precision/demand pricing so as to more accurately value goods and services, and thus increase efficiency in matching supply and demand, but such pricing practices also enable companies to extract rents, especially in oligopolistic markets.

25 WTO, note 5 above, at 42, 142. In addition, under this market dynamic, it is harder for niche companies to create profitable niches, which reduces the likelihood that some consumers will be served. Winner-takes-all companies acquire small companies to foreclose competition and, in the process, reduce consumer choice.

in China.[26] In parallel, it enables "surveillance capitalists" to steer us toward products to maximize their profits.[27] Not only can our data be automated, but we can too. When social media become constitutive of social participation, we become increasingly numb to companies and governments knowing everything about us, while we know nothing about how and what they know.[28] We as consumers are consumed. We participate in our commoditization to fuel trading in data to make the commodities that we buy. It is law that helps constitute that relationship, including through protecting company algorithms through property law.[29] Law could, for example, ban particular algorithmic practices and otherwise require disclosure and monitoring of algorithms so that they can be contested, whether for different forms of bias or for their social consequences.

Third, the data revolution poses massive problems for democracies. To start, the dynamic of increased economic inequality facilitates conditions for decreased social solidarity and increased social conflict, which can erode democracies. More specifically, the data revolution enables others to manipulate our views, including through the proliferation of "fake news" that harnesses predictive power regarding our psychology and behavior.[30] Tech developed and harnessed by groups such as Cambridge Analytica relentlessly targets individual vulnerabilities and spurs "thinking fast" tribal responses, thus manipulating behavior to win elections and embed leaders in power.[31] Foreign authoritarian powers can harness these mechanisms, creating "vast numbers of fake persons orchestrated by shadowy intelligence warfare units building momentum for online paranoia and conspiracy theories."[32] In addition, entrepreneurs can profit by targeting search results from prior preferences,

26 K Strittmatter, *We Have Been Harmonised: Life in China's Surveillance State* (London, Old Street Publishing, 2019) ; K Wong and A Dobson, "We're Just Data: Exploring China's Social Credit System in Relation to Digital Platform Ratings Cultures in Westernised Democracies" (2019) 4 *Global Media and China* 220, at 221.

27 S Zuboff, *The Age of Surveillance Capitalism: The Fight for a Human Future at the New Frontier of Power* (New York, Public Affairs, 2019), at 8 ("Surveillance capitalism unilaterally claims human experience as free raw material for translation into behavioral data ... fabricated into '*prediction products*' that are traded in '*behavioral futures markets*,' creating incentives '*to herd behavior to profitable outcomes*'"); J Cohen, "The Biopolitical Public Domain: The Legal Construction of the Surveillance Economy" (2018) 31 *Philosophy & Technology* 213, at 231 ("a commercial future in which consumer surplus is extracted 'from each according to his abilities,' while goods and services flow 'to each according to his [manufactured] needs'").

28 F Pasquale, *The Black Box Society* (Cambridge, MA, Harvard University Press, 2016).

29 Pistor, note 11 above, at 129–131.

30 L Diamond, *Ill Winds: Saving Democracy from Russian Rage, Chinese Ambition, and American Complacency* (New York, Penguin Press, 2019); R Hasen, *Election Meltdown: Dirty Tricks, Distrust, and the Threat to American Democracy* (New York, Yale University Press, 2020); D Kaye, *Speech Police: The Global Struggle to Govern the Internet* (New York, Columbia Global Reports, 2019).

31 J Bartlett, *The People vs Tech: How the Internet Is Killing Democracy* (New York, Dutton, 2018) at 1 ("In the coming years either tech will destroy democracy and the social order as we know it, or politics will stamp its authority over the digital world").

32 V Buterin and J Lanier, "Foreword," in E Posner and EG Weyl, *Radical Markets: Uprooting Capitalism and Democracy for a Just Society* (Princeton, NJ, Princeton University Press, 2018), at xxv.

which divides societies into information bubbles, leading to increased social fragmentation and political polarization. While foreign governments target conspiracy theories at vulnerable groups to create social chaos, entrepreneurs do so to profit from "clickbait."[33] As Larry Diamond documents, antidemocratic politics are spreading globally.[34] Democracies risk becoming a shell, unless governments, companies, and societies rise to the regulatory challenge.

Fourth, data and AI pose national security challenges, in part because the refined data and technology have dual uses, giving rise to a shift in trade analysis toward geopolitics and "geoeconomics."[35] This shift places traditional trade liberals, with their analysis of trade's mutual benefits, on the defensive. At the core of the USA–China trade war is technology, which will determine the global leaders of tomorrow and whether those leaders are Chinese or American. As part of this competition, China competes with the United States, Europe, and Japan in creating standards for the data-driven economy, such as for 5G infrastructure and the future of manufacturing. The US contestation of China's 2025 innovation initiative, in part, is because China threatens to take the lead in "smart manufacturing" at the cutting edge of technology. Yet that technology also can be used for military purposes. Sales of Huawei 5G infrastructure, for example, become security concerns not only because they facilitate espionage but also because a country's economy can be held hostage under the threat of a shutdown of wireless services. Technology can be "weaponized" by withholding key components in a trade war or in an actual conflict.[36]

Fifth, the technology poses significant systemic concerns regarding the risks of system vulnerability, integrity, and availability.[37] If the 5G network were to shut

33 C Silverman and L Alexander, "How Teens in the Balkans Are Duping Trump Supporters with Fake News" (*BuzzFeed*, 3 November 2016), https://perma.cc/9JNN-YJBT; A Higgins et al., "Inside a Fake News Sausage Factory: 'This Is All About Income'" (*New York Times*, 25 November 2016), https://perma.cc/CF85-JQEQ; N Pelroth, "A Former Fox News Executive Divides Americans Using Russian Tactics" (*New York Times*, 21 November 2019), https://perma.cc/9UJ6-C2WU.

34 Diamond, note 30 above.

35 R Blackwill and J Harris, *War by Other Means: Geoeconomics and Statecraft* (Cambridge, MA, Harvard University Press, 2016) (geoeconomics as the "use of economic instruments to promote and defend national interests, and to produce beneficial geopolitical results"); A Roberts et al., "Toward a Geoeconomic World Order in International Trade and Investment" (2019) 22 *Journal of International Economic Law* 655 (using the term "to describe a macro level change in the relationship between economics and security in the regime governing international trade and investment").

36 H Farrell and A Newman, "Weaponized Interdependence: How Global Economic Networks Shape State Coercion" (2019) 44 *International Security* 42.

37 Engineers refer to three types of risks known as CIA: confidentiality, integrity, and availability. Confidentiality refers to data privacy and security (i.e. unauthorized information release). Integrity refers to the ability of a third party to enter and compromise a program or device, such as a self-driven vehicle, a heart monitor, the electrical grid, or a nuclear power reactor (i.e. unauthorized information modification). Availability refers to the ability to shut down a device or system (i.e. unauthorized denial of use). These three risks are connected and thus referenced in terms of a triangle. For example, a breach of a system's integrity can compromise confidentiality as well as availability. AI, for example, can be very brittle, subject to compromise of its integrity so that a minor tweak can lead to serious malfunction, potentially leading to dire consequences. The CIA triad is codified in the United States

down without a backup, social chaos could spread, giving rise to a Margaret Atwood MaddAddam dystopia.[38] Economics, ecology, engineering, and psychology – from their different vantages – all stress the importance of resilience to guard against system collapse,[39] which the risks of the COVID-19 virus exemplify. The so-called global financial crisis was not in fact global because China and Chinese banks were less ensnared in the market disintegration triggered by the US housing and mortgage-backed securities bubble. Countries could sell their products to China, enabling the global economy to staunch contagion and recover more quickly. Imagine the counterfactual if China's economy had been "just like us" (i.e. the United States) in 2008, with free capital flows and globally integrated banks, and had crashed as well. Because it differed, there was greater resilience for the global economy, benefiting everyone. This experience holds lessons for the risks posed by a global economy dependent on single technological systems, regardless of whether geoeconomic conflict can be managed.

Sixth, the technological revolution can lead to "premature deindustrialization" of developing countries, possibly trapping them at low-income levels in services sectors, widening the global economic divide by a "digital divide."[40] Development economists worry about the consequences for development since manufacturing helped make many developing countries, particularly in Asia, richer.[41] With deindustrialization, smart manufacturing enterprises operate more like software companies, requiring employees to design, program, operate, and debug "smart" machines. That know-how will more likely reside in a few leading countries, with the United States, Europe, China, and a few others vying for leadership. In the winner-takes-most economy, large countries that require data localization, such as China, can grant privileged access to their nationals' data to national companies. That is why populous countries such as India, Indonesia, and Brazil envy Chinese Internet companies' fortunes. The calculus for smaller developing countries is less favorable. They most likely benefit from free data flows for foreign companies

Code in 44 U.S.C. §3552 (Definitions). Y Cherdantseva and J Hilton, A *Reference Model of Information Assurance Security* (2013) 2013 *Int'l Conf. on Availability, Reliability and Security* 546, at 546–555 (2013) (providing a history of the triad); N Kobie, "To Cripple AI, Hackers Are Turning Data Against Itself" (*Wired*, 11 September 2018), https://perma.cc/5FKF-NZFW.

[38] Atwood's MaddAddam trilogy consists of *Oryx and Crake* (2003), *The Year of the Flood* (2009), and *MaddAddam* (2013).

[39] R Bhamra et al., "Resilience: The Concept, a Literature Review and Future Directions" (2011) 49 *International Journal of Production Research* 5375, at 5386, 5393 (noting "the conceptual linkages between vulnerability, resilience and adaptive capacity"); Y Sheff, "Building a Resilient Supply Chain" (2005), https://perma.cc/W6PA-SK8L; J Diamond, *Collapse: How Societies Choose to Fail or Succeed* (London, Penguin Books, 2011).

[40] WTO, note 5 above, at 8.

[41] Deindustrialization is "premature" because developing countries lose the benefits of manufacturing jobs before "catching up" to the wealth and prosperity of "post-industrialized" nations. D Rodrik, "Premature Deindustrialization" (2015) NBER Working Paper Series No. 20935, at 3.

serving their constituents, but they will also face foreign monopolists' economic clout.

Seventh, because of rising inequality within countries (which the data-driven economy facilitates), combined with declining inequality between the West and a few emerging powers (notably China with its massive investments in AI and data-linked technology), social conflict both within and between countries could rise. Violence looms, threatening national civic and global peace. For some, the link between the threat of violence and this combination of increasing inequality within countries and decreasing inequality between them may seem paradoxical. Within national contexts, rising domestic inequality increases domestic social conflict. US President Trump's references to the prospect of "civil war" were he to be impeached are symptomatic,[42] as are the mass protests of the "yellow vest" movement in France.[43] At the international level, declining inequality between the United States and China threatens US hegemony and, possibly in turn, the stability of the international system to the extent that it depends on one country being hegemonic (per "hegemonic stability theory").[44] In parallel, populist leaders harness US and European workers' lost sense of status from the shift of jobs to China and the East, harnessing nationalist fervor. Scholars now warn of the "Thucydides Trap" in which a rising power and an incumbent heedlessly and inescapably march toward war.[45]

Eighth, and finally, there are risks to personal privacy and dignity. We have so far stressed societal risks as opposed to individual ones, as the latter have been most frequently addressed in legal scholarship.[46] Yet many of these societal risks build on individual ones. Even if societal risks are addressed, the risks to individuals regarding their privacy, dignity, and safety can be ruinous, whether the individual are coerced by authoritarian governments or privately, such as through social media.[47]

42 M McCord, "Armed Militias Are Taking Trump's Civil War Tweets Seriously" (*Lawfare*, 2 October 2019), https://perma.cc/8KE3-D3TY. As Diamond also writes, "Trump suggested that if his democratically nominated rival, Hillary Clinton, won, the only way to stop her from picking liberal, pro-gun-control judges would lie with 'the Second Amendment people' – a clear reference to gun violence and assassination." Diamond, note 30 above, at 78–79.

43 P Goodman, "Inequality Fuels Rage of 'Yellow Vests' in Equality-Obsessed France" (*New York Times*, 15 April 2019), https://perma.cc/3NC7-KURS.

44 "Hegemonic stability theory" posits that the international system will be more stable if one country is a dominant power or hegemon, as was the United States following the end of the Cold War. R Gilpin and JM Gilpin, *Global Political Economy: Understanding the International Economic Order* (Princeton, NJ, Princeton University Press, 2001).

45 G Allison, "The Thucydides Trap: Are the U.S. and China Headed for War?" (*The Atlantic*, 24 September 2015), https://perma.cc/5V8L-9YSA.

46 See, for example, B Schneier, *Data and Goliath: The Hidden Battles to Collect Your Data and Your World* (New York, W.W. Norton & Company, 2015); DJ Solove and PM Schwartz, *Information Privacy Law* (New York, Wolters Kluwer, 2017); C Kuner, *Transborder Data Flows and Data Privacy Law* (Oxford, Oxford University Press, 2013).

47 In this vein, Europe (as well as others) has recognized a "right to be forgotten" in recognition of individual privacy and dignity. *Google Spain SL, Google Inc. v Agencia Española de Protección de Datos, Mario Costeja González* (2014). Compare Daniel Citron, *Hate Crimes in Cyberspace* (Cambridge, MA, Harvard University Press, 2016).

III THE CURRENT NEGOTIATING CONTEXT

Trade negotiations often take a mercantilist orientation where trade negotiators aim to protect domestic industries while opening foreign markets. Through the mechanism of reciprocity, these negotiations, complemented by litigation, have led to greater trade liberalization over time. For those focused on reciprocally opening markets, their starting point is no different for data than it is for goods and services – how to free up flows, in this case data flows that are intrinsic to the new data-driven economy. In this way, trade law can reduce transaction costs for business and the costs of segmented markets.[48]

Trade scholars have focused on the fit of current trade rules with developments in the new economy, finding the fit wanting.[49] The same conclusion applies to international law more generally,[50] rendering the challenges for trade law even greater. Given that World Trade Organization (WTO) rules were negotiated over a quarter of a century ago, before the Internet existed, scholars naturally conclude that trade rules must be updated. WTO rules still address primarily goods, a legacy of the 1948 General Agreement on Tariffs and Trade (GATT), an era where industrial manufacturing represented the commanding heights of the economy. In 1995, with the creation of the WTO and its inclusion of a General Agreement on Trade in Services (GATS), the trade regime partially and indirectly addressed services that are linked to the digital economy, as well as technical regulations affecting trade in goods.[51] But that too was a quarter of a century ago and technology has changed radically. Today, services constitute the largest and fastest-growing part of the global economy in terms of output, value added, and employment.[52] The GATS only rudimentarily addresses digital issues where the line between a "good" and a "service" blurs and could eventually disappear.[53] Not only are an increasing number of goods now inextricably linked with "services" (the Internet of Things),

48 At the WTO ministerial meeting in Buenos Aires in 2018, a group of members issued a Joint Statement on Electronic Commerce to commence negotiations. WTO, *Joint Statement on Electronic Commerce*, WT/L/1056, 25 January 2019.

49 Meltzer, note 18 above; AD Mitchell and N Mishra, "Data at the Docks: Modernizing International Trade Law for the Digital Economy" (2018) 20 *Vanderbilt Journal of Entertainment & Technology Law* 1073; M Burri, "The Regulation of Data Flows Through Trade Agreements" (2017) 48 *Georgetown Journal of International Law* 407.

50 B Kingsbury, "Infrastructure and InfraReg: On Rousing the International Law 'Wizards of Is'" (2019) 8 *Cambridge University Law Journal* 171, at 184.

51 The WTO included a more detailed agreement governing product regulation, the Agreement on Technical Barriers to Trade, but it was drafted before the rise of the data-driven economy and does not address data regulation.

52 P Buckley and R Majmudar, "The Services Powerhouse: Increasingly Vital to World Economic Growth" (*Deloitte*, 12 July 2018), https://perma.cc/3KZA-E7DM; S Lund et al., "Globalization in Transition: The Future of Trade and Value Chains" (2019), https://perma.cc/9X9F-KSJR, at 109.

53 Mitchell and Mishra, for example, note the limitations of the GATS classification system, and the fact that the main restrictions on Internet-based services are regulatory. Mitchell and Mishra, note 49 above.

but know-how and data have become the most valuable components of trade across borders.[54]

While WTO negotiations have failed to fill key regulatory gaps for digital trade, countries have negotiated bilateral and plurilateral trade agreements to instill their priorities and values into standards for the digital economy. Trade negotiations reflect competition between systems, since countries' positions reflect their internal policies. One can broadly speak of three distinct approaches for digital governance advanced by the WTO's three most powerful members – the United States, the European Union (EU), and China.[55]

The United States has trumpeted a world of free "data flows" that would benefit its companies.[56] The United States-Mexico-Canada Agreement, which entered into force on 1 July 2020, illustrates the US approach.[57] Chapter 19 of the agreement is on "Digital Trade," and it represents the first time that a trade agreement has a chapter with such a title. Although this change is, in part, semantic since the chapter borrows significantly from chapter 14 of the earlier Trans-Pacific Partnership (TPP) agreement on "Electronic Commerce," the title signifies a broader concern than trade in goods, and the chapter indeed further tightens rules in favor of US technology companies. It includes provisions mandating free movement of data, a permanent moratorium on customs duties, and bans on data localization requirements, forced disclosure of source codes, and other forced technology transfers. It also includes a new provision providing that Internet platforms should not be held civilly liable for their users' actions, which is modeled on section 230 of the US Communications Decency Act.[58]

Although the EU has advanced liberalization objectives, it imposes significant restraints on the free flow of data on privacy grounds. The EU's position is reflected in its General Data Protection Regulation (GDPR), together with EU judicial oversight of its negotiation of "adequacy decisions" with third countries, such as through "safe harbors" and "privacy shields," in order for data on European citizens to leave the continent. On 16 July 2020, the European Court of Justice invalidated the US-EU Privacy Shield because it provides inadequate protection to EU citizens' privacy from surveillance, just as the court had in October 2015 as regards the

54 McKinsey Global Institute, note 4 above.

55 Ciuriak and Ptashkina present an excellent table comparing US, EU, and Chinese approaches across issue areas based on the Trans-Pacific Partnership (TPP), the EU-Canada Comprehensive Economic and Trade Agreement (CETA), and the China-Australia Free Trade Agreement. Ciuriak and Ptashkina, note 2 above, at table A1 in annex 2.

56 The United States is home to the top ten Internet brands, seven out of the ten Internet companies with the largest market value worldwide, and four US companies provide more than half of the world's cloud computing capacity. SA Aaronson and P Leblond, "Another Digital Divide: The Rise of Data Realms and Its Implications for the WTO" (2018) 21 *Journal of International Economic Law* 245, at 253.

57 Agreement between the United States of America, the United Mexican States, and Canada (USMCA), chapter 19, 10 December 2019 (entered into force 1 July 2020).

58 Ibid., at art. 19.17; and Communications Decency Act of 1996 § 230, 47 U.S.C. § 230.

previous US-EU "Safe Harbor Privacy Principles."[59] Because the EU lacks leading digital firms, it is politically easier for it to champion such regulation.[60]

China, in contrast, applies "data localization" requirements on sovereignty grounds, rather than the protection of citizen rights. In this way, the Chinese state and Chinese companies control data over China's 1.4 billion citizens, facilitating social control while creating a competitive advantage for Chinese enterprises.[61] A result is the rise of Chinese information technology titans such as Alibaba and Tencent.

Other countries choose among these three models, although those "choices" occur within negotiating contexts that can involve highly asymmetric power. In this way, these different models are adopted around the globe. Japan has adopted the US approach, as reflected in the 2019 US-Japan Trade Agreement.[62] Australia and Canada have hybrid approaches that include stronger data privacy protection as under the EU model, while India, Indonesia, and Brazil are enticed by China's requirements of data localization to create national champions.[63]

A question arises regarding how these models will interface. It is conceivable that the United States and EU could negotiate a further compromise. Although the EU will periodically challenge US tech giants, it unlikely will develop its own. Nonetheless, the EU generally favors a single market for data flows, subject to adequate privacy and consumer protection. The United States and China, however, are less likely to negotiate a compromise (unless it includes significant carve-outs on national security and other public policy grounds) given the advantages for China of requiring data localization so that foreign companies do not gain access to the Chinese data trove. India will likely follow this route.[64] Economic behemoths from just a few countries could dominate the globe. From an economics perspective, the global market will not be based on perfect competition

59 Court of Justice of the European Union Press Release 91/20, The Court of Justice Invalidates Decision 2016/1250 on the Adequacy of the Protection Provided by the EU-US Data Protection Shield (16 July 2020); Case C311/18, Data Prot. Comm'r v. Facebook Ireland Ltd. ECLI:EU:C:2020:559 (16 July 2020).

60 There are no European firms among the top fifteen digital firms by market value, and US firms control some 54 percent of the EU's digital market. Aaronson and Leblond, supra 56 above, at 258.

61 Mitchell and Mishra, note 49 above. While the United States and European Union have been exporting their approach through free trade agreements (FTAs), Chinese FTAs do not contain binding rules on data flows or language to limit digital protectionism. Rather, China has encouraged e-commerce, a sector where it is very competitive with firms like Alibaba and JD.com. For example, China included provisions for facilitating cross-border e-commerce in its updated FTA with Chile. Ibid., at 268. China is the world's largest digital market, accounts for more than 40 percent of e-commerce transactions, and by 2021 more than half its economy will be digital. Ibid., at 262.

62 See "Fact Sheet on U.S.-Japan Trade Agreement," Office of the United States Trade Representative (2019), https://perma.cc/SVZ4-JAKJ.

63 Mitchell and Mishra, note 49 above, at 1084–1087.

64 "US Criticises India's Data Localisation Norms, Draft E-commerce Policy" (*The Economic Times*, 9 April 2019), https://economictimes.indiatimes.com/news/economy/foreign-trade/us-criticises-indias-data-localisation-norms-draft-e-commerce-policy/articleshow/68794927.cms?from=mdr.

reflected in neoclassical models, but rather "strategic trade" in which a few countries compete to support national champions that reap oligopolistic and monopolistic profits, potentially having positive spillover effects for their national economies.

IV GOVERNANCE FRAMEWORK FOR A WAY FORWARD: A CALL FOR MODESTY

Although the challenges are severe, if they are to be met, law must play a critical role nationally, internationally, and transnationally. This section provides a framework for addressing the challenges posed. It places trade law in a broader regulatory context that involves competing ways to frame the "problem" to be addressed in a world characterized by uncertainty and rapid technological change. It then applies it to particular issues.

Addressing the challenges requires regulation. Two key issues are: (i) at what level regulation should occur; and (ii) what form and content such regulation should take. In practice, regulation can occur at multiple levels and take different forms, public and private, hard and soft. Moreover, regulation in any one country will have impacts on constituencies outside that country, so that countries have incentives to address these externalities. In parallel, common problems may require regulatory coordination among countries to address it. The key questions thus can be reframed as: (i) What regulation, if any, should occur at the international level and how should it interface with national regulation? (ii) What forms should regulation take and how should these forms interface?

1. **Three Governing Principles.** To determine a framework for governance of the respective challenges, we start with three principles. First, traditional trade agreements are not optimal for regulatory agreements and thus trade agreements need to be viewed as part of a *broader ecology of governance* of the new data-driven economy, which creates links between different rule-making and monitoring bodies at different levels of social organization. Second, for most of the issues raised in Section II, there should be *no single system of hierarchical rules*. Rather, in a world of radical uncertainty and different preferences regarding the regulation of these issues, countries will benefit from experimentation with different regulatory approaches. A diversity of regulatory approaches provides greater resilience against the systemic risks posed when single systems fail. Third, given the transnational impacts of the risks, as well as of national regulation addressing (or failing to address) them, there is a need for *systems of regulatory coordination* over options and experiences that will facilitate trade while enhancing regulatory efficacy, learning, and adaptation. Once one turns to issues of coordination and the interface of different national regulatory systems, one is in a world of transnational legal ordering that is not just top-down but also bottom-up, horizontal, and transversal.

Elsewhere I have developed a theory of transnational legal orders with the sociologist Terence Halliday.[65] That approach focuses on how problems are framed, norms develop transnationally in response to such framings, and norms settle and unsettle as part of recursive processes of interaction between different levels of social organization, from the international to the national and local. That framework has been predominantly positivist in its approach, aimed at generating empirical research for how legal norms develop, diffuse, and change transnationally.

Such an approach, however, also has normative payoffs when combined with what has been called new governance theory regarding systems of adaptive regulation in light of uncertainty involving changing problems and regulatory contexts. New governance theory, when applied transnationally, emphasizes the need for the development of new transnational institutional structures for regulation comprising a common forum for deliberation, principles to guide discussions, an open menu of options for addressing regulatory choices, and peer review and information sharing to enhance trust and learning.[66] Through such structured processes of regulatory dialogue, both hard and soft international law norms can develop.[67] The question becomes: How can trade law help to facilitate and channel these processes?

Under a new governance approach, countries jointly create regulatory goals and measures to gauge achievement and permit variation in how regulatory agencies pursue the attainment of these goals. These agencies then report to each other and participate in peer-review processes regarding regulatory outcomes, aimed at continual improvement and potential reassessment of goals in light of experience.[68] This approach, in the pragmatist tradition, entails ongoing mutual scrutiny of outcomes and their effectiveness based on continuous information exchange by regulators committed to regulatory improvement and attentive to risk, including potentially catastrophic risks. Under this approach, regulators exchange information, conduct joint trials and risk assessments, monitor results, and adapt regulatory

65 T Halliday and G Shaffer, *Transnational Legal Orders* (Cambridge, Cambridge University Press, 2015).

66 C Sabel and J Zeitlin, "Learning from Difference: The New Architecture of Experimentalist Governance in the EU," in C Sabel and J Zeitlin (eds), *Experimentalist Governance in the European Union: Toward a New Architecture* (Oxford, Oxford University Press, 2012) (theorizing, describing, and giving examples of new governance mechanisms in the EU); G de Burca and J Scott (eds), *Law and New Governance in the EU and the US* (Oxford, Hart, 2006), at 2; V Nourse and G Shaffer, "Empiricism, Experimentalism, and Conditional Theory" (2014) 67 *Southern Methodist University Law Review* 141.

67 The Organisation for Economic Co-operation and Development (OECD) breaks down the full range of options into eleven approaches that include these regulatory options. See OECD, *International Regulatory Cooperation: Rules for a Global World* (2012); J Wiener and A Alemanno, "The Future of International Regulatory Cooperation: TTIP as a Learning Process toward a Global Policy Laboratory" (2015) 78 *Law & Contemporary Problems* 103.

68 CF Sabel and WH Simon, "Minimalism and Experimentalism in the Administrative State" (2011) 100 *Georgetown Law Journal* 53, at 55; Nourse and Shaffer, note 66 above.

practices.[69] Transparency is central to this model through processes of information sharing, peer review, questioning, and response. Through regulatory learning, norms and practices can recursively change.

At the global level, Charles Sabel and Bernard Hoekman note the possibility of open plurilateral trade agreements that could create frameworks for developing such a regulatory approach. A core group of countries initially would join the agreement, but others could join it subsequently.[70] In June 2020, Chile, New Zealand, and Singapore signed a Digital Economy Partnership Agreement that aims to develop mechanisms that build trust in data flows, which is open for other parties to join.[71] More broadly, the United States and EU discussed the development of new transatlantic regulatory mechanisms in their negotiations to create a Transatlantic Trade and Investment Partnership.[72] The EU proposed the creation of a new transatlantic body, called a Regulatory Cooperation Body, to support specific regulatory cooperation initiatives and oversee them. Hoekman noted how other institutions, including private ones, could complement it in particular regulatory domains.[73] Through ongoing interactions, national regulators eventually could recognize each other's regulations as functionally equivalent, facilitating trade. These programs could lead to the institutionalization of broader sectoral frameworks, giving rise to cooperative regulatory systems that reduce barriers to trade while enhancing regulatory responsiveness in an increased number of domains. Food safety is one area where such a system has been applied transnationally.[74] The governance challenges posed by the digital economy beckon for new institutional initiatives in this vein.

New governance theory is particularly useful in a world of radical regulatory uncertainty. Given the risks, uncertainties, and differences in values, interests, and priorities, international trade law must not foreclose experimentation and variance. Yet, given these very same risks, uncertainties, and differences, international trade law and institutions are needed to foster cooperation, deliberation, and exchange of

69 See C Sabel and W Simon, "Contextualizing Regimes: Institutionalization as a Response to the Limits of Interpretation and Policy Engineering" (2012) 110 *Michigan Law Review* 1, at 18, 20.

70 C Sabel and B Hoekman, "Open Plurilateral Agreements, International Regulatory Cooperation and the WTO" (2019) 10 *Global Policy* 297. See also B Hoekman and C Sabel, "In a World of Value Chains: What Space for Regulatory Coherence and Cooperation in Trade Agreements," in B Kingsbury et al. (eds), *Megaregulation Contested: Global Economic Ordering After TPP* (Oxford, Oxford University Press, 2019).

71 The Digital Economy Partnership Agreement (DEPA) (2019), www.mfat.govt.nz/assets/Uploads/DEPA-Signing-Text-11-June-2020-GMT.PDF.

72 G Shaffer, "Alternatives for Regulatory Governance Under TTIP: Building from the Past" (2016) 22 *Columbia Journal of European Law* 1.

73 Hoekman, for example, recommended the creation of "knowledge platforms" that bring together "academics, regulators, government agencies, and NGOs." B Hoekman, "Fostering Transatlantic Regulatory Cooperation and Gradual Multilateralization" (2015) 18 *Journal of International Economic Law* 609, at 615. He similarly notes the potential role for supply chain councils that would identify regulatory policies that generate unnecessary costs in light of regulatory objectives. Ibid., at 618.

74 Sabel and Hoekman, note 67 above.

ideas. International trade law must foster transnational engagement, while not foreclosing regulatory policy space to engage with the challenges posed. Seeking and adjusting the "right" balance between coordination, harmonization, and experimentation will be an ongoing challenge.

2. **Electronic Commerce.** Regarding electronic commerce, a WTO trade agreement is most achievable if it adopts a decentralized model that accommodates regulatory flexibility in which countries of varying levels of development have different implementation periods conditioned on regulatory capacity building and technical assistance. The WTO's 2017 WTO Trade Facilitation Agreement offers a model of how this can be done.[75] The Trade Facilitation Agreement provides for flexibility in relation to a country's level of development, and it facilitates provision of technical assistance and resources for developing countries to adapt their regulatory systems. A new digital trade agreement could have a similar structure, in this case organized to accommodate not only countries at different levels of development but also to support the interface and interoperability of different regulatory systems that reflect varying national practices and preferences.[76] It could establish digital norms to ensure the validity of contracts, recognition of electronic authorizations and signatures, protection against fraudulent practices, and the banning of unsolicited commercial messages. In this way, parties would commit both to foster consumer trust by protecting information and preventing fraud, and to cooperate to tackle transnational problems, such as spam generated from abroad.[77] Developing country adherence to them, however, would be subject to the receipt of technical assistance, as under the Trade Facilitation Agreement.

These norms could be negotiated and developed in conjunction with other venues, such as before the United Nations Commission on International Trade Law (UNCITRAL), the United Nations Conference on Trade and Development (UNCTAD), the Organisation for Economic Co-operation and Development (OECD), and the G20, each of which has ongoing programs to develop, share, assess, and provide capacity building for the adoption of e-commerce regulations.[78] Though developed elsewhere, the norms could be incorporated by reference into the trade agreement and be updated over time. They could constitute minimum

[75] The Trade Facilitation Agreement was concluded at the WTO Ministerial Conference in Bali in December 2013, but it did not enter into force until 22 February 2017. A Eliason, "The Trade Facilitation Agreement: A New Hope for the World Trade Organization" (2015) 14 *World Trade Review* 643, at 644.

[76] This also could be addressed through a "reference paper on digital trade," which is attached to a WTO members' schedule of commitments under the GATS, where there is a basic text that provides for variation in members' commitments, analogous to the Trade Facilitation Agreement. M Burri, "Towards a Treaty on Digital Trade" 55 *Journal of World Trade* 1 (2021, in press).

[77] R Wolfe, "Learning about Digital Trade: Privacy and E-Commerce in CETA and TPP" (2019) 18 *World Trade Review* 63.

[78] I Lianos et al., "The Global Governance of Online Consumer Protection and E-Commerce, Building Trust" (2019), https://perma.cc/3LLE-GG39.

standards, while permitting countries to deviate from them on legitimate regulatory grounds. There is precedent for this approach in WTO and other trade agreements. Within the WTO, the Agreement on Sanitary and Phytosanitary Standards references standards developed by Codex Alimentarius and other standard-setting bodies, and the Agreement on Technical Barriers to Trade references international standards more generally, including those developed in the International Organization for Standardization (ISO). More directly on point, in the EU-Canada agreement known as CETA (Comprehensive Economic and Trade Agreement), the parties agree that they "shall take into due consideration international standards of data protection of relevant international organizations of which both Parties are members."[79] In each case, they permit parties to apply more stringent standards for legitimate regulatory reasons.

Such an agreement could also include provisions that are standard in trade agreements. It could require nondiscrimination between domestic and foreign digital products, potentially subject to negotiated product and sectoral carve-outs and general exceptions on regulatory policy grounds, including national security. It could incorporate basic due process commitments, including the right to be heard and to receive reasoned justifications before administrative and judicial processes. It could address (and either ban or otherwise limit) customs duties on electronic transmissions. It could likewise cover the use of digital taxes, possibly, once more, by reference to standards developed elsewhere, whether in the OECD or otherwise.[80] It also could clarify and enhance parties' market access commitments to services that affect digital trade, which is currently being negotiated in the form of a Trade in Services Agreement on a plurilateral basis among a subset of twenty-three WTO members, including the United States and EU.[81]

Such an agreement could include an ongoing new governance component as well. It could require regulatory transparency and create a framework for

[79] Comprehensive Economic and Trade Agreement (CETA), Art. 16.4. Parts of CETA went into provisional effect in September 2017, pending ratification.

[80] A trade agreement could incorporate by reference rules on digital taxes developed elsewhere, such as the OECD or G20. Many developing countries are wary of such liberalization, including the banning of customs duties on electronic transmissions, fearing they will lose revenue and competitiveness. U.N. Conference on Trade and Development, *Rising Product Digitilisation and Losing Trade Competitiveness*, 15–18, Doc No. UNCTAD/GDS/ECIDC/2017/3 (2017). As for revenue, however, they still could apply nondiscriminatory sales and value-added taxes on such transmissions.

[81] For many digital services, it is unclear how they should be classified under the GATS. Burri, note 49 above, at 413–414. Where countries want even greater constraints on data and digital-related regulation, such as prohibiting data localization and source code transfers (subject to possible exceptions, such as on national security and public order grounds), they can address them in bilateral and regional agreements. Even the United States, for example, will wish to retain authority to access source code to guard against money laundering or economics sanctions evasion. See, for example, the Comprehensive and Progressive Agreement for Trans-Pacific Partnership (CPTPP), Art. 14.17; USMCA, Art. 19.16; US-Japan Trade Agreement. On the range of data localization policies that vary in their strictness, see S Sacks and J Sherman, "Global Data Governance" (*New America*, 16 December 2019), https://perma.cc/3FNT-V8DA, at 8.

regulators, standard setters, and commercial enterprises to engage with and learn from each other to address the uncertainties that new technologies pose and share information through peer-to-peer processes.[82] Although WTO committee and working group processes offer one means,[83] these groups also can work in coordination with other international organizations and standard-setting bodies where the primary regulatory peer review could be done. These latter bodies could then report to the WTO committee. In parallel, bilateral and plurilateral trade agreements can serve as learning laboratories for the development of norms.

3. **Cybersecurity and Resilience.** To turn to the other challenges raised in Section II, they will be more difficult. For example, concerns over resilience represent a critical reason why a very "ambitious" trade agreement would be problematic at this stage. Governments must be free to regulate and require different standards, product controls, and even product bans, on security grounds to ensure resilience. States and companies will need to develop backup, modular, and exit systems involving redundant and diverse infrastructure that is adaptive to 5G communications and other breakdowns.[84] It is a critical question for engineering and for regulatory policy. There are always tradeoffs in product performance and costs, on the one hand, and security, on the other. But here it is not a question of simple market failure and "second-best" government intervention to "correct" it. Rather, the risks can be catastrophic. Regulation of these concerns should thus be left predominantly at the national level, addressed primarily by security and not trade law professionals.

The current GATT Article XXI exception on national security grounds was not drafted with cybersecurity concerns at stake and it will need to be updated to address cyber threats.[85] The article currently refers to "action … taken at time of war or other emergency in international relations." National cybersecurity precautions do not neatly fall within this text. It accordingly should be expanded to grant governments greater flexibility to define their security policies in relation to new threats (beyond immediate "emergencies"), while remaining subject to oversight through peer-review mechanisms and (possibly) judicial application of proportionality analysis on a deferential basis. For example, article 17.13 of the Regional Comprehensive Economic Partnership now includes measures "taken so as to protect critical public infrastructure,

82 Sabel and Hoekman, note 70 above.

83 A Lang and J Scott, "The Hidden World of WTO Governance" (2009) 20 *EJIL* 575, at 589.

84 "EU Coordinated Risk Assessment of the Cybersecurity of 5G Networks Report" (9 October 2019), https://perma.cc/CS9S-FZLG; "Overview of Risks Introduced by 5G Adoption in the United States" (31 July 2019); J-P Kleinhans, "Whom to Trust in a 5G World? Policy Recommendations for Europe's 5G Challenge" (2019), https://perma.cc/VHA7-ZT9E.

85 For an excellent article on alternative institutional arrangements to address national security issues, see B Heath, "The New National Security Challenge to the Economic Order" (2020) 129 *Yale Law Journal* 924.

including communications, power, and water infrastructures" under the list of legitimate national security concerns.[86]

The bulk of such regulatory efforts must be national where regulators and politicians are most easily held to account. Nonetheless, given the externalities of one country's regulations on others and given reciprocal regulatory concerns, there is a role for regulatory architectures where countries adopting different economic models, holding different preferences, and advancing different interests can cooperate. That calls, on the one hand, for the retention of policy space, including the development of "regulatory sandboxes" to keep up with a rapidly changing digital world in which diverse countries may gain regulatory experience and develop alternative regulatory models.[87] On the other hand, it calls for the development of new oversight and peer-review mechanisms, together with standard setting, possibly on a voluntary, soft-law basis. Such standard setting and oversight can be allocated between the ISO, the International Electrotechnical Commission, the WTO, and other organizations, catalyzing interlinked networks of institutional oversight and peer review to foster policy learning, cooperation, and coordination.

In a world of increasing geoeconomic competition and accompanying national security concerns, there are limits to what trade agreements can accomplish. Because technological shifts give rise to automated and wirelessly connected products that are vulnerable to hacking, trade in such products acquires a greater security dimension. The US blacklisting of Huawei and other Chinese companies, the banning of the use of Huawei's 5G technology for their wireless networks by Australia, Japan, New Zealand, and the United Kingdom, and Europe's internal debates exemplify the concerns. In this area, the 2017 US national security plan declares, "economic security is national security."[88] Trade wars and the decline of the rule of law for trade could follow.[89]

And yet, law can be structured to alleviate some of these concerns by facilitating international coordination. To start, rising US concerns over national security suggest that the US position also is shifting toward more expansive exceptions to free data flow commitments.[90]

86 Regional Comprehensive Economic Partnership, article 17.13. The new USMCA goes further in constraining judicial review, providing that "nothing in this Agreement shall be construed to . . . preclude a Party from applying measures that it considers necessary for . . . the protection of its own essential security interests." USMCA, article 32.2. As a result, invocation of "essential security interests" is no longer limited to an enumerated list of matters under the USMCA, unlike under GATT Article XXI.

87 Ciuriak, note 3 above, at 7.

88 "National Security Strategy of the United States of America" (December 2017), https://perma.cc/Q3KH-RYTH, at 17 (citing Donald Trump, "Economic security is national security," as epigraph).

89 G Shaffer, "A Tragedy in the Making? The Decline of Law and the Return of Power in International Trade Relations" (2019) 44 *Yale Journal of International Law Online* 37.

90 For example, the US government is concerned about Chinese companies transmitting data on US consumers back to China. J Nicas et al., "TikTok Said to Be Under National Security Review"

This shift potentially could facilitate agreement, provided the exceptions are broad enough to encompass privacy and public order interests advanced by the EU, China, and others. In addition, a transnational governance architecture that convenes regulators to address common problems can enhance deliberation, reduce tensions, and thus (indirectly) be more conducive to peace. The approach set forth in this chapter is vastly preferable to the current situation in which trust that underpins a cooperative international trade legal order is eroding.

4. **Competition Law.** Similarly, policymakers are reevaluating competition policy in response to digitalization and the data-driven economy.[91] Policy options include regulating property rights in data,[92] blocking oligopolists' expansion through acquisitions that preempt competition, breaking up companies, and regulating oligopolists like utilities or fiduciaries.[93] There is considerable debate

(*New York Times*, 1 November 2019), https://perma.cc/8UZQ-SXAP (noting "evidence of the app sending data to China"). At the WTO, the United States has proposed three categories of exceptions relating to the Joint Statement Initiative on e-commerce: a general exception (which would include public morals and thus privacy); a national security exception; and a prudential/monetary exception. H Monicken, "China's E-commerce Proposal Includes Privacy Protections, Lacks Data Flow," 37 *Inside US Trade* 20 (2019).

91 T Philippon, *The Great Reversal: How America Gave Up on Free Markets* (Cambridge, MA, Harvard University Press, 2019). It is sometimes argued that "the nature of competition in digital markets differs from that in traditional markets as it tends to be based first-and-foremost on innovation rather than pricing," although welfare losses may be high as monopolists become entrenched. R Anderson et al., "Competition Policy, Trade and the Global Economy: Existing WTO Elements, Commitments in Regional Trade Agreements, Current Challenges and Issues for Reflection" (2018) WTO Staff Working Papers ERSD-2018–12, at 47.

92 The legal construct of property rights in data is subject to debate. For example, should data that is generated by user interaction with a product (say, a rented driverless vehicle) be owned by the user, the producer (of the vehicle), or a third-party service provider (such as the rental company, the provider of GPS services, or the provider of insurance)? Should individuals retain ownership rights in their data? Should data be socialized so that large companies are forced to share it with competitors to combat monopolization? Should oligopolistic companies holding data be regulated like utilities? Should governments create state-owned enterprises to profit from citizens' data that the government holds? Or should there be bans on the collection and use of some data so that it does not become property at all? Compare L Weinar, *Blood Oil: Tyrants, Violence, and the Rules That Run the World* (Oxford, Oxford University Press, 2016) (critiquing the role of property law in legitimizing theft by corrupt leaders of a people's natural resources); and F Pasquale, "The Second Wave of Algorithmic Accountability" (*Law and Political Economy Blog*, 25 November 2019), https://perma.cc/F376-5GBT (contending that some algorithms should be banned).

93 For example, some propose granting competitive access to data to alleviate consumer "switching costs" of moving from one platform to another, which otherwise lock in consumers. World Trade Report 2018, at 42. Article 20 of the EU's General Data Protection Regulation provides for "data portability" of raw data provided by the data subject, but it likely will have limited impact since the value of data lies in how it has been processed. Regulation 2016/679, of the European Parliament and of the Council of 27 April 2016 on the protection of natural persons with regard to the processing of personal data and on the free movement of such data, and repealing Directive 95/46/EC (General Data Protection Regulation), 2016 O.J. (L 119/1), 68. Nonetheless, government-mandated information sharing will be critical to retain competitive markets. Australia, for example, began consultations on a "mandatory information-sharing scheme between international automakers and Australia's independent repair and service sector" after its national competition authority found that car

regarding them.[94] Winner-takes-most companies profit globally through trade, raising tensions between the companies' home countries and third countries regulating them, as in the case of the EU investigating the practices of US data-exploiting multinational companies such as Google.[95] Countries deploying competition law to discipline foreign companies will continue to trigger trade conflicts.[96] Given divisions on competition policy, especially between the United States and EU, and given divisions in economic theory, including in relation to the diversity of social contexts, it may be difficult to address this issue in a trade agreement. Nonetheless, the issue calls for dialogue and regulatory response, including within the International Competition Network (ICN), the OECD, and UNCTAD, as well as the WTO's system of committees and working groups. Although the OECD has organized a series of sessions on these issues and the ICN spent its annual meeting in 2019 at Cartagena addressing them, much more work needs to be done regarding the competition law challenges that digitalization poses.[97]

5. **Data Privacy.** As regards data privacy regulation, countries' approaches again will diverge based on different preferences. Nonetheless, structures can be developed where countries discuss their common concerns and work to free data flows so long as core concerns are met. The European Court of Justice's invalidation of the US-EU Privacy Shield, while upholding the validity of the EU's "standard contractual" clauses for data transfers, illustrates the challenges posed.[98] Nonetheless, bilateral negotiations, complemented by the development

manufacturers withheld the computerized information from mechanics to favor their dealership networks. N Toscano, "Win for Local Mechanics with Plan to Make World's Car Makers Share High Tech Data" (*The Sydney Morning Herald*, 12 February 2019), https://perma.cc/YG2X-BANH. See also Mayer-Schonberger and Ramge, note 21 above, at 167–169 (calling for "progressive data sharing").

94 Compare J Tirole and S Rendall, *Economics for the Common Good* (Princeton, NJ, Princeton University Press, 2019) (chapters 14 and 15); "What if Large Tech Firms Were Regulated Like Sewage Companies?" (*The Economist*, 23 September 2017), https://perma.cc/VJZ9-2BHM; P Swire, "Should the Leading Online Tech Companies Be Regulated as Public Utilities?" (*Lawfare*, 2 August 2017), https://perma.cc/BF4F-CB6Q; D Ghosh, "Don't Break Up Facebook – Treat It Like a Utility" (2019), https://perma.cc/7XDK-NQFE; G Sitamaran, "Too Big to Prevail: The National Security Case for Breaking Up Big Tech" (*Foreign Affairs*, March/April 2020), https://perma.cc/NDV3-66P5; J Balkin, "Information Fiduciaries and the First Amendment" (2016) 49 *UC Davis Law Review* 1183 (treating online companies as fiduciaries of private information, giving rise to fiduciary obligations of care and loyalty); J Balkin and J Zitrain, "How to Exercise the Power You Didn't Ask For" (2018), https://hbr.org/2018/09/how-to-exercise-the-power-you-didnt-ask-for; and Posner and Weyl, note 32 above (chapter 5) (proposing granting stronger rights in data "as labor" so that individuals can extract greater rent from the use of their data).

95 Zuboff, note 27 above, at 134–138.

96 DJ Gifford and RT Kudrle, *The Atlantic Divide in Antitrust: An Examination of US and EU Competition Policy* (Chicago, IL, University of Chicago Press, 2015); D Sokol, "Troubled Waters between U.S. and European Antitrust" (2017) 115 *Michigan Law Review* 955.

97 ICN, "2019 Annual Conference Press Release" (*ICN*, 17 May 2019), www.internationalcompetitionnetwork.org/featured/2019-annual-conference-press-release ("clear focus is on two topics, first, on the digital economy").

98 Court of Justice of the European Union Press Release 91/20, note 61 above; Case C311/18, Data Prot. Comm'r v. Facebook Ireland Ltd., ECLI:EU:C:2020:559, note 61 above.

of common international principles and standards, together with ongoing judicial oversight, present a path forward. In practice, jurisdictional conflicts, including the assertion of de facto or de jure extraterritorial jurisdictional power, must be managed continuously.[99] In these cases, a key challenge for all countries will be how to protect individual information in a world where AI increasingly can identify individuals even when data is processed to be anonymized and deemed "nonpersonal."[100] Given the transnational implications of any policy, and given the role of companies in governing data usage, there is a need not only for governments to develop rules, but also for domestic and transnational civil society organizations to be incorporated within governance mechanisms to engage with governments and corporations.[101] Once more, structures can be developed outside the WTO for information exchange, peer review, and norm development to address privacy regulation concerns. But the WTO committee system also can be engaged in coordination with such other international bodies.

6. **Inequality.** Not to be forgotten, societies face rising inequality that the data-driven economy exacerbates. Like trade in goods, free flow of data enhances efficiency and thus welfare gains, but also facilitates economic processes that exacerbate inequality in ways that can threaten social stability and international cooperation. Liberalization of data flows should not be addressed without complementary social policies. For conventional trade theorists, social equality and trade adjustment assistance should be left entirely to the national level. Many reference Scandinavian social welfare and job flexicurity policies to show how this can be done.[102] Again, such regulatory power should reside predominantly at the national level, which is most democratically legitimate. However, trade agreements can facilitate governments' ability to address social inclusion policies.[103] At a minimum, trade agreements should not directly or indirectly constrain governments from adopting necessary policies domestically. They must accommodate (and not foreclose) mechanisms that enable states to address labor and other social

[99] G Shaffer and D Bodansky, "Transnationalism, Unilateralism and International Law" (2012) 1 *Transnational Environmental Law* 31. For example, the European Court of Justice ruled in favor of Google that French rules on the "right to be forgotten" could not be applied to Internet searches conducted outside of the EU. "'Right to be Forgotten' on Google Only Applies in the EU, Court Rules" (*The Guardian*, 24 September 2019), https://perma.cc/B5SS-SLJ8.

[100] L Rocher et al., "Estimating the Success of Reidentifications in Incomplete Datasets Using Generative Models" (2019) 10 *Nature Communications* 3069 (finding "that 99.98% of Americans would be correctly re-identified in any dataset using 15 demographic attributes"); see also Chapter 10 in this volume.

[101] David Kaye, former UN Special Rapporteur on the Promotion and Protection of the Right to Freedom of Opinion and Expression, stresses this point regarding the regulation of speech in his book *Speech Police*. Kaye, note 30 above.

[102] Flexicurity policies combine labor market flexibility, lifelong learning, active labor market policy, and social security. G Shaffer, "Retooling Trade Agreements for Social Inclusion" (2019) 1 *University of Illinois Law Review* 17, at 23–24.

[103] Ibid., at 17.

concerns.[104] Such agreements also should address (or support addressing) tax evasion and avoidance so that governments can fund social welfare and job flexicurity policies.[105] These agreements should be developed primarily outside of the WTO. However, since these policies implicate trade, trade liberalization initiatives for the digital economy could be made contingent on their conclusion. Similarly, trade agreements could explicitly recognize the ability of countries to address social dumping concerns, as most recently developed in the United States–Mexico–Canada Agreement.[106] Otherwise, the economic dynamics of trade liberalization in the digital economy could further increase inequality, undercut domestic solidarity, and, in turn, empower nativist and politically populist domestic movements that undermine international cooperation and good will, as well as national democratic systems.

V CONCLUSION

The world needs international institutions to enhance international deliberation, cooperation, and exchange, but international institutions must be careful not to overreach. Normatively, there are efficiency and fairness reasons for agreements to accommodate policy space so that governments may respond effectively to different preferences and priorities. Politically, when international trade law overreaches, it can spur populist backlash so that the system unravels.

The challenges raised in Section II will not be resolved through a traditional trade agreement alone. The data-driven economy is developing at a rapid pace for which governments lack regulatory experience. Given the risks – ranging from systemic risks to risks to democratic institutions, national security, and personal privacy – trade negotiators should proceed with caution and humility. The issues raised are not clearly protectionist, as with tariffs, but rather entail regulation addressing diverse public policy concerns. While one of the purposes of international trade agreements is for national political bodies to "tie themselves to the mast" to avoid the siren call of protectionism,[107] this rationale is inapt when applied to regulation. Democracies should be able to elect leaders that change orientation regarding the appropriate mix of free data flow and regulation to protect security, privacy, and other concerns. Trade agreements constraining their ability to do so curtail democracy. Because governments weigh tradeoffs regarding the balance between free data flow and other policies in different ways, each country should be free to change its mind. International trade law should not foreclose these domestic debates and choices.

104 Ibid., at 33–39.
105 Ibid., at 17–22.
106 Agreement between the United States of America, the United Mexican States, and Canada (entered into force on 1 July 2020), chapter 23.
107 G Maggi and A Rodríguez-Clare, "A Political-Economy Theory of Trade Agreements" (2007) 97 *American Economic Review* 1374.

At the same time, governance mechanisms are needed in an interdependent world to address common challenges and the externalities that one country's regulations pose for others. Governments should be required to provide equal treatment and due process to affected foreigners domestically, and to provide public policy justifications for the regulations they adopt before transnational peer review and other mechanisms. Section IV advanced a pragmatist, transnational governance architecture focused on regulatory cooperation and learning as an essential complement to WTO "hard" rules backed by dispute settlement.[108] This form of international governance can interact with national regulation in ways that enhance trade, with its accompanying welfare benefits, as well as regulatory efficacy, learning, and adaptation. It is the best way for trade law to address the challenges raised by the data-driven economy.

The approach set forth in this chapter differs significantly from the "grand bargains" that characterized the creation of the WTO. It is much humbler, grounded in uncertainty regarding the digital world and what it means for societies and individuals. Trade agreements, in turn, should approach the issues with caution, leaving regulation predominantly at the national level, while recognizing common standards in some areas to facilitate trade in goods and services (such as regarding electronic signatures and authorizations), coupled with structures that catalyze experimentation and exchange of knowledge and practices regarding the challenges that all societies will continue to face and to which they must respond. These processes can facilitate learning and, possibly but not necessarily, convergence over time.

There are clear limits to this governance alternative. Commercial interests and countries will contend that there is certainty regarding "best" policies and they will attempt to use leverage and persuasion to extend these policies globally. "Learning" is difficult to facilitate where interests have strong incentives to think otherwise. Yet, even then, such processes will make differences more transparent, while still leaving open the possibility of learning from experience that, potentially, can lead to policy adaptation.

The future can be governed in worse ways or better. Law at the international and national levels and their transnational interaction will help constitute that world. In the face of uncertainty, there is a critical need for agonistic deliberation, debate, and policy experimentation. Karl Polanyi in his book *The Great Transformation* described what occurred when governments lost control of unleashed markets in the first half of the last century.[109] We know how that ended. With the data revolution and the rise of AI, the risks are high. The choices societies make today will shape which science fiction remains fiction. It is a brave new world. A future will arrive that we have yet to imagine, but that (hopefully) we can muddle through.

108 G Shaffer and M Pollack, "Hard vs Soft Law: Alternatives, Complements and Antagonists in International Governance" (2010) 94 *Minnesota Law Review* 706.

109 K Polanyi, *The Great Transformation: The Political and Economic Origins of Our Time* (2nd ed., Boston, MA, Beacon Press, 2001).

3

Global Law in the Face of Datafication and Artificial Intelligence

Rolf H. Weber

I INTRODUCTION

Law is regularly challenged by new societal developments. Therefore, its stabilizing function is at risk in the globalized world if technology moves fast and changes the bases of human interactions. Eventually, law is no longer able to provide support for the reorientation of civil society in the context of a potentially highly dynamic environment. However, in a transnational legal system, such as the international trade regime, the evolution of expectations in world society must be channeled in order to avoid social differences that lead to disruptions.[1] Therefore, law cannot disregard technological developments.[2] This contribution examines challenges to the global legal framework caused by recent (primarily technological) developments. At the outset, the characteristics of the law as a structural system are outlined. Thereafter, potentially changing factors, such as technology-driven datafication (big data, cloud computing) and artificial intelligence (AI), will be briefly addressed. Based on this foundation, the main component of this contribution analyzes a desirable digital governance and the regulatory principles of a data-driven world with regard to the establishment of global legal standards in the international trade context.

II LEGAL FRAMEWORK AND TECHNOLOGICAL ADVANCES

A *Law as a Structural System*

Law as a structural system gives guidance about desired behavior, thereby stabilizing normative expectations.[3] In principle, legal concepts can help to support

[1] S-Y Peng, "The Rule of Law in Times of Technological Uncertainty: Is International Economic Law Ready for Emerging Supervisory Trends?" (2019) 22 *Journal of International Economic Law* 1, at 13.

[2] This assessment is not new; twenty years ago, Lawrence Lessig had already pointed to the importance of technical architecture. L Lessig, *Code and Other Laws of Cyberspace* (New York, Basic Books, 1999).

[3] RH Weber, *Realizing a New Global Cyberspace Framework, Normative Foundations and Guiding Principles* (Zürich, Schulthess Juristische Medien, 2014), at 33.

adequate normative reasoning, since the addressees of legal provisions are supposed to acknowledge the authority of the rule-making body and comply with the law.[4] The functions of law are crystallized in rules and institutions that underpin civil society, facilitate orderly interactions, and resolve disputes and conflicts that arise in spite of such rules.[5] The normative framework allows people and businesses in a community to determine the limits of what can and cannot be done in the collective interest.[6] Therefore, the rule of law helps to achieve a high, discretion-limiting degree of certainty and predictability in social relations and transactions.[7]

Irrespective of the manner in which norms actually influence behavior, law-making bodies must understand the different processes that facilitate legal developments, insofar as law often proves to be path-dependent.[8] This assessment corresponds to the reality that the legal system is linked to other social systems, such as technological advances or ethical relations; that is, law only enjoys relative autonomy and is confronted with technological uncertainty.[9] The structural coupling that occurs between and among the legal system and other systems requires the implementation of mechanisms that allow a change of law called for because of societal needs and circumstances.[10] Only when such mechanisms are institutionalized can the continuous existence of the legal system be secured over time.[11] In other words, even if the law requires predictability and a stable structure, the adaptability of legal rules keeps the law intact in cases of social variation.[12]

Nevertheless, some substantive legal values are so fundamental that their abolition would totally undermine the function of law in society. On the one hand, human rights, such as the freedom of expression or the nondiscrimination principle, represent major (even untouchable) constitutional values. On the other hand, legal order can hardly function without property rights and privacy rights.[13] As a consequence, certain legal pillars may not be "overruled" by technological developments.

These pillars of law as a structural system must be mirrored against the challenges caused by recent technological advances in order to avoid "clashes" that may harm civil society.

4 Weber, note 3 above, at 34 with further references.

5 RH Weber, "The Role of Law in Constituting Financial Markets" (2017) 32 *Journal of International Banking Law and Regulation* 253, et seq.

6 HLA Hart, *The Concept of Law* (2nd ed., Oxford, Oxford University Press, 1997), at 55–57.

7 RH Weber, *Regulatory Models for the Online World* (Zürich, Kluwer Law International, 2002), at 38.

8 Weber, note 5 above, at 254.

9 Weber, note 3 above, at 35; Peng, note 1 above, at 12.

10 N Luhmann, *Das Recht der Gesellschaft* (Frankfurt, Suhrkamp, 1993), at 93, 283, 441.

11 Weber, note 5 above, at 254.

12 Weber, note 3 above, at 34–35.

13 See also OECD, "Algorithms and Collusion: Background Note by the Secretariat" (2017), https://perma.cc/5R7T-8JTB, at 43.

B *Datafication as a Technological Trend*

The term "datafication" was coined by Mayer-Schönberger and Cukier in 2013, primarily with respect to the then-new phenomenon of big data.[14] Datafication, which has become a buzzword in the new IT world, refers to a technological trend that is able to "convert" many aspects of modern life into computerized data.[15] Hereinafter, not only are big data and cloud computing addressed but also new developments in the AI context.

1 Big Data and Cloud Computing

Over the past few decades, an immense amount of data has been generated through the (cross-border) flow of information, humans, products, services, and capital. These developments have resulted in data protection concerns, as well as the specific problem of users of online goods and services "paying" for products offered by disclosing data without assessing the nature and value of the data. The recent European Union (EU) Directive on digital content even regulates the payment of online services through the provision of data.[16] Furthermore, data holders are often unaware of how much data is collected and stored about them.

Big data is a term coined for datasets whose size is beyond the ability of commonly used software tools to capture, curate, manage, and process within a tolerable degree of time. The phenomenon of big data analytics is often characterized by four elements, namely volume, variety, velocity, and veracity (the "4 V"). "Volume" refers to the especially large amount of data; "variety" makes it clear that the data is derived from manifold sources and formats; "velocity" mirrors the high speed of the data processing; and "veracity" reflects the reliance on the correctness of the data. A special feature of big data from a legal perspective is the fact that the traditional concept of causation is replaced by the concept of correlation.[17]

For some years, international organizations such as the Organisation for Economic Co-operation and Development (OECD), as well as academic voices, have assumed that big data is potentially a key driver of innovation, productivity growth, and economic competitiveness.[18] The global exchange of data requires unrestricted cross-border data flows in order to realize its merits. In this context, big data analytics is able to improve the outcome of data processing in manifold

14 V Mayer-Schönberger and K Cukier, *Big Data: A Revolution That Will Transform How We Live, Work and Think* (London, John Murray, 2013), at 73 et seq.

15 RH Weber, "Digitalisierung und der Kampf ums Recht," in A Dal Molin-Kränzlin et al. (eds), *Digitalisierung – Gesellschaft – Recht, Analysen und Perspektiven von Assistierenden des Rechtswissenschaftlichen Instituts der Universität Zürich* (Zürich/St. Gallen, Dike, 2019), 3, at 6.

16 Directive (EU) 2019/770 on certain aspects concerning contracts for the supply of digital content and digital services of 20 May 2019, OJ 2019 L 136 of 22 May 2019, 1 et seq.

17 Mayer-Schönberger and Cukier, note 14 above, at 50 et seq.

18 See also RH Weber, "Data Portability and Big Data Analytics, New Competition Policy Challenges," in Concorrenza e Mercato 23/2016, 59, at 61/62.

areas.[19] Examples include the automotive industry, which evaluates ideas submitted through its "virtual innovation agency," and the health sector, which collects data on larger populations in order to reduce disease, bringing rapidly and accurately identified drugs to the market and providing better healthcare by enabling the application of evidence-based interventions.[20]

A further technical innovation is cloud computing, which facilitates cross-border data flows in order to take advantage of cheaper on-demand computer capacity that can be scaled and paid for as needed. Cloud services encompass software and access to processing, email, storage, and other computer resources. From a business perspective, cloud computing turns a fixed IT cost into a variable operating cost, and from the angle of human resources, cloud computing underpins the capacity of people to work remotely.[21] Major challenges include connectivity and the compliance of cross-border data flows with data protection and data security requirements.[22]

2 Artificial Intelligence

Algorithms are able to automate the "production" of goods/services and to facilitate the selection and filtering of information in various ways, thereby attributing relevance to certain data and moderating content. Algorithms are the foundation of AI as a machine-based system that is capable of influencing the environment by making recommendations and predictions without human input.[23] An AI system lifecycle encompasses various phases, such as the design and modeling of data, the verification and validation of data, as well as the deployment, operation, monitoring and storage of data.[24]

AI allows for the implementation of a "regime" of automated decision-making to be conducted in a highly timely and effective manner. Such automation is primarily feasible in situations that do not require a specific human intervention. The new technologies can also transform traditional manufacturing into smart manufacturing, focusing on digitization from early product design through maintenance at the product's end of life by using advanced sensors and big data analytics.[25] As examples, and only at the very beginning of data-driven innovation potential, the following phenomena can be identified: (i) driverless cars will

19 Weber, note 3 above, at 6–7.

20 J Meltzer, "Governing Digital Trade" (2019) 18 *World Trade Review* 23, at 31.

21 Ibid.

22 For an overview, see DN Staiger, *Data Protection Compliance in the Cloud* (Thesis, Zurich, 2017), at 268 et seq.

23 RH Weber, "Socio-ethical Values and Legal Rules on Automated Platforms: The Quest for a Symbiotic Relationship" (2020) 36 *Computer Law & Security Review* 1 et seq.

24 See also OECD, "Recommendation of the Council on Artificial Intelligence" (2019), https://perma.cc/EW3K-FE6R.

25 Meltzer, note 20 above, at 29.

become a reality, and (ii) robotics will move forward to become a widespread industry tool based on rapidly advancing AI.

Notwithstanding the fact that AI has many benefits, some risks also cannot be overlooked. Therefore, from a normative concept of civil society, a few questions must be considered in an interdisciplinary manner:[26] (i) Do AI processes comply with fundamental constitutional principles? (ii) Is the AI application based on a sufficient legal foundation? (iii) Do AI processes comply with the applicable requirements of data protection laws? (iv) Who is in charge of monitoring the socially responsible use of AI, and who is liable in case of a failure caused by an algorithm?

These questions merit appropriate answers, even if solid responses that serve the needs of global society are not easy to find. Nevertheless, a reconciliation of AI's chances and risks must be kept in mind if an adequate legal framework for digital governance in global relations, particularly in the international trade regime, is to become a reality.

III RECONCILING GLOBAL TRADE WITH GLOBAL LAW

A *Rule-Making in the Digital World*

1 Globalization and Governance

Globalization is not a clearly defined term; its concrete meaning depends on the given substantive component of societal life.[27] (i) Legal globalization concerns the harmonization of states' normative orders, or the implementation of cross-border legal rules. (ii) Cultural globalization addresses those issues related to manifold social policies. (iii) Commercial globalization reflects the existence of increased transnational businesses and economic activities. Global law as an aspect of legal globalization is confronted with new concepts, examining institutional differentiations and elaborated procedural techniques.[28]

The term "governance," which stems from the Greek word "*kybernetes*" and the Latin word "*gubernator*," means a steersman, and it must be recognized for its importance. Governance can be addressed from the perspective of different disciplines; nevertheless, at whatever level of social organization it may take place, governance refers to the appropriate business conduct of a private or a public body. In this context, some key questions must be asked and answered:[29] (i) Who

26 Weber, note 23 above, at 1.
27 See JA Scholte, *Globalization: A Critical Introduction* (New York, St. Martin's Press, 2000); S Caney, *Justice Beyond Borders* (Oxford, Oxford University Press, 2005).
28 B Kingsbury and L Casini, "Global Administrative Law Dimensions of International Organizations Law" (2009) 6 *International Organizations Law Review* 319 et seq.
29 RH Weber, *Shaping Internet Governance: Regulatory Challenges* (Zurich, Schulthess Juristische Medien, 2009), at 2.

is entitled to set the rules? (ii) In whose interest are the rules? (iii) By which mechanisms are the rules created? (iv) For which purposes are the rules designed? There is a need to develop overarching networks and negotiation systems between different stakeholders, thus forming a "cooperative approach to governance" that includes the entire society, hence dividing responsibilities between public and private actors.

Based on the described notions of "globalization" and "governance," the development of a broader rule-making approach encompassing the needs of the international trade regime and of the digital environment of today's societies appears to be unavoidable and equally justified.

2 A Broader and Better-Coordinated Rule-Making Approach

Assessing the dichotomy of regulatory sources and the emergence of new regimes introduced by civil society, adapted transnational concepts must be developed in the global law environment.[30] Institutions can lead states to more cooperative behavior than they otherwise might have adopted, building mutual connections from peripheral points in federative or associate forms.[31] In realizing an appropriate governance framework, civil society involvement should be strengthened. The facilitation of networking opportunities and public support from concerned persons and organizations in the relevant policy field should also be considered; that is, a policy vision must be developed.[32]

In the Internet governance context, a new approach has been developed and applied in part, namely the multistakeholder participation model, which attempts to involve all concerned persons and organizations in the public and private sphere in the discussions and negotiations of the regulatory framework.[33] Practical experience has shown that some basic challenges need to be addressed in order to ensure that the multistakeholder concepts are successful. Four fundamental questions must be tackled:[34] (i) How do governance groups best match challenges with organizations and networks? (ii) How can governing bodies/entities be most able to help develop legitimate, effective, and efficient solutions? (iii) How should the flow of information and knowledge necessary for successful governance be structured? (iv) How can different governance groups approach coordination between available governance networks in order to avoid conflicting interests?

30 Weber, note 3 above, at 111.

31 M Senn, *Non-State Regulatory Regimes, Understanding Institutional Transformation* (Heidelberg, Springer, 2011), at 215–216.

32 RH Weber, "Visions of Political Power: Treaty Making and Multistakeholder Understanding," in R Radu et al. (eds), *The Evolution of Global Internet Governance, Principles and Politics in the Making* (New York, Springer, 2014), 95, at 102 et seq.

33 Weber, note 3 above, at 126 et seq.

34 U Gasser et al., "Multistakeholder as Governance Groups: Observations from Case Studies" (2015) Berkman Center for Internet & Society Research Publications No. 2015-1.

Over the last few years, the globalization of the international legal framework, among other fields in international trade law (particularly due to the "outdated" classification regime in the World Trade Organization (WTO) Agreements), and equally in the area of Internet law (due to a stronger emphasis on state sovereignty), has suffered some setbacks. In light of the fact that the legal fragmentation caused by national laws jeopardizes an appropriate design of global law in a network society, coherence between different initiatives should be strengthened in order to overcome trends leading to various forms of fragmentation or distorted regulatory regimes.

The recently developed term "legal interoperability" addresses the process of creating legal rules that cooperate across jurisdictions.[35] This objective can be realized in a matter of degrees, as many options exist between a full harmonization of normative rules and a complete fragmentation of legal systems.[36] As is so often the case in the real world, striking the correct balance is of utmost importance. While an excessively high level of interoperability could cause difficulties in the management of the harmonized rules and fail to acknowledge social and cultural differences, a level too low could present challenges to smooth social interaction.[37]

B *Regulatory Principles for the Data-Driven World*

In view of these technological innovations, the legal order is confronted with the need to establish an international regulatory framework for the data-driven world that implements the following basic regulatory principles.

1 Transparency

All involved stakeholders should promote a culture of transparency, enshrining the disclosure of data logics and access to the applied algorithms and datasets.[38] Transparency is usually defined as "easily seen through ... evident, obvious, clear."[39] Transparency means understandable and forward-looking information, appropriate to the context and the state of the art, in order to make stakeholders aware of their interactions (in an ex ante or ex post data-centered decision-making process).[40]

Transparency requires robust and general rules, not necessarily more regulation; that is, the improvement of transparency does not mean a quantitative increase in

35 J Palfrey and U Gasser, *Interop: The Promise and Perils of Highly Interconnected Systems* (New York, Basic Books, 2012).

36 RH Weber, "Legal Interoperability as a Tool for Combatting Fragmentation" (2014) Global Commission on Internet Governance Paper Series No. 4, at 6.

37 Ibid., at 7–9.

38 Council of Europe, Report on Artificial Intelligence, T-PD(2018)09Rev, Strasbourg, 3 December 2018, at 11/12.

39 Oxford English Dictionary Online, 1989.

40 Weber, note 29 above, at 122/123.

information, but rather "more" in terms of higher information quality.[41] A future-oriented understanding of transparency should observe the following elements:[42] (a) the existence of publicly reliable information; that is, substantive quality standards related to information, supported by an adequate legal framework; (b) the designation of the information recipient as a holder of rights and an essential component for perception and transparency; and (c) the availability of disclosure procedures and observance of the time element; that is, transparency implies constant visibility of information.

Providing information about the type of input data and the expected output, explaining the variables and their weight, and shedding light on analytics architecture usually contribute to transparency with respect to AI algorithms.[43] Nevertheless, a generic statement on the use of AI does not allow for the easy assessment of all challenges and risks; concrete circumstances do play a role, which means that solutions focused on disclosing specific information about the applied algorithms may be the best option.[44]

2 Accountability

All stakeholders involved in datafication and AI mechanisms should be accountable for the proper functioning of the systems employed, as well as the integrity of the regulatory environment.[45] Accountability helps to ensure an environment in which individuals and enterprises assume their respective responsibilities. The first legislative attempts to meet this requirement can already be seen: for example, in the field of data protection, the EU General Data Protection Regulation calls upon organizations to apply a "Privacy by Design/Default" approach and – under certain circumstances – to conduct a "Data Protection Impact Assessment."[46]

Accountability encompasses the obligation of one person to another, according to which the former must give an account of, explain, and justify his/her actions and decisions against criteria of the same kind.[47] Therefore, the proportionality principle, which inspires an adequate and appropriate deployment of big data analytics and AI, should apply.[48] Accountability also relates to good governance, which was previously addressed. The development of respective concepts in public institutions

[41] C Kaufmann and RH Weber, "Transparency of Central Banks' Policy," in P Conti-Brown and RN Lastra (eds), *Research Handbook on Central Banking* (Cheltenham, Edward Elgar Publishing, 2018), 518, at 520.

[42] Weber, note 29 above, at 121 et seq., 131.

[43] Council of Europe, note 38 above, at 12; for further details see Weber, note 23 above, at 6–7.

[44] See also OECD, note 24 above, at no. 1.3.

[45] Weber, note 3 above, at 78 et seq.

[46] The details are contained in article 25 and article 35 of the General Data Protection Regulation (GDPR).

[47] For further details see Weber, note 23 above, at 7.

[48] Weber, note 29 above, at 137 et seq. with further references.

and private enterprises requires publicly assessable accounts as a precondition for a sustainable society.[49]

The obligation to be accountable encompasses the task of disclosing information about the actual AI processes. To improve respective foreseeability, standards should be developed and introduced that moderate the behavioral requirements in a concise manner. Furthermore, the responsibility of the accountable person to ensure that concerned individuals are protected from damages when having suffered a detriment is to be legally developed in a precise way.[50]

3 Safety and Robustness

Technological innovations must be safe and robust throughout their entire lifecycle so that data-driven communications and transactions can overcome adverse conditions or foreseeable potential misuse. Safety and robustness also extend to the terms of security and resilience. Therefore, the traceability of the datasets, processes, and decisions must be secured. Furthermore, the risks with respect to safety and robustness should be managed throughout the entire process of hardware or software applications. Consequently, the execution of impact assessments with respect to technological risks is necessary.[51]

International instruments already state that the likely impact of AI on civil society must be adequately taken into account in order to safeguard fundamental rights. For example, the Recommendation of the OECD Council on Artificial Intelligence refers in part 1.4 to robustness, security, and safety as follows:[52]

> AI systems should be robust, secure and safe throughout their entire lifecycle so that, in conditions of normal use, foreseeable use or misuse, or other adverse conditions, they function appropriately and do not pose unreasonable safety risk. To this end, AI actors should ensure traceability, including in relation to datasets, processes and decisions made during the AI system lifecycle, to enable analysis of the AI system's outcomes and responses to inquiry, appropriate to the context and consistent with the state of art.

Furthermore, the use of AI through modern data-processing techniques and the trend toward implementation of data-intensive processes require a more advanced understanding of risk assessment by individuals, businesses, and public organizations, since possible adverse outcomes stemming from data processes cannot be excluded.[53]

49 See C Kaufmann and RH Weber, "The Role of Transparency in Financial Regulation" (2010) 13 *Journal of International Economic Law* 779, at 789.

50 Weber, note 29 above, at 147.

51 For a comprehensive discussion of new forms of impact assessments, see A Mantelero, "AI and Big Data: A Blueprint for Human Rights, Social and Ethical Impact Assessment" (2018) 34 *Computer Law & Security Review* 754 et seq.

52 OECD, note 24 above, at no. 1.4; for further details see Weber, note 23 above, at 7–8.

53 Council of Europe, note 38 above, at 13.

Risks and compliance assessments are not only justified by collective social and ethical values, as well as the nature of fundamental rights and treatments affected by AI application. They also represent an opportunity to better foster public trust as a key objective of the information society.[54]

4 Interim Assessment

As stated earlier, the use of modern data-processing techniques and the trend toward implementation of information-intensive data analytics require a more advanced understanding of risk assessment. In particular, the fact that automated decision-making may have an impact on fundamental rights (including the nondiscrimination principle), as well as collective social and ethical values, must be addressed.[55] AI programs can affect various human rights, i.e. the right to human dignity, the principle of nondiscrimination, privacy rights, and the guarantee of self-determination.[56]

Furthermore, risks and compliance assessments are not only justified by the nature of the rights and freedoms potentially affected by datafication (or big data analytics), as well as AI applications. In a participatory environment such assessment can contribute to an increased level of trust.[57] As the most recent political developments in the political arena have shown, trust plays an important role in the context of the international trade regime. Trust can even be seen as a central pillar of the globalized governance, as previously discussed.

C *Combatting Distortive Interferences*

In the digital society and economy, the factual possession and control of data is key. New technologies, such as datafication and AI, lead to situations in which the data control function is primarily assumed by large private enterprises and by governments. The use of big data results and the application of algorithms give these entities information power,[58] which can be exercised in either a good or bad way. Improvement in healthcare or the strengthening of measures to protect cybersecurity undoubtedly have a positive effect. However, the misuse of data is also possible, for example with the objective of spreading inaccurate, embarrassing, or misleading information or controlling the data exchange for one's exclusive benefit, insofar as

54 O O'Neill, *Justice, Trust and Accountability* (Cambridge, Cambridge University Press, 2005).

55 See also RH Weber, "Ethics in the Internet Environment" (2016) Global Commission on Internet Governance Paper Series No. 39, at 7.

56 FA Raso et al., "Artificial Intelligence and Human Rights: Opportunities and Risks" (2018) Berkman Klein Center for Internet & Society at Harvard University Research Publication No. 2018-6, at 14 et seq.

57 See O'Neill, note 54 above, at 61 et seq.

58 On the phenomenon of information power, see D Kuehl, *Defining Information Power*, 1997 (June, No. 115) Strategic Forum, at 1 et seq. More recently, the initiatives introduced by political bodies and particularly by antitrust authorities against the US giants (GAFA: Alphabet (Google), Amazon, Facebook, and Apple) clearly show the sensitivity of the problem.

the holder of data can become a "data demagogue,"[59] contradicting the basic principles of an appropriate international trade regime.[60]

1 Anticompetitive Behavior

From the perspective of competition law, different issues are at stake. An initial aspect concerns the changed market parameters. Digital markets, as well as the exchange of communications in a digital society, should increase the possibilities for participation among all interested individuals and organizations/businesses. However, the markets tend to be dominated by a few firms (Alphabet (Google), Amazon, Facebook, and Apple (GAFA)). Similar experiences are found in East Asia (Alibaba, Tencent).

The overwhelming dominance of a few players in digital markets causes anticompetitive concerns, which are primarily due to the risk that a market-dominant position has been misused.[61] The oligopolistic market structure is now challenged by competition authorities (for example, the Directory Competition of the EU), as well as political bodies in the United States and Europe. The outcome of these interventions is unresolved for the time being.

Other behavioral problems are also on the horizon – for example, the tacit collusion by big firms through the use of parallel algorithms.[62] For good reasons, primarily the OECD, as one of the most important international organizations in the economic field, is thoroughly analyzing the respective challenges.[63] So far, competition law does not appear to be fully fit to tackle these problems. The lack of general competition law principles in the WTO framework must be seen as another disadvantage for the international trade regime.[64] Furthermore, the lack of coherent competition policies among jurisdictions leads to the disadvantage that national competition authorities are ill equipped to effectively address the anticompetitive data practices; the need for more streamlined standards between antitrust regimes is obvious.

59 RS Neeraj, "Trade Rules for Digital Economy: Charting New Waters at the WTO" (2019) 18 *World Trade Review* 121, at 129.

60 This subchapter uses the title "distortive interference," not "data demagogues," in order to avoid any preliminary assessment, particularly because the remarks must remain relatively short.

61 Neeraj, note 59 above, at 129.

62 RH Weber, "Disruptive Technologies and Competition Law," in K Mathis and A Tor (eds), *New Developments in Competition Law and Economics* (Cham, Springer International Publishing, 2019), 223, at 232 et seq.

63 See for example OECD, "Algorithms and Collusion, Competition Policy in the Digital Age" (2017), https://perma.cc/WZR9-7M4T; OECD, "Rethinking Antitrust Tools for Multi-sided Platforms" (2018), https://perma.cc/V7VD-7X2E.

64 RH Weber, "Unfinished Business: Competition Law and the WTO," in J Chaisse and T-Y Lin (eds), *International Economic Law and Governance, Essays in Honour of Mitsuo Matsushita* (Oxford, Oxford University Press, 2016), at 201–215.

2 Denial of Network Neutrality

A second issue is network neutrality: all market participants (providers of goods and services, as well as consumers) should have unfettered access to the digital infrastructure.[65] The preferential treatment of some businesses or individuals results in the risk of competition distortion. Therefore, discrimination toward certain market participants must be considered unjustified.

In some countries (for example, in the EU), network neutrality provisions do exist.[66] The national implementation of the neutrality principle, however, does not always cover existing needs. In the United States, the trend has moved away from regulatory intervention because of the existing political climate. Obviously, rules cannot replace the market. However, illegitimate discrimination does have a substantial negative effect on the international trade framework.[67]

3 Data Localization

A third challenge, more due to efforts of governments than private enterprises, concerns data localization requirements. Around the globe, such requirements are implemented in a variety of forms.[68] Information and communications technology companies may be obligated to host all subscriber and consumer data locally within the country; in some instances, only information covering certain substantive areas (for example, health) must be stored in the country.

Data localization reduces access to data and digital technologies and may also be counterproductive. Requiring data localization in relation to cybersecurity increases data vulnerability in a single jurisdiction, making it easier to target and possibly preventing data backups in globally distributed data centers.[69] Obviously, such provisions raise the costs of access to, and use of, data, thereby reducing gains from digital trade.

4 Interim Assessment

As the aforementioned deliberations demonstrate, global law is exposed to "data demagogues" who strive to interfere with cross-border data flows. Various forms of

65 Neeraj, note 59 above, at 138.

66 See for example Article 3(3) of the Telecom Single Market Regulation (EU) 2015/2120; for further information on the EU regulations on network neutrality see https://perma.cc/P7SF-GS4K.

67 A full review of the literature on network neutrality cannot be done in this chapter; for the EU see note 66; for the US, see T Wu, "Network Neutrality, Broadband Discrimination" (2003) 2 *Journal on Telecommunications and High Technology Law* 141 et seq.; more recently CS Yoo, "Wireless Network Neutrality: Technological Challenges and Policy Implications" (2017) 31/2 *Berkeley Technology Law Journal* 1409 et seq.

68 Meltzer, note 20 above, at 25, 36; Neeraj, note 59 above, at 138–139; A Chander, "The Internet of Things: Both Goods and Services" (2019) 18 *World Trade Review* 14 et seq.

69 Meltzer, note 20 above, at 25.

unjustified market interventions, such as anticompetitive behavior, denial of network neutrality, and data localization provisions, can have a competition distortion effect. Such an outcome must be avoided or, at the very least, mitigated by the regulator.

In addition, legal uncertainty, caused by technological advances, leads to discretionary power that is not always consistent with the rule of law.[70] This fact primarily concerns governments and other regulatory bodies. However, private enterprises can also have power in factual forms. A balance between differing interests is often difficult to find, but efforts to reconcile such interests appear to be unavoidable.[71]

D *New Digital Trade Regime*

1 Outdated Goods and Service Classifications

So far, a commonly agreed-upon definition of what represents digital trade does not exist. The WTO has addressed the "production, distribution, marketing, sale, or delivery of goods and services by electronic means" as part of digital trade in its Work Programme on Electronic Commerce of 1998.[72] Cross-border data flows enabling digital trade have not played a major role in the previous discussions, notwithstanding the fact that their appearance is important.

Legal scholars of WTO law have been tackling the distinction between goods (General Agreement on Tariffs and Trade, GATT) and services (General Agreement on Trade in Services, GATS) for many years, since it is not clear which "product category" and consequently which Agreement would be suitable in addressing digital assets.[73] The differentiation is practically important, since the GATT offers less room for maneuvering to member states that are unwilling to liberalize digital markets than the GATS.[74]

The WTO itself is well aware of the existing problems, and efforts have been initiated to remedy the situation. In the context of the 11th Ministerial Conference (December 2017, Buenos Aires), a short "Joint Statement on Electronic Commerce" was adopted, inviting participating member states to undertake further work on digital trade.[75] Most developed countries have agreed to this Joint Statement; China did it almost at the last minute. However, no concrete outcome can be

70 Peng, note 1 above, at 13–14.
71 Ibid., at 14–15.
72 World Trade Organization, Work Programme on Electronic Commerce, adopted by the General Council on 25 September 1998, Geneva.
73 See RH Weber, "Digital Trade and E-commerce: Challenges and Opportunities of the Asia-Pacific Regionalism" (2015) 10 *Asian Journal of WTO & International Health Law and Policy* 321 et seq.
74 Ibid., at 332; for further details see RH Weber, "A New International Trade Framework for Digital Assets" in M Kolsky Lewis et al. (eds), *A Post-WTO International Legal Order* (Cham/Switzerland, Springer, 2020), 277, at 280 et seq.
75 WTO, WT/MIN(17)/60 of 13 December 2017.

seen for the time being, even though several proposals have been submitted and discussed in the WTO forum. The World Trade Report 2018 of the WTO also intensively addressed digital trade, pointing to the further transformation of the global trade regime. As a result of these investigations, the WTO has pleaded for a technology-induced reshaping of the regulatory environment.[76] Nevertheless, a solution to the existing problems may not surface in the near future.

2 New Data-Oriented Regulatory Approaches in World Trade Organization Law

An important component of the regulatory challenges concerns cross-border data flows. Foundational principles of data regulation in international trade law must be developed.[77] The elements encompass fostering digital trust and ensuring interoperability and transparency, in support of the free flow of information. Therefore, a hybrid regulatory approach based on a polycentric governance model[78] appears to be suitable.

New business models must become part of the trade rule framework. For example, digital platforms should be able to overcome barriers that have prevented small companies from participating in international trade, and from facilitating the building of trust in global transactions.[79] In summary, regulatory support for the implementation of digital platforms that are stable and trustworthy is an objective that must be pursued.

The WTO rules typically do not refer to private standards, industry best practices, or multistakeholder institutions.[80] However, these models are commonplace in the digital world and therefore must also be incorporated in international trade law. Self-regulation and – possibly – coregulation do have important merits; therefore, it appears to be worthwhile for WTO bodies to cooperate with international organizations and associations that are involved in the development of international trade standards.

Another issue concerns ongoing discussions about digital trade barriers.[81] The respective objectives are often at least partly founded in sound policy or social reasoning. Examples include cross-border cooperation on cybersecurity issues, the

[76] World Trade Organization, "World Trade Report 2018: The Future of World Trade: How Digital Technologies Are Transforming Global Commerce" (2018), https://perma.cc/NKD3-BT7E, at 130 et seq.

[77] Weber, note 74 above, 285 et seq.; AD Mitchell and N Mishra, "Regulating Cross-Border Data Flows in a Data-Driven World: How WTO-Law Can Contribute" (2019) 22 *Journal of International Economic Law* 389 et seq.

[78] See Weber, note 3 above, at 92 et seq.

[79] Meltzer, note 20 above, at 33.

[80] Mitchell and Mishra, note 77 above, at 404–405; see generally J Pauwelyn, "Rule-Based Trade 2.0? The Rise of Informal Rules and Standards and How They May Outcompete WTO Treaties" (2014) 17 *Journal of International Economic Law* 739 et seq.

[81] Meltzer, note 20 above, at 35–36.

implementation of an appropriate privacy framework, and the integration of consumer trust-enhancing measures.[82]

Finally, legal scholars are generally of the opinion that the WTO framework should be expanded in the light of smart goods and smart services, constituting the Internet of Things.[83] Apart from horizontal obligations on cross-border data flows and data localization,[84] efforts must be undertaken to amend the international trade regime by way of new provisions that enable digital innovation and promote business trust.[85] For example, technical standards for digital services that are consistent with internationally recognized standards should be adopted.

E *International Regulatory Cooperation*

Cross-border data flows and digital trade are in the process of transforming the global legal framework. In contrast, experience over the last five years has shown that many governments have become less inclined to agree on new, internationally accepted rules and are increasingly restricting cross-border data flows.[86] The discussed data localization requirements can be seen as a new form of digital protectionism that extends beyond justified objectives, such as protection of privacy, law enforcement needs, and cybersecurity concerns. Fragmentation of the Internet is another widely discussed topic.[87]

The developments identified herein are leading us in the wrong direction. Rather, efforts should be undertaken to strengthen international regulatory cooperation. Therefore, the interplay between global needs and national interests should be better analyzed, and should also lead to an appropriate design of such cooperation.[88] Legal interoperability (for example, through mutual recognition understandings) must become a regulatory objective,[89] and a convergence toward principles and standards in areas such as privacy and cybersecurity is desirable.[90] Such developments can only be successful if international regulatory cooperation between actively public and private cross-border organizations is improved (in the form of interagency coordination and compliance management measures).

In the light of growing nationalism and deepened sovereignty interests in many large and small states around the globe, international regulatory cooperation represents a difficult stand. Nevertheless, from an academic and political perspective,

82 For further details see Mitchell and Mishra, note 77 above, at 407 et seq.
83 Weber, note 74 above, at 288; Neeraj, note 59 above, at 127–128.
84 Mitchell and Mishra, note 77 above, at 6–7.
85 Ibid., at 3; see also M Burri and R Polanco, "Digital Trade Provisions in Preferential Trade Agreements: Introducing a New Dataset" (2020) 23 *Journal of International Economic Law* 187 et seq.
86 Meltzer, note 20 above, at 25/26.
87 M Mueller, *Will the Internet Fragment? Sovereignty, Globalization and Cyberspace* (Cambridge, Polity Press, 2017).
88 See Palfrey and Gasser, note 35 above, at 178 et seq.
89 Weber, note 36 above, at 6 et seq.
90 Meltzer, note 20 above, at 47.

coordination is always better than confrontation. This assessment should motivate policymakers to place more emphasis on the harmonization of international bodies' activities.

IV OUTLOOK

Overarching key elements of global law in the context of the international trade regime are transparency, trust, and traceability. An optimal design for a balanced policy environment in the global trade ecosystem must consider aspects including risk assessment and ethical considerations, thereby strengthening the trust of all involved stakeholders in the global legal framework.

Regulation should become an enabler of digital innovation and should not limit business activities in an undue way. Interoperability, with respect to technical standards, data models, and AI processes, may help in the design of an appropriate normative framework. Governance measures that avoid further fragmentation may also help to realize a globally accepted legal environment. The difficulties ahead are remarkable, but not insurmountable. However, a new way of thinking is needed, setting traditional sovereignty considerations aside and moving toward new intellectual concepts.

4

Trading Artificial Intelligence

Economic Interests, Societal Choices, and Multilateral Rules

Dan Ciuriak and Vlada Rodionova

I INTRODUCTION

After technology's decade of disillusion, societies confront the decade of decision: how to address the myriad issues already encountered with digital technology in reality or conceptualized in virtual realities, as use cases proliferate and as applications gain power. As a general-purpose technology with applications that can touch on virtually any human endeavour, the integration of artificial intelligence (AI) into social and economic frameworks poses particularly thorny issues. The full extent to which it will be embraced and the terms and conditions under which it will be allowed into our lives will likely vary across jurisdictions, reflecting differences in governance structures, societal preferences, and economic interests, with regulatory decisions being made in a context of limited experience, highly imperfect information, and at best a rudimentary understanding of the complex feedbacks that will be unleashed as the integration of AI proceeds.

From a trade perspective, regulatory decisions concerning the operation of AI within societies will constitute non-tariff measures (NTMs) that condition market access for the hyper-specialized AI applications that are already in use and the many more that are under development and slated to be brought to markets over the coming years.

The multilateral trade system has some experience addressing issues encountered with the introduction of new technologies, including the range of considerations bearing on risk tolerance, such as, inter alia, the use of available scientific evidence, the factors to be considered in assessing risk, the role of international standards in establishing acceptable levels of risk, and even in providing flexibility for differences in consumer tastes and preferences (i.e. political choice, including involvement of civil society) with regard to risk, including through the invocation of the precautionary principle.

At the same time, the "dual-use" character of AI[1] and the data that train it[2] make national security entanglements seemingly unavoidable and perhaps even ultimately unbounded in scope, while the prospect of large valuable economic rents from AI applications incentivizes strategic trade and investment policies.[3]

With AI and machine learning (ML), we are navigating largely uncharted waters. The Stanford 100-year project on AI (Stanford AI100) advised against premature regulation on the grounds this could prevent the development of potentially beneficial technologies, stifle innovation, and/or drive innovation to less restrictive jurisdictions.[4] However, given the geopolitical AI arms race currently underway, and given the lure of large prospective economic rents, there is no likelihood of the pace of development and deployment of AI actually slowing down. By the same token, the terms and conditions under which AI accesses markets will be developed through a learning-by-doing process in which societies conduct natural experiments in allowing applications while "regulatory sandboxes" are used to develop the rules that in turn pave the way for international market access.

In this chapter, we discuss the rites of passage of AI as it enters the trading system. The next section discusses the challenge of getting AI applications to market and how they are being handled. Section III then discusses the hurdles that societal impacts may throw up, including national security, political choice, and income distribution. The final section ventures a discussion of how the integration of AI into international commerce might unfold.

II GETTING ARTIFICIAL INTELLIGENCE TO MARKET: NAVIGATING THE REGULATORY FRAMEWORK

A *The Artificial Intelligence Future Is Here*

If we replace the term "AI" with "smart", we realize immediately that AI is already all around us: AI applications power the smart assistants on cell phones, the range of smart home applications now widely in use, proliferating smart applications in business, and above all increasingly intelligent machines that combine a plethora of AI-driven functions to acquire increasingly flexible, human-like capabilities, up to and including humanoid robots

1 G Allen and T Chan, "Artificial Intelligence and National Security" (2017) Belfer Center for Science and International Affairs, www.belfercenter.org/sites/default/files/files/publication/AI%20NatSec%20-%20final.pdf.

2 L Bezuidenhout, "Data Sharing and Dual-Use Issues" (2013) 19(1) *Science and Engineering Ethics* 83.

3 D Ciuriak, "Economic Rents and the Contours of Conflict in the Data-Driven Economy" (2020) Centre for International Governance Innovation, www.cigionline.org/publications/economic-rents-and-contours-conflict-data-driven-economy.

4 P Stone et al., "Artificial Intelligence and Life in 2030" (2016), http://ai100.stanford.edu/2016-report.

carrying on conversations on stage[5] and AI television news anchors reading the news.[6]

Stanford AI100 places widespread introduction of ML in software services and mobile devices as starting in 2000,[7] even before the breakthroughs in technology that powered the development of modern AI. Kelly identifies these breakthroughs as follows:[8] the development of "deep learning" based on stacked neural networks by Geoffrey Hinton in 2006 (which effectively industrialized learning); the application of parallel processing computer chips to neural networks by Andrew Ng and his team at Stanford in 2009; and the accumulation of big data, which greatly increased with the mobile revolution that followed the introduction of the iPhone in 2007. Agrawal, Gans, and Goldfarb[9] place the commercial debut of AI only in 2012. Ciuriak and Ptashkina[10] place the dawn of the data-driven economy circa 2010, more or less coincident with the breakthroughs that powered the commercial application of AI.

Well before these breakthroughs, the development of regulatory frameworks and quality assurance systems for AI were already underway, since the basic issues raised in developing standards for AI were already encountered in developing quality assurance for "expert systems", which date back to the 1960s.[11] These systems were based either on data (encoded knowledge of a very specific area) or deep learning based on comprehensive structural knowledge of the subject matter, and used an "inference engine" that sought to mimic the decision-making process of a human expert.[12] The generic problems raised by these applications are as follows:

- The validation of an expert system requires human experts, who are in some sense more expert than the expert system itself. But leading human experts do not always agree, experts might not be available, and some might be biased; and the ethical contribution to a decision might be different from expert to expert.[13] And how does one validate AI that performs at levels superior to humans?

5 See, for example, "DIA 2019 Munich, Robot Sophia Interview", www.youtube.com/watch?v=YoHkIG2x4FU.

6 See, for example, "Xinhua Unveils World's First Female AI News Anchor", www.youtube.com/watch?v=5iZuffHPDAw.

7 See history timeline in the Stanford 100-year project on AI, "One Hundred Year Study on Artificial Intelligence (AI100), History" (Stanford University), https://ai100.stanford.edu/history-1.

8 K Kelly, "The Three Breakthroughs That Have Finally Unleashed AI on the World" (27 October 2014), www.wired.com/2014/10/future-of-artificial-intelligence.

9 A Agrawal et al., *Prediction Machines: The Simple Economics of Artificial Intelligence* (Boston, MA, Harvard Business Review Press, 2018).

10 D Ciuriak and M Ptashkina, "The Data-Driven Economy and the Role of the State", in B Haggart et al. (eds), *Contests for Power and Authority in Internet Governance: Return of the State* (Routledge, in press) .

11 E Feigenbaum, "Expert Systems: Principles and Practice", in BW Wah (ed), *The Encyclopedia of Computer Science* (New York, Wiley, 1992).

12 J Rushby, "Quality Measures and Assurance for AI Software" (NASA Contract Report 4187, Washington, DC, 1988), www.csl.sri.com/papers/csl-88-7/csl-88-7r.pdf.

13 For a discussion of ethical inputs into AI decisions, see A Etzioni and O Etzioni, "AI Assisted Ethics" (2016) 18 *Ethics and Information Technology* 149.

- AI trained on data can only draw inferences within the scope and experience base of those data. But there is no way to definitively specify what is comprehensive coverage of the knowledge required to draw an expert inference. For example, humans often reason by analogy; how does one code the intuition that informs when an analogy is apt?
- Conventional validation requires precise testing of outputs. But definitive assessments are not possible with AI that will draw inferences from new information, even though the AI can be tested for repeatability and stability with given data inputs.

In the modern era, where AI is developed in non-deterministic processes through training on big data, in which the decision-making process cannot be broken down into sub-programs that can be individually tested, the problem becomes still more complex. While "black box" testing approaches have been developed, these are considered to be more "workarounds" than solutions to the problem of quality assurance.[14] Notably, an AI chatbot trained on Twitter quickly became a foul-mouthed racist and had to be shut down,[15] highlighting the issues raised for regulation by open-ended training data.

Notwithstanding these essentially unbounded concerns, use cases for AI through expert systems have proliferated and myriad applications have, as noted, already passed the applicable regulatory procedures and industry-established quality benchmarks without apparently encountering significant problems in terms of accessing international markets. How was this done? We turn to this question next.

B *Horizontal Standards*

The modern era of powerful AI emerged in a regulatory context informed by the experience acquired developing quality assurance for expert systems within the software engineering stream, under the auspices of the International Organization for Standardization (ISO) and the International Electrotechnical Commission (IEC). The ISO/IEC 90003 Software Engineering standards for expert systems date back to 1998. At the industry level, relevant quality assurance approaches include Total Quality Management (TQM), Six Sigma, and a number of others.

With technology rapidly advancing, many AI-specific standards are being developed at the national and international levels. For example:

[14] ME Mehle, "Quality Assurance for AI Software and Machine Learning" (*Cosylab*, 5 April 2020), www.cosylab.com/2020/04/05/qa-for-ai-and-ml.

[15] E Hunt, "Tay, Microsoft's AI Chatbot, Gets a Crash Course in Racism from Twitter" (*The Guardian*, 24 March 2016), www.theguardian.com/technology/2016/mar/24/tay-microsofts-ai-chatbot-gets-a-crash-course-in-racism-from-twitter.

- The US National Institute of Standards and Technology (NIST) has released a Plan for Federal Engagement in AI Standards Development,[16] which lists nine areas of focus, including human interactions, performance testing, and trustworthiness. The US approach is generally "light touch", relying on self-regulation by industry, and emphasizing commercial opportunity.
- China's Standardization Administration of China (SAC) has released a White Paper to support China's international engagement on AI standards for key technologies and interoperability, including on algorithmic transparency, liability, bias, and privacy, among other ethical and security issues.[17]
- The European Commission has, inter alia, issued a White Paper on AI; a report on safety and liability implications of AI, the Internet of Things (IoT), and robotics; and, through a High-Level Expert Group, ethical guidelines for trustworthy AI.[18]
- Japan has established an Advanced Integrated Intelligence Platform Project (AIP), which features a comprehensive programme on AI, including standards.[19]
- The United Nations has been active on the human rights aspects of AI, developing recommendations on ethical issues raised by the development and application of AI.[20]
- The Organisation for Economic Co-operation and Development (OECD) Ministerial Council has agreed a set of high-level OECD Principles on Artificial Intelligence.[21]
- As regards the deeper issues raised by ML, international standards under development include the ISO/IEC CD 23053 ("Framework for Artificial Intelligence Systems Using Machine Learning") and the ISO/AWI TR 23348 ("Statistics – Big Data Analytics – Model Validation"). These may provide a common approach for assessing compliance of AI software in high-risk applications in regulated industries.[22]

16 NIST, "U.S. Leadership in AI: A Plan for Federal Engagement in Developing Technical Standards and Related Tools" (2019), www.nist.gov/system/files/documents/2019/08/10/ai_standards_fedengagement_plan_9aug2019.pdf.

17 J Ding et al., "Chinese Interests Take a Big Seat at the AI Governance Table" (*New America*, 20 June 2018), www.newamerica.org/cybersecurity-initiative/digichina/blog/chinese-interests-take-big-seat-ai-governance-table.

18 European Commission, "Artificial Intelligence" (2020), https://ec.europa.eu/digital-single-market/en/artificial-intelligence.

19 "About AIP" (*Riken*), https://aip.riken.jp/about-aip.

20 "Elaboration of a Recommendation on the Ethics of Artificial Intelligence" (*UNESCO*), https://en.unesco.org/artificial-intelligence/ethics; J Pielemeier, "AI and Global Governance: The Advantages of Applying the International Human Rights Framework to Artificial Intelligence" (2019) United Nations University Center for Policy Research.

21 "Forty-two Countries Adopt New OECD Principles on Artificial Intelligence" (OECD, 22 May 2019), www.oecd.org/science/forty-two-countries-adopt-new-oecd-principles-on-artificial-intelligence.htm.

22 Mehle, note 13 above.

Trustworthiness standards are of particular interest as they cover a gamut of difficult issues, including accuracy, explainability, resiliency, safety, reliability, objectivity, and security.[23] The ISO technical committee on AI published its first overview of trustworthiness in AI only on 28 May 2020.[24] While this document discusses these various aspects of trustworthiness, the specification of *levels* of trustworthiness for AI systems remains beyond the scope of the ISO process. And, of course, it is precisely the level of trustworthiness where social and political choice is decisive, as demonstrated by the heated debate over the use of facial recognition by public authorities.[25]

Progress in these areas is being driven by necessity because AI is being deployed commercially and regulation cannot wait. For example, the European Union's (EU's) General Data Protection Regulation (GDPR) establishes explainability as a right: under the GDPR, individuals have a right to ask businesses that use their personal data for automated processing how decisions that affect them were made – and businesses must be able to explain to be compliant. Moreover, the GDPR establishes the right to request human intervention for review of an AI decision, and grants new investigatory, advisory, corrective, and punitive powers to the EU's data protection authorities, putting firms on notice.[26] Explainability has also engaged the attention of the military in developing protocols for military use of AI.[27] "Explainable AI" has thus become an important frontier for research[28] – and, indeed, has acquired its own acronym, "XAI".

In short, while horizontal AI-specific regulations were largely missing in action in the early phase of integration of AI into the economy and society, this gap is fast being filled.

23 NIST, note 15 above, at 3.

24 Technical Committee ISO/IEC JTC 1/SC 42 on Artificial Intelligence, www.iso.org/obp/ui/#iso:std:iso-iec:tr:24028:ed-1:v1:en.

25 M Andrejevic and N Selwyn, "Facial Recognition Technology in Schools: Critical Questions and Concerns" (2020) 45 *Learning, Media and Technology* 115; M Hirose, "Privacy in Public Spaces: The Reasonable Expectation of Privacy against the Dragnet Use of Facial Recognition Technology" (2016) 49 *Connecticut Law Review* 1591; J Greene, "Microsoft Won't Sell Police Its Facial-Recognition Technology, Following Similar Moves by Amazon and IBM" (*Washington Post*, 22 June 2020), www.washingtonpost.com/technology/2020/06/11/microsoft-facial-recognition.

26 For a sceptical view of the reality of the "right of explainability" under the GDPR, see S Wachter et al., "Why a Right to Explanation of Automated Decision-Making Does Not Exist in the General Data Protection Regulation" (2017) 7 *International Data Privacy Law* 76; for a view that the overall scheme "provides a muscular 'right to explanation' with sweeping legal implications for the design, prototyping, field testing, and deployment of automated data processing systems", see B Casey et al., "Rethinking Explainable Machines: The GDPR's 'Right to Explanation' Debate and the Rise of Algorithmic Audits in Enterprise" (2019) 34 *Berkeley Technology Law Journal* 145.

27 M Turek, "Explainable Artificial Intelligence (XAI)" (*DARPA*, 2020), www.darpa.mil/program/explainable-artificial-intelligence.

28 AB Arrieta et al., "Explainable Artificial Intelligence (XAI): Concepts, Taxonomies, Opportunities and Challenges Toward Responsible AI" (2019) 58 *Information Fusion* 82; D Gunning et al., "XAI – Explainable Artificial Intelligence" (2019) 4 *Science Robotics* 7120.

C *Vertical or Industry/Product-Specific Standards – Mechanical Functions*

The largely unimpeded commercial progress of AI to date has arguably reflected several characteristics of the market, in addition to the general absence of restrictive horizontal standards:

- Industrial applications were developed by highly sophisticated companies working with sophisticated clients, including government agencies, with the AI embedded in machinery that was subject to an industry- or sector-specific (hence "vertical") regulatory framework.
- Consumer-facing applications were embedded in products marketed mostly by "superstar" firms (e.g. cell phones with "smart" assistants and other AI-powered applications) and subject to product-specific standards and regulations administered by designated agencies with deep expertise in regulating on behalf of unsophisticated households.

The least problematic applications from a standards perspective are those where AI performs purely mechanical functions; performance in these types of functions tends to be measurable and the behaviour of the AI, even with learning, converges to an observable standard. AI applications that replace human cognitive/decision functions and involve agency on the part of the AI (i.e. where the AI makes autonomous decisions with real-world impacts) attract more regulatory attention. Applications can of course combine mechanical and cognitive functions. Accordingly, certification for domestic markets of particular AIs may involve a multiplicity of approvals.

One of the most straightforward uses of AI is to automate routine business or production processes or to reassign specific human functions to machines for accuracy. These types of applications have been adopted rapidly and widely and spread globally, without seemingly encountering barriers.

Industry is already familiar with industrial robots. Integrating AI into an industrial robot makes the robot more intelligent in the sense of being able to perform more complex functions. In such traditional industrial robotic applications, robots can substitute for particular human roles entirely and even work in isolation from humans. A quintessential example is provided by the role of AI in supply chain management automation. The integration of AI, improved sensors, sophisticated warehouse management software, IoT telecommunications systems, and automated robotic technology effectively allows warehouses to operate autonomously on a literally "lights-out" basis.[29]

More commonly, AI applications in workplace settings support human–robot interaction within a shared workspace. Instead of replacing people with autonomous modules, such collaborative AIs (so-called cobots), trained with ML techniques and

[29] R Bowles, "Warehouse Robotics: Everything You Need to Know in 2019" (*Logiwa*, 24 August 2020), www.logiwa.com/blog/warehouse-robotics.

big data, work with humans, providing extra precision, speed, and consistency without fatigue in routinized tasks, while leaving the less routine aspects to humans. There are many examples of cobot applications already in use.[30] One example is "pick and place" functions, which involve mundane repetitive tasks that require cognition and result in errors due to boredom; such jobs can be more efficiently (and more safely given the propensity for repetitive strain injuries) done by robots with advanced vision systems and trained by AI, while the human member of the team focuses on aspects that require decisions. Another is "packaging and palletizing", which includes a range of functions from shrink-wrapping and boxing to placing products on a pallet for shipment.

Routine quality inspection functions are also being turned over to cobots that inspect finished parts by comparing images from multiple high-resolution cameras that capture all angles of a product simultaneously and are not prone to mental fatigue. More sophisticated cobot applications under development include an aircraft inspection assistant cobot in the "Hangar of the Future", which automates aircraft inspection as part of maintenance, repair, and overhaul operations.[31] Trucking is likely to go down this route with AI systems taking over the long-haul highway portions, leaving the first and last mile which involve more complicated environments to human drivers.

While many (if not most) of these tasks involve AI enabling the replacement of physical labour by robots, there are other cases where the AI replaces the skilled function. It is typically the case in these instances that the AI is hyper-competent and the AI's work is superior to the human's. This is likely the future for much assembly-type manufacturing that requires precision work such as automotive and aircraft assembly – see, for example, the use of AI and ML techniques to refine the installation of aircraft skins by Boeing.[32] Healthcare has emerged as a major use case for cobots where the AI is hyper-competent in this sense, particularly surgery-assisting cobots that use AI to improve the precision of surgical procedures.[33]

Other interesting examples of this include Sony's Hawkeye in tennis, which uses AI to make line calls. In tennis, the AI over-rules the human line caller in a challenge. In the 2020 US Open, AI made all the line calls on fifteen of the

[30] Robotics Online Marketing Team, "Robotic Surgery: The Role of AI and Collaborative Robots" (*Robotics Online Blog*, 9 July 2019), www.robotics.org/blog-article.cfm/Robotic-Surgery-The-Role-of-AI-and-Collaborative-Robots/181.

[31] "Hangar of the Future: Excelling in MRO" (Airbus, 6 December 2016), www.airbus.com/newsroom/news/en/2016/12/Hangar-of-the-future.html.

[32] H Solan, "Artificial Intelligence, Machine Learning Advances Hit Factory Floor" (Boeing), www.boeing.com/features/innovation-quarterly/feb2019/people-aifactory.page.

[33] Robotics Online Marketing Team, note 29 above; V Chalmers, "Scientists Develop a Ground-Breaking Robot 'Which Could Revolutionise Spinal Surgery' Because It Can Drill Holes with 0.1mm Accuracy - Better Than EVER Recorded for Humans" (*Daily Mail*, 7 January 2019), https://med.news.am/eng/news/20680/scientists-develop-a-ground-breaking-robot-which-could-revolutionise-spinal-surgery-because-it-can-drill-holes-with-01mm-accuracy–better-than-ever-recorded-for-humans.html.

seventeen courts;[34] meanwhile, in the 2020 French Open, the failure to deploy the AI line-calling system was decried following an apparent mis-call at a critical moment in the match between Canada's Denis Shapovalov and Spain's Roberto Carballes Baena, leading to a rising tide of sentiment within the professional ranks in favour of the system. A retail market version ("InOut") is already in use.[35] Similar applications have been developed for goal-line decisions in football.[36] Baseball is experimenting with turning over the ball-strike calls to AI based on analysis that human umpires incorrectly call pitches (e.g. Chen et al. find that umpires call only about 60 per cent of close pitches accurately and show systematic bias due to effects such "anchoring" or the "gambler's fallacy"[37]). In its first baseball application, the human is advised by the AI and it is the human that makes the definitive call.[38]

Clearly, such AI applications have navigated complex sector-specific regulatory systems to get to market (such as those for medical devices or civil aviation) – or none at all (such as those for sports). From a trade perspective, the technology typically enters a new market either through foreign direct investment or through a transaction between a sophisticated supplier and a sophisticated buyer with considerable tailoring of the application to the specific circumstances and needs of the buyer. Accordingly, the future for the international dissemination of such AI applications does not appear to be any more problematic than its experience to date has been.

D *Vertical or Industry/Product-Specific Standards – Cognitive/Decision Functions*

AI that performs human cognitive/decision functions, in contexts where agency is involved and the decision criteria are less clear-cut and the consequences more significant than making a ball/strike call in baseball or a line call in tennis, will likely face substantially higher hurdles to achieve acceptance. The essential analogue would be competence regulation for human experts. Depending on the nature of the judgements the AI would be called to make, how it is trained might come into play.

34 C Clarey, "Automated Line Calls Will Replace Human Judges at U.S. Open" (*The New York Times*, 3 August 2020), www.nytimes.com/2020/08/03/sports/tennis/us-open-hawkeye-line-judges.html.

35 "In/Out v2.0: The Portable Line Call Device with Millimeters Accuracy" (Inout), https://inout.tennis/en/index.htm.

36 L Silkin, "Artificial Intelligence: The New Driving Force Behind Sports Performance and Entertainment" (Lexology, 13 February 2019), www.lexology.com/library/detail.aspx?g=7d3990a1-0a9e-4f2b-8a6d-2a2b5b035730.

37 D Chen, TJ Moskowitz, and K Shue, "Decision-Making under the Gambler's Fallacy: Evidence from Asylum Judges, Loan Officers, and Baseball Umpires" (NBER Working Paper No. 22026, February 2016).

38 J Bogage, "Baseball's Robot Umpires Are Here. And You Might Not Even Notice the Difference" (*Washington Post*, 10 July 2019), www.washingtonpost.com/sports/2019/07/10/baseballs-robot-umpires-are-here-you-might-not-even-notice-difference.

In the legal domain, for example, the amount of unstructured data mobilized for legal cases is enormous. It is no surprise that natural language processing (NLP) and image recognition techniques lend themselves to extract efficiencies in the preparation of legal cases. As the marketing of these tools is between sophisticated businesses, there are no apparent issues.

At the same time, deploying advanced algorithms in actual legal procedures raises concerns related to the core principles and guarantees of judicial systems. In this regard, the European Commission for the Efficiency of Justice (CEPEJ) adopted the first European Ethical Charter[39] on the use of AI in the justice system in 2018. The charter outlines principles to guide policymakers, legislators, and justice professionals to help them to embrace and, where needed, confront the spread of AI applications in judicial systems. These principles aim to ensure compliance with fundamental rights, non-discrimination, quality and security, transparency, and controllability.

In the latter regard, international practice already shows the wide range of possibilities in how societies might act: China has established an AI Internet court presided over by an AI judge for cases involving legal disputes in the digital domain;[40] Estonia has launched a project to build a robot judge to preside over small claims disputes involving sums of less than € 7,000;[41] the United States allows a limited yet still controversial[42] use of AI in informing legal decisions concerning whether to incarcerate defendants pending trial; but France, on the other hand, has banned the use of AI in legal proceedings.[43] This effectively spans the waterfront of possible positions on AI's role from full agency, to supporting role, to outright ban.

Healthcare is also witnessing pioneering developments of AI applications, given the availability of enormous amounts of data that greatly exceeds human cognitive capacity to effectively manage,[44] increases in computational power, and the

39 "European Ethical Charter on the Use of Artificial Intelligence in Judicial Systems and Their Environment" (2018), https://rm.coe.int/ethical-charter-en-for-publication-4-december-2018/16808f699c.

40 G Du and M Yu, "Big Data, AI and China's Justice: Here's What's Happening" (*China Justice Observer*, 1 December 2019), www.chinajusticeobserver.com/a/big-data-ai-and-chinas-justice-heres-whats-happening.

41 V Kumar, "AI Moves to Court: The Growing Footprints of AI in the Legal Industry" (*Analytics Insight*, 23 January 2020), www.analyticsinsight.net/ai-moves-court-growing-footprint-ai-legal-industry.

42 "Using risk assessment tools to make fair decisions about human liberty would require solving deep ethical, technical, and statistical challenges, including ensuring that the tools are designed and built to mitigate bias at both the model and data layers, and that proper protocols are in place to promote transparency and accountability. The tools currently available and under consideration for widespread use suffer from several of these failures", Partnership on AI, "Report on Algorithmic Risk Assessment Tools in the U.S. Criminal Justice System" (2019), www.partnershiponai.org/report-on-machine-learning-in-risk-assessment-tools-in-the-u-s-criminal-justice-system.

43 See Legifrance (2019), www.legifrance.gouv.fr/jorf/article_jo/JORFARTI000038261761?r=nrSLylJGaZ. The Justice Reform Act, Article 33 limits judicial analytics. "The identity data of magistrates and members of the registry cannot be reused with the object or effect of evaluating, analyzing, comparing or predicting their actual or supposed professional practices" [free translation].

44 ME Matheny et al., "Artificial Intelligence in Health Care: A Report from the National Academy of Medicine" (2020) 323 *Journal of the American Medical Association* 509.

development of ML techniques to retrieve information from unstructured data as well as in imaging and signal detection tasks. As a result, the healthcare system provides many examples of AI that are already widely deployed in areas such as radiology, oncology, and ophthalmology,[45] and even general medical decision-making, such as triaging patients in a hospital setting;[46] and AI-powered chatbot triage services as an alternative to telephone helpline services to dispense healthcare advice and direct patients to local and out-of-hours medical services.[47]

Not all AI products for healthcare face significant regulatory oversight – for example, consumer-facing platforms or assistants that dispense conventional advice (e.g. guiding patients in their preparation for surgery or through the recovery process). Such applications that are already widely distributed involve modern versions of expert systems that are embedded in online products and that are relatively simple in terms of the understanding of terminology, data protection, human involvement, safety, and risk management. The level of trustworthiness can be decided by market competition which fosters industry standards as regards accuracy, robustness of technical capabilities, and other application-specific criteria. Standards can be overwritten by authorities if any concerns arise.

The US Food and Drug Administration (FDA) has taken the lead in developing a regulatory framework for approval of AI/ML medical devices in more critical applications.[48] It has established three levels of clearance for AI/ML-based medical applications, namely:

- a 510(k) which clears Class I or II devices for market if they can be established to be at least as safe and effective as another similar, legally marketed device;
- pre-market approval for Class III devices that require greater regulatory evaluation of the scientific evidence because of potential risks to health (e.g. pacemakers); and
- a de novo pathway for novel medical devices for which there are no legally marketed counterparts, for which the FDA performs a risk-based assessment to establish safety and effectiveness.

Already we can see the potential for differing conclusions across major regulatory jurisdictions as to what is sufficiently safe and effective to be put on the market, given the scope for differing risk tolerances, including for devices requiring pre-market clearance where there is potential for different regulatory agencies to reach different conclusions; and even more so for de novo devices.

45 S Benjamens et al., "The State of Artificial Intelligence-Based FDA-Approved Medical Devices and Algorithms: An Online Database" (2020) 3 *Digital Medicine* 1.

46 S Horng et al., "Creating an Automated Trigger for Sepsis Clinical Decision Support at Emergency Department Triage Using Machine Learning" (2017) 12 *PLOS One* 1.

47 S O'Hear, "Babylon Health Partners with UK's NHS to Replace Telephone Helpline with AI-Powered Chatbot" (TechCrunch, 4 January 2017), https://techcrunch.com/2017/01/04/babylon-health-partners-with-uks-nhs-to-replace-telephone-helpline-with-ai-powered-chatbot.

48 Benjamens et al., note 43 above.

An example of embedded AI that provides a glimpse into the regulatory framework through which it moves is provided in the aviation sector, where aircraft incorporate a myriad of systems that co-share flying operations with human pilots,[49] performing both mechanical and cognitive functions. In the Boeing 737 Max case, a faulty sensor resulted in incorrect information being fed into an AI system (the automated flight-control system, Maneuvering Characteristics Augmentation System, or MCAS), which resulted in two crashes.[50] An international panel of experts[51] was formed to review the causes of the breakdowns in Boeing's internal safety disciplines and the US Federal Aviation Authority's certification and oversight procedures. The panel made a dozen recommendations,[52] which established de facto conditions for the re-entry into service of this Boeing aircraft around the world.

E *The Locked Versus the Unlocked*

Since the first AI/ML device received FDA approval (a wearable-tech monitoring system introduced in 2012),[53] some sixty-four AI/ML-based medical devices and algorithms have received FDA approval and been put on the market. While this early experience is encouraging, a still more complex issue has been encountered in this area. The current regulatory approach for medical devices was designed for devices that are "locked" (i.e. devices that give the same answer each time the same inputs are presented) and feature only discrete modifications from time to time. It is now recognized that this needs to be adapted for algorithms that *learn* with each application.[54]

In this regard, the FDA has put out a discussion paper setting out a proposed regulatory framework for modifications to AI/ML-based Software as a Medical

[49] L Eliot, "Boeing 737 MAX 8 and Lessons for AI: The Case of AI Self-Driving Cars" (AI Trends, 22 March 2019), www.aitrends.com/ai-insider/boeing-737-max-8-and-lessons-for-ai-the-case-of-ai-self-driving-cars.

[50] R Kraus, "'Aggressive and Riskier' A.I. – and Bureaucracy – Caused the Boeing Crashes, Report Says" (Mashable, 2 June 2019), https://mashable.com/article/boeing-737-max-aggressive-risky-ai.

[51] The Joint Authorities Technical Review (JATR) comprised experts from two US agencies (the Federal Aviation Authority and the National Aeronautics and Space Administration), and civil aviation authorities from Australia, Brazil, Canada, China, Europe, Indonesia, Japan, Singapore, and the United Arab Emirates.

[52] W Bellamy III, "International Regulators Submit Joint Technical Review of 737 MAX Flight Control System to FAA" (*Aviation Today*, 14 October 2019), www.aviationtoday.com/2019/10/14/international-regulators-submit-joint-technical-review-737-max-flight-controls-faa.

[53] "Bringing to Market Solutions Based on Their Health Platform That Incorporates Mobile, Tablet, Cloud and Physiological Monitoring Technologies for Early Screening and Diagnosis through Completion of Care, Preventice Is Helping Health Care Providers Achieve Higher-Quality Outcomes" (CEOCFO, 7 January 2013), www.ceocfointerviews.com/interviews/Preventice12-CEOCFO-Article.pdf.

[54] Benjamens et al., note 43 above.

Device (SaMD), which involves a total lifecycle approach to regulation, based on four principles:[55]

- establish clear expectations on quality systems and good ML practices (GMLP);
- conduct pre-market review for those SaMD that require pre-market submission to demonstrate reasonable assurance of safety and effectiveness and establish clear expectations for manufacturers of AI/ML-based SaMD to continually manage patient risks throughout the lifecycle;
- monitor the AI/ML device and incorporate a risk management approach and other guidance in development, validation, and execution of algorithm changes; and
- transparency to users and FDA using post-market real-world performance reporting for maintaining continued assurance of safety and effectiveness.

These principles – in particular the third, which requires a continual programme of monitoring and validation – highlight the issues posed by the inherent fluidity of deployed AI/ML devices and algorithms that are undergoing continuous modification with acquired experience. Coupled with the ubiquitous concerns about bias and data security, this fluidity underscores the need to establish and maintain a high-trust environment between the creators of the AI, the user community, and the regulators. Similar levels of confidence and transparency will be required between national regulatory bodies to ensure international market access. However, as AI will rely heavily on trade secrets to protect the intellectual property in AI applications (e.g. algorithms and data), the issues concerning the quality and biases inherent in the data used to train AI algorithms may prove to become points of friction in international trade.

III GETTING ARTIFICIAL INTELLIGENCE TO MARKET: NAVIGATING SOCIETAL CHOICE AND INSECURITY

While the integration of AI into the trading system has been more or less seamless at the technical level, as it begins to have systemic significance, new hurdles are likely to emerge. Three of these in particular loom large as potential points of friction: societal impacts, national security concerns, and the question of the impact of AI on jobs. We address these next.

A *Societal Impacts*

The nexus of AI/ML/big data not only impacts at the micro level on individuals and firms but also drives a complex co-evolution of technology, the economy, and society

[55] FDA, "Proposed Regulatory Framework for Modifications to Artificial Intelligence/Machine Learning (AI/ML)-Based Software as a Medical Device (SaMD)" (2019), www.fda.gov/medical-devices/software-medical-device-samd/artificial-intelligence-and-machine-learning-software-medical-device.

that takes on its own dynamic, as captured in the title of Kevin Kelly's 1994 book, *Out of Control: The New Biology of Machines, Social Systems, and the Economic World*. The pace of evolution in machine space is dictated by the resources committed to innovation and thus is almost arbitrarily fast. The technological instinct is indeed to move fast and disrupt; however, with disruptive technological change, the co-evolution of societal structures and of the economy ensures that, along with all that is gained, there is also much that is lost. Moreover, governance systems that evolved in an age of much slower technological change are not well equipped to get out in front of the implications of new technologies. The result is system friction:

> The shift of our economy and society online is taking place without referendum. What could go wrong? As it turns out, plenty.[56]

This friction surfaced in the "techlash" that flared in the second half of the 2010s.[57] There were numerous contributing factors beyond the pace of change. For example, there was widespread apprehension about the potentially dystopian directions of change,[58] many of which were popularized by the television series, *Black Mirror*, and even amplified by Elon Musk who said in an interview, "With artificial intelligence we're summoning the demon".[59] The fragility of democracy in silico was underscored by the revelation of manipulation of electorates in historical events such as the Brexit Referendum and the 2016 Trump presidential campaign by firms such as Cambridge Analytica using Facebook data and applying AI-driven quantitative social psychology tools.[60]

Even more fundamentally, the concentration of wealth enabled by the data-driven economy irrevocably altered the balance of power within modern societies. This is underscored by the fact that a company like Facebook has 2.5 billion clients

[56] D Ciuriak and B Wylie, "Data and Digital Rights: More Questions Than Answers – But Enumerating the Questions Is Essential" (2018), https://papers.ssrn.com/abstract=3300263.

[57] R Botsman, "Dawn of the Techlash" (*The Guardian*, 11 February 2018), www.theguardian.com/commentisfree/2018/feb/11/dawn-of-the-techlash; E Smith, "The Techlash Against Amazon, Facebook and Google – and What They Can Do" (*The Economist*, 20 January 2018), www.economist.com/briefing/2018/01/20/the-techlash-against-amazon-facebook-and-google-and-what-they-can-do; RD Atkinson et al., "A Policymaker's Guide to the 'Techlash' – What It Is and Why It's a Threat to Growth and Progress" (Information Technology and Innovation Foundation, 28 October 2019), https://itif.org/publications/2019/10/28/policymakers-guide-techlash.

[58] W Hartzog and E Selinger, "Facial Recognition Is the Perfect Tool for Oppression" (2018), http://cyberlaw.stanford.edu/publications/facial-recognition-perfect-tool-oppression.

[59] G Kumparak, "Elon Musk Compares Building Artificial Intelligence to 'Summoning The Demon'" (TechCrunch, 26 October 2014), https://techcrunch.com/2014/10/26/elon-musk-compares-building-artificial-intelligence-to-summoning-the-demon.

[60] RD Atkinson et al., note 56 above. C Cadwalladr, "The Great British Brexit Robbery: How Our Democracy Was Hijacked" (*The Guardian*, 7 May 2017), www.theguardian.com/technology/2017/may/07/the-great-british-brexit-robbery-hijacked-democracy; T Gross, "Reporter Shows the Links Between the Men Behind Brexit and the Trump Campaign" (National Public Radio, 19 July 2018), www.npr.org/2018/07/19/630443485/reporter-shows-the-links-between-the-men-behind-brexit-and-the-trump-campaign.

for its applications[61] – more than the populations of the United States, the EU, and China combined. This change in power relations was evidenced in the behaviour of the technology CEOs who did not fail to sense their new status:

> By displacing the print and broadcast media in influencing public opinion, technology is becoming the new Fourth Estate. In our system of checks and balances, this makes technology co-equal with the executive, the legislature, and the judiciary. When this new Fourth Estate declines to appear before [the International Grand Committee] – as Silicon Valley executives are currently doing – it is symbolically asserting this aspirational co-equal status. But it is asserting this status and claiming its privileges without the traditions, disciplines, legitimacy or transparency that checked the power of the traditional Fourth Estate.[62]

These factors combined to generate pushback on the technology companies, their CEOs, and indeed the practical implementation of the technology nexus of AI/ML and big data.

At the national level, the likely source of issues for international trade will be invocation of the precautionary principle to exclude certain uses or technologies altogether based on societal preferences. The international community has some practical experience with this. Generally, under the World Trade Organization (WTO) Agreement, in particular the Technical Barriers to Trade (TBT) Agreement and the Agreement on the Application of Sanitary and Phytosanitary Measures (the "SPS Agreement"), countries have the right to set higher standards than accepted international standards,[63] although they are subject to general tests of reasonableness such as avoiding arbitrary or unjustifiable distinctions in risk tolerance across different situations (including, of course, not discriminating against imports compared to domestic products). At the same time, where relevant scientific evidence is insufficient, a WTO member may provisionally apply restrictive measures based on available pertinent information subject to the requirement that a more objective assessment of risk is made within a reasonable period.[64] While not directly referencing the precautionary principle that is formally incorporated in multilateral environmental agreements such as the Cartagena Protocol on Biosafety, the WTO Agreement thus does allow for precaution in setting rules.[65]

61 A Hutchinson, "Facebook Climbs to 2.5 Billion Monthly Active Users, But Rising Costs Impede Income Growth" (*Social Media Today*, 30 January 2020), www.socialmediatoday.com/news/facebook-climbs-to-25-billion-monthly-active-users-but-rising-costs-imped/571358.

62 J Balsillie, "Jim Balsillie: 'Data Is Not the New Oil – It's the New Plutonium'" (*Financial Post*, 28 May 2019), https://financialpost.com/technology/jim-balsillie-data-is-not-the-new-oil-its-the-new-plutonium.

63 S Charnovitz, "The Supervision of Health and Biosafety Regulation by World Trade Rules" (2000) 13 *Tulane Environmental Law Journal* 271.

64 Article 5.7 of the SPS Agreement.

65 The panel in the WTO dispute on marketing approvals by the EU for genetically modified organisms referred to the "precautionary approach" (WTO Panel Report, *EC – Approval and Marketing of Biotech Products*, para. 7.3065).

This base of experience, particularly the extensive debate concerning the precautionary principle,[66] helps prepare us for the challenges of carving out legitimate policy-based derogations for trade in AI from the freedom of commerce that international economic law defends.

A likely more challenging aspect of the pushback is at the sub-national level. A quintessential example of this, given the breadth of issues raised, was the communitarian response to the ambitious, futuristic smart city proposal for the Toronto waterfront Quayside district put forward by Sidewalk Labs, a subsidiary of Alphabet/Google, which aimed to essentially "disrupt the neighbourhood" in multiple dimensions.[67] This proposal was eventually withdrawn after a concerted battle by community activists.[68]

Governance flashpoints in the Sidewalk Toronto case included the proposal to claim a share of property taxes (essentially privatizing municipal governance); privacy concerns about the capture of the enormous flow of data that the district would generate through ubiquitous sensors (concerns which led to the resignation of the privacy adviser, Ann Cavoukian);[69] and more general governance concerns given that the administration of the smart city district would involve a private firm replacing regulations established through democratically accountable processes with its own frameworks[70] and digital incentives (e.g. one element of the plan was to grant residents access to certain spaces based on how much data they provide, or rewarding them for "good behaviour"[71]).

Another set of objections focused on the financial aspects of the proposal, starting with the inside track that Alphabet/Google appeared to have had for the project,[72]

66 IM Goklany, *The Precautionary Principle: A Critical Appraisal of Environmental Risk Assessment* (Washington, DC, Cato Institute, 2001); J Tait, "More Faust Than Frankenstein: The European Debate about the Precautionary Principle and Risk Regulation for Genetically Modified Crops" (2001) 4 *Journal of Risk Research* 175; G Majone, "What Price Safety? The Precautionary Principle and Its Policy Implications" (2002) 40 *Journal of Common Market Studies* 89; CR Sunstein, "Beyond the Precautionary Principle" (2003) 151 *University of Pennsylvania Law Review* 1003; CJ Pereira Di Salvo and L Raymond, "Defining the Precautionary Principle: An Empirical Analysis of Elite Discourse" (2010) 19 *Environmental Politics* 86.

67 C Crowe, "Disruptor of the Year: Sidewalk Labs" (Smart Cities Dive, 9 December 2019), www.smartcitiesdive.com/news/smart-city-disruptor-sidewalk-labs-alphabet-toronto-dive-awards/566277; N Ahmed, "The City vs. Big Tech" (*Briarpatch Magazine*, 2 July 2019), https://briarpatchmagazine.com/articles/view/the-city-vs.-big-tech.

68 Ibid.

69 J O'Kane, "Privacy Expert Ann Cavoukian Resigns from Sidewalk Toronto Smart-City Project: 'I Had No Other Choice'" (*Globe and Mail*, 2018), www.theglobeandmail.com/business/article-privacy-expert-ann-cavoukian-resigns-from-sidewalk-toronto-smart-city.

70 For example, Sidewalk Labs proposed designing a system for Digital Transparency in the Public Realm to facilitate what it termed "the co-creation of prototypes that can advance digital transparency and enable agency in the world's public spaces". "Designing for Digital Transparency in the Public Realm" (Sidewalk Labs), www.sidewalklabs.com/dtpr.

71 Ahmed, note 66 above.

72 D Skok, "Cracks in the Sidewalk" (MacLeans, 1 April 2019), https://archive.macleans.ca/article/2019/4/1/cracks-in-the-sidewalk.

which evoked the sense of overweening influence wielded by "big tech"; the vast asymmetry in information between the Canadian government bodies negotiating the deal and Sidewalk Labs, in particular concerning the ownership and ultimate monetization of the intellectual property and data that the smart city would generate;[73] and the economic power that the administering company, a multinational digital "superstar" firm, would have had over the district, which raised the omnipresent sceptre of market failure to which the data-driven economy is inherently susceptible.[74]

The Sidewalk Toronto example highlights the likely role of cities and communitarian activism in mediating social acceptance of AI. We have already seen communitarian activism drive policy on single-use plastics and Styrofoam products, with some US states and cities banning their use; and, highlighting the frictions, we have also seen some states imposing pre-emptive laws to *prevent* their cities from banning such products.[75] The use of AI for facial recognition has similarly met with divergent policies, with embrace in some states and bans in others[76] – and even international sanctions for alleged human rights abuses.[77] Reflecting the reading of public opinion, Microsoft, Amazon, and IBM publicly committed not to sell facial recognition to police departments because of human rights concerns over surveillance and racial profiling in the context of Black Lives Matters protests, until there is federal legislation that regulates its use and takes into account human rights issues.[78]

The scope for sub-national variance of treatment is also illustrated by regulations being developed for autonomous vehicles. Husch and Teigen highlight the many differences in the rules frameworks that have been adopted in the United States, where regulation of autonomous vehicles falls to the states.[79] Since 2012, there has been inconsistent acceptance, with some forty states having enacted legislation related to autonomous vehicles, implemented an executive order, or both.[80]

With urbanization growing steadily and expected to raise the share of the world's population living in cities from over 55 per cent in 2020 to 68 per cent

73 J Hinton and N Raffoul, "For Economic Outcomes of Sidewalk Toronto We Need to Talk about Intellectual Property" (*The Globe and Mail*, 18 February 2019), www.theglobeandmail.com/business/commentary/article-for-economic-outcomes-of-sidewalk-toronto-we-need-to-talk-about.

74 D Ciuriak, "The Economics of Data: Implications for the Data-Driven Economy" (2018), https://papers.ssrn.com/abstract=3118022.

75 CT Schlachter, "Regulation Trends on Plastic Bag Bans and Preemptions" (2019) Working Paper.

76 K Hill, "The Secretive Company That Might End Privacy as We Know It" (*New York Times*, 18 January 2020), www.nytimes.com/2020/01/18/technology/clearview-privacy-facial-recognition.html.

77 R Orol, "Can Sanctions Keep China's Surveillance Market in Check?" (CIGI, 12 November 2019), www.cigionline.org/articles/can-sanctions-keep-chinas-surveillance-market-check.

78 Greene, note 45 above.

79 B Husch and A Teigen, "Regulating Autonomous Vehicles" (2017) 25 Legis Brief.

80 "Autonomous Vehicles, Self-Driving Vehicles Enacted Legislation" (National Conference of State Legislatures, 18 February 2020), www.ncsl.org/research/transportation/autonomous-vehicles-self-driving-vehicles-enacted-legislation.aspx.

by 2050,[81] cities will gain increasing clout in governance and will be looking for technological solutions to the infrastructure and administrative challenges posed by newly highlighted pandemic risks, environmental sustainability imperatives, and income inequality. They will thus be both the *demandeurs* for AI technology and the battlegrounds for its acceptance.

B *National Security*

The digital transformation, the advent of the data-driven economy, and particularly the coming implementation of fifth-generation telecommunications networks (5G) and IoT applications, which 5G will power, combine to fundamentally transform the concept of national security. This reflects in the first instance the proliferation of vulnerabilities to cyber attacks, whether from state actors, from criminal elements (e.g. ransomware attacks on cities and public institutions), or even from university students gaming the system (e.g. the infamous Mirai bot event that crippled the Internet in 2016 was initially thought to be the work of a state actor before being traced to US college students).[82] As 5G and growing AI applications transform the backbone infrastructure of an economy (i.e. transportation, telecommunications, energy, and finance) from a passive utility into an interactive "central nervous system",[83] national security principles have to be updated quite fundamentally.

Importantly from a trade perspective, these vulnerabilities are fundamentally different from those that informed the crafting of the current WTO national security exception as set out in the General Agreement on Tariffs and Trade (GATT) Article XXI. The framers of the GATT had World War II and the use of nuclear bombs in mind when providing examples of issues that might reasonably trigger the Article – circumstances that relate to fissionable materials (that is, nuclear weapons), traffic in arms, or measures taken in time of war or other emergencies in international relations.

By contrast, cyber attacks are high-frequency and relatively low-cost events, mostly carried out by bots with limited attributability to anyone, including to state actors. Security firm F-Secure, which deploys decoy servers to attract such attacks (so-called honeypots), recorded 5.7 billion attacks in 2019, up from 1.0 billion in 2018.[84]

81 "68% of the World Population Projected to Live in Urban Areas by 2050, Says UN" (UN, 16 May 2018), www.un.org/development/desa/en/news/population/2018-revision-of-world-urbanization-prospects.html.

82 B Bours, "How a Dorm Room Minecraft Scam Brought Down the Internet" (*Wired*, 13 December 2017), www.wired.com/story/mirai-botnet-minecraft-scam-brought-down-the-internet.

83 J Balsillie, "Six Recommendations for the International Grand Committee on Disinformation and 'Fake News'" (CIGI, 7 November 2019), www.cigionline.org/articles/six-recommendations-international-grand-committee-disinformation-and-fake-news.

84 J Stattler, "Attack Landscape H22019" (F-Secure, 4 March 2020), https://blog.f-secure.com/attack-landscape-h2-2019-an-unprecedented-year-cyber-attacks.

Sacramento-based Sutter Health reported 87 billion cyberthreats encountered in 2018.[85]

The cyber context resembles that of a biological immune system in a biosphere full of viruses, mostly fighting them off, but sometimes catching a cold – unpleasant but with consequences that fall far short of those associated with kinetic war (let alone nuclear war). The first suspected death attributable to a nonstate cyber attack occurred in 2020 in Duesseldorf, when a ransomware attack on a university hospital forced redirection of emergency cases elsewhere, delaying critical care.[86] The financial costs of such attacks are estimated in the millions of dollars but the overall cost at the economy level for the United States in 2019 amounted to only perhaps USD 7.5 billion or 0.036 per cent of US GDP.[87]

To be sure, the costs of disruption of infrastructure by state actors could be substantially higher – for example, a "kill switch" on an electrical grid being triggered. This possibility appears to have been established by infiltrations by governments of rivals' systems.[88] However, given the multiple sources of risks (including human, software, and hardware), it is far from clear that these concerns (or related concerns of cyber espionage) warrant extreme measures that preclude trade, such as the US' "5G Clean Path" programme that aims to freeze Chinese telecommunications equipment suppliers out of 5G systems outside of China.[89]

The WTO has little experience in dealing with national security issues as an exception.[90] One reason is that "trade restrictions during the Cold War period mainly related to non-Members, and there was no great need for justification under GATT".[91] Another is that countries were reluctant to set

85 N Wetsman, "Health Care's Huge Cybersecurity Problem" (*The Verge*, 4 April 2019), www.theverge.com/2019/4/4/18293817/cybersecurity-hospitals-health-care-scan-simulation.

86 N Wetsman, "Woman Dies During a Ransomware Attack on a German Hospital" (*The Verge*, 17 September 2020), www.theverge.com/2020/9/17/21443851/death-ransomware-attack-hospital-germany-cybersecurity.

87 A Hope, "Ransomware Costs in 2019" (*CPO Magazine*, 15 January 2020), www.cpomagazine.com/cyber-security/ransomware-costs-in-2019.

88 D Volz and T Gardner, "In a First, U.S. Blames Russia for Cyber Attacks on Energy Grid" (*Reuters*, 15 March 2018), www.reuters.com/article/us-usa-russia-sanctions-energygrid-idUSKCN1GR2G3.

89 This programme is framed as an attempt to "address the long-term threat to data privacy, security, human rights and principled collaboration posed to the free world from authoritarian malign actors". The programme effectively blacklists vendors, such as ZTE and Huawei. The initiative not only prevents US companies from buying services and products from untrusted vendors but also requires the leading US and foreign companies to remove their apps from the Huawei app store. See "The Clean Network" (US Department of State), www.state.gov/the-clean-network.

90 D Ciuriak and M Ptashkina, "Toward a Robust Architecture for the Regulation of Data and Digital Trade" (2020) CIGI Paper No. 240; JB Heath, "National Security and Economic Globalization: Toward Collision or Reconciliation?" (2019) 42 *Fordham International Law Journal* 1431.

91 T Cottier and P Delimatsis, "Article XIV bis GATS: Security Exceptions", in R Wolfrum et al. (eds), *WTO – Trade in Services: Max Planck Commentaries on World Trade Law: Vol. 6* (Leiden, Nijhoff, 2008).

precedents that might be used against them, and thus figuratively opening Pandora's box.[92]

Not surprisingly, the framing of national security exemptions in trade agreements is evolving. For example, the recent update of the North American Free Trade Agreement (NAFTA) – the US-Canada-Mexico Agreement (USMCA) – included a GATT Article XXI-type exception but dropped the examples. Unfortunately, it provided no alternative language, leaving fully open the question of what kinds of national security risks in this digital age would support an abrogation of trade commitments. This gap is especially problematic given the evolution of the global system of production and trade into a "made in the world" system of global value chains.

Decoupling and repatriation of international supply chains comprise one possible solution to national security concerns, but this would come at some considerable economic efficiency cost, would not actually remove the vulnerabilities from the IoT framework, and would in any event not be a realistic option for any economy other than perhaps the United States, the EU, or China.

AI finds itself in the eye of this particular storm. It is central to the national security frameworks of the major powers. As a practical example, China has indicated it would block the transfer of the AI algorithm underpinning the ByteDance TikTok operation.[93] The problem in this instance is not that the AI cannot get into a market, but rather that it cannot leave a market. This risk will hang over other companies – will Tesla, for example, be allowed to transfer its Chinese-developed technology to the USA if US bans on transfer of US technology to China continue? At the same time, control of AI that is in a position of influence over popular opinion in a country clearly will not be allowed for companies from countries that are considered strategic competitors.

Accordingly, national security could be a conversation killer for AI when market access comes up in an international trade context.

C *Labour Markets and the New "Guilded Age"*

AI can be thought of as a new form of productive capital – machine knowledge capital. As such, it is likely to complement human skills in some tasks and compete with them in others. If we think of "jobs" as packages of "tasks",[94] automation of tasks results in partial automation of all jobs. Consistent with the experience of skill-biased

[92] S Kho and T Peterson, "Turning the Tables: The United States, China, and the WTO National Security Exception" (*China Business Review*, 16 August 2019), www.chinabusinessreview.com/turning-the-tables-the-united-states-china-and-the-wto-national-security-exception.

[93] Z Xin and T Qu, "TikTok's Algorithm Not for Sale, ByteDance Tells US: Source" (*South China Morning Post*, 13 September 2020), www.scmp.com/economy/china-economy/article/3101362/tiktoks-algorithm-not-sale-bytedance-tells-us-source.

[94] M Arntz et al., "The Risk of Automation for Jobs in OECD Countries: A Comparative Analysis" (2016) OECD Social Employment and Migration Working Papers No. 189.

technological change over the past several decades,[95] income inequality is likely to increase as workers whose skills are mainly complemented by AI will realize rising returns to their human capital, while those whose skills are mostly substituted by AI will face job loss or strong downward competitive pressure on wages.[96]

Various scenarios have been suggested for the impact of AI on labour markets. Pessimistic scenarios[97] conclude there will be heavy job destruction. Less pessimistic scenarios[98] conclude that automation will mainly transform jobs rather than destroy them, but that low-qualified workers will likely bear the brunt of the adjustment costs since a greater proportion of their tasks can be automated compared to highly qualified workers. The main challenges in this scenario are facilitating job/task transition with training and addressing income inequality. Meanwhile, technology optimists conclude that AI will create jobs.[99]

Regardless of which scenario ultimately obtains, it seems clear that a new factor of production will claim its share of national income – and since this new factor primarily competes with human brain work, it follows that this share of income will be clawed away from today's white-collar work force. The current organization of society and economy in advanced countries in terms of status and income is based on human capital. People invest heavily to acquire both the knowledge capital and the credentials. Even though student debt is often crippling, the overall returns to a university degree are still very substantial: an estimate of the net present value of a university degree in the United States in 2018 was, on average, USD 344,000.[100] At the same time, at a price point where the annual cost of college equals USD 50,000, the odds of the investment in a college degree paying off fall to about 50–50.[101]

What happens in this context when the rents to higher education are eroded – that is, when the incomes that drive the net present value of a degree fall? The answer is, of course, structural adjustment along many margins – demand for higher education falls, prices fall, and the supply of this service contracts. Universities and colleges are pillars of their local economies. So these college towns would suffer as well from the multiplier effects. In this regard, the AI shock to white-collar work and the social organization around it in the advanced economies would resemble the China shock to industrial work and the social organization around it in the advanced countries in

95 See for example, E Berman et al., "Implications of Skill-Biased Technological Change: International Evidence" (1998) 113 *Quarterly Journal of Economics* 1245.

96 J Blit et al., "Automation and the Future of Work: Scenarios and Policy Options" (2018) CIGI Papers No. 174.

97 CB Frey and MA Osborne, "The Future of Employment: How Susceptible Are Jobs to Computerisation?" (2017) 114 *Technological Forecasting & Social Change* 254.

98 Arntz et al., note 93 above.

99 B Reese, "AI Will Create Millions More Jobs Than It Will Destroy. Here's How" (Singularity Hub, 1 January 2019), https://singularityhub.com/2019/01/01/ai-will-create-millions-more-jobs-than-it-will-destroy-heres-how.

100 D Webber, "Is College Worth It? Going Beyond Averages" (Third Way, 18 September 2018), www.thirdway.org/report/is-college-worth-it-going-beyond-averages.

101 Ibid.

the first decades of the twenty-first century[102] – except that the AI shock will likely be larger and likely come faster.

The political ramifications of this in the advanced countries can only be guessed at; however, the best guide perhaps is what happened with the China shock to industrial jobs and incomes – protectionism of all sorts. AI should expect a similar welcome as it starts to make serious inroads into the rents currently captured by white-collar work and to undermine the social edifice built on those rents.

In pre-industrial times, the protection of rents flowing to skilled artisans was through craft guilds. In their day, these acted as professional associations, restricting entry to capture rents, but also enforcing quality standards, preserving and transferring knowledge inter-generationally through the apprenticeship system, and providing financial support for their members.[103] Modern professions such as law, medicine, accounting, and architecture replicate guild practices by requiring a licence, passing a qualifying exam, or acquiring a diploma from a formal programme of study.[104] The modern guilds have been able to resist international services trade liberalization and may be expected to mobilize to moderate the entry of AI into their functions to protect the rents that flow to knowledge credentials. From this perspective, the age of AI – at least in its early years and decades – may be a new "guilded age" in which the professions find ways (which trade economists would see as non-tariff barriers) to restrict market entry.

IV DISCUSSION AND CONCLUSIONS

AI has made impressive inroads into our economy and society, but this was far from an overnight success, as it struggled through many decades and several AI winters, disappointing many hopes and prognostications along the way. With the emergence of the data-driven economy, the technological conditions for AI to blossom were finally in place – and blossomed it has. AI is now all around and contributes importantly to the value of internationally traded goods and services.

For the most part, AI has navigated the regulatory path to market entry without problems. However, as AI has become more powerful, high-level concerns have started to mount about its impact on society, national security, and the livelihoods of those who will compete with it. Based on the experience to date, regulatory concerns that could create market barriers to AI in the future are likely to align with the Pareto principle (the "80–20" rule), whereby most of the issues will prove to be easily handled at least at the technical level, allowing the integration of AI into economic

[102] David Autor et al., "The China Shock: Learning from Labor-Market Adjustment to Large Changes in Trade" (2016) 8 *Annual Review of Economics* 205.

[103] SR Epstein, "Craft Guilds, Apprenticeship, and Technological Change in Preindustrial Europe" (1998) 58 *The Journal of Economic History* 684.

[104] MS Larson, *The Rise of Professionalism: A Sociological Analysis* (Berkeley, CA, University of California Press, 1977).

and social life to proceed apace, while a smaller subset of cases that generate cross-cutting societal impacts and raise security and economic distributional concerns will generate most of the headaches.

The transition of AI from executing instructions to exercising agency, which raises thorny issues for legal doctrines,[105] still lies largely ahead and raises rather open-ended questions about social acceptance, alongside the already thorny issues raised by its use as a tool for political influence and social regulation. Also mostly ahead are the impacts of AI on the job market – in particular on white-collar work and the social structures built around human capital in the advanced economies (although blue-collar work will not be entirely spared either, as AI combined with robots will make the latter more flexible and more competitive with blue-collar workers).

A complicating factor (as if the above were not complicated enough!) is that AI is being developed at a pace that exceeds the ability of regulators to regulate it. This has stalled deployment of AI in domestic contexts (e.g. several major US firms have declined to supply AI for facial recognition until federal regulations are established) and promises to be still more problematic internationally, given that trust is at a nadir internationally – particularly between China and the United States, the two leading AI/ML centres. While this state of affairs seems unpromising for future collaboration, it might be noted that professional exchanges between the Chinese and US epidemiological communities during the COVID-19 crisis were as cordial and forthcoming as the political relations were not. Science transcends national boundaries and with AI/ML we will be dealing with truly cutting-edge science. Moreover, the issues of trust between humans might become rather moot when AI clearly surpasses individual human expertise. The path for AI into practice has generally been cleared by simple demonstrations of its capacity to do better.

The potential difficulty of untangling these issues is well illustrated by the US ban on the TikTok app based on its ownership by China's ByteDance. This case has triggered commentaries focused on the societal risks of the app itself,[106] the alleged national security risks posed by the data it collects,[107] and the value of the company (as much as USD 50 billion[108]).

History has been described as one damn thing after another. The first decade of the data-driven economy proved to be one of increasingly dense history, with

[105] Y Bathaee, "The Artificial Intelligence Black Box and The Failure of Intent and Causation" (2018) 31 *Harvard Journal of Law & Technology* 889.

[106] J Ochs, "The Negative Impact of TikTok on Teens" (Smart Social, 21 January 2020), https://smartsocial.com/negative-impact-tiktok.

[107] J Sherman, "Unpacking TikTok, Mobile Apps and National Security Risks" (Lawfare Blog, 2 April 2020), www.lawfareblog.com/unpacking-tiktok-mobile-apps-and-national-security-risks.

[108] E Wang et al., "Exclusive: ByteDance Investors Value TikTok at $50 Billion in Takeover Bid – Sources" (*Reuters*, 29 July 2020), www.reuters.com/article/us-bytedance-tiktok-exclusive-idUSKCN24U1M9.

the year 2020 serving up a perfect storm of historical developments. The technology nexus of AI/ML/big data played a not insignificant role in generating that history and also found itself an increasingly divisive bone of contention. As new applications proliferate, the discussion in this chapter suggests that the path of AI to international markets will become more complicated.

PART II

Reconceptualizing World Trade Organization Law for the Artificial Intelligence Economy

5

Trade Rules for Industry 4.0

Why the Technical Barriers to Trade Agreement Matters Even More

*Aik Hoe Lim**

I INDUSTRY 4.0: THE WHOLE IS GREATER THAN THE SUM OF ITS PARTS

Aristotle is credited for having said "the whole is greater than the sum of its parts".

Correctly or incorrectly attributed to Aristotle, those words have beguiled philosophers for many a century. If Aristotle did indeed say those words,[1] he probably did not have Industry 4.0 in mind.

Yet, his thoughts are rather prescient. They are prescient in the sense that the concept that "the whole is greater than the sum of its parts" underpins the notion of "emergence", a key idea in the debate over what is consciousness and artificial intelligence (AI).[2] It is indeed a very good description of what we are witnessing with the convergence[3] of AI, robotics, additive manufacturing (3D printing), blockchain and the Internet of Things (IoT) into digitally connected networks of production, communication and consumption. The effects of technological innovation are creating immense transformations in the way companies and countries organize production, trade goods, invest capital and develop new products and processes.

The third industrial revolution brought us the power of the microprocessor and the personal computer with the capacity to store, organize and retrieve vast amounts of data, and undertake cumbersome repetitive tasks in milliseconds. As each

* This chapter is based on my keynote address at the 6th Biennial Conference of the Asian International Economic Law Network: "International Trade Regime for the Data-Driven Economy: How Will Artificial Intelligence Transform International Economic Law?" (26–27 October 2019, Chinese Taipei). The views expressed are mine and cannot be attributed to the World Trade Organization, the Secretariat or its members. I am grateful to Lauro Locks, Devin McDaniels, Mateo Ferero and Maryam Aldoseri for their comments and assistance in undertaking background research.

1 Even if not that exact phrase, Aristotle's writings do indeed seem to indicate he was perhaps the first to introduce this very idea. See "No, Aristotle Didn't Write 'A Whole Is Greater Than the Sum of Its Parts'" (*Sententiae Antiquae*, 6 July 2020), https://perma.cc/JD7N-HKZW.

2 See B Reese, *The Fourth Age: Smart Robots, Conscious Computers, and the Future of Humanity* (New York, Atria, 2018), at 52, 71; and M Tegmark, *Life 3.0: Being Human in the Age of Artificial Intelligence* (London, Penguin Books, 2017), at 300.

3 See generally R Baldwin, *The Great Convergence: Information Technology and the New Globalization* (Cambridge, MA, The Belknap Press of Harvard University Press, 2016).

"disruptive technology"[4] improved on the hardware and software of computing, the costs of PC ownership were rapidly brought down, giving households access to computing power previously only enjoyed by large institutions. By connecting individual computers together in the worldwide web, the Internet was created, and a new paradigm of communication and data became possible. And this continuing acceleration of technological deployment is now coupled with an equally rapid process of diminishing costs. Indeed, it has been estimated that "[b]efore 2050, the price of a computer with the computational power of everyone on the planet combined will be less than what you paid for your smartphone in 2018".[5]

The fourth industrial revolution and Industry 4.0[6] extends this march of technology as digital networks of hardware and software become more sophisticated and integrated. Fueled by data and algorithms, and aided by sensors, machines and computers can autonomously communicate with each other, and are increasingly doing tasks and taking decisions without human involvement.[7]

Take the modern car, which is fast resembling a computerized hub of sensors with wheels. Fully or semiautonomous vehicles collect, exchange and analyze data that is then used to take decisions that can be better or faster than the human brain: braking before a collision, shifting from two to four wheels or, in the ultimate case, driving itself. And the amount of data that can be collected is immense: it has been estimated that "a single car will generate about as much data as 3,000 people do in a similar period day".[8] All this data can in turn be fed back into the production process to design better hardware, software and algorithms.

The same model of data connectivity, convergence and advanced analytics is being applied to heavy machinery, health equipment, buildings, consumer devices, logistics, supply management and so forth. Customers on e-commerce platforms generate vast amounts of data, which AI can use to better anticipate consumer demand and behavior. A German online retailer that uses machine learning algorithms to predict what customers are going to buy has developed a system so reliable

[4] World Trade Organization (WTO), "World Trade Report 2018: The Future of World Trade – How Digital Technologies Are Transforming Global Commerce" (2018(hereinafter WTO 2018)), https://perma.cc/EV7G-QVJH, at 158 ("New disruptive technologies are affecting firm production decisions and reshaping global patterns of trade and investment").

[5] Reese, note 2 above, at 188.

[6] "Industry 4.0" (*Wikipedia*), https://perma.cc/87K8-3AYL ("Industry 4.0 is the subset of the fourth industrial revolution that concerns industry . . .. Although the terms 'industry 4.0' and 'fourth industrial revolution' are often used interchangeably, 'industry 4.0' factories have machines which are augmented with wireless connectivity and sensors, connected to a system that can visualise the entire production line and make decisions on its own"). On the fourth industrial revolution more generally, see K Schwab, *The Fourth Industrial Revolution* (Geneva, World Economic Forum (WEF), 2016).

[7] For a general overview of the different industrial revolutions, see Schwab, note 6 above, at 11–13. See also E Schulze, "Everything You Need to Know about the Fourth Industrial Revolution" (CNBC, 22 January 2019), https://perma.cc/N6X4-59EZ.

[8] T Wheeler, *From Gutenberg to Google* (New York, Brookings Institution Press, 2019), at 224.

that it can predict with 90 percent accuracy what will be sold within the following thirty days.[9]

Industry 4.0 is rapidly demonstrating that the whole is indeed greater than the sum of its parts. And it is in ensuring that the "whole" does come together that the World Trade Organization (WTO) Agreement on Technical Barriers to Trade (TBT) has a key role to play.

The TBT Agreement addresses regulatory interventions that may affect trade in products. This will be the case for many Industry 4.0-related standards and regulations. The unparalleled speed and breadth of the current "revolution" unfolds every day with new digital products being invented ready to fulfill needs we did not even know we had. These developments invariably expose a "dark side" of new technology; of risks that we also did not know could even exist. You may have heard that "IoT toasters" may be misused and turned into "weapons of mass destruction". Are such concerns far-fetched or legitimate? If they are legitimate, how should such concerns be regulated? Could governments be tempted to influence the evolving global governance framework through setting regulations that give their industry a first mover or competitive advantage?

The TBT Agreement, by promoting global regulatory coherence (harmonization via international standardization) and global regulatory cooperation (via good regulatory practices, equivalence and mutual recognition), will assume even greater importance as standards and regulations are developed for Industry 4.0. As the 2020 World Trade Report notes:

> Cooperation on technical standards is also especially important when confronting novel regulatory challenges and risks, such as those related to "dual use technologies" (i.e. both for civil and defence purposes) or to the area of AI. Technical standards applying to dual-use technologies, for instance with respect to radio, telecommunication and network security, or autonomous vehicles and aircraft, are notified by WTO members under the TBT Agreement.[10]

More than ever, we will need to ensure that the interconnectivity and interoperability[11] required by Industry 4.0 are not hampered by discriminatory or unnecessarily divergent standards and regulations.

[9] "How Germany's Otto Uses Artificial Intelligence" (*The Economist*, 12 August 2017), https://perma.cc/6LTL-UUJJ.

[10] World Trade Organization (WTO), "World Trade Report 2020: Government Policies to Promote Innovation in the Digital Age" (2020), at 137 (original footnotes omitted). www.wto.org/english/res_e/booksp_e/wtr20_e/wtr20_e.pdf (hereinafter WTO 2020).

[11] Indeed, "[a] lack of international standards for the development of smart manufacturing can limit the interconnection of distributed manufacturing facilities and services, hampering export opportunities. Inefficient customs procedures, barriers to express delivery services, and tariffs also raise the costs of exporting goods that are purchased on digital platforms". J Meltzer, "Governing Digital Trade" (2019) 18 *World Trade Review* 23, at 36–37.

II HOW WILL INDUSTRY 4.0 IMPACT TRADE?

WTO's 2018 World Trade Report[12] explored some of the most immediate changes that we can envisage for the near future and concluded that new technologies have the potential to profoundly transform: (1) the way we trade; (2) who trades; and (3) what is traded. Understanding how these technologies may impact world trade is essential to thinking about the role of trade rules in maximizing gains and minimizing friction.[13]

Firstly, on the way we trade, we have seen the impressive rise of e-commerce, which has reshaped what and how we purchase and consume. In 2016, the value of e-commerce transactions was estimated to be US$27.7 trillion, of which US$ 23.9 trillion was business-to-business e-commerce transactions.[14] The convergence of physical and digital worlds will create new economic opportunities, many of which have not yet been conceived. McKinsey forecasts that the IoT will add between US$ 2.7 trillion and US$ 6.2 trillion in economic value annually through 2025 and improve manufacturing productivity by up to 5 percent. Cisco estimates that the IoT will have a global economic impact of US$ 14.4 trillion between 2013 and 2022.[15]

Secondly, advances in the way we trade will also reduce international trade costs.[16] WTO projections predict that trade could grow yearly by 1.8–2 percentage points until 2030 as a result of falling trade costs, amounting to a cumulated growth of 31–34 percentage points over fifteen years. Gains are expected to come in several ways:[17]

- Cargo and transport logistics are optimized by the combination of vehicle telematics, robotization and AI. IoT[18] sensors, for example, can reduce the costs of global trade by increasing the efficiency of transport and logistics. By

12 WTO 2018, note 4 above.

13 For a recent comprehensive study on how trade rules (including those under the TBT Agreement) relate to innovation in the digital age, and how they reinforce and affect each other, see WTO 2020, note 10 above.

14 In 2017, global e-commerce transactions generated $29.267 trillion, including $25.516 trillion for business-to-business transactions and $3.851 trillion for business-to-consumer sales. "Global E-commerce Sales Surged to $29 Trillion" (*UNCTAD*, 29 March 2019), https://perma.cc/WQA7-36H7.

15 E Gerwin, "Industry 4.0: Trade Rules for the Internet of Things" (TradeVistas, 22 June 2017), https://perma.cc/79D6-2UYV.

16 B Lewis, "How to Tackle Today's II Security Risks" (ISO, 10 January 2019), https://perma.cc/M2LQ-453V. See also J Meltzer, "A WTO Reform Agenda: Data Flows and International Regulatory Cooperation" (2019), https://perma.cc/ASQ7-7655, at 4 (stating that "E-commerce provides a potentially significant opportunity to increase small business participation in international trade. For instance, having a website gives small businesses an instant international presence without having to establish a physical presence overseas").

17 WTO 2018, note 4 above.

18 As noted by the Organisation for Economic Co-operation and Development (OECD), there is no single, established global definition for "IoT". For a new overarching IoT definition, see OECD, "IoT Measurement and Applications" (2018), https://perma.cc/F2WC-4AGN, at 5.

being able to track in real time, fewer goods will be lost in transport. Companies will also be able to optimize routes to efficiently use shipping containers.[19]

- The automation of warehousing, trailer and container unloading and packing will add to time and cost savings. Combined with AI algorithms, the use of advanced robotics minimizes the cost of storage and speeds up distribution to final customers.[20]
- It is not just transport and logistics that affect cross-border trade. Layers of procedures and customs regulations can add to costs. At the most basic, information and communications technologies (ICTs) can help reduce paperwork, streamline procedures and reduce the costs of crossing borders. In more advanced applications, AI is already being used to help businesses to continually monitor, analyze and comply with regulatory changes.[21]
- Harnessing blockchain's decentralized, distributed digital ledger that is secured using various cryptographic techniques could help improve trust. Information, once added to a blockchain, is time-stamped and cannot be easily modified, making it easy to track attempted changes, and transactions are recorded, shared and verified on a peer-to-peer basis by anyone with the appropriate permissions. While much of its potential is yet to be fully realized, it is expected that this technology could help the trading community to better access information and gain trust in cross-border transactions, which would in turn reduce the cost of transactions.[22]

Thirdly, the Internet and the reduction of trade costs has made trade more inclusive and reduced some of the challenges of size and geography. Services offered by online platforms have, for instance, facilitated the direct participation of micro, small and medium enterprises in export activities. The decline in information and transaction costs can help firms in developing countries that tend to face higher costs for obtaining information and guaranteeing transactions. The WTO estimates foresee that developing countries' share in global trade could grow from 46 percent in 2015 to 57 percent by 2030.[23] Much depends on whether appropriate complementary policies are put in place and challenges related to technology diffusion and regulation are addressed.

Fourthly, the composition of what is traded may change. 3D printing – the key element of "additive manufacturing" – may paradoxically reduce trade in intermediate parts and components. This may mean further reductions in transport and

[19] WTO 2018, note 4 above, at 68.

[20] Ibid., at 67.

[21] Ibid., at 71.

[22] Ibid., at 7, 71–72. See also E Ganne, "Can Blockchain revolutionize international trade?" (2018), www.wto.org/english/res_e/booksp_e/blockchainrev18_e.pdf; and, more recently, E Ganne and D Patel, "Blockchain and DLT in Trade: Where do we stand?" (2020), www.wto.org/english/res_e/booksp_e/blockchainanddlt_e.pdf.

[23] Ibid., at 5.

logistics costs, and a consolidation of global value chains as 3D printing is used to locally manufacture complex or customized inputs. In time, this could lead to a shift toward more digital and localized supply chains with reduced need for a back room where inventories are stored.[24]

IT has also allowed for the "digitalization" of certain goods, where physical products have been progressively replaced by digital equivalents. For example, the digital distribution of books, films and music has increasingly replaced physical transactions, a trend that is blurring the traditional boundary between trade in goods and trade in services. The importance of services in the composition of trade is expected to increase, with the share of services trade to grow from 21 percent to 25 percent by 2030. Trade in information technology products has tripled in the past two decades, reaching US$ 1.6 trillion in 2016.[25]

Yet achieving the great promise of Industry 4.0 is neither guaranteed nor automatic. The great convergence promised by the IoT requires, not least, solutions to many technical and practical barriers. Different devices, software and siloed systems based on varying standards must be enabled to interconnect, interoperate and communicate securely. There are also significant numbers of different policy concerns – not only the obvious ones like human safety but also others like national security, cybersecurity, impacts on market concentration, privacy and the digital divide[26].

III HOW CAN TRADE AND WORLD TRADE ORGANIZATION RULES HELP SHAPE THE FUTURE?

These are very important questions that have a trade rules dimension. It is also a vast canvas of issues. At the WTO, in terms of existing rules, "WTO agreements reached a quarter of a century ago proved to be remarkably forward-looking in providing a framework that helped to foster the development of an ICT-enabled economy in countries across all levels of development, while preserving policy space for countries to pursue different models of digital development."[27]

In terms of new rules, at the WTO, much of the discussion has been on what rules are needed to support e-commerce. While e-commerce is not "new" in the WTO, lately there have been very active discussions, particularly under the "Joint

[24] See "Global Value Chain Development Report 2019: Technological Innovation, Supply Chain Trade and Workers in a Globalized World" (2019), https://perma.cc/J6KV-XRUT, at 73.

[25] WTO 2018, note 4 above, at 5.

[26] According to a recent WTO Secretariat note, the current COVID-19 pandemic "has highlighted the glaring need to bridge the digital divide, both within and across countries, given the central role the digital economy has played during the crisis". The Note also observed that, due to the pandemic, "[m]any traditional obstacles have been accentuated and have continued to hamper greater participation in e-commerce activities by small producers, sellers and consumers in developing countries, particularly in least-developed countries (LDCs)". "E-Commerce, Trade and the COVID-19 Pandemic – Information Note" (WTO, 4 May 2020), https://perma.cc/BFV8-J64U.

[27] WTO 2020, note 10 above, at 11.

Statement Initiative on E-commerce", currently involving some eighty-six WTO members.[28]

Under those discussions, text-based proposals are being discussed under five broad themes: digital trade facilitation and logistics; access to Internet and data; business trust; capacity building and cooperation; and market access. In these discussions, one key consideration has been on how cross-border data flows are affected by diverse localization, privacy and security requirements. Analyses of existing WTO rules that have relevance for e-commerce have tended to focus on the General Agreement on Trade in Services (GATS).

E-commerce in services encompasses not only the end-to-end electronic delivery of services, such as Internet and other telecommunications, themselves a service supplied electronically, but also the many other services that can be transmitted in digitized form. There are also online distribution services, such as e-commerce web portals, through which goods or services are ordered electronically, even if subsequently delivered in physical form. Some services sectors are, in themselves, part of the infrastructure for e-commerce. These include telecommunications and distribution services; postal and delivery services; financial services; and transport and logistics. While the GATS is clearly an important instrument in respect of e-commerce, I would like to take a different tack and reflect on the "goods" angle.

Industry 4.0 "smart manufacturing" means that goods are affected and improved by services as much as services are affected and improved by goods. Indeed, for some, this may even challenge the very definitions of, and boundaries between, goods and services, which in turn may impact assessing ed which specific WTO disciplines apply to measures affecting Industry 4.0.[29] Besides the GATS, a plethora of other

[28] In January 2019, at the WEF in Davos, a group of 76 WTO members issued a joint statement confirming their "intention to commence WTO negotiations on trade-related aspects of electronic commerce" (WT/L/1056, 25 January 2020). As of December 2020, the number of participating members stood at eighty-six. In a recent statement, JSI participants informed that on 7 December 2020 they circulated among them a "consolidated negotiating text that captures progress so far" and that this text "will form the basis of the next stage of negotiations". They added that this "consolidated text" was "based on Members' proposals" covering the "following themes: enabling electronic commerce; openness and e-commerce; trust and e-commerce; cross-cutting issues; telecommunications; market access; and scope and general provisions". ("Joint Statement Initiative on E-Commerce: co-conveners' update", https://perma.cc/8HFV-9NU9). See also "E-commerce co-convenors release update on the negotiations, welcome encouraging progress" (WTO, 14 December 2020), https://perma.cc/HW52-S66J and "Negotiations on e-commerce continue, eyeing a consolidated text by the end of the year" (WTO, 23 October 2020), https://perma.cc/ESE2-7RGX. See further "E-Commerce, Trade and the COVID-19 Pandemic – Information Note" (WTO, 4 May 2020), https://perma.cc/BFV8-J64U.

[29] See A Chander, "The Internet of Things: Both Goods and Services" (2019) 18 *World Trade Review* 9 (positing that if "IoT consists in goods, then the [GATT], as well as the [TBT Agreement], will discipline trade barriers to the flow of goods [but if] IoT consists in services, then the [GATS] will apply, though generally to different barriers than those covered by GATT"; and then concluding that, in fact, "IoT consists in *both* goods and services, therefore calling into application *multiple* WTO disciplines, with the specific agreements that are applicable dependent on the particular measure subject to challenge" (p. 3 – emphasis added). See also Shin-yi Peng, "A New Trade Regime for the

WTO disciplines may be at play here,[30] including the TBT Agreement but also, among others, the General Agreement on Tariffs and Trade (GATT), Sanitary and Phytosanitary (SPS) Agreement (food safety and animal plant health), Trade Facilitation Agreement (TFA) (facilitating customs procedures), Trade-Related Aspects of Intellectual Property Rights (TRIPS) (intellectual property)[31] and Import Licensing Agreement.

For the purpose of my chapter here, I will focus on the WTO's TBT Agreement. In doing so, I would like to reflect on some challenges and opportunities; in particular, on how the existing principles and disciplines in the TBT Agreement as well as practices and guidance developed by the WTO TBT Committee over the years are likely to be relevant for Industry 4.0.[32]

A *Coverage of Technical Barriers to Trade and Industry 4.0: Examples of Industry 4.0-Type Technical Barriers to Trade Notifications*

Recent notifications of draft regulations to the TBT Committee show that Industry 4.0-related regulations are increasing in number and variety, and that members, by submitting such notifications, consider them as falling within the scope of the TBT

Servitization of Manufacturing: Rethinking the Goods-Services Dichotomy" *Journal of World Trade* 54, no. 5 (2020): 699–726 (stating that the "age of industry 4.0" is witnessing "increasing complementarities between goods and services," which is in turn leading to government interventions (regulations) in this area that are increasingly of a "dual nature," thus leading to "problems related to the concurrent application of the goods/services trade rules"). See also P Sauvé, "To Fuse, Not to Fuse, or Simply Confuse? Assessing the Case for Normative Convergence Between Goods and Services Trade Law" (2019) 22 *Journal of International Economic Law* 355. Sometimes, the "blurring" may even be between goods and intellectual property (IP). For instance, sometimes TBT (standardization) and TRIPS (IP) may be intrinsically entangled. See R Pudszun, "Standard Essential Patents and Antitrust Law in the Age of Standardisation and the Internet of Things: Shifting Paradigms" (2019) 50 *IIC – International Review of Intellectual Property and Competition Law* 720.

30 WTO 2018, note 4 above. A useful summary of this Report's description of each of these different disciplines is provided in this PowerPoint presentation: "An In-Depth Look at the World Trade Report 2019" (2018), https://perma.cc/X4NP-DVCE.

31 On the IP angle see WTO 2018, note 4 above; "WIPO Technology Trends 2019: Artificial Intelligence" (2019), https://perma.cc/S85A-P6HK; J Meltzer, "Artificial Intelligence Primer: What Is Needed to Maximize AI's Economic, Social and Trade Opportunities" (2019), https://perma.cc/W83F-PFFC ("For AI to develop also requires an enabling environment that includes new regulation in areas such as AI ethics and data access and revisiting existing laws and regulation in areas such as privacy and intellectual property (IP) rights to ensure that they work for AI").

32 For detailed descriptions of the different reasons why TBT may be relevant to digital trade, see P Cihon, "Standards for AI Governance: International Standards to Enable Global Coordination in AI Research and Development" (2019), https://perma.cc/XL5S-D2EU; J Meltzer, note 11 above; J Meltzer, note 16 above; J Meltzer, note 31 above; J Trachtman, "The Internet of Things Cybersecurity Challenge to Trade and Investment: Trust and Verify?" (Draft, 2019), https://perma.cc/NY8R-JYCL; SY Peng, "Private Cybersecurity Standards? Cyberspace Governance, Multistakeholderism, and the (Ir)relevance of the TBT Regime" (2018) 51 *Cornell International Law Journal* 445.

Agreement. Novel technologies are being regulated for a variety of policy reasons and in different ways. Here are a few examples.

1 Internet of Things

In the last few years, there has been an increase in notified TBT measures dealing with IoT, concerned with their safety, interoperability, national security/cybersecurity, performance and quality.[33] The challenge is that the IoT is not a single product as such but rather the integrated system of products linked to each other. At the core of the IoT regulatory problem is the very fact that IoT devices are connected devices, and so even if a single device is compromised, this could risk cyber-intrusion for the whole network.

2 5G Technology

Recently notified TBT measures on 5G (fifth-generation cellular network) technology[34] – the essential technological backbone that will make IoT possible and ubiquitous – indicate different reasons why governments are intervening in this area, including "national security" and "interoperability".

3 3D Printing

There have also been some recent notifications covering 3D printing machines/devices.[35] Interestingly, some of the objectives behind the notifications have less to do with the safety of the machines themselves and are more about potential illegal misuse (e.g. producing weapons).

4 Drones

There has been an increase of notified TBT measures dealing with drones (more specifically, small unmanned aerial vehicles) in the last few years.[36] Many of these notifications are concerned not only with risks for humans/consumers and interoperability problems, but also with national security risks. Again, the issue may not be the product safety of the drone itself but potential abuses leading to public safety and national security concerns (e.g. recent incidents at airports).

[33] G/TBT/N/USA/1597; G/TBT/N/TPKM/399; G/TBT/N/TPKM/400; G/TBT/N/JPN/610; G/TBT/N/KOR/776; G/TBT/N/EU/567.

[34] G/TBT/N/BRA/975; G/TBT/N/BRA/976; G/TBT/N/BRA/977; G/TBT/N/TPKM/399; G/TBT/N/TPKM/400; G/TBT/N/JPN/627/Add.1; G/TBT/FRA/191 G/TBT/FRA/192; G/TBT/FRA/193.

[35] G/TBT/N/THA/479.

[36] G/TBT/N/CHE/233; G/TBT/N/FRA/186; G/TBT/N/FRA/187.

5 Autonomous Vehicles

Not surprisingly, we are also seeing an increase of notified TBT measures dealing with autonomous vehicles, mostly concerned with their safety and performance.[37] Much has been discussed on autonomous vehicles for private use, but there is a marked increase of use by industry as well.

B *The Regulatory Challenge*

Faced with the mindboggling rapidity and complexity of these transformations, governments struggle to react to them in a timely and coordinated fashion. Globally, this may generate a plethora of different regulations and technical standards across countries. This is a problem – in particular, when differences are unnecessary and ill founded – from the perspective not only of its trade impacts but also of consumers, industry and society in general.

TBT disciplines are unique in the way they put into practice the overarching goal of balancing the right to regulate and the avoidance of unnecessary technical barriers.[38] They are intended to impact members' entire regulatory lifecycle preventively, reactively and self-correctively. Industry requires regulations that address market failures but do not stifle innovation and competitiveness.[39] The public requires regulation that fosters trust and confidence in products' quality, performance and safety; and trading partners require regulations that are nondiscriminatory, not protectionist and not more trade restrictive than is necessary.

37 G/TBT/N/KOR/827; G/TBT/N/USA/1283/Add.1.

38 This balance is enshrined in the preamble of the TBT Agreement. As observed by the Appellate Body, the TBT Agreement's "objective of avoiding the creation of unnecessary obstacles to international trade through technical regulations, standards, and conformity assessment procedures [stated in its preamble's fifth recital] is, however, qualified in the sixth recital by the explicit recognition of Members' right to regulate in order to pursue certain legitimate objectives" (Appellate Body Report, *US – Clove Cigarettes*, para. 94). See also "The WTO Agreement Series: Technical Barriers to Trade", www.wto.org/english/res_e/booksp_e/tbt3rd_e.pdf (hereinafter "TBT Handbook"), at 28 ("the Agreement also gives members the sole prerogative to determine the 'level of protection' they deem appropriate under a legitimate objective. At the same time, this right should be balanced against the need to ensure that TBT measures are not prepared, adopted or applied so as to create 'unnecessary obstacles to international trade'. This means that the Agreement does not prohibit all 'obstacles to international trade', but rather only those that are 'unnecessary'.").

39 As already mentioned, international standards can play a positive pivotal role in shaping up national regulatory frameworks for Industry 4.0. As further explained later, the TBT Committee encourages international bodies to observe a set of principles and procedures (the "6 Principles") when developing and adopting international standards. See specifically Principle 4 on *Effectiveness and Relevance*. G/TBT/1/Rev.9, part I, section III (at 10–12) and annex B (at 37–39). See also E Wijkström and D McDaniels, "International Standards and the WTO TBT Agreement: Improving Governance for Regulatory Alignment" (2013) Staff Working Paper ERSD-2013-06, at 10, 18; see also TBT Agreement, preamble, third recital and eighth recital. On the "6 Principles", see also notes 43, 53–54, 60 and 65 below.

This characteristic of balancing between needs makes TBT particularly well suited to addressing regulatory challenges in these times of rapid and radical technological and societal changes.

C *Transparency on Nascent Regulation*

TBT obligations start early in the regulatory process. The TBT Agreement becomes relevant once the decision to regulate is taken by a member. When this happens, the Agreement subjects members to a series of disciplines aimed at preserving members' policy space while ensuring that the regulation is the least trade-restrictive possible.

1 Early Notification of Draft Measures Helps Prevent Friction and Fosters Cooperation

Recognizing the tensions between trade and regulation, the TBT Agreement has important transparency obligations that apply throughout the regulatory lifecycle of a measure. Transparency is the key element of the "preventive" nature of TBT disciplines, which is particularly needed in times of rapid technological change. Unique in the WTO system, the TBT (and SPS) Agreement requires members to notify proposed measures (technical regulations and conformity assessment procedures) and to provide an opportunity for comment. This opens an opportunity for cooperation between regulators to gain valuable feedback toward better-quality regulations, seek clarification and avoid potential trade frictions.

Timing is at the heart of TBT transparency: the notification must take place as early as possible when comments by any stakeholders (including from any other WTO member) can still be meaningfully considered, and possible changes made more easily.

The TBT transparency mechanism is a success story in the WTO.[40] Year on year, an increased number of draft measures are notified to the WTO, demonstrating members' commitment to transparency. A total of 3,337 notifications were submitted in 2019, as compared to 3,000 in 2018. Harnessing the notification process can support a smoother implementation of Industry 4.0 regulations and avoid trade frictions.

2 Technical Barriers to Trade Committee Practices Create Needed Deliberative Spaces

The working practices of the TBT Committee reinforce this "preventive" nature of TBT transparency. When regulations are notified in draft form at early stages of their development, they can be discussed amongst all WTO members.

40 Marianna B. Karttunen, "Transparency in the WTO SPS and TBT Agreements: The Real Jewel in the Crown" (Cambridge, 2020). See also the presentations made at the book launch of 19 June 2020, as the opening event of the WTO's "TBT@40 Dialogue Series", www.wto.org/english/tratop_e/tbt_e/booklauchtbtspsjewelcrow_e.htm.

Over the years, the TBT Committee has been used by members to raise "specific trade concerns" (STCs) with respect to each other's TBT measures. This practice, combined with the early notification of draft measures, facilitates regulatory dialogue, helps ensure that other views are taken into consideration and, in the best cases, creates opportunities for regulatory cooperation, which can in turn lead to improved and more effective regulations.[41]

Since all this takes place in the multilateral setting of the TBT Committee, it carries an additional "preventive" benefit; one especially important with respect to nascent regulations addressing challenges stemming from new and rapidly evolving technologies, including Industry 4.0. Concerns raised in the TBT Committee also serve as a bellwether on new regulatory trends and point to areas where early dialogue is required on evolving regulation. In fact, as far back as the early 2000s the Committee was already discussing concerns with Internet-related regulations.[42]

3 Transparency Is Not a "One-Off" Obligation

But not everything can be addressed preventively. Regulations are based on issues, risks and techno-scientific knowledge available at the time of their development and adoption. Risks can change, sometimes rapidly and continuously so. Regulations may therefore need to change accordingly, and these changes may sometimes themselves constitute trade barriers.

The TBT Agreement contains disciplines aimed at situations when regulations need to evolve and adapt.[43] For instance, Article 2.3 of the Agreement states that measures may not be maintained if the circumstances or objectives giving rise to their adoption no longer exist or can be addressed in a less trade-restrictive manner.

In other words, if, upon reassessment, in light of new scientific (or other relevant) information, a perceived risk is deemed to be nonexistent, it may be necessary to review the measure.[44] For instance, the TBT Committee recommended that members submit "follow-up notifications" to track the progress of a measure through the

41 For a recent discussion about the important role of STCs as ways for addressing regulatory trade frictions cooperatively rather than litigiously, see "WTO TBT Committee and regulatory measures: prevention, not litigation", TBT@40 Dialogue Series (2 September 2020), www.wto.org/english/tratop_e/tbt_e/tbt_t40_20920_e.htm.

42 "Korea: Regulation on Wireless Internet Platform for Interoperability – STC n. 89", G/TBT/M/29, para. 54–56.

43 This principle is equally applicable to international standard-setting processes. In fact, it is highly relevant because under the TBT Agreement international standards should normally be the basis of regulations, and because of the special role international standards should and will play in Industry 4.0 regulations. As further explained later, the TBT Committee has provided some guidance and principles on various aspects related to international standard-setting. One of these principles – "Effectiveness and Relevance" (Principle 4) – stresses the importance of international standardizing bodies taking account of "relevant regulatory or market needs, as feasible and appropriate, as well as scientific and technological developments in the elaboration of standards". On the "6 Principles", see also note 39 above, and 53–54, 60 and 65 below.

44 TBT Handbook, note 38 above.

regulatory lifecycle, and to provide new comment periods following substantial revisions. The Committee has also recommended that the availability of the final adopted text should be notified as a follow-up to the original notification.

In the ideal case, transparency by fostering regulatory cooperation can help avoid technical barriers to trade and improve the quality of the regulation. As governments start to regulate AI and other technologies driving Industry 4.0, it becomes even more important to utilize the tools provided by the TBT Agreement to shed more light on emerging national governance frameworks.

D *Data and Dataflows: Is There a Technical Barriers to Trade Angle?*

Despite competitive tensions, international cooperation is needed if Industry 4.0 is to succeed. AI needs to be able to access vast amounts of data. Volume matters because machine learning needs to be able to incorporate into future predictions as many past outcomes as possible.[45] Much of this data is obtained from both national and cross-border Internet activity and digital platforms. Businesses and governments are also important sources of data. The McKinsey Global Institute estimates that in 2014 global data flows were more valuable than trade in goods,[46] and PricewaterhouseCoopers predicts that by 2030, AI could raise global GDP by over $15 trillion.[47]

Discussions on e-commerce at the WTO are illustrative of the challenges faced on the global governance of data and the implications for Industry 4.0. At the risk of missing out important nuances, views on the question of data appear to fall into three camps.

There are those who are generally opposed to data localization requirements and restrictions on cross-border data flows, unless such measures would fall under limited exceptions. There are others who, while in general opposing these restrictions, wish to reserve the right to adopt appropriate safeguards to protect personal data and privacy, including rules on the cross-border transfer of personal data. Finally, some appear to favor wide latitude to exercise cyberspace sovereignty in pursuit of public policy objectives.[48]

While the TBT Agreement's scope is on trade in goods and not on cross-border data flows per se, there are some important data-related considerations. With the IoT, products have embedded sensors that collect, transmit and exchange information in real time over a network regardless of their location. Since such sensors and the accompanying source code could be said to be a characteristic of the product,

45 Meltzer, note 31 above.

46 Meltzer, note 11 above, at 23.

47 Ibid.

48 Following the categorization by Niall Meagher and Vitaly Pogoretskyy in the presentation on WTO Negotiations on E-commerce: General Overview – Workshop for the Informal Group of Developing Countries (AWCL, 16 September 2019) (on file with the author).

any technical regulation on source codes would probably be within the scope of the TBT Agreement.

Members in the TBT Committee have discussed around sixteen "specific trade concerns" related to a range of "cybersecurity measures", covering ITC products and network equipment, vehicles, civil aviation, banking and insurance, amongst other sectors. Concerned members voiced issues about requirements that could discriminate against foreign technology and equipment, lack of clarity of the measures, inconsistency with international standards and best practices and the need for duplicative in-country testing of imported products.[49]

The challenge is: how do we square the right to take measures necessary for the protection of essential security interests and not create unnecessary obstacles to international trade? Here, there are important principles and obligations in the TBT Agreement that are worth recalling, especially in terms of promoting good regulatory practices and regulatory cooperation, and the use of international standards.

E *Role of International Standards in Support of Regulatory Alignment*

International standards are critical for achieving the full potential of Industry 4.0, while avoiding unnecessary barriers to trade in these technologies.[50] Alignment of regulations for connected devices to international standards will facilitate trade by providing a common benchmark, enhancing competition and lowering prices for consumers.

The TBT Agreement is a driving force for harmonization and coordination at a global scale, through its provisions that strongly promote alignment of national regulations to international standards. The pivotal role of international standards to the attainment of the TBT Agreement's principles and objectives is already reflected in various parts of its preamble. There, the Agreement "encourage[s] the development of international standards", listing "important contributions" these documents can make to "improving efficiency of production and facilitating the conduct of international trade" and promoting "the transfer of technology from developed to developing countries".[51]

49 G/TBT/M/71, paras. 2.9–2.22; G/TBT/M/72, paras. 3.4–3.10; G/TBT/M/73, paras. 2.4–2.6; G/TBT/M/72, paras. 3.27–3.30; G/TBT/M/72, paras. 3.31–3.35; G/TBT/M/72, paras. 3.11–3.17; G/TBT/M/67, paras. 2.51–2.56; G/TBT/M/65, paras. 2.16–2.22; G/TBT/M/64/Rev.1, paras. 2.53–2.54; G/TBT/M/57, paras. 76–79; G/TBT/M/55, paras. 39–42; G/TBT/M/53, paras. 85–96; G/TBT/M/52, paras. 9–14; G/TBT/M/48, paras. 49–53; G/TBT/M/44, paras. 34–37; G/TBT/M/32.

50 On international standards generally, see TBT Handbook, note 38 above, at 33–36; see also "Facilitating Trade Through Regulatory Cooperation: The Case of the WTO's TBT/SPS Agreements and Committees", https://perma.cc/WH9N-Q5VX.

51 "International standards can be seen as 'evidence-based' documents codifying scientific and technical knowledge developed at the global level. Their development and use can thus be an important means of disseminating knowledge and fostering innovation." TBT Handbook, note 38 above, at 34. See also WTO 2020, note 10 above, at 135–137 and 151–152 (stating, for instance, that the TBT Agreement also

1 Alignment with International Standards

More specifically, the Agreement:

(i) requires members to use relevant international standards as a basis for national regulations (except when the international standard would be ineffective or inappropriate to accomplish a member's legitimate objective);
(ii) incentivizes members to fully harmonize measures with international standards (presuming TBT consistency); and
(iii) strongly encourages members to participate in the development of international standards.

Therefore, the TBT Agreement acts as a catalyst for alignment of national product regulations based on voluntary international standards set by specialized non-WTO bodies. In principle, the use of international standards by governments brings regulatory requirements and systems closer to one another, thereby reducing the prevalence of unnecessary differences.[52]

2 No Definition of International Standards but Six Principles Instead

But there is a catch. The TBT Agreement does not contain a definition of international standards. Nor does it contain a list of recognized international standardizing bodies, as is the case under the SPS Agreement. This has created some debate and tension in the WTO, given the degree of uncertainty about the identification of the benchmark for alignment. But at the same time it has also given members flexibility.

In order to provide additional guidance, in 2000 the TBT Committee took a decision on the "Principles for the Development of International Standards, Guides and Recommendations, with Relation to Articles 2, 5 and Annex 3 of the TBT Agreement".[53] This decision, commonly known as the "six principles", encourages international standard-setting bodies to observe a set of principles and procedures when international standards, guides and recommendations are elaborated to ensure: (i) transparency; (ii) openness; (iii) impartiality and consensus; (iv) effectiveness and relevance; (v) coherence; and (vi) the development dimension.[54]

recognizes the pivotal role of technical standards, in particular of international standards, in "technology development and dissemination"). Ibid., at 135.

52 See Wijkström and McDaniels, note 39 above.

53 G/TBT/1/Rev.9, part I, section III (at 10–12) and Annex B (at 37–39). On the "6 Principles", see also notes 39 and 43 above, and 54, 60 and 65 below.

54 For a recent appraisal of the relevance of the "6 Principles" since its adoption more than twenty years ago, and on whether they still "remain fit for purpose in a world of rapid change", see "TBT Committee's Six Principles for the development of international standards: Are they still relevant?" TBT@40 Dialogue Series (14 October 2020). www.wto.org/english/tratop_e/tbt_e/tbt_six_principles_e.htm.

International standards that are developed in line with these principles are more likely to be considered as "relevant international standards" for the purposes of the TBT Agreement. Adherence to these so-called six principles will continue to be vital for standardization with respect to Industry 4.0.[55]

The process of international harmonization set out in the Agreement is not, however, a rigid one. It gives members space to deviate from international standards under certain conditions. The TBT Agreement gives members the leeway not to use international standards as a basis for a regulation if they would be "ineffective" or "inappropriate". For instance, "fundamental climatic or geographic factors" or "fundamental technological problems" may sometimes render an existing international standard an unsuitable basis for properly addressing the objectives of a regulation a member intends to prepare and adopt.[56]

3 An Incentive to Use International Standards

The Agreement also provides a strong incentive to use international standards. When technical regulations are "in accordance with" relevant international standards, they are "rebuttably presumed" not to create unnecessary obstacles to international trade (i.e. they are presumed not to be more trade-restrictive than necessary and thus consistent with Article 2.2). It provides a "safe haven" for measures conforming to international standards with the objective of "harmonizing" technical regulations, conformity assessment procedures (CAPs) and (national) standards "on as wide a basis as possible".[57] The Agreement puts a particular emphasis on the fact that this goal can only be attained if the international standard-setting process is as inclusive and participative as possible, in particular by developing country members.[58] In other words, "Members shall play a full part, within the limits of their resources, in the preparation by appropriate international standardizing bodies of international standards, guides and recommendations relevant to technical regulations or conformity assessment procedures they adopted or are expected to

[55] See also WTO 2020, note 10 above, at 136 (referring to evidence that, in fact, the "six principles" have benefited the digital age since its inception: "Karachalios and McCabe (2013) argue that the success of the internet has benefitted from the bottom-up, globally open, market-driven system of standardization as supported by the TBT Committee's [6 Principles]").

[56] Under the second part of Article 2.4 of the TBT Agreement, a member may depart from a relevant international standard when it would be an "ineffective or inappropriate means for the fulfilment of the legitimate objectives pursued" by the domestic regulation. In addition, on special and differential treatment, see Art. 12.4.

[57] As stated in Articles 2.6, 5.5 and Annex 3.G, respectively.

[58] See TBT Technical Assistance (TA) and Special and Differential Treatment (S&D) provisions on improving participation in international standard-setting: Articles 11.2, 12.5 and 12.6. See also Walshe et al., "AI and Big Data Standardization: Contributing to United Nations Sustainable Development Goals", *Journal of ICT*, 8_2 (2020), 77–106, at 88 (stating that international standards "provide a universal language, thus breaking down technical barriers to international trade allowing developing countries to compete more easily in the global marketplace").

adopt".[59] This has been challenging for many developing countries and it could be even more so with rapidly developing standards for new technologies.[60]

4 Voluntary vs. Mandatory: To What Extent Is This an Issue?

One concern that is frequently highlighted is the implications of being a voluntary national standard or a "mandatory" technical regulation. This is an important issue for Industry 4.0 as there are many actors out there developing standards that could potentially shape the sector. The disciplines on technical regulations arguably bite deeper, but it is worth recalling that there are also disciplines in the TBT Agreement on "voluntary" national standards. These disciplines, which are a combination of Article 4 and Annex 3 to the Agreement (the Code of Good Practice for the Preparation, Adoption and Applications of Standards – "Code of Good Practice"[61]), contain substantive provisions on discrimination, trade restrictiveness, use of international standards and so on, largely mirroring those for technical regulations.

The obligation works in a two-pronged manner: (i) members shall ensure that their central government standardizing bodies have to accept and comply with Annex 3 of the Code of Good Practice; and (ii) members shall take reasonable measures as may be available to them to ensure that their local (as well as regional) and nongovernmental standardizing bodies also comply and accept. So, while Annex 3 is open to acceptance by any standardizing body, which includes a "non-governmental body", Article 4 creates an obligation on members to ensure that they do so. Since Article 14.4 on dispute settlement covers Article 4, this avenue could be pursued where a member considers that another member has not achieved satisfactory results.

A question that is different from whether there are disciplines on "voluntary" standards is what is to be understood by a "non-governmental body". The definition

[59] TBT Agreement, Articles 2.6 and 5.5.

[60] In order to address such challenges, the TBT Agreement contains detailed provisions tailored specifically to developing and least-developed members on Technical Assistance (Article 11) and Special and Differential Treatment (Article 12). Also relevant is the TBT Committee "6 Principle" decision on international standards, which addresses these challenges in "Principle 6" (on "Development Dimension"). On the "6 Principles", see notes 39, 43, 53–54 above, and 65 below.

[61] Under Article 4.1 (first sentence), members shall ensure that their "central government standardizing bodies" not only *accept* but, more importantly, also *comply* with all principles and obligations of the Code of Good Practice (Annex 3). Such obligations include, for instance, that standards adopted by central bodies shall: not be discriminatory (Annex 3.D); not create "unnecessary obstacles to international to trade" (Annex 3.E); and be based on "international standards" (Annex 3.F). The Code (see Annex 3.B) also covers standards adopted by "local government bodies" and "non-governmental bodies" as well as those by "regional standardizing bodies". However, members' obligations with respect to these other bodies are less stringent: members shall only "take such reasonable measures as may be available to them" to ensure that these bodies accept and comply with the Code (Article 4.1, second sentence). "Central government", "local", "non-governmental" and "regional" bodies are defined in Annex 1 of the Agreement.

of a nongovernmental body in the Agreement is illustrative. It defines it in the negative as a "body other than a central government body or a local government body, including a non-governmental body which has legal power to enforce a technical regulation".[62] What about other nongovernmental bodies; that is, those that do not have legal power? And what should be understood by "non-governmental"? These are issues for further consideration.

F *Improving Coherence*

Coherence in standards development is a major challenge for Industry 4.0. Entire batches of standards are being developed to underpin AI, the IoT, blockchain and autonomous systems (e.g. cars, trucks, trains, drones), to name just a few.[63] These standards will all need to "talk" to each other, and interoperability will be critical to ensure performance, privacy, safety, etc. Imagine one autonomous vehicle trying to avoid an accident with another autonomous vehicle. If the other vehicle is following a different standard, the vehicles will not be able to communicate, and this could inadvertently provoke a crash.[64] So, as this process unfolds, standards will be essential to keep the "parts" interoperable and contributing to the "whole".

If, for example, two international bodies decide, independently and without talking to each other, to develop differing standards for addressing issues related to the safety of autonomous vehicles, they may well end up adopting two significantly different – or worse, conflicting – international standards addressing the same issue. Trade will be very difficult, if not impossible, between countries that have not used the same international standard as a basis for their regulations.

The TBT Committee "six principles" highlight the importance of coherence,[65] in order to avoid duplication or overlap between the work of international standardizing bodies. Cooperation and coordination are essential. A lack of coherence is also a barrier to participation by developing countries in international standardization as their scarce resources cannot cover participation in duplicative processes.

Lock-in and path dependencies in standards for one technology can also quickly lead to fragmentation and duplication in standards for other technologies. This translates to higher trade costs and impediments to innovation. Forward-looking cooperation between standards development organizations and between regulators can help chart a path toward convergence.

62 TBT Agreement, Annex 1.8.

63 WTO 2020, note 10 above, at 135 (discussing the relevance of "technical standards" in these areas).

64 "DDG Wolff Urges Standards Bodies to Boost Support for Multilateral Trading" (WTO, 28 September 2018), https://perma.cc/9XJM-H97P.

65 As already mentioned above, another principle of particular relevance for Industry 4.0 is "Effectiveness and Relevance" (Principle 4), which complements the need to attain "coherence". See in particular recommendations (a) to (c). On the "6 Principles", see notes 39, 43, 53–54 and 60 above.

G Good Regulatory Practice

Good regulatory practice (GRP) describes best practices and procedures developed by governments and organizations to improve the quality of regulation.[66] It must therefore also be an indispensable component of the Industry 4.0 regulatory process. A key feature of the fourth industrial revolution are technologies that straddle multiple sectors, jurisdictions and institutions. Regulation, on the other hand, tends to be organized along traditional sectoral lines. As new regulations are formulated, or existing ones redesigned, the impact on trade could be considerable. GRP provides governments with a toolkit of approaches and processes that can help them identify and address the trade impacts of their regulatory action.[67]

Examples of GRP include internal coordination (whole-of-government approach), transparency and public consultations, and regulatory impact assessment. Much work has been done in this area, both at the WTO and elsewhere, including in the context of the Asia-Pacific Economic Cooperation (APEC), the Organisation for Economic Co-operation and Development (OECD) and the World Bank.[68] Application of GRP can help ensure the design of high-quality, cost-effective regulations that are consistent with the goal of open trade. Moreover, the wider dissemination of GRP can contribute to the establishment of a common, predictable framework for regulatory intervention, thereby facilitating international regulatory cooperation and harmonization.[69]

The TBT Committee has recognized that "GRP can contribute to the improved and effective implementation of the substantive obligations under the TBT Agreement".[70] GRP discussions in the TBT Committee have emphasized the transparency and accountability of regulatory processes.[71] Strengthening transparency and accountability can help avoid unnecessarily trade-restrictive regulatory outcomes. Other areas of GRP considered by the TBT Committee include analysis and review of regulatory alternatives (including the option not to regulate) and the design of regulations, including the advantages of simple, responsive and flexible regulations. Members have also stressed that GRP is an important element of capacity-building initiatives[72] and that preparing GRP guidelines could be particularly helpful for developing countries.[73]

66 See TBT Handbook, note 38 above, at 30.

67 See R Basedow and C Kauffmann, "International Trade and Good Regulatory Practices: Assessing the Trade Impacts of Regulation" (2016) OECD Regulatory Policy Working Papers No. 4, https://perma.cc/F44S-YFN2.

68 Ibid.

69 G/TBT/26, para. 14. See also "Facilitating Trade through Regulatory Co-operation: The Case of the WTO's TBT/SPS Agreements and Committees" (WTO-OECD 2019), at 9–10 (hereinafter "WTO-OECD 2019").

70 G/TBT/26, para. 5, at 2. See also WTO-OECD 2019, note 69 above, at 10.

71 G/TBT/32, para. 4.

72 G/TBT/26, para. 59.

73 See TBT Handbook, note 38 above, at 30–32. See also, generally, WTO-OECD 2019, note 69 above.

The TBT Agreement's provisions on transparency and discussions on GRP are closely linked. For instance, "early notice", notification, comments, publication and entry into force are all processes that should lead to better regulation. Incorporating the transparency processes of the TBT Agreement into the regulatory lifecycle of a specific measure is a powerful means of fostering GRP, which has transparency and consultation as one of its fundamental components.[74] At the same time, greater utilization of GRP could help contribute to avoiding unnecessary and unintentional regulatory barriers to trade.

H *Regulatory Dialogue and Cooperation*

Besides harmonization via international standard-setting processes, the TBT Agreement provides members with "sign-posts" to engage in other forms of cooperation through various mechanisms, such as "equivalence" or "arrangements for conformity assessment".[75] These are additional mechanisms for encouraging the reduction of regulatory diversity and associated trade costs[76] – key challenges of Industry 4.0.

Equivalence refers to an arrangement in which members recognize that, although each other's product specifications and rules are different, they achieve the same result. When this happens, they can decide to accept the rules of the trading partner as "equivalent".[77]

This facilitates trade by allowing firms to produce according to domestic requirements and still directly access foreign markets without having to meet another set of requirements. It does not require regulations to be changed from the preferred domestic policy. The way that members choose to cooperate through equivalence agreements may vary depending on trade flows, their respective levels of protection, the costs of demonstrating achievement of the appropriate level of protection in light of risk and the possibility of unilateral or mutual recognition of equivalence.[78]

The TBT Agreement sets out a framework for members to reach "equivalence agreements" on their TBT-related technical regulations.[79] The Agreement does this not by requiring but by encouraging members to "give positive consideration to accepting as equivalent technical regulations of other Members, even if these regulations differ from their own, provided they are satisfied that these regulations adequately fulfil the objectives of their own regulations".[80]

74 See TBT Handbook, note 38 above, at 30.
75 WTO-OECD 2019, note 69 above, at 44.
76 Ibid.
77 Ibid.
78 Ibid.
79 Ibid., at 45.
80 TBT Agreement, Article 2.7. See also WTR 2020, note 10 above, at 136 and 151 (stressing the importance of TBT's encouragement to "equivalence").

I *Facilitating Acceptance of Conformity Assessment Results*

Divergent systems that trading partners use to verify conformity to applicable standards and regulations can create impediments to trade.[81] Around half of specific trade concerns raised at the TBT Committee over the last ten years have been on CAP. Duplication of testing and certification (due to nonrecognition of results) is a frequent source of trade friction. It is likely that conformity assessment will become even more complex with Industry 4.0.[82] Developing countries face particular challenges in the digital age, as systems and laboratories are not always available or as effective as they could be.[83]

The TBT Agreement, of course, requires members to ensure that their CAPs, among other obligations, do not create unnecessary obstacles to international trade.[84] But the way to achieve this result is far from obvious.

Governments greatly prize their freedom to regulate as a sovereign right and they have a responsibility to do so. No government wants to be told by another government (let alone an international organization) how to protect their security interests, consumers or the environment, or what tests or certificates to accept and from whom, or what results to follow. They may be unwilling to accept a test report or certificate from a foreign body that they do not know or may not trust.

Moreover, limited development of National Quality Infrastructure (e.g. standardization, metrology, accreditation, conformity assessment procedures), supporting laws and policy frameworks in some economies may limit options available to regulators when choosing their conformity assessment procedures.[85]

This can make it difficult to strike the balance between, on the one hand, the strictness of the procedures put in place to assess conformity to a given regulation's objectives, and, on the other, the risks that "nonconformity" with those objectives would create.[86] This challenge is not unique to Industry 4.0-related products, but achieving the appropriate balance may be particularly difficult for new technologies for which the risks are still not fully understood. Here, the TBT Agreement encourages the use of several tools to build trust and confidence.

These include recognition of conformity assessment results and the use of international and regional systems for conformity assessment. The TBT Agreement encourages members to recognize the results of CAP of other members, recognizing that this needs to be built upon cooperation between them, including in respect of the adequate and enduring technical competence of the relevant conformity

81 WTO-OECD 2019, note 69 above, at 45.

82 See J Rosenberg, "Conformity Assessment: An Industry Perspective" (2015), https://perma.cc/6LUH-T6BL.

83 See B Zhai and W Aranki, "Quality Infrastructure (QI): A Rising Topic for Development" (IAF Outlook, 30 June 2020), https://perma.cc/CKS9-2KA9.

84 TBT Agreement, Article 5.1.2. See also WTO-OECD 2019, note 69 above, at 45.

85 WTO-OECD 2019, note 69 above, at 45.

86 Ibid.

assessment bodies in the exporting member.[87] The Agreement provides a basis for cooperation, stating that prior consultations might be needed to arrive at a mutually satisfactory understanding on recognition.[88]

The TBT Agreement mentions accreditation as one means to build trust and confidence in the technical competence of foreign bodies providing CAP results.[89] It also encourages members to allow foreign conformity assessment bodies to participate in their national conformity assessment procedures on a national treatment and most-favored-nation basis.[90] The potential of accreditation to lower the costs of conformity assessment by eliminating the need for duplicative tests and certifications is not reached automatically: regulators have to be willing to rely on accreditation within their conformity assessment schemes.

Further, the TBT Agreement encourages members to enter into negotiations to conclude agreements on mutual recognition (MRAs) of the results of each other's conformity assessment procedures.[91] MRAs are one regulatory cooperation mechanism that allows parties to recognize specific results (e.g. test reports or certificates) in specific sectors.[92] While little is known about the actual implementation and functioning of MRAs, they can require significant time and costs to negotiate and maintain.[93] MRAs have been most successful in specific sectors like electrical and electronic products (e.g. the Association of Southeast Asian Nations MRA).

The TBT Agreement requires members, wherever practicable, to formulate and adopt, as well as participate as members of, international systems for conformity assessment.[94] This can help to strengthen regional and international regulatory cooperation between members in the area of CAP.[95]

These types of international and regional systems have grown in importance since the entry into force of the TBT Agreement in 1995. In the TBT Committee, members have discussed a range of systems based on arrangements between accreditation and conformity assessment bodies, including those operated by the International Laboratory Accreditation Cooperation, the International Accreditation Forum and the International Electrotechnical Commission (e.g. the IECEE CB scheme[96]), as well as other organizations. In the TBT Committee,

87 Ibid., at 46.

88 TBT Agreement, Article 6.1. See also WTO-OECD 2019, note 69 above, at 46.

89 TBT Agreement, Article 6.1.1. See also WTO-OECD 2019, note 69 above, at 46.

90 TBT Agreement, Article 6.4. See also WTO-OECD 2019, note 69 above, at 46.

91 TBT Agreement, Article 6.3. See also WTO-OECD 2019, note 69 above, at 46.

92 See also WTO 2020, note 10 above, at 135–136 (stressing the importance of TBT rules on MRAs, including as useful "tools by which the multilateral trading system fosters co-operation on digital technologies").

93 See also WTO-OECD 2019, note 69 above, at 46.

94 TBT Agreement, Article 9.1. See also WTO-OECD 2019, note 69 above, at 46.

95 See also WTO-OECD 2019, note 69 above, at 46.

96 International Electrotechnical Commission for Electrical Equipment Certification Body scheme. This is an international system for mutual acceptance of test reports and certificates dealing with the safety of electrical and electronic components, equipment and products.

members have discussed how to increase regulators' reliance on these types of systems to facilitate trade.[97]

IV CONCLUDING REMARKS

There is much in the TBT toolkit of disciplines, decisions, recommendations and practices that can be used to support Industry 4.0 by avoiding unnecessary regulatory diversity and reducing trade costs. Yet the converging and multidisciplinary nature of Industry 4.0, as well as the fast pace of technological changes associated with it, might mean that simply emphasizing better application of WTO rules by each member may not be enough.

Industry 4.0 instead requires broad, concerted, cooperative regulatory discussions; it also requires these discussions to be flexible, as well as both preventive (focus on drafts) and forward looking (detecting trends, constant updating, revisions, etc.), so as to minimize unnecessary barriers to trade. The WTO TBT Agreement and Committee practice could be used to support cooperation. But there are also issues that will need further consideration:

- Transparency is key, particularly given TBT transparency's unique preventive and self-corrective nature. How can these be better used and harnessed so as to shed more light on Industry 4.0-related regulation?
- International standardization is also key for Industry 4.0 regulatory processes. But sometimes full harmonization is not possible, or even desirable (e.g. difficult to harmonize nontechnical, societal issues like morality, religion and privacy, now also forming the basis of Industry 4.0 regulations on both goods and services). WTO will not be the place to set standards, but the TBT decision on six principles can help guide such development. However, we also need to recognize that international standardization will have difficulty in harmonizing cases where there are widely divergent underlying values and approaches. What can be done in the absence of international standards?
- This brings into focus other tools such as regulatory cooperation and good regulatory practices. Industry 4.0 regulation is dynamic and ever-evolving: there is a pressing need to establish a constant dialogue for better identifying what the convergences and differences in Industry 4.0 are and to discuss how to deal with some of them. How can we ensure coherence, avoid measures that are unnecessary and cope with those that are necessary?
- Some Industry 4.0 issues have already been raised at the TBT Committee through the notification and specific trade concerns process. Should and can more be done in terms of Industry 4.0 issues? This is a matter for further deliberation by WTO members. Some issues might lend themselves more to horizontal approaches (decisions and recommendations) as well as vertically

[97] G/TBT/1/Rev.13, Section 3.1, at 14. See also WTO-OECD 2019, note 69 above, at 46.

(in terms of how best to improve the STC process – a topic already under consideration in discussions on WTO reform).

- There is also the question of the cross-cutting nature of the challenge of convergence. Apart from the TBT Committee, Industry 4.0-related issues are surfacing either in whole or in part in different bodies and processes in the WTO (e.g. TRIPS Council; Joint Statement on E-Commerce; E-commerce Work Program; the GATS). How do we ensure coherence in approaches and avoid fragmentation in the discussion?

There are undoubtedly many more issues, many of which have already been raised in this book. In the future, AI will have written and possibly delivered this address. And it will undoubtedly have done a better job. And, very possibly, AI will also have negotiated the trade agreements that are needed to help it flourish. Until then, we will have to rely on the one thing that has helped us as humans, with all our limitations, to survive and thrive – our ability, despite all the dissonance on trade, to develop instruments for large-scale, vast networks of cooperation.

6

Autonomous Vehicle Standards under the Technical Barriers to Trade Agreement

Disrupting the Boundaries?

Shin-yi Peng

I INTRODUCTION

Following the highlight of the World Trade Organization's (WTO's) 2018 World Trade Report regarding how artificial intelligence (AI) can be used to "increase efficiency in the production of goods and services,"[1] former WTO Director-General Roberto Azevêdo, in his official capacity, claimed that technologies such as the Internet of Things (IoT), AI, and connected and autonomous vehicles (CAVs) have the potential to profoundly transform "the way we trade, who trades and what is traded."[2] This chapter focuses on CAVs as a case study to explore the question of how to modernize the Technical Barriers to Trade (TBT) Agreement in the age of AI.

Cars have been driving themselves in science fiction films and TV shows for decades. If you've ever dreamed of owning a car like KITT of *Knight Rider*,[3] your dream is about to come true. Fitted with cameras, sensors, and communication systems, CAVs are able to learn from each other and to see, hear, think, and make decisions just like human drivers do.[4] Driving automation can refer to a broad range of vehicle technologies and uses.[5] A general concept of CAVs, as defined in policy papers, is "vehicles that are capable of driving themselves without being controlled or monitored by an individual for at least part of a journey."[6] CAVs have been

[1] World Trade Organization, "World Trade Report 2018: The Future of World Trade – How Digital Technologies Are Transforming Global Commerce" (2018), https://perma.cc/F6SR-3XCW, at 3–6.

[2] R Azevêdo, "The Global Trading System Today Is More Important Than Ever" (The Permanent Mission of Japan to the International Organizations in Geneva, 3 April 2018), https://perma.cc/5GPX-U3QG.

[3] *Knight Rider* was a popular TV series that aired on NBC from 1982 to 1986. It featured KITT, which was an artificially intelligent car.

[4] CAVs may be able to communicate with their occupants, other vehicles, road users, and all Internet-based applications. CAVs are equipped with an algorithm that processes data regarding what is right, wrong, safe, and unsafe for the car to perform. See C Skinner, *Digital Human: The Fourth Revolution of Humanity Includes Everyone* (Singapore, Marshall Cavendish Business, 2018), at 117–121.

[5] See generally "Publications" (SAE International), https://perma.cc/8XFJ-PCXZ.

[6] "Automated Vehicles" (Law Commission), https://perma.cc/3NAK-HPW3.

described by governmental agencies as "a combination of sensors, controllers and onboard computers, along with sophisticated software, allowing the vehicle to control at least some driving functions, instead of a human driver."[7] Overall, a CAV can be seen as "a combination of various IoT devices with the capability to communicate with its surrounding physical and digital environment."[8] Depending on the features incorporated, the concept ranges from technologies that assist human drivers to vehicles that drive themselves with no human control or intervention.[9] The McKinsey Global Institute Report predicts that the automotive industry will be one of the most technologically progressive industries in incorporating AI into design and manufacturing processes.[10] As the brain of CAVs, AI is becoming an absolute necessity to ensure that CAVs function safely. More specifically, deep learning technology, a technique used to implement machine learning, will play a central role in the CAV market.[11]

This study relies on the technical report issued by the Society of Automotive Engineers International (SAE) as the foundation for analysis.[12] With the goal of providing common terminologies to describe the respective roles of human drivers at different levels of automation, the classification of "SAE levels" has been widely used by policymakers as an analytical tool to identify the respective policy considerations of automated driving systems.[13] To illustrate, the SAE has divided the system into six levels, ranging from "no automation," where the human driver performs all of the driving tasks (level 0), to "full automation" (level 5), where human intervention is not required. A key transition takes place when the functions of monitoring the driving environment shift from the human driver (level 2) to conditional automation, where automated driving systems perform all aspects of the driving tasks but the human driver is expected to respond when necessary (from level 3 upward).[14]

7 Deloitte, "Cybersecurity for Connected and Autonomous Vehicles: Considerations and Opportunities for Growth" (2019), https://perma.cc/YWF5-GLDN, at 3.

8 M Sinanian, "Jailbreak! What Happens When Autonomous Vehicle Owners Hack into Their Own Cars" (2017) 23 *Michigan Telecommunication and Technology Law Review* 357.

9 "Automated Vehicles: A Joint Preliminary Consultation Paper" (2018), https://perma.cc/NC4K-6RBX, at 3–5, 11–12. (Hereinafter "the UK CAV Consultation Paper.")

10 F Kanafani, "Why Artificial Intelligence Is a Key Component of Autonomous Cars" (Business Transformation, 6 September 2019), https://perma.cc/M8Z4-F7BE.

11 Ibid.

12 "Publications," note 5 above.

13 Ibid.

14 Ibid. See also "Summary of Levels of Driving Automation for On-Road Vehicles" (Cyberlaw, Standard), https://cyberlaw.stanford.edu/files/blogimages/LevelsofDrivingAutomation.pdf. The six SAE levels, which are generally followed globally, can be summarized as follows:

Level 0: No automation (human driver). The human driver performs all aspects of all driving tasks.

Level 1: Driver assistance (feet off). The system can either carry out the steering or acceleration/deceleration, but a human driver performs the remaining tasks.

Level 2: Partial automation (hands off). The system can carry out both steering and acceleration/deceleration while a human driver remains actively engaged in other tasks, including monitoring the driving environment.

Major automotive companies have claimed that they will deliver full "level 5" CAVs by 2021,[15] when there will be no need for a steering wheel, accelerator, or brakes, and the vehicle will be able to drive itself with no human input or intervention. Moving toward the 2021 new world, Ford, for example, announced its intention to deliver highly autonomous vehicles for ridesharing (level 4) in advance, featuring CAVs without a steering wheel and gas and brake pedals for use in commercial mobility services, such as ridesharing within geo-fenced areas.[16] In yet another example, BMW and Mercedes-Benz have joined forces, committing autonomous technicians to the goal of accelerating the timeline to release level 3 CAVs.[17] In fact, the installation rate of AI-based systems for new vehicles is rapidly increasing. The growth of the adoption rate is expected to rise by 109 percent in 2025, compared to 8 percent in 2015.[18] According to Gartner, more than 250 million cars will soon be connected to each other (V2V), and to the infrastructure around them, through vehicle-to-everything (V2X) communication systems.[19] Research firm IHS Markit also predicts that China alone will sell an estimated 14.5 million autonomous cars by 2040.[20] It should also be noted that CAVs, by their very nature, are heavily reliant on data. At present, telecom operators across several countries are preparing to launch 5G networks,[21] which will be instrumental in spurring further developments, including scale, in CAVs.

The large-scale use of driving automation systems may have significant implications and create a range of legal issues. CAVs bring new opportunities, challenges, and risks. The more AI technologies challenge the existing automotive industry, the greater the demand for new business models and regulatory frameworks tailored to their adoption. Governments all around the world are considering the potential disruptive impacts of CAVs.[22] The current debates surrounding standards/interoperability,

Level 3: Conditional automation (eyes off). The system is capable of performing all of the driving tasks, but the human driver is expected to respond and intervene when and where necessary.

Level 4: High automation (mind off). The system can perform all of the driving tasks within defined geographic cordons.

Level 5: Full automation (passengers only). The vehicle is capable of performing all driving functions under all environmental conditions.

15 See "Tesla Autopilot" (Tesla), www.tesla.com. Tesla, of course, also announced that the company has "pushed a software update" that will enable it to build "no steering wheel, no pedals" CAVs by 2021.

16 "Ford Targets Fully Autonomous Vehicle for Ride Sharing in 2021; Invests in New Tech Companies, Doubles Silicon Valley Team" (Ford, 16 August 2016), https://corporate.ford.com/articles/products/autonomous-2021.html.

17 "The Path to Autonomous Driving" (BMW, 30 June 2020), https://perma.cc/APF4-NYRA.

18 S Gadam, "Artificial Intelligence and Autonomous Vehicles" (Medium, 20 April 2018), https://medium.com/datadriveninvestor.

19 T Koslowski, "U.S. Government Must Clarify Its Terms to Boost V2V Technology Adoption" (Gartner Research, 10 February 2014), https://perma.cc/2TYA-QTPV.

20 N Chow, "Chinese Government Drafts Policies for Autonomous Vehicles" (IHS Markit, 25 January 2018), https://perma.cc/E2RN-ST38.

21 The bandwidth for 5G operators must be at least 80MHz to 100MHz. The first wave of 5G licenses were issued in Taiwan in the first half of 2020.

22 See Unmanned Vehicles Technology Innovative Experimentation Act 2018 (Taiwan) (UV Act). The UV Act was promulgated on 19 December 2018.

privacy/security, intellectual property/ethics, product liability/legal compliance risk management, integrity/trust, and business model/market strategies indicate that forward-thinking vision toward the AI age is more necessary than ever. Indeed, if the full potential of CAVs is to be realized, the necessary infrastructure and policies must be in place.[23]

In the context of international economic law, the impact of AI/CAVs on the regimes of both trade in goods and trade in services is gradually emerging. Domestic regulations will serve as major determinants of how AI-based goods or services will be traded. Relevant regulations, if overreaching or overly restrictive, may constitute behind-the-border trade barriers. More specifically, products that incorporate AI will require the development of a range of new standards. CAVs, under this movement, are facilitating the standardization process. This chapter uses the case of CAV standards as a window to explore how this "disruptive innovation" may alter the boundaries of international trade agreements.[24] Amid the transition to a driverless future, the transformative nature of disruptive innovation renders the interpretation and application of trade rules challenging. The author argues that disruptive technologies have a greater fundamental and structural impact on the existing trade regime.

II CONNECTED AND AUTONOMOUS VEHICLE (RE)CLASSIFICATION

A *Data-Driven Business Models*

The automotive industry is in transition where business model changes are concerned.[25] "Traditional" automotive manufacturers are now transforming into a new mobility ecosystem – from a mass-produced goods-sale business into highly customized data-based service suppliers.[26] In order to address changing consumer demand, the automotive industry is becoming less and less industrial and, simultaneously, increasingly intent on services, especially the operation and maintenance of vehicles.[27] Moving toward data-driven business models, AI

[23] It should be noted that at the international level, Article 8.5 of the Vienna Convention has requirements that are relevant to CAVs, including that every vehicle must have a driver. See Convention on Road Traffic, chapter xi: Transport and Communications, https://perma.cc/4UKK-QG93.

[24] See generally P Armstrong, *Disruptive Technologies: Understand, Evaluate, Respond* (London, Kogan Page, 2017).

[25] S Corwin and DM Pankratz, "Forces of Chance: The Future of Mobility" (2017), at 4–7 (hereinafter "Deloitte Analysis").

[26] G Lay, *Servitization in Industry* (New York, Springer, 2014), at 50, 109. AD Javan and SH Touri, *Servitization: Challenges, Classification and Categorization* (Saarbrücken, LAP Lambert Academic Publishing, 2012). See also Kanafani, note 10 above.

[27] Kanafani, note 10 above. See also Tim Baines and Howard Lightfoot, *Made to Serve: How Manufacturers Can Compete Through Servitization and Product Service Systems* (New York, Wiley, 2013), at 112.

further shatters the boundaries between the physical and the remaining components of the CAV.[28]

At the same time, another significant transformation in the automotive industry is the use of CAVs to supply Mobility as a Service (MaaS) solutions. Vehicle manufacturers will play an important role in MaaS services.[29] On the one hand, the transportation environment will be increasingly dominated by car-sharing, ride-hailing, and related services. In this context, being driven by CAVs will represent the essential nature of future transportation, and automotive firms will supply car-sharing and ad hoc use applications to drive up utilization rates. On the other hand, revenues generated by MaaS may become the core source of shareholder value creation when traditional car sales decline.[30] To summarize, the data-driven economy enabled by CAVs will displace vehicle ownership with MaaS, leading to a new transport system landscape.[31]

In light of these changes, business models for CAVs will become increasingly complex. Considering the trends toward MaaS, the typical business model will be based on a function that combines tangible vehicles and intangible services. Automotive firms will offer services to adjust existing functionalities and update software to increase the automated capabilities of a vehicle. Because the economic value of CAVs relies on their use value, throughout their operational life, tangible vehicles and intangible services must be combined to jointly fulfill customers' needs.[32] In this respect, it is fair to say that the higher the level of automated driving systems, the more service-oriented the automotive industry. Despite this reality, most CAVs, especially levels 1–4 of driving automation, fall in between traditional "goods" and "services."

B *Integrated Technical Features*

CAV systems are highly integrated, both internally and externally. In terms of internal integration, a CAV may contain several driving automation features that have individual, narrow-use specifications, but which together may provide

[28] See generally S-Y Peng, "A New Trade Regime for the Servitization of Manufacturing: Rethinking the Goods-Services Dichotomy" (2020) 54(5) *Journal of World Trade*, at 699–726.

[29] Mobility as a Service refers to "integrated mobility and multimodal transportation offerings based on a single contract, which will shift the transportation from vehicle ownership, taxi use, rental car use and public transport to the use of third-party transportation services based on autonomous vehicles." G Seiberth and W Gründinger, "Data-Driven Business Models in Connected Cars, Mobility Services and Beyond" (2018) BVDW Research No. 01/18, at 24.

[30] Deloitte Analysis, note 25 above, at 4. In fact, Japanese carmaker Toyota indicated that it expects CAV taxis to be operational by 2020. BMW and Mercedes are also working together on "Reach Now," which is an app that bundles different types of mobility. In addition to classic car-sharing, this also includes rental bikes and ridesharing.

[31] Ibid., at 8–10.

[32] L Fontagne and AE Harrison, *The Factory: Free Economy* (Oxford, Oxford University Press, 2017), at 86.

advanced automated driving functions. Technically speaking, a combination of automation features means that an aggregate level of safety is necessary for CAVs. In other words, part-based standards, for example steering wheels, no longer make any sense.[33] CAVs should be regulated at the system level to ensure the overall safety of the entire driving system. Only an aggregate "measure of safety" can cope with the challenges of "cumulative" automation features and therefore adequately protect CAV safety.[34] The "target" of safety regulation, therefore, should be gradually shifted from "auto parts" (goods) to integrated CAVs (overlapping boundaries of goods and services).

In terms of external integration, vehicles are rapidly transforming into "connected devices." Under the technological trends of V2X, a CAV is merely one component of the entire transport ecosystem. Depending on the level of automation, a CAV may be able to communicate with its occupants, other vehicles, road users, the surrounding transportation physical infrastructure, and all other Internet-based devices and applications. Indeed, in the extreme, in the age of AI, the world we are living in can be described as a convergence of all "IoT devices." CAVs will always be data-driven – by digitally connecting to one another and their surroundings. By interacting with the external physical and digital environment through V2X communications, CAVs are literally "components" of a holistic transport landscape.[35] This complex transport ecosystem requires a regulatory framework that considers security convergence, namely the combination of physical security and cybersecurity.

Despite this reality, security risks are particularly complex for CAVs, because they operate across both the physical and the digital world.[36] Compared to conventional vehicles, risks to a CAV involve threats related to the integrated environment. When communicating with other vehicles and infrastructure, CAVs become a channel for attack and an opportunity for hackers. Hackers can target the CAV itself, the servers supporting it, or the external systems that communicate with the CAV. It is also technologically possible for attackers to seize control of an entire fleet of CAVs by breaching the infrastructure.[37] In this context, the internal and external integration of CAVs may lead to complex security concerns. There is a need not only for "device" security but also for entire ecosystem security, with a strategic approach to threats. Regulators must ensure that CAVs are safe, both mechanically and in terms of protection from cyber attacks.[38]

33 After all, one key challenge facing CAV developers is the installation of effective software. SD Adkisson, "System-Level Standards: Driverless Cars and the Future of Regulatory Design" (2018) 40 *University of Hawaii Law Review* 1, at 1, 35–40.
34 Ibid., at 36–37.
35 Sinanian, note 8 above, at 361.
36 Ibid., at 359–365.
37 Ibid., at 359.
38 Ibid., at 360. Deloitte, note 7 above, at 2–3.

C *Technical Barriers to Trade Agreement or General Agreement on Trade in Services?*

Considering their business models and technical features, CAV-related safety standards may disrupt the scope of coverage of the TBT Agreement. Are CAVs goods or services?[39] Classification determines whether and to what extent the TBT Agreement rules are applicable. When "goods" and "services" converge as a package in the CAV market, the same is true for relevant safety standards.[40] The integrated CAV system, under which services are embedded with the physical body of the CAVs, is disrupting the traditional boundaries of trade regimes in terms of standards.

It should be noted that WTO case law generally supports the existence of a "boundary" between trade in goods and trade in services.[41] The Appellate Body has repeatedly stressed that whether a specific measure is scrutinized under the General Agreement on Tariffs and Trade (GATT), the General Agreement on Trade in Services (GATS), or both is a matter that can only be determined on a case-by-case basis.[42] Here, the Singapore Standard Council, for example, has issued a Technical Reference related to an enhanced cybersecurity framework for CAVs.[43] The Technical Reference, among other things, requires CAV developers to provide comprehensive documentation for a security-by-design review, to conduct cybersecurity assessment, and to comply with "cybersecurity principles" throughout the full lifecycle of CAVs, including design, development, operations, maintenance, and decommissioning.[44] The purpose of this Technical Reference is to provide rules to govern the cybersecurity assessment framework of CAVs on public roads. Toward that end, drawing from best practices in the industry, the Technical Reference provides standards. These standards apply to "a cyber-physical vehicle system," which includes embedded control systems and "a coupling between the computational elements and physical elements."[45] In this particular instance, is the standard under Singapore's Technical Reference for Autonomous Vehicles a measure of goods or services?[46]

[39] See, generally, P Sauvé, "To Fuse, Not to Fuse, or Simply Confuse? Assessing the Case for Normative Convergence Between Goods and Services Trade Law" (2019) 22(3) *Journal of International Economic Law* 355; A Chander, "The Internet of Things: Both Goods and Services" (2019) 18(S1) *World Trade Review* S9.

[40] Peng, note 28 above, at 703–705.

[41] Ibid., at 707–709. See also F Smith and L Woods, "A Distinction without a Difference: Exploring the Boundary Between Goods and Services in the World Trade Organization and the European Union" (2005) 12 *Columbia Journal of European Law* 1.

[42] Appellate Body Report, *Canada – Certain Measures Affecting the Automotive Industry* (Canada – Autos), WT/DS139/AB/R, WT/DS142/AB/R, adopted 19 June 2000, para. 159.

[43] Singapore Standard Council, Technical Reference for Autonomous Vehicles, TR68. Part II: Safety and Part III: Cybersecurity Principles and Assessment Framework (2019), https://perma.cc/7CK5-R5Q8.

[44] Ibid., at 8.

[45] Ibid., at 9. See also Deloitte, note 7 above, at 2–3.

[46] Hypothetically, if China were to bring a WTO dispute settlement case based on the TBT Agreement, claiming that Singapore's Technical Reference constitutes regulatory trade barriers for Chinese

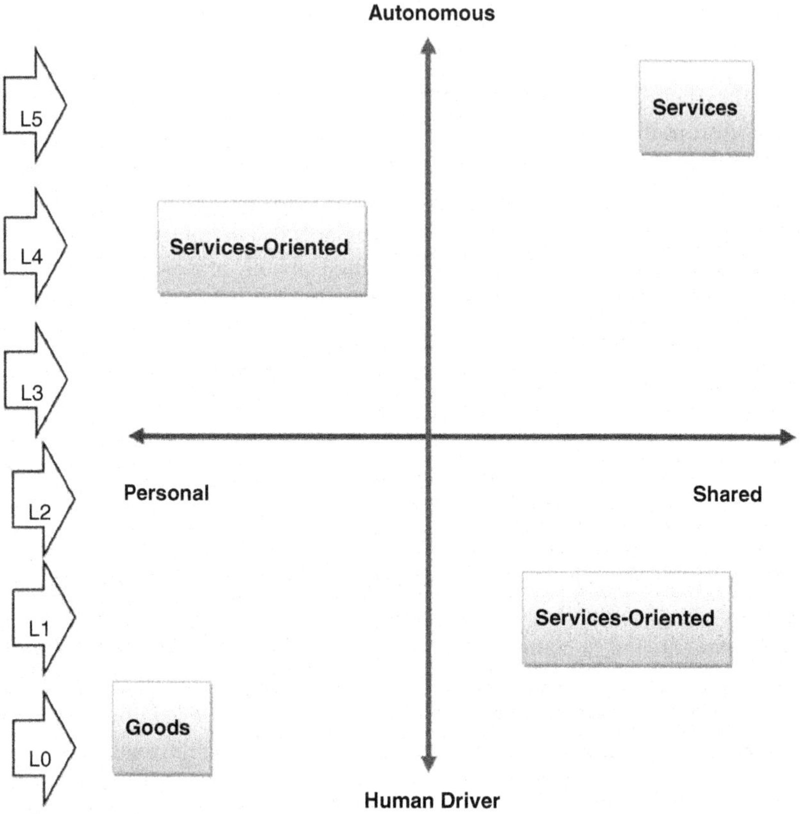

FIGURE 6.1 (Re)classification of connected and autonomous vehicle standards

Figure 6.1 demonstrates the evolution of CAV standards.[47] At the core of the issue is whether the regulations under the emergence of a new ecosystem of mobility should be subject to the TBT Agreement. Based on the factors delineated earlier regarding the transformation of the auto industry, the MaaS, the cumulative automation features of integrated CAVs, and the complex security concerns involved, the classification or reclassification of CAVs – in the context of the SAE's six levels (levels 0–5) – will prove an interesting case. At one extreme, level 0 (no automation, human driver), representing conventional, "personally owned" vehicles,[48] should be classified as goods and thus fall within the lower-left quadrant. At the other extreme,

CAVs in the Singapore market, how would the nature of the "measure at issue" be determined? The primary issue is whether these CAV standards should be subject to the rules under the TBT.

47 See Deloitte Analysis, note 25 above, at 3–5. The Deloitte paper created an analytical framework to identify the four potential future states of CAVs. The goods vs. services analysis in this article is based on the level of automation.

48 Ibid., at 3.

level 5 (full automation, "passengers only"),[49] representing shared CAVs, should be classified as services and thus fall within the upper-right quadrant. The remaining levels of CAVs (levels 1–4) comprise both goods and services under this four-quadrant analytical framework. During this time of transitional human–vehicle cooperation, CAV measures govern "trade in goods" but also affect "trade in services."

As shown in Figure 6.1, as CAVs evolve from level 0 to level 5, more and more domestic regulations will be subject to GATS. That said, CAV standards are arguably a "technical standard" within the meaning of Article VI:4.[50] The requirements in GATS Article VI:5, including "reasonable" and "not more burdensome than necessary," should be further explored in relation to high-level CAV standards.[51] However, the GATS contains too few trade rules to handle level 5 CAVs.[52] More importantly, in the interim, regarding levels 1–4, how should CAV standards be reclassified? The obligations under the TBT are far more substantial than those under the GATS. The danger of legal unpredictability may be imminent. To conclude, automation systems are "disruptive" in the way that they challenge existing governance frameworks and disrupt the boundaries of the TBT Agreement.

III CONNECTED AND AUTONOMOUS VEHICLE CO-GOVERNANCE

A *Industry-Driven Standardization Process*

One noteworthy angle in the ongoing process of CAV standardization is the industry-led approach. Such a regulatory scheme emphasizes market incentives rather than top-down regulation.[53] Government agencies consider themselves to be in partnership with developers in pursuit of the safe and rapid deployment of CAVs. One outstanding example is the subtitle of the US National Highway Traffic Safety Administration (NHTSA) guidelines: "Accelerating the Next Revolution in Roadway Safety."[54] By stressing its role as a facilitator in the exchange of information among CAV stakeholders, the US government does not play an exclusively dominant role in shaping the standards of automation systems.

This privatization of governance is attributable, in part, to governments' lack of requisite technical expertise, as well as the flexibility necessary to address ever more

49 Ibid.

50 *Informal Note by the Chairman, Disciplines on Domestic Regulation Pursuant to GATS Article VI:4*, Working Party on Domestic Regulation, Room Document (18 April 2006), para. II:5.

51 Ibid.

52 See generally P Sauvé, "Been There, Not Yet Done That: Lessons and Challenges in Services Trade," in M Panizzon et al. (eds), *GATS and the Regulation of International Trade in Services* (Cambridge, Cambridge University Press, 2008), at 617–620.

53 See generally F Fletcher et al., "Initial Scan of Policy: Issues Relevant to Autonomous Vehicle Development and Deployment" (2018), https://perma.cc/4RTK-LXJM.

54 JL Mashaw and DL Harfst, "From Command and Control to Collaboration and Deference: The Transformation of Auto Safety Regulation" (2017) 34 *Yale Journal on Regulation* 167, at 272.

complex regulatory tasks.[55] One of the potential legal hurdles that might slow the deployment of CAVs is bureaucracy, which often moves much more slowly than technological changes. Relevant agencies are aware that CAV development is taking place in a remarkably complex and dynamic technological environment, and that governments are currently in no position to provide mandatory performance standards for these emerging technologies.[56] Indeed, the development of CAV standards requires timely action. The scheme under which the private sector leads the standardization process has proven to be a more effective approach.

Procedurally and practically, the concept of "co-governance" has increasingly been advocated.[57] The CAV ecosystem comprises a variety of interconnected stakeholders, including the automotive industry and software businesses.[58] Governments must govern alongside private and civic sectors in a more inclusive, collaborative, and dynamic manner to drive cross-industry discussion. Through a relatively inclusive and transparent process,[59] governmental agencies participate on an equal footing with stakeholders.[60] In a world in which technological development is firmly in the control of industry, "regulated" parties should be treated as committed partners.[61] The collaborative approach may prove perfectly sensible.

B *Voluntary Standards*

An empirical survey reveals that in most jurisdictions, CAV standards go by many names, including "guidance," "guidelines," "recommendations," "informal standards," "best practices," and "codes of conduct."[62] These informal regulatory mechanisms, which in general are created to be "morally" or "politically" binding, can be considered to fall under the broad umbrella of "soft law."[63] This demonstrates how CAVs have been "regulated" in the loosest sense of the term.

55 Ibid., at 262. See also S-Y Peng, "'Private' Cybersecurity Standards? Cyberspace Governance, Multistakeholderism, and the (Ir)relevance of the TBT Regime" (2018) 51 *Cornell International Law Journal* 445.

56 See "Automated Vehicles for Safety" (NHTSA), https://perma.cc/PV94-RG8W.

57 W Mattli, "Beyond the State? Are Transnational Regulatory Institutions Replacing the State?" in S Leibfried et al. (eds), *The Oxford Handbook of Transformations of the State* (New York, Oxford University Press, 2015), at 289–297.

58 Deloitte, note 7 above, at 3.

59 J Pauwelyn, "Rule-Based Trade 2.0? The Rise of Informal Rules and International Standards and How They May Outcompete WTO Treaties" (2014) 17(4) *Journal of International Economic Law* 739, at 748–751.

60 Ibid., at 748.

61 See G Shaffer, *Defending Interests: Public-Private Partnerships in WTO Litigation* (Washington, DC, Brookings Institution Press, 2003), at 12–14. See also Mashaw, note 54 above, at 260.

62 KPMG, Autonomous Vehicles Readiness Index (2018), https://perma.cc/S97G-P4ZS, at 12–38.

63 See, generally, GC Shaffer and MA Pollack, "Hard vs. Soft Law: Alternatives, Complements, and Antagonists in International Governance" (2010) 94 *Minnesota Law Review* 706, at 710. See also R Hagemann et al., "Soft Law for Hard Problems: The Governance of Emerging Technologies in an Uncertain Future" (2018) 17 *Colorado Technology Law Journal* 37.

Empirical studies also demonstrate that more and more jurisdictions aim to minimize mandatory governmental regulation and favor voluntary, industry-led, nonbinding standards to enhance CAV safety.[64] In the UK, for example, the Automated and Electric Vehicles Act 2018 received Royal Assent on 19 July 2018.[65] The UK's Law Commission completed its first round of consultation in February 2019, which focused on regulatory frameworks, namely how to ensure safety when using CAVs, and how current road rules should be adapted for AI.[66] The primary considerations identified in the consultation paper identify areas in which there may be ambiguity in the law, as well as potentially necessary reforms. Stakeholders have actively responded to the key questions raised in the consultation paper, including, among other items, how to allocate civil and criminal responsibility when control is shared between the automated driving system and a human user, impacts on other road users, and protection from risks.[67] More importantly, the government has already published a "Code of Practice" to provide "guidance" for CAV testing. Although, by the very nature of the code, compliance is voluntary, it nevertheless sets out "principles" and details "recommendations" that the government believes should be followed to minimize potential risks and maintain safety.[68]

On the other side of the Atlantic, the US NHTSA and the US Department of Transportation (DOT) jointly issued the Federal Automated Vehicles Policy in September 2016.[69] The Policy was designed to "set forth a proactive approach to providing safety assurance and facilitating innovation."[70] The NHTSA issued "Automated Driving Systems: A Vision for Safety 2.0" (Guidance 2.0) in September 2017,[71] which, based on the comments of key stakeholders (e.g., the automotive industry) as they considered "best practices," offers a "flexible, non-regulatory approach" to CAV safety.[72] In October 2018, the DOT released "Preparing for the Future of Transportation: Automated Vehicles 3.0" (Guidance

64 KPMG, note 62 above, at 53.

65 The Automated and Electric Vehicles Act 2018 received Royal Assent on 19 July 2018. Its commencement date is subject to appointment by the Department for Business, Energy and Industrial Strategy (BEIS) (The Automated and Electric Vehicles Act 2018 (UK)).

66 See the UK CAV Consultation Paper, note 9 above, at 4.

67 Ibid., at 185–191.

68 Ibid., at 69.

69 At the same time, most state governments, which typically administer driving and car registrations, had passed legislation relating to CAVs. Relevant rules in different states, however, vary to some extent. The industry has been aggressively pushing for federal actions to create one standard instead of different state versions.

70 NHTSA, "Automated Vehicles for Safety," https://perma.cc/52AQ-9YKV.

71 The NHTSA has repeatedly made clear that the Policy is "not mandatory," and it has no intention to convert the voluntary guidelines into legally binding regulations. The NHTSA's hesitancy in imposing mandatory safety standards on CAV manufacturers is evident. T Pearl, "Hands on the Wheel: A Call for Greater Regulation of Semi-Autonomous Cars" (2018) 93 *Indiana Law Journal* 713, at 727.

72 Ibid. The NHTSA's Principles for improving motor vehicle cybersecurity represent another striking example. The NHTSA's 2017 guidelines discuss vehicle cybersecurity standards in general, which merely "encourage" manufacturers "to consider and incorporate voluntary guidance, best practices, and design principles" published by the National Institute of Standards and Technology (NIST).

3.0), which again serves as "voluntary guidance" and "is intended to be flexible."[73] As advanced by some commentators, the NHTSA's CAV guidelines are indeed "an exuberant celebration of volunteerism."[74]

In Asia, one striking case is China's CAV roadmap. Following the "New Generation Artificial Intelligence Development Plan," issued by the State Council in 2019, the Ministry of Industry and Information Technology announced a Three-Year Plan for Promoting Development of a New Generation of the Artificial Intelligence Industry (MIIT), implemented to detail action plans for the development of driver assistance systems, vehicle intelligence algorithms, and automotive smart chips.[75] Further, the MIIT has published "communication guidelines," which cover ninety-two standards, with a focus on CAV technology.[76] The government also announced that more than thirty key standards that are critical to autonomous driving systems will be introduced in the coming years.[77] China's approach to CAV development is systematic. Following China's top-down standardization process, the government continues to take primary responsibility in terms of standardization development. However, in the case of CAVs, the government has been working closely with the CAV industry, including the China Industry Innovation Alliance for the Intelligent and Connected Vehicles, to ensure the "relevance and flexibility" of standards.[78] The alliance, together with other industry associations, has been commissioned by the MIIT to develop a common set of "protocols" for CAVs.[79]

To summarize, most countries maintain CAV safety policies while emphasizing the voluntary nature of standards and safety assessments.[80] Governments tend to refrain from mandating CAV-specific design features and performance standards. In addition, relevant authorities are inclined to offer nonregulatory approaches to CAV safety. CAV

[73] US Department of Transportation, "Preparing for the Future of Transportation: Automated Vehicle 3.0," www.transportation.gov/av/3. It should be noted, however, that although the testing of CAVs is generally permitted, some states mandate that a licensed human driver be present and capable of taking manual control of a CAV at all times. Some states limit who may test a CAV and under what circumstances. Several states restrict CAV operations to sandbox projects preapproved by relevant authorities. Many states merely require that CAV owners notify state regulators prior to operating on public roads. See JA Carp, "Autonomous Vehicles: Problems and Principles for Future Regulation" (2018) 4 *University of Philadelphia Journal of Law & Public Affairs* 81.

[74] Mashaw, note 54 above, at 266.

[75] X Tan, "China's Race to Develop Autonomous Vehicles" (*New Security Beat*, 28 February 2019), https://perma.cc/2S3A-KATZ.

[76] Ibid. First-tier cities such as Beijing and Shanghai have already allowed CAV road testing. "Beijing Adds Area for Self-Driving Vehicle Tests with Passengers" (*Xinhua*, 30 December 2019), https://perma.cc/F74U-SD84.

[77] Ibid. See also, KPMG, note 62 above, at 32.

[78] Ibid. See also F Li, "Country Issues National Standards for Autonomous Vehicle Testing" (*China Daily*, 13 August 2018), https://perma.cc/RK6S-UR5Y; "China Issues National Standards for the Testing of Autonomous Vehicles" (Intelligent Transport, 14 August 2018), https://perma.cc/UNE5-DNKP.

[79] Ibid.

[80] Mashaw, note 54 above, at 266.

developers may "consider" the guidance as they develop, test, and deploy CAVs on public roadways. They are also "encouraged" to submit a "safety self-assessment," describing their treatment of each guideline.[81] This chapter is not the place to provide a detailed analysis of whether existing approaches can meet CAV safety needs. However, a few general comments bear emphasis. To some extent, the voluntary approach seems realistic. Standards of a soft law nature offer advantages over traditional command-and-control regulation because they provide greater flexibility and adaptability and lower compliance and administrative costs, directly address industry-specific and consumer issues, and adapt to the rapidly changing political landscape.[82]

C *Technical Barriers to Trade Agreement: In or Out?*

The proliferation of "soft" safety standards in the CAV industry reveals a pattern of self-regulation. In 2018, the SAE formed a committee of stakeholders, took the lead, and published the CAV safety "principles."[83] In 2019, industry leaders across the CAV technologies also published "Safety First for Automated Driving," a nonbinding framework for the development, testing, and validation of safe CAVs.[84] The distinguishing feature of these standards is their legally nonbinding nature, which strongly correlates to the self-regulation of nonstate actors. Indeed, they were literally drawn up by the private entity that is to be regulated.[85]

This ongoing shift to voluntary co-governance raises an important question: Under what conditions can the complaining party invoke the dispute settlement system against nonbinding CAV standards that have developed by the private entities?[86] In Figure 6.2, the vertical axis represents the relative level of governmental involvement in the standardization process, while the horizontal axis represents the relative degree of the binding effects of the standards. At the crux of the matter is this: the emerging CAV standards have implications for the boundaries of the TBT Agreement. First, the fact that the CAV standardization process may lack sufficient governmental involvement raises the question of whether the TBT Agreement will apply. Second, these CAV

81 KPMG, note 62 above, at 53.

82 Hagemann, note 63 above, at 59.

83 S Abuelsamid, "SAE International Ready to Tackle Automated Vehicle Safety Testing Standards" (*Forbes*, 1 August 2018), https://perma.cc/3PFZ-E82Y.

84 These eleven leaders – Aptiv, Audi, Baidu, BMW, Continental, Daimler, FCA US LLC, HERE, Infineon, Intel, and Volkswagen – comprise a broad representation of the CAV industry. "Automotive and Mobility Industry Leaders Publish First-of-Its-Kind Framework for Safe Automated Driving System" (*Businesswire*, 2 July 2019), https://perma.cc/K557-8UWC.

85 K Creutz, "Law versus Codes of Conduct: Between Convergence and Conflict," in J Klabbers and T Piiparinen (eds), *Normative Pluralism and International Law: Exploring Global Governance* (Cambridge, Cambridge University Press, 2013), at 191.

86 TBT, Annex 1: For the purpose of the TBT Agreement, the following definitions shall apply: 1. Technical regulation: Document which lays down product characteristics or their related processes and production methods, including the applicable administrative provisions, *with which compliance is mandatory* (emphasis added).

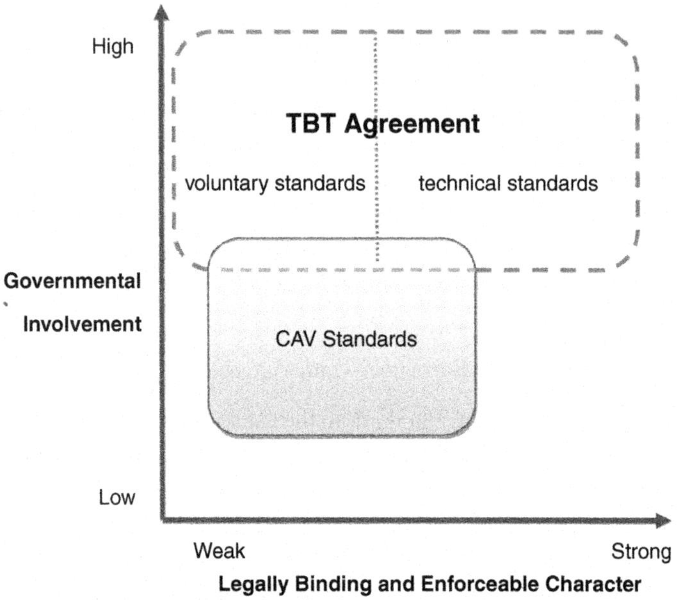

FIGURE 6.2 Co-governance of connected and autonomous vehicle standards

standards may fall outside the definition of "technical regulation" in the TBT Agreement. As clearly argued by Lim in Chapter 5 of this book, the first issue is more important than the second, because although the TBT disciplines on technical regulations are relatively deeper, voluntary standards are still subject to Article 4 and Annex 3 of the Agreement.[87] Nevertheless, as shown in Figure 6.2, the transformative nature of disruptive innovation renders the interpretation and application of TBT rules challenging.

To illustrate, the WTO provides a dispute settlement mechanism whereby a member considers that its benefits under the covered agreements are being impaired by "measures" taken by another member.[88] In this context, any act or omission "attributable" to a WTO member can serve as a "measure" of that member for purposes of dispute settlement proceedings.[89] "A complainant must clearly establish that the alleged measure is attributable to the responding Member."[90]

87 I share Lim's view that the key issue here is the definition of "non-governmental body." However, this chapter also argues that the concepts of "governmental involvement" and "legally binding" are to a certain extent intertwined. See Aik Hoe Lim, Chapter 5 of this book. See also A Arcuri, "The TBT Agreement and Private Standards," in Tracey Epps et al. (eds), *Research Handbook on the WTO and Technical Barriers to Trade* (Cheltenham, Edward Elgar, 2013), at 505.

88 Article 3.3 of the Dispute Settlement Understanding.

89 Appellate Body Report, European Communities – *Selected Customs Matters*, WT/DS315/AB/R, adopted 11 December 2006, para. 133.

90 Appellate Body Report, United States – *Countervailing Measures on Supercalendered Paper from Canada*, WT/DS505/AB/R, adopted 5 March 2020, paras. 5.17, 5.6.

The decisive factor here is "the degree of governmental involvement."[91] WTO case law indicates that "private actions" may fall within the scope of the TBT Agreement if the support provided by a government is sufficient to become a "governmental act."[92] Considering the approaches taken by WTO panels and the Appellate Body in past disputes,[93] the conduct of the private body may come under WTO disciplines if there is a demonstrable link between the government and such "conduct."[94] To summarize, a nexus must exist between the responding member and the "measure" – regardless of whether it is an act or an omission.[95]

At the core of the question is whether the standards published by a nongovernmental body at the request of the government, or with some degree of government support, can be viewed as a measure of a member government.[96] Is there an adequate connection between a private entity's self-regulation and government action? To what extent should a tribunal impose the responsibility of WTO members with regard to industry standards? The emergence of the self-regulating, collaborative approach for CAV standard-setting therefore leads to the question of how the TBT Agreement should respond to the trend of public–private convergence in the standardization process.[97] As shown in Figure 6.2, the CAV case study demonstrates that the co-governance model, in which governments "more or less" "work together" with stakeholders of the CAV ecosystem, arguably falls into the middle-lower portion of the "Governmental Involvement" axis.

Furthermore, even if sufficient governmental involvement can be found in the CAV standard-setting process, the next question is whether these "standards" can constitute "technical regulation" within the meaning of the TBT Agreement, therefore allowing a set of deeper trade disciplines to apply.[98] In past WTO cases, the panels and the Appellate Body elaborated on the term "mandatory," indicating that it includes "binding as well as obligatory, compulsory, not discretionary," or

91 PC Mavroidis, "Private Standards and the WTO: Reclusive No More" (2017) 16(1) *World Trade Review* 1, at 10.

92 Arcuri, note 87 above, at 497. A Kudryavtsev, *Private-Sector Standards as Technical Bakeries in International Trade in Goods: In Search of WTO Disciplines* (Nijmegen, The Netherlands, Wolf Legal Publishers, 2015), at 238–239.

93 See, for example, Panel Report, *European Union and Its Member States – Certain Measures Relating to the Energy* Sector (EU – Energy Package), WT/DS476/R, 10 August 2018, para. 7.640.

94 See, for example, Appellate Body Report, *United States – Sunset Review of Anti-Dumping Duties on Corrosion Resistant Carbon Steel Flat Products from Japan*, WT/DS244/AB/R, adopted 9 January 2004, paras. 81–82. Appellate Body Report, *United States – Definitive Anti-Dumping and Countervailing Duties on Certain Products from China*, WT/DS379/AB/R, adopted 25 March 2011, para. 292.

95 Appellate Body Report, *United States – Measures Affecting the Cross Border Supply of Gambling and Betting Services*, WT/DS285/AB/R, adopted 20 April 2005, para. 121.

96 Panel Report, Japan – *Measures Affecting Consumer Photographic Film and Paper*, WT/DS44/R, adopted 22 April 1998, paras. 10.43, 10.45–51.

97 Peng, note 55 above, at 462.

98 The distinction between technical regulations and standards is that compliance is mandatory with the former and voluntary with the latter. TBT, Annex 1.

"required by law or mandate; compulsory."[99] However, as clarified in several disputes, "the mandatory character of the measure may result from a combined effect of various measures or actions attributable to the Member in question."[100] In other words, a "voluntary and non-mandatory" measure may become "mandatory" as a result of "some other governmental action" or "some other action attributable to the Member concerned."[101] As shown in Figure 6.2, the industry-driven, voluntary standards of CAVs may be determined to fall outside the definition of "technical standards" under the TBT Agreement because of its private and soft nature, unless compliance with the standards becomes de facto mandatory because of "some other action attributable to the Member concerned."

That said, CAV standardization is indeed an interesting case study in the determination of "*de facto* mandatory."[102] In terms of administrative actions, CAV safety guidance, although industry-led and nonbinding, may become a core requirement for "duty of safety" and may also have important evidentiary value in regulatory investigations. The UK's CAV consultation paper, for example, indicates that "there is a rebuttable presumption that a product is safe if it conforms to voluntary standards published by the Commission."[103] In terms of judicial litigation, depending on the level of automation, courts need legal standards to determine liability when CAVs crash. More specifically, for levels 1–4, in which humans and CAVs are codrivers, determining "cause" during the transition to a driverless future will become increasingly complex in lawsuits related to negligence or product liability. Did the CAV properly alert the human driver?[104] Should the CAV have been designed to automatically reduce vehicle speed on a snowy road? Or should the system prevent driving altogether?[105] In a negligence or product liability lawsuit involving CAVs, the key issues will be whether the design of the CAV is defective in nature. This will inevitably lead to an inquiry into the "standard of care" that is imposed on CAVs, or the definition of a "design defect" for CAVs.[106] How do manufacturers address "reasonable care" when designing the automated driving system? What safety standards should apply to CAVs?[107]

99 The notion of "mandatory" may encompass the legally binding and enforceable character of the instrument. Panel Report, *United States – Measures Concerning the Importation, Marketing and Sale of Tuna and Tuna Products* (US – Tuna II), WT/DS381/R, adopted 13 June 2012, as modified by Appellate Body Report WT/DS381/AB/R, para. 7.173.

100 Panel Report, *United States–Measures Concerning the Importation, Marketing and Sale of Tuna and Tuna Products*, WT/DS381/R, Sept. 15, 2011, paras. 7.102–106.

101 Ibid., para. 7.173.

102 Kudryavtsev, note 92 above, at 60–63.

103 Law Commission (UK), "Automated Vehicles: Background Papers to the Preliminary Consultation Paper" (2018), https://perma.cc/6NSG-JXAG, at para. 2.96.

104 DA Riehl, "Car Minus Driver, Part II" (2017) 73 *Journal of the Missouri Bar* 264.

105 Ibid., at 266.

106 Ibid., at 88–89.

107 Pearl, note 71 above, at 728.

In practice, the industry-led voluntary standards provide a baseline for judges in the evaluation of appropriate levels and evidence of CAV safety prior to deployment,[108] which may become a strong incentive for CAV manufacturers to comply with "guidance," "best practice," or "codes of conduct," thereby demonstrating a commitment to meeting expert safety expectations.[109] More specifically, compliance with industry standards can provide convincing evidence regarding whether there is a defect.[110] CAV manufacturers may be able to partially mitigate the legal risk by demonstrating conformity to industry safety standards. At the same time, judges may resort to industry standards when evaluating the duty of safety in tort cases.[111] In brief, self-regulation is being afforded legal status through complementary evidence.[112] As a result, private soft law is no longer merely a self-imposed corporate obligation. It can also constitute a source of law in court proceedings.

To conclude, compliance with CAV standards may become de facto mandatory, which somehow blurs the line between mandatary/voluntary standards. The key question, however, remains: Is the TBT Agreement capable of addressing de facto mandatory "self-regulation"? To what extent should a WTO tribunal assume the responsibility of members with regard to CAV safety standards that are prepared and published by a private entity? How should the TBT Agreement respond to the trend of private standardization processes in which the government involvement per se is often minimum, if not nominal? Evidently, the development of disruptive innovation inherently involves changes in governance frameworks and calls for new governance approaches that break the boundaries of existing trade disciplines.

IV CONCLUDING REMARKS

CAVs will have far-reaching implications across numerous areas of policy-making.[113] To fully realize the benefits of CAVs, a vast array of legal issues must be addressed, corresponding to the developmental phases of CAVs.[114] This chapter reviewed legal issues related to CAVs in the context of international trade law, with a view toward offering a critical assessment of the two systematic issues – the goods/services boundaries and the public/private sector boundaries. Looking to the future,

108 Ibid., at 118.

109 Ibid., at 466. See also Kudryavtsev, note 92 above, at 496; Arcuri, note 92 above, at 503.

110 Pearl, note 71 above, at 95–96.

111 T Buthe and W Mattli, *The New Global Rulers: The Privatization of Regulation in the World Economy* (Princeton, NJ, Princeton University Press, 2011), at 205.

112 Creutz, note 85 above, at 191.

113 See KPMG, note 62 above, at 7.

114 For example, the data generated by CAVs presents particular legal challenges. Among others, one of the toughest policy decisions concerns the data-sharing requirement. Concerns about algorithmic accountability are starting to convince automotive manufacturers that some form of transparency might be important. Toyota is currently working on an algorithmic transparency project called "The car can explain." G Sussman and L Kagal, "The Car Can Explain!" (CSAIL), https://perma.cc/QXF7-2NPD.

regulations governing CAVs will become increasingly complex, as the level of systemic automation evolves into levels 3–5. Domestic standards and conformity assessment procedures may become potential technical barriers to CAV trade.[115] The TBT regime must be modernized to reflect current standardization trends, and to safeguard its important role in global economic governance in the twenty-first century.

115 Turning back to the example regarding Singapore's CAV Technical Reference, if we proceed on the assumption that the CAV standards are "technical regulation," potential issues regarding TBT Article 2.1 claims include whether imported and domestic CAVs are "like products" if national security is taken into account. However, it would be more difficult for a complaining party to win TBT Article 2.2 claims. A WTO member contesting Singapore's failure to comply with TBT Article 2.2 must present evidence showing that it would be possible to achieve the same objective through a less trade-restrictive measure.

7

Convergence, Complexity and Uncertainty

Artificial Intelligence and Intellectual Property Protection

*Bryan Mercurio and Ronald Yu**

I INTRODUCTION

Artificial intelligence (AI) is integral to many systems we use today – from the recommendation engines on entertainment platforms to facial recognition software on mobile phones to systems driving progress on the future of autonomous vehicles. What was once thought of as science fiction – an AI creating copyrightable content, registerable designs or potentially patentable inventions – or even creating non-existent but realistic-looking persons[1] – has morphed into reality.[2]

AI is also changing the nature of the process of buying goods and services on e-commerce platforms in a way that has important implications for commerce and market competition. For example, AI assistants, search engines, customer service bots and online marketplaces play an important role in shaping the consumer decision-making process. The manner in which a consumer interacts with the online marketplace through AI may result in the presentation of only a limited number of brands to a consumer or other alterations to the way that consumers view and make product selections.[3]

Presently, a non-human cannot in most jurisdictions be named as an inventor for something it invented or enjoy copyright rights for the creation of works. With this background, it is not difficult to see how AI sits uneasily in the construct of the intellectual property (IP) system. The question of AI and IP is both contemporary and

* This article was produced as part of a project funded by the Hong Kong Policy Innovation and Co-ordination Office's Public Policy Research Funding Scheme for a project entitled *Regulating Cross Border Data: A Public Policy Framework for Hong Kong* (Project No. 2019.A4.064.19D)

1 M Zhang, "This AI Creates Photo-Realistic Faces of People Who Don't Exist" (Petapixel, 17 November 2017), https://perma.cc/HUH8-JXHQ.

2 For example, a Paris-based collective called "Obvious" created the work "Portrait of Edmond de Belamy" that sold at auction for $423,500 in October 2018, using Generative Adversarial Networks. See J Newman and SM Gibson, "Blurring the Lines: When AI Creates Art, Is It Copyrightable?" (Patent Lawyer Blog, 13 May 2020), https://perma.cc/UMR5-QSQA.

3 WIPO Secretariat, "Revised Issues Paper on Intellectual Property Policy and Artificial Intelligence", WIPO/IP/AI/2/GE/20/1 REV, https://perma.cc/9PDM-DY35.

pressing. In fact, the issue has been deemed so important and urgent that the World Intellectual Property Office (WIPO) held a "Conversation on IP and AI" event in September 2019, followed by a public consultation in which it received over 250 submissions, a consultation paper,[4] an event in February 2020 on "Copyright in the Age of Artificial Intelligence"[5] and a second "Conversation on IP and AI" in July 2020.

Some of the urgency behind this activity lies in the fragmentation of norms stemming from a lack of international guidance. The matter is made even more urgent by the notoriety surrounding the recent rejection of the granting of patents by patent offices in the USA, UK and Europe to an AI named DABUS (which stands for "Device autonomously bootstrapping uniform sensibility"), who the owner claims invented "food container" and a "device and method for attracting enhanced attention" autonomously without any form of human intervention.[6]

The time is thus ripe to address the profound role the IP system has in AI, not only because it can protect but also serve to block access to key AI technologies (for example, by patent holders preventing others from using patented technologies). This chapter first defines the concept before evaluating the state of play in regards to AI and patents, trade secrets and copyright. In so doing, the chapter raises substantive issues relating to AI which challenge the norms and standards of the IP system. Next, the chapter evaluates issues concerning IP in the data used by an AI system. Finally, the chapter briefly touches on the profound question of the purpose of IP, and the consequences of AI as an IP holder.

II DIFFICULT TO DEVISE AND DEFINE

Before even thinking of how to address issues relating to AI and IP, it is necessary to understand some of the more esoteric aspects of IP and how these could affect policy decisions regarding AI inventions. In order to do so, however, it is necessary to first agree on certain definitions. This was likely one of the first set of challenges that WIPO encountered when launching its consultation. Defining AI for legal purposes is not straightforward, given the wide range of ideas and opinions as to what constitutes "AI". To avoid any lengthy debates, this chapter will simply adopt the definitions WIPO used in its consultation paper:

- AI is a discipline of computer science that is aimed at developing machines and systems that can carry out tasks considered to require human intelligence, with

4 See "Artificial Intelligence and Intellectual Property Policy" (World Intellectual Property Organization (WIPO)), https://perma.cc/587U-WN49. The Consultation Paper was subsequently heavily revised in May 2020 on the basis of comments and further reflection.

5 See "Copyright in the Age of Artificial Intelligence" (Copyright.gov, 5 February 2020), https://perma.cc/LKB8-7VEG.

6 See "AI 'DABUS' Autonomous Inventor, But Not Official" (Meyer-Dulheur MD Legal Patentanwalte Partg MBB, 17 February 2020), https://perma.cc/57CV-SYSH; K Baretto, "'DABUS MACHINE': The Harbinger to Debates on Artificial Intelligence as an 'Inventor' under Patent Law" (RGNUL Student Research Review, 22 February 2020), https://perma.cc/9EWW-TKJP.

limited or no human intervention. AI generally equates to "narrow AI" which is techniques and applications programmed to perform individual tasks. Machine learning and deep learning are two subsets of AI.[7]

- "AI-generated" and "generated autonomously by AI" are terms that are used interchangeably and refer to the generation of an output by AI without human intervention. This is to be distinguished from "AI-assisted" outputs that are generated with material human intervention and/or direction.[8]

While these definitions are sufficient for our purposes, it should be noted that defining what constitutes an AI-generated invention or creation is far more difficult than it appears at first glance, given both the wide continuum between AI that was created autonomously[9] and with some human input (which itself may have been augmented, for example with artificial creativity augmentation[10] or other AI). The full set of arguments as to what is or is not an AI-generated invention is beyond the scope of this chapter,[11] but suffice to say that the definition of AI is perhaps not completely finalized and static.

III ARTIFICIAL INTELLIGENCE AS AN INTELLECTUAL PROPERTY HOLDER

With AI defined, we can now proceed to examine the questions of:

- whether AI-generated inventions, creations or designs can be granted IP protection;
- how such inventions, creations and designs should be treated in legislation or by governmental agencies; and
- whether the law should require that a human being be named as an inventor or author or whether it should permit an AI application to be named as the inventor (which naturally raises the question of whether an AI could have legal personhood).

Of course, a large part of the problem here is that current laws never envisaged a situation where AI systems could create and invent on their own, with a minimal nexus with a human being. In such a circumstance, a human could not technically

7 Deep learning is regarded by some as a subset of machine learning. See, for example, "Uniformed Search Algorithms" (Javatpoint), https://perma.cc/64NU-AKM4.

8 WIPO Secretariat, WIPO Conversation on Intellectual Property (IP) and Artificial Intelligence (AI), Second Session, Revised Issues Paper on Intellectual Property and Artificial Intelligence, WIPO/IP/AI/2/GE/20/1 REV, 21 May 2020.

9 It should be noted that there is a human connection in fully autonomous systems and as long as computers rely on instructions defined by a human as to how to solve a problem, the separation between human and non-human (algorithmic) ingenuity is, in itself, artificial.

10 On this topic, see N-M Aliman and L Kester, "Artificial Creativity Augmentation", paper delivered at AGI-20 Conference, 25 June 2020, https://perma.cc/SR2Z-UMEK.

11 Those wishing to explore a more robust discussion on this subject should read the excellent paper by D Kim, "'AI-Generated Inventions': Time to Get the Record Straight?", 69 GRUR International 443.

be listed as author or inventor. Yet current laws in most jurisdictions also prevent the AI from being named an author or inventor, and thus AI inventions are left in a lacuna without legal protection, which returns us to the question of whether AI-generated content, inventions and the like warrant IP protection. If AI inventions and creations are allowed IP protection, should there be new systems of examination (for patents) or protection (for copyright) for such works? Finally, if AI inventions and creations are denied IP protection, would this incentivize organizations and individuals to conceal the involvement of AI, and if AI were involved, how could it even be detected? On top of these, there are questions specifically related to patents, trade secrets and copyrights which will be addressed in subsections A to D.[12]

A *Patents and Trade Secrets*

At first glance, obtaining patent protection for an AI-generated invention appears straightforward; such an invention would be patentable if it meets the definition as set out by Article 27.1 of the Trade-Related Aspects of Intellectual Property Rights (TRIPS) Agreement and domestic legislation:

> patents shall be available for any inventions, whether products or processes, in all fields of technology, provided that they are new, involve an inventive step and are capable of industrial application . . . and patent rights enjoyable without discrimination as to the place of invention, the field of technology and whether products are imported or locally produced.

Thus, in order to qualify for protection, an invention must meet the following conditions:

- novelty – meaning it is not part of the state of the art (as defined by the relevant patent law);
- inventiveness (or non-obviousness); and
- utility (or industrial applicability) – which means, among other things, that it is capable of actually working in the real world (e.g. an invisibility cloak, similar to what one might see in *Star Trek* or *Harry Potter*, would not meet this test).

These conditions distinguish an invention from a mere discovery of, say, a naturally occurring phenomenon or equation.[13] Thus, discovering that a wave coming from the earth's core that interferes with satellite broadcasts is useful, but not

[12] Other important questions regarding the ramifications inventorship and ownership would have on related issues such as infringement, liability or dispute resolution – or even how, if an AI were an inventor, it could enter into contracts – are beyond the ambit of this chapter. On the latter, see A Chan, "Can an AI Be an Inventor? Not Yet" (*MIT Technology Review*, 8 January 2020), https://perma.cc/JNU8-EYLJ.

[13] See, for example, *Diamond v Chakrabarty* 447 U.S. 303 (1980); *J.E.M. Ag Supply v. Pioneer Hi-Bred Int'l* (USSC (2001)).

patentable, whereas inventing a device which filters the interference would be a patentable invention.

Inventiveness (and novelty) are judged from the standard of a person skilled in the art (i.e. the "skilled person") standard.[14] The skilled person is a legal fiction of a person who knows everything about a particular field yet is not creative or imaginative. While the standard of the skilled person differs across jurisdictions,[15] Laddie, J. discussed the nature of the skilled (but non-inventive) person in the art in the case of Pfizer Ltd.'s patent:

> This is not a real person. He is a legal creation. He is supposed to offer an objective test .... He is deemed to have looked at and read publicly available documents and to know of public uses in the prior art. He understands all languages and dialects. He never misses the obvious nor stumbles on the inventive. He has no private idiosyncratic preferences or dislikes. He never thinks laterally. He differs from all real people in one or more of these characteristics. A real worker in the field may never look at the piece of prior art – for example he may never look at the contents of a particular public library – or he may be put off because it is in a language he does not know. But the notional addressee is taken to have done so.[16]

AI potentially challenges the standard of inventiveness in three ways. First, many AI systems work by sifting through vast amounts of data to find patterns, which some liken to the process of discovery, which is problematic as it is generally accepted that utilizing something that already exists in nature is a "discovery", and therefore not patentable.[17] Second, as an AI has far greater capacity to analyse vast amounts of data trained with specific data from designated fields of art than any human, such an AI not only will more easily find inventions obvious but, if taken to its logical extreme, it could not only become a skilled person but might also find all inventions obvious.[18] Third, as AI is increasingly employed in research and development (R&D), there is the potential to raise the standard of inventiveness of developers and those skilled in the art. What these potential issues mean is that in order to accommodate AI, there may have to be a re-think of the inventiveness standard – this will be difficult and lead to many unintended consequences. For example, raising the bar for inventiveness

14 In the USA the skilled person is known as "A person having ordinary skill in the art" (PHOSITA).

15 N Khanna and J Gulati, "Knowledge/Skill Standards of a 'Person Skilled in Art': A Concern Less" (2018) 17 *John Marshall Review of Intellectual Property Law* 588.

16 *The Asia File Products Sdn Bhd v. Brilliant Achievement Sdn Bhd & 2 Ors*, MTKL GS No. 05 (IP)-22–47 (2010), citing [2001] FSR 201.

17 For further analysis, see R Yu, "Should an Invention Created by Machine Learning Be Patentable?" (WIPO Public Consultation on AI and IP Policy – Submissions, 15 December 2019), https://perma.cc/AV9W-XPC5.

18 R Abbott, *The Reasonable Robot: Artificial Intelligence and the Law* (Cambridge, Cambridge University Press, 2020), at 93. The concern that the "skilled person" should need to be raised in light of AI or that inventive AI might even represent the skilled person has been raised in recent literature. See R Abbott, "Everything Is Obvious" (2018) 66 *UCLA Law Review* 2.

would ensure information and discoveries are not locked away but may make it harder for ordinary human inventors to acquire a patent.[19]

In addition to the three standards of patentability, a patent application must also provide for sufficient disclosure of the invention to enable a skilled person to reproduce the invention.[20] This is in keeping with the patent system's other goal to promote social and technical advancement and increase public welfare through the disclosure of inventions to the public for the benefit of the public at large. AI-related issues pose a significant challenge to the system in this regard – simply stated, what does one need to disclose when dealing with an AI-generated invention? The answer is not as simple as one might think given that the outcomes of an AI invention might change depending on the input data and/or the algorithms.[21] Additional questions involve unique complexities and will lead to divergences of opinion, such as: must algorithms used by the AI be disclosed as part of a patent application by an AI? Should data used by the AI also be disclosed as well, and if so, how much data? Does the human expertise used to select and curate the data and train the algorithm be disclosed, and if so, to what extent? Requiring strict standards which demand inventors to supply greater detail and precise information may mean inventors simply bypass the patent system in favour of maintaining the invention as a trade secret. This in turn may not be to society's benefit. In short, the difficulties with enablement/disclosure should not be underestimated given the potential size of the data sets involved.[22]

Finally, the Trade-Related Aspects of Intellectual Property Rights (TRIPS) Agreement allows (but does not require) members to create exceptions to patentability, such as inventions "necessary to protect *ordre public* or morality, including to protect human, animal or plant life or health or to avoid serious prejudice to the environment",[23] and diagnostic, therapeutic and surgical methods for the treatment of humans or animals as well as plants and animals other than micro-organisms, and essentially biological processes for the production of plants or animals other than

19 J Wu, "High Patent Quality Standards Have Caused U.S. to Lose Technological Advantages" (IP Watchdog, 8 August 2017), https://perma.cc/T52C-YMSN.

20 See *Biogen v. Medeva* [1997] RPC, at 1.

21 On the issue of explainability, see AD Selbst and S Barocas, "The Intuitive Appeal of Explainable Machines" (2018) 87 *Fordham Law Review* 1085.

22 As a reference, Amazon gathers data on every one of its customers while they use the site including what they buy, what they look at, their shipping addresses and whether they leave reviews/feedback. Amazon's Buyer Fraud Service system collects more than 2,000 real-time and historical data points for each order and uses machine learning algorithms to detect and prevent those with a high probability of being fraudulent. Multiply these by the millions of orders Amazon processes daily and one gets some idea of the amount of data the company collects on a daily basis. See "Amazon: Using Big Data to Understand Customers" (Nernard Marr & Co.), https://perma.cc/7RAV-3RM5; and Amazon, "Amazon.com Buyer Fraud Service Gains Scalability, Cuts Costs in Half Using AWS", https://perma.cc/SDD2-GTEL.

23 TRIPS, Article 27.2.

non-biological and microbiological processes.[24] While these lines may appear straightforward, the reality is not quite so simple and distinctions can be blurred.[25]

Compounding the issue is the fact that exceptions from patentability are defined at the regional and national level. In regard to AI, this raises issues involving software and business methods. These forms of invention are excluded from patentability in some nations, meaning that software or computer program-related inventions may be patentable in one jurisdiction but not in another.[26] The result of disunity could be more forum shopping whereby organizations, inventors or creators actively seek jurisdictions whose laws are more favourably disposed to protecting their inventions or creations, in this case created or generated by AI. Moreover, this connects to the issue of broader societal benefits resulting from inventions; if AI applications or algorithms are excluded from patentability, developers and organizations would essentially have no choice but to keep such AI as a trade secret, thereby undermining the goal of the patent system to disseminate technical knowledge.

To date, applications for patent protection when the inventor is named as an AI system have been rejected. For instance, the UK Intellectual Property Office (UKIPO), European Patent Office (EPO) and US Patent and Trademark Office (USPTO) all recently denied applications for patents that named an AI, called DABUS, as the inventor in December 2019, January 2020 and April 2020, respectively. These applications, for a warning light and food container, were made on behalf of Stephen Thaler, CEO of Imagination Engines, by the Artificial Inventor Project.[27] In rejecting the application, the UKIPO hearing officer decided that the UK Patents Act 1977 requires an invention by a natural person.[28] The EPO likewise rejected the applications on procedural grounds as an application for a European patent must designate an inventor and "state the family name, given names and full address of the inventor". In so holding, the EPO found this requirement was consistent with a "clear legislative understanding that the inventor is a natural person" and consistent with EPO and national decisions.[29] Similarly, the USPTO held that the US patent statutes preclude interpretation of "inventor" to cover

[24] Ibid., at Article 27.3. Members must, however, provide for the protection of plant varieties either by patents or by an effective sui generis system or by any combination thereof.

[25] Compare, for instance, the Canadian Supreme Court decisions in *Harvard v. Canada* [2002 SCC 76] and *Monsanto Canada Inc. v. Schmeiser* [2004] 1 S.C.R. 902, 2004 SCC 34.

[26] For example, Art. 52 of the European Patent Convention states that computer programs are not patentable per se, but in the USA no specific exclusion of software from patentable subject matter exists.

[27] As noted earlier, Stephen Thaler claims that the AI created the inventions autonomously and without human intervention.

[28] See Intellectual Property Office, BL O/741/19, 4 December 2019, https://perma.cc/HK2V-6XFB.

[29] See Grounds for the EPO decision of 27 January 2020 on EP 18 275 163, https://perma.cc/T3NS-S2GV; Grounds for the EPO decision of 27 January 2020 on EP 18 275 174, https://perma.cc/6KTW-PL3C ("The designation of an inventor is mandatory as it bears a series of legal consequences, notably to ensure that the designated inventor is the legitimate one and that he or she can benefit from rights linked to this status. To exercise these rights, the inventor must have a legal personality that AI systems or machines do not enjoy").

machines because "the plain reading" of words such as "whoever", "himself", "herself" and "individual", as well as the requirement that an inventor executes an oath, is as a "person". The USPTO also cited US case law which holds that inventors cannot be states or corporations.[30]

This leaves trade secrets as the more likely avenue for protection of AI inventions. Trade secrets protect information that is secret, of commercial value, imparted in a situation of confidentiality and subject to reasonable efforts to protect its secrecy. In some ways, trade secrets better suit the companies which develop AI as such inventions do not require registration and can last indefinitely, provided they are kept secret.[31] Moreover, given the fast pace of development and difficulty in reverse engineering AI systems, companies are in fact increasingly relying on trade secrets to protect investments and developments in AI. AI companies also rely on trade secrets to protect their valuable algorithms given their inability to acquire patent protection for algorithms and reluctance to disclose the algorithm in a patent application,[32] and because copyright law protects expression and not the underlying idea behind an algorithm, effectively rendering copyright unsuitable for protecting the functional aspects of algorithms.[33]

While one cannot register a trade secret – doing so would itself alert others to its presence and provide for public disclosure – there are systems in place to prove the existence of a trade secret without disclosing the secret. An example of this is WIPO Proof, which provides tamper-proof evidence of the existence of a trade secret by providing a data- and time-stamped digital fingerprint of a digital file containing the trade secret and a repository of these fingerprints (which WIPO refers to as tokens).[34]

B *Copyright*

The TRIPS Agreement (Article 9.2) states that copyright attaches to original works which are "expressions and not to ideas, procedures, methods of operation or

30 The USPTO also noted this was consistent with the approach to inventorship in the USPTO's Manual of Patent Examining Procedure. See M Hervey, "USPTO Denies Patent Application for Invention by AI" (Gowling WLG, 4 May 2020), https://perma.cc/96XJ-S4HW.

31 For background, see JC Frome, "Machines as the New Oompa-Loompas: Trade Secrecy, the Cloud, Machine Learning, and Automation" (2019) 94 *New York University Law Review* 706.

32 Companies go to great lengths to protect algorithms, not only with physical security and legal means such as non-disclosure agreements but also with technological methods – for example, frequent changes to algorithms. In 2018 Google reportedly made 3,234 changes to its search algorithms (see "Google Algorithm Update History" (Moz), https://perma.cc/J6Y5-H2DB). There are, however, some efforts underway to erode companies' reliance on trade secrets to protect, for example, algorithms. For example, at the time of writing, India proposed rules to require tech companies like Google, Amazon and Facebook to provide source code and algorithms. See R Montti, "Google Might Have to Give Algorithm Access to India" (*Search Engine Journal*, 6 July 2020), https://perma.cc/ZJ53-87KH.

33 This is often referred to as the idea–expression distinction (or dichotomy) which limits the scope of copyright protection by differentiating an idea from the expression or manifestation of that idea. Unlike patents, which may confer proprietary rights in relation to general ideas and concepts per se when construed as methods, copyright does not confer such rights.

34 "WIPO PROOF – Trusted Digital Evidence" (WIPO), https://perma.cc/5HDF-GSRJ.

mathematical concepts as such." In the context of software, this makes clear that expressions are protected, whereas the underlying ideas in the software or computer programs – that is, the AI algorithms and other processes – would not be eligible for protection.

Originality (which is different from the novelty standard in patent law which requires that the invention not be part of the prior art) – the aspect of a created or invented work that makes it new or novel, and thereby distinguishes it from reproductions, clones, forgeries or derivative works[35] – remains a basic prerequisite in copyright law.[36] The question in regards to our inquiry is whether an AI-generated work can be regarded as original. The Berne Convention references "authors",[37] which may not be determinative but perhaps lends itself to the conclusion that there must be a human involved in the process. Indeed, courts in several countries have interpreted originality as requiring a fairly significant degree of human ingenuity. For instance, in the famous case of *Naruto v. Slater*, the 9th Circuit Court in the USA held that "[t]o qualify as a work of 'authorship' a work must be created by a human being".[38] In that case, it was not enough for a photographer to place cameras in strategic locations and tempt the animals to pick up the camera and take pictures. Likewise, in *Acohs Pty Ltd v. Ucorp Pty Ltd* the Full Federal Court of Australia found that data sheets created by a computer program (a simple data-collecting mechanism) were not subject to copyright because there was not a sufficiently involved human author.[39]

These judgments indicate that copyright over computer programs and software will generally vest with whoever created the source code of that software. Likewise, content generated by "AI-like" software which performs functions based on programmed rules but without exhibiting true intelligence or originality, for example a "smart-home" device that can dim lights or check the weather forecast on command, would likely remain the copyright of the author of the program's code or the person making the input. The same would likely apply for programs used as part of an artistic or technical process but which are ultimately controlled by human choices.

35 "Originality in Copyright" (US Legal), https://perma.cc/4NH7-XD9W.

36 J Dratler and SM McJohn, *Intellectual Property Law: Commercial, Creative and Industrial Property* (vol. 1, New York, Law Journal Press, 2006), at 5–71.

37 The Berne Convention deals with the protection of works and the rights of their authors. Its first paragraph states: "The countries of the Union, being equally animated by the desire to protect, in as effective and uniform a manner as possible, the rights of authors in their literary and artistic works." See "Berne Convention (1971 Paris Act plus Appendix), Berne Convention for the Protection of Literary and Artistic Works", https://perma.cc/6WWA-8Q9J.

38 *Naruto v. Slater*, No. 16–15469 (9th Cir. 2018), where the US 9th Circuit Court affirmed the district court's dismissal of copyright infringement claims brought by the People for the Ethical Treatment of Animals (PETA), which filed suit as a friend to Naruto the crested black macaque, alleging copyright infringement over selfies he took on a wildlife photographer's unattended camera.

39 *Acohs Pty Ltd v. Ucorp Pty Ltd* (2012) 201 FCR 173 (Full Federal Court).

That being the case, while the creator of the AI program would retain copyright over original source code, that individual may have no rights to original work created by the software that they did not envision or program. Thus, for instance, while the source code of an AI program designed to create original music or generate business recommendations would be subject to copyright, the decisions and work generated by that AI may not be copyrightable if there is not a sufficient level of human input. The more distant the human involvement from the ultimate original work (as the AI continues to evolve), the less likely it would be that copyright would attach to the individual.

Whereas the US Copyright Office and others apply a "human authorship policy" that prohibits copyright protection of works that are not generated by a human author,[40] not all jurisdictions concur with this interpretation. For instance, UK law acknowledges the possibility that works could be "computer-generated"[41] and provides that the author of a computer-generated work is deemed to be the person "by whom the arrangements necessary for the creation of the work are undertaken".[42] Interestingly, China may also be heading towards protection for AI as a court decision in Guangzhou in January 2020 awarded RMB1500 in damages for infringing a financial article written by Tencent's robot Dreamwriter without authorization: "the article's form of expression conforms to the requirements of written work and the content showed the selection, analysis and judgment of relevant stock market information and data … the article's structure was reasonable, the logic was clear and it had a certain originality".[43] What remains unclear in jurisdictions which hold that AI-generated work can enjoy copyright protection is, among other things, whether such protection extends to other related copyright rights such as sound recordings, broadcasts, performances or adaptations. This is an important question, but as of yet undecided and untested.

Yet another interesting question is whether copyright law ought to be used to regulate deep fakes – the generation of simulated likenesses of persons and their attributes, such as their appearance or voice.[44] Deep fakes raise complicated copyright questions such as whether deep fakes created by information that may be copyright protected should benefit from copyright, and if they should, to whom the copyright in the deep fake should belong; and whether the person whose likenesses

40 R Abbott, "The Artificial Inventor Project" (*WIPO Magazine*, December 2019), https://perma.cc/AZR4-N86Y.

41 Defined as "generated by computer in circumstances such that there is no human author of the work" (Copyright Designs and Patents Act 1988 (UK) Sec. 178).

42 Copyright Designs and Patents Act 1988 (UK) Sec. 9(3).

43 See A Guadamuz, "Impact of Artificial Intelligence on IP Policy", https://perma.cc/7RPS-GEW9.

44 Such systems have improved dramatically in the last few years. See A Liszewski, "Disney's Developed Movie-Quality Face-Swapping Technology That Promises to Change Filmmaking" (Gizmodo, 29 June 2020), https://gizmodo.com/disneys-developed-movie-quality-face-swapping-technolog-1844202003.

and performances are used in the deep fake ought to receive compensation, and if so, how this could be done.

More fundamentally, other questions involving the term of protection and liability of the copyright owner will also need to be addressed. In terms of the former, many copyright laws provide specific periods of time during which the work and the rights arising thereof are legally protected that are usually determined in reference to the lifetime of the work's author, and exceptionally the work's first publication or transmission. The life of the author cannot be used when AI is the author, given the theoretically indefinite lifespan of the system,[45] but consensus has not yet emerged on the appropriate length of protection. In regards to liability, unlike an original work written by a person, some AI systems store their information in a form that cannot easily be read by humans or reverse engineered. Given this, it may be impossible to discover why a system made a particular decision or produced a particular output. In such cases, liability will likely attach to the person or entity that controls or directs the actions of the AI. This is difficult, however, and may not always be apparent where one party has created the AI and another has decided what data to put into it or what questions to ask it. In the interim, the practical reality is that business entities will need to ensure that there are contractual indemnities in place for any actions of the AI that infringe copyright work.[46]

C *Intellectual Property in the Data*

A thorough discussion of AI and IP cannot ignore the important issue of data, as there may be IP in the data and there certainly is IP in the systems that manage and handle data. Developers rely on vast troves of data in the initial training of AI systems as well as for personalization, product improvement or localization (i.e. adapting AI systems to work in a variety of different local conditions). Considerable resources must be spent finding suitable training data, correcting training errors or ensuring the data has not been corrupted (for example, by a cyberattack).

Yet IP protections for data are limited save for some sui generis legislation and the limited protection offered by copyright law for databases as collections.[47] In the USA, for example, databases may be protected by copyright law not as such but as compilations which are defined as a "collection and assembling of preexisting

45 G Gurkaynak et al., "Questions of Intellectual Property in the Artificial Intelligence Realm" (2018) 3 *The Robotics Law Journal* 9.

46 Similarly, businesses will also need to ensure they know the source of the data used in the AI system to avoid infringing third parties' IP rights or misusing confidential information.

47 Databases may be protected by copyright and under sui generis legislation; see, for example, the EU Database Directive which defines a database as "a collection of works, data or other independent materials arranged in a systematic or methodical way and capable of being individually accessed by electronic or other means". The definition of database is sufficiently wide to include collections of material on the website. However, use of data by an AI has yet to be judicially tested and sui generis database rights are territorial. See G Smith, *Internet Law and Regulation* (5th ed., London, Sweet & Maxwell, 2020), at 2–110.

materials or of data that are selected in such a way that the resulting work as a whole constitutes an original work of authorship".[48] Such protection is of limited value, however, as the US Supreme Court held that a compilation of facts is copyrightable *only* if the selection or arrangement "possesses at least some minimal degree of creativity".[49] Pre-existing materials or data included in the database therefore may be protected by copyright, or may be unprotectable facts or ideas.[50] In contrast, Europe grants copyright protection to databases which, as such, by reason of the selection or arrangement of their contents, constitute the "author's own intellectual creation". However, additional sui generis protection afforded under the Database Directive[51] is granted to reward the substantial investment of the database maker in creating the database and prevent free-riding on somebody else's investment in creating the database, and exists in parallel to the copyright protection on the structure of the database.[52]

That there is weak IP protection for data and no system of property rights raises numerous questions regarding the equity of current setups among AI companies that take freely provided data from individuals, then use this data to create products that those same individuals are charged to use.[53] This situation is analogous to the one lesser-developed countries experienced decades ago when they complained that developed countries had appropriated their traditional knowledge (TK)[54] without adequate compensation, thereby exacerbating the wealth gap between developed and developing countries.[55] TK does not enjoy IP protection, though sui generis legislation in some countries does grant protection. But unlike the international north–south divide that characterized the TK debates decades ago, the current debate on remuneration to data providers is both international and intra-national

48 17. U.S.C. § 101.

49 *Feist Publications, Inc. v. Rural Telephone Service Co.*, 499 U.S. 340 (1991).

50 A fundamental principle of intellectual property law is that no one should be given a monopoly on facts, ideas or other building blocks of knowledge, thought or communication. See JE Cohen and WM Martin, "Intellectual Property Rights in Data", in DJ Richards, BR Allenby and WD Compton (eds), *Information Systems and the Environment* (Washington, DC, National Academy Press, 2001), at 51.

51 Directive 96/9/EC of the European Parliament and of the Council of 11 March 1996 on the legal protection of databases.

52 J Debussche and J César, "Big Data and Issues and Opportunities: Intellectual Property Rights" (Bird & Bird, March 2019), https://perma.cc/8S5Z-NVMQ.

53 A Yang, "Make Tech Companies Pay You for Your Data" (*Los Angeles Times*, 27 June 2020), https://perma.cc/H7MD-MS7C.

54 According to WIPO, TK is a living body of knowledge passed on from generation to generation within a community. It often forms part of a people's cultural and spiritual identity. See "Traditional Knowledge", https://perma.cc/69VC-VHMX.

55 A comprehensive review of IP and TK is beyond the scope of this chapter, but for additional information see T Cottier and M Panizzon, "Legal Perspectives on Traditional Knowledge: The Case for Intellectual Property Protection" (2004) 7 *Journal of International Economic Law* 371; G Dutfield, "Protecting Traditional Knowledge: Pathways to the Future" (2006) ICTSD Issue Paper No. 16; and S Ragavan, "Protection of Traditional Knowledge" (2001) 2 *Minnesota Intellectual Property Review* 1.

(though the challenge now could be characterized as a struggle between the tech giants who have both the data and the technological infrastructure and those companies who do not possess such assets).

Granting property rights in the data raises a host of challenging issues, which are raised but not analysed here, including adequate compensation for use, restriction on use (and whether prevention of data transfer without compensation falls afoul of obligations undertaken in free trade agreements) and whether and the extent to which property rights in data hinder innovation. Another IP-related aspect to data worth considering is that there is IP in the form of know-how (or other trade secrets) in the use of data for AI. Because of the growing liability concerns and other issues associated with faulty AI systems,[56] organizations employing AI systems will need to become more careful about the implementations of such systems, and will need to ensure the quality of the data used to train and update such systems to ensure that the data is appropriate for the task at hand, that it was not tampered with and that it is accurate (the last point is a problem given that the sources of data companies rely upon for, say, digital marketing may be suspect).[57] Thus there is IP in the curation of data – to ensure the data has been validated, is appropriate for the purpose at hand and has not been tampered with – as well as IP in the creation of AI applications and deployment of AI technologies (that may be protected by IP rights or block their use by others' IP rights). The importance of these IP-related data issues will only grow in relevance, yet current levels of protection are limited and it is uncertain whether greater levels of protection would lead to clearer outcomes or enhanced levels of innovation.

D *The Profound Question*

IP refers to creations of the mind[58] used in commerce, and the IP system is designed to encourage creation and invention and reward creators and inventors through IP rights. As per Stephen Thaler's claim that an AI is capable of autonomously creating a patentable invention (DABUS) without any human intervention, the most fundamental question which requires resolution is whether AI's lack of corporeal

[56] For example, a faulty facial recognition match led to a man's arrest for a crime he did not commit. K Hill, "Wrongfully Accused by an Algorithm" (*New York Times*, 25 June 2020), https://perma.cc/23BC-87T3.

[57] For example, much of the data used by digital marketers to profile users was actually created by AI bots and not human users. See A Fou, "Are Marketers Wasting Money on Adtech Myths?" (*Forbes*, 4 June 2020), https://perma.cc/4JA9-MEDB.

[58] Interestingly, the question of what constitutes a "mind" has not arisen in recent discussions of AI and IP. Does "mind" refer to a single monolithic mind which characterizes human and most AI systems, a symbiosis of human minds and AI, a hive mind or swarm intelligence? This is beyond the ambit of this chapter, but for more information see L Rosenberg, "The Rise of the Human Hive Mind, Disruption Hub" (Disruption Hub, 28 June 2017), https://perma.cc/8L72-5CTL; and G Beni and J Wang, "Swarm Intelligence in Cellular Robotic Systems", in P Dario, G Sandini and P Aebischer (eds), *Robots and Biological Systems: Towards a New Bionics?* (Berlin, Springer, 1993), at 703–712.

existence is sufficient to deny it IP rights. This conundrum forces us to confront a related question – is the IP system, which until now has been intimately associated with the human creative and inventive spirit with its respect and reward for the encouragement of human innovation and creativity – more about advancing creative and technological progress or upholding human rights?

Dr Francis Gurry, immediate past Director General of WIPO, noted that "intellectual property is key to economic development",[59] and studies have shown that IP rights benefit developing as well as developed nations.[60] There have always been developmental and commercial aspects to IP, even with the fundamental objective of the patent system being to encourage investment of human and financial resources and risk taking in generating inventions that may positively contribute to the welfare of a society, promote creations, distinguish the origin of goods and services and prevent consumer confusion.[61] Even national constitutions promote IP; for example, the American Constitution's Patent and Copyright Clause states that "[The Congress shall have power] to promote the progress of science and useful arts, by securing for limited times to authors and inventors the exclusive right to their respective writings and discoveries";[62] AI could undoubtedly increase the pace of innovation and creation.

There is potential benefit to the signalling value of protecting the IP of AI-generated creations and inventions, including that jurisdictions which permit the registration of IP rights to an AI for its inventions or creations would be seen as pro-innovation and perhaps attract more development, investment and employment opportunities. Likewise, a lack of IP protection for AI-generated inventions might discourage companies from investing in AI technologies and prevent breakthroughs in important areas like drug discovery.[63]

What is certain is that a lack of protection will lead to greater use of trade secrets, which could serve to further retard innovation and knowledge dissemination. While limiting the use of trade secrecy could potentially mitigate this potential problem, attempts to do so could violate obligations undertaken in free trade agreements[64] and

59 "Intellectual Property Key to Economic Development" (Zimbabwe Situation, 5 November 2019), https://perma.cc/M3QT-CXY5.

60 JM Barnett, "Patent Tigers: The New Geography of Global Innovation" (2017) 2 *Criterion Journal on Innovation* 429. For a more nuanced view, see B Mercurio, "Reconceptualising the Debate on Intellectual Property Rights and Economic Development" (2010) 3 *The Law and Development Review* 65.

61 WIPO Secretariat, note 3 above.

62 US Constitution, Article I Section 8, Clause 8.

63 See Chan, note 12 above.

64 The Intellectual Property Chapter of the recently negotiated United States-Mexico-Canada Agreement (USMCA), also referred to as the "new NAFTA", contains the most comprehensive treatment of trade secrets in any free trade agreement, with provisions against the misappropriation of trade secrets, the possibility for criminal and civil procedures, penalties and remedies, prohibitions against impeding licensing of trade secrets, judicial procedures to prevent disclosure of trade secrets during the litigation process and penalties against government officials for the unauthorized disclosure of trade secrets. See USMCA, Section I (Article 20.69–20.77).

would definitely meet fierce resistance by tech giants and other AI companies dependent on the protection of confidential algorithms and other information for business pursuits. Moreover, countries considering weakening trade secrecy laws would do well to remember India's past attempt to emasculate trade secrecy – when India attempted to force Coca-Cola to release its secret recipe under its Foreign Exchange Regulation Act of 1973, Coca-Cola refused and simply left the country.[65]

But the question remains unanswered whether prioritizing innovation and creation over people is fair or wise. As AI continues to increase in sophistication, society may be unwilling to sacrifice individual rights at the altar of innovation. Industry promises to protect the rights of marginalized groups and individuals, but such promises often ultimately ring hollow as history has shown that such self-regulation can be woefully inadequate at protecting people, particularly those in marginalized communities who are frequently targeted by manipulation campaigns.[66] Furthermore, in times of global economic crisis the priority may be coping with the significant socio-economic challenges brought about by the COVID-19 health crisis.[67]

In sum, there are countless legal, technical and policy arguments for and against ownership of IP by an AI in the areas of patents, copyrights, design rights and trade secrets, as well as questions regarding property rights in the data or whether to establish a sui generis system for original content, and posing one question in one area can generate many others elsewhere. At one level, there is no practical need to let an AI become an IP holder. After all, one could simply name a human in an application the way some companies designate their chief engineer in patent applications, even though the actual inventors were other employees; or it has been suggested that the system could treat AI as we would treat a pet, arguing that pets have intelligence and a certain level of autonomy but not legal personhood. Similarly, the AI operator legitimately controls, confines and possesses the AI during conception and thus ownership of the AI invention should be held by the AI operator, their employer (work-of-hire) or successor.[68] While the latter approach allows for easy identification of the origin of the invention and a true entity entitled to the exclusive right, it does not suffer from problems of wrongful credibility (i.e. truthfully showing the involvement of an AI, and avoiding divisive discussions of

65 See K Obermeier, "When India Kicked Out Coca-Cola, Local Sodas Thrived, Some Still Reign Today" (*Atlas Obscura*, 15 February 2019), https://perma.cc/ESM8-R5A4. Curiously, India may be attempting to do so again by requiring foreign tech companies to disclose their algorithms. See R Montti, "Google Might Have to Give Algorithm Access to India" (*Search Engine Journal*, 6 July 2020), https://perma.cc/DJ4V-NF5B.

66 AccessNow, "Human Rights in the Age of Artificial Intelligence" (2018), https://perma.cc/MC4L-CMJD.

67 The economic situation in Spain, for example, has deteriorated to the point that the country has already taken steps to implement universal basic income. See K Ng, "Spain Approves National Minimum Income Scheme" (*Independent*, 29 May 2020), https://perma.cc/Y82L-HP8F.

68 ZW Lin, "Finding a Way Forward: Analyzing Approaches to Artificial Intelligence Inventorship" (*IP Watchdog*, 20 June 2020), https://perma.cc/Q9XE-K7RK.

legal personhood[69]). This model, however, may not work or may seem unfair where human intervention is minimal.

The final challenge to address is how the question of IP rights affects business investment. Some have claimed that the USA's more permissive software patenting regime than Europe is a primary reason why more software development took place in America.[70] This may be overblown, as the USA did not see an outflow of investment, innovation or talent following the effective raising of standards after the US Supreme Court's decision in *Alice Corp. v. CLS Bank International*, where the court avoided giving a clear definition of the expression "software patent" and held that "merely requiring generic computer implementation fails to transform [an] abstract idea into a patent-eligible invention".[71] Similarly, the 2018 report on the impact of the Database Directive[72] made no mention of any great new flows of technological investment into the European Union as a result of the Directive.

IV CONCLUSION

How the IP system deals with AI is far more complicated and involved than it might initially appear because there are many difficult matters that are at once esoteric and, in some cases, profoundly consequential, plus a mixture of technical, legal, data-related, social and societal issues to juggle. Even the question of how to deal with disclosure in a patent application involving an AI-generated invention is complex – and that is only one of many such problems. AI and IP bring together many technological, legal, data and societal policy questions in a complex, messy convergence that is not easy to untangle. In short, AI makes for an uneasy fit with the existing structures and norms of the IP regime. Thus, developers of AI would be well advised to secure the benefits of their investment and mitigate IP risks associated with AI by contract. Developers would be well advised to select an appropriate jurisdiction for the development of AI, contractually define such matters as the ownership of IP and inventions akin to IP, and assign and break down all foreseeable risks created by AI via insurance clauses or other mechanisms.

69 This is something the European Union discovered when it examined the issue of legal personality for robots. See J Delcker, "Europe Divided Over Robot 'Personhood'" (*Politico*, 13 April 2018), https://perma.cc/Y2DA-JHEC.

70 See "Which Countries Allow Software Patents?" (Patsnap, 25 January 2017), https://perma.cc/K6L3-3AVB; M Guntersdorfer, "Software Patent Law: United States and Europe Compared", https://perma.cc/X9C3-ZNYD; and E Robert Yoches et al., "How Will Patent Reform Affect the Software and Internet Industries?" (2011), https://perma.cc/B2FF-RJSY.

71 *Alice Corp. v. CLS Bank International*, 573 U.S. 208 (2014). In 2019 the USPTO issued new guidelines to applicants with software-related patent applications that increased the burden on applicants to provide a more robust disclosure for computer-related claims. See further M Henry-Nickie, K Frimpong, HS Friday, "Trends in the Information Technology Sector" (Brookings Institute, 29 March 2019), https://perma.cc/8HG8-79A9.

72 European Commission, Evaluation of Directive 96/9/EC on the legal protection of databases, Brussels 25.4.2018.

8

Are Digital Trade Disputes "Trade Disputes"?

Yuka Fukunaga

I INTRODUCTION

Since the issuance of a joint statement in January 2019, eighty-six World Trade Organization (WTO) members have confirmed their intention to commence WTO negotiations on trade-related aspects of electronic commerce. Additionally, several have submitted concept papers and text proposals, and many more have engaged in exploratory discussions on a wide range of issues surrounding electronic commerce. In December 2020, the consolidated negotiating text was circulated to the participating members. There is a growing expectation that a new Agreement on Trade-Related Aspects of Electronic Commerce (TREC Agreement) that will be either multilateral or plurilateral in nature will be adopted in the not-so-distant future.[1]

One key question that has been left out in the process of negotiating the TREC Agreement is how disputes concerning electronic commerce should be settled. The assumption may be that the rules and procedures of the WTO Dispute Settlement Understanding (DSU) apply to disputes under the TREC Agreement.[2] However, the validity of this assumption is questionable, because disputes arising under the proposed TREC Agreement would differ from conventional trade disputes, as discussed in this chapter. As a result, special or additional dispute settlement procedures must be developed to properly settle disputes under the TREC Agreement.

This chapter highlights key differences between conventional trade disputes and their digital counterparts and proposes special or additional dispute settlement rules and procedures that may be incorporated in the TREC Agreement. For the sake of convenience, this chapter uses the term "digital trade disputes" to represent disputes that would likely arise under the TREC Agreement. It does not seek to define the term "digital trade," which may include not only trade in digital products but also

[1] Compare SA Aaronson and P Leblond, "Another Digital Divide: The Rise of Data Realms and Its Implications for the WTO" (2018) 21 *Journal of International Economic Law* 245, at 251–253, 270–271.

[2] Compare M Burri, "The Governance of Data and Data Flows in Trade Agreements: The Pitfalls of Legal Adaptation Symposium – Future-Proofing Law: From RDNA to Robots" (2017) 51 *UC Davis Law Review* 65, at 95–97.

digitally enabled trade in goods and services.[3] Nor does it discuss substantive rules to be included in the TREC Agreement.[4] Instead, this chapter infers the nature of digital trade disputes arising under the TREC Agreement by examining rules on digital trade provided in recently concluded regional trade agreements (RTAs); that is, the United States-Mexico-Canada Agreement (USMCA), the Trans-Pacific Partnership (TPP) Agreement, as incorporated in the Comprehensive and Progressive Trans-Pacific Partnership (CPTPP) Agreement, and the Japan-European Union Economic Partnership Agreement (JEEPA).[5] This chapter argues that differences in the nature of conventional trade rules under the WTO agreements and digital trade rules under the TREC Agreement,[6] as well as their underlying techno-social discrepancies, will result in differences in the nature of disputes arising under these rules.

More specifically, this chapter examines two key differences between conventional trade disputes and digital trade disputes. The first difference is the significant diversity of stakeholders in digital vis-à-vis conventional trade disputes. A conventional trade dispute is typically brought by an exporting WTO member against an importing WTO member when businesses of the former complain about trade practices of the latter. While a digital trade dispute may arise under similar situations, it often takes more diverse forms involving various stakeholders. For

[3] JL González and M-A Jouanjean, "Digital Trade: Developing a Framework for Analysis" (2017) OECD Trade Policy Papers No. 205, at 12–18. In addition, digital trade takes various modes. For example, Ciuriak and Ptashkina categorize activities that fall within the scope of e-commerce or digital trade into five different modes. D Ciuriak and M Ptashkina, "The Digital Transformation and the Transformation of International Trade" (2018), https://perma.cc/WMF3-L6DP, at 5–8. In the WTO work programme on electronic commerce, "electronic commerce" is defined as "exclusively for the purposes of the work programme, and without prejudice to its outcome," as the "production, distribution, marketing, sale or delivery of goods and services by electronic means." WTO, *Work Programme on Electronic Commerce: Adopted by the General Council on 25 September 1998*, WT/L/274 (30 September 1998), at para. 1.3.

[4] The WTO members discussing the TREC Agreement do not share the idea of what substantive rules should be included in the TREC Agreement. While some African countries prefer to limit the scope to what has been dealt with under the WTO e-commerce working group, others seek to go further. SA Aaronson, "Data Is Different: Why the World Needs a New Approach to Governing Cross-Border Data Flows" (2018) CIGI Paper No. 197, at 8. Furthermore, while developed countries, such as the United States and the European Union, have moved to access to cross-border flows of data, China takes a very different approach by restricting the free flow of data. H Gao, "Digital or Trade? The Contrasting Approaches of China and US to Digital Trade" (2018) 21 *Journal of International Economic Law* 297.

[5] Although digital trade rules under these RTAs are diverse, there are some common elements that indicate the common nature of digital trade disputes arising under the rules. For a quantitative analysis of digital trade provisions in preferential trade agreements, see M Burri and R Polanco, "Digital Trade Provisions in Preferential Trade Agreements: Introducing a New Dataset" (2020) 23 *Journal of International Economic Law* 187. For a term-frequency analysis of digital trade provisions in RTAs, see I Willemyns, "Agreement Forthcoming? A Comparison of EU, US, and Chinese RTAs in Times of Plurilateral E-Commerce Negotiations" (2020) 23 *Journal of International Economic Law* 221.

[6] Compare T Streinz, "Digital Megaregulation Uncontested? TPP's Model for the Global Digital Economy", in B Kingsbury et al. (eds), *Megaregulation Contested: Global Economic Ordering After TPP* (Oxford, Oxford University Press, 2019), at 324–329.

example, a business entity may challenge a domestic regulation of its own government, or consumers may raise concerns with an Internet giant over data privacy issues. This chapter argues that these various stakeholders should be allowed to participate in digital trade dispute settlement mechanisms made available under the TREC Agreement.

The second difference arises from the unique nature of the balance between trade and non-trade values. Under conventional trade rules, exceptions – such as Article XX of the General Agreement on Tariffs and Trade (GATT) – are incorporated to ensure a balance between WTO members' obligations to not restrict trade and right to regulate in order to achieve legitimate non-trade policy objectives. Therefore, WTO members are entitled to adopt otherwise inconsistent measures for legitimate policy objectives, such as the protection of human life and health or the preservation of the environment, and subsequently applied in accordance with certain conditions. Meanwhile, under the TREC Agreement, the protection of certain non-trade values, such as privacy protection, may be regarded as among the principal objectives of the Agreement and would therefore be fashioned as an obligation rather than an exception. In other words, a contracting party to the Agreement would be *required* to take trade-restrictive measures to protect non-trade values. Thus, a balance between the obligation to promote digital trade and the obligation to restrict it to protect non-trade values would need to be struck under the TREC Agreement. This chapter argues that the unique nature of the balance between trade and non-trade values under the TREC Agreement would require different weighing and balancing exercises between trade and non-trade values in digital trade dispute settlements.

With these differences in mind, this chapter then considers appropriate dispute settlement mechanisms to resolve digital trade disputes. More specifically, it discusses what special or additional dispute settlement rules and procedures should be incorporated into the TREC Agreement to fill those gaps in the existing DSU with regard to the handling of digital trade disputes.

II DIGITAL TRADE DISPUTES UNDER THE EXISTING WORLD TRADE ORGANIZATION DISPUTE SETTLEMENT PROCEDURES

Before exploring the key differences between conventional trade disputes and digital trade disputes, this section briefly reviews whether existing WTO dispute settlement procedures can properly resolve digital trade disputes in accordance with the existing rules of the WTO.

Although the Internet was almost non-existent when the WTO agreements were drafted, some of the WTO rules are applicable to digital trade, and disputes may arise regarding whether certain measures to restrict digital trade are inconsistent with these rules.[7] For example, a WTO member may claim that another WTO

7 J Meltzer, "Governing Digital Trade" (2019) 18(S1) *World Trade Review* s23, at s37–s46.

member's restrictions to cross-border transfers of personal data are inconsistent with its market access and national treatment commitments under the General Agreement on Trade in Services (GATS). In response, the respondent member may argue that even if they are inconsistent with its commitments, its measures are justified under paragraph (a) or (c) of Article XIV of GATS.[8]

Some issues related to the consistency and justifiability of digital trade measures under the GATS have been raised in *US – Gambling*. In this case, the panel and the Appellate Body first reviewed whether the United States' total prohibition of the cross-border supply of gambling and betting services was inconsistent with its obligations under Article XVI:1 and Article XVI:2(a) and (c) of the GATS. Having found the United States in violation of these obligations, they next examined whether the measure was justified under Article XIV(a) or (c) of the GATS. The Appellate Body found that although the challenged measures were "necessary to protect public morals or to maintain public order" relevant to paragraph (a) of Article XIV, they were not justified, because they did not meet the conditions under the chapeau of Article XIV.[9]

The findings in *US – Gambling* appear to suggest that some digital trade disputes can be handled under the existing rules and exceptions in the relevant dispute settlement procedures, although there may be difficulties in applying the conventional trade rules to digital trade disputes.[10] In some respects, the conventional trade rules simplify the settlement of a digital trade dispute involving the protection of other legitimate objectives into a matter involving the balance between members' rights to liberalize trade and members' rights to regulate non-trade issues. The mandate for panels and the Appellate Body is to determine, by the weighing and balancing of relevant factors, the counterpoise, where relevant legitimate objectives are protected without overly interfering with trade.[11]

However, digital trade disputes will likely raise far more complicated matters of balance involving multiple stakeholders with diverse policy objectives, especially if the TREC Agreement seeks to provide comprehensive rules on digital trade governance, as do recently concluded RTAs. The diversity of stakeholders and the complexity of the balance between trade and non-trade values under the TREC

[8] N Mishra, "Privacy, Cyber Security, and GATS Article XIV: A New Frontier for Trade and Internet Regulation?" (2019) *World Trade Review* 1, at 9–20; A Mattoo and J Meltzer, "International Data Flows and Privacy: The Conflict and Its Resolution" (2018) 21 *Journal of International Economic Law* 769, at 780–782.

[9] Appellate Body Report, *United States – Measures Affecting the Cross-Border Supply of Gambling and Betting Services*, WT/DS285/AB/R, 7 April 2005.

[10] First, there are difficulties in determining which rules should be applied to digital trade. Restrictions to flows of data may be subject to either the GATT or the GATS depending on whether to characterize data as goods or services. N Sen, "Understanding the Role of the WTO in International Data Flows: Taking the Liberalization or the Regulatory Autonomy Path?" (2018) 21 *Journal of International Economic Law* 323, at 327–331. Moreover, data flows may not be properly categorized into a single mode of transaction and a single classification under the GATS classification system. Ibid., at 331–335.

[11] Ibid., at para. 310.

Agreement would render the mandates of panels and the Appellate Body extremely difficult, if not impossible.

III STAKEHOLDERS

In both conventional trade in goods and services and in digital trade, the direct economic beneficiaries are private parties, such as businesses and consumers. However, their legal status will likely differ under conventional trade rules in the WTO agreements versus digital trade rules in the proposed TREC Agreement.

Under conventional WTO rules, the primary stakeholders are the member governments, in the sense that these rules principally establish the rights and obligations of the members. Violations of the rules result in disputes between member governments, and such disputes can be properly settled through intergovernmental WTO dispute settlement procedures.

Under the TREC Agreement, rules pertaining to the rights and obligations of private entities would be equally important as those of the governments of the contracting parties, as established in this section. As a result, disputes under the TREC Agreement would arise between various stakeholders, and their settlement would require the involvement not only of governments, but also private entities. The special or additional rules and procedures under the WTO agreements designed to resolve multi-stakeholder disputes provide useful guidance as to how digital trade disputes should be settled.

The following subsections A to B contrast stakeholders in conventional trade disputes arising under the WTO agreements with stakeholders in digital trade disputes arising under the TREC Agreement.

A *Stakeholders in Conventional Trade*

1 Trade in Goods

The WTO agreements primarily establish the rights and obligations of the members. For example, the Marrakesh Agreement Establishing the World Trade Organization (Marrakesh Agreement) states that the WTO provides "the common institutional framework for the *conduct of trade relations among its Members*" (emphasis added).[12] The central role of the members is also signified by the shared recognition that the WTO agreements reflect the balance of benefits among WTO members. The primary stakeholders under the WTO agreements are the members – more specifically, the governments of the members, in the sense that they are the subject of the WTO rules.

The stakeholders in the WTO agreements become clearer when the addressee of specific rules is examined. For example, GATT Articles I and III prohibit

[12] Marrakesh Agreement, Art. II:1.

a discriminatory measure against a certain product of a member rather than a certain product of an individual exporter or producer. A less favourable treatment of a certain product or item offered by a specific individual exporter from a member does not necessarily constitute a violation of the non-discrimination principles, unless it amounts to discrimination towards a product from that member.[13] This is because the WTO agreements protect the rights of the members rather than the rights of individual exporters or producers. It follows that WTO disputes arise between member governments and are properly settled through inter-governmental dispute settlement procedures.

Some disputes under certain WTO rules may arise between private parties and WTO member governments. More specifically, disputes under the Agreement on Implementation of Article VI of the General Agreement on Tariffs and Trade 1994 (Anti-Dumping Agreement) may arise between exporters or foreign producers and the government of an importing member conducting anti-dumping investigations and imposing anti-dumping measures, because the interests of the former are directly affected by these investigations and measures.

The rules of the Anti-Dumping Agreement provide for the obligations of the relevant authorities of WTO members that are in charge of conducting anti-dumping investigations and imposing anti-dumping measures, and they are expected to ultimately protect the interests of exporters and foreign producers from abusive anti-dumping investigations and measures. Moreover, some rules of the Anti-Dumping Agreement, such as Article 6, explicitly require the authorities of the members to ensure that the procedural rights of private parties are properly protected. Thus, the stakeholders in the Anti-Dumping Agreement include not only the governments of members, but also private parties that may be subject to anti-dumping investigations and measures.

Given that the interests and procedural rights of exporters and foreign producers are protected under the Anti-Dumping Agreement, violations of the Agreement can provoke disputes between members conducting anti-dumping investigations and imposing anti-dumping measures and exporters or foreign producers that are subject to such investigations and measures. The governments of these exporters or producers may bring such a dispute to the WTO for dispute settlement on their behalf. Conversely, governments may choose not to do so if their interests do not coincide with the interests of the WTO. In order to allow exporters and foreign producers to directly challenge anti-dumping investigations and measures of WTO members on their own, additional dispute settlement procedures are stipulated in the Anti-Dumping Agreement, which is revisited in Section V.

[13] Compare Appellate Body Report, *Japan – Taxes on Alcoholic Beverages*, WT/DS8/AB/R, WT/DS10/AB/R, WT/DS11/AB/R, 4 October 1996, p. 16; Appellate Body Report, *European Communities – Measures Affecting Asbestos and Asbestos-Containing Products*, WT/DS135/AB/R, 12 March 2001, at para. 100.

2 Trade in Services

Although the GATS generally shares the features of the GATT in that the primary stakeholders are the governments of members, it takes a different approach from the GATT with regard to the position of private entities. More specifically, some rules under the GATS, such as Article VIII:1 and Article IX:1, provide for discipline regarding the conduct of service suppliers, albeit indirectly, through domestic laws and regulations of WTO members.

These provisions are incorporated into the GATS based on the recognition that the anti-competitive practices of service suppliers could restrict trade in services. This does *not* mean that the anti-competitive practices of producers of *goods* could *not* restrict trade in goods. On the contrary, the anti-competitive practices of producers of goods could also be trade restrictive and, for this reason, it would be appropriate to incorporate regulations on anti-competitive practices related to trade in goods as well.[14] Nevertheless, it is undeniable that certain service sectors are more susceptible to monopolization and other anti-competitive practices than the goods sectors. Therefore, the inclusion of competition regulations is needed more in the GATS than in WTO agreements on trade in goods. As a panel once suggested,[15] trade barriers in trade in services, especially those related to basic infrastructure, include not only governmental measures, but also anti-competitive practices of service suppliers. Although these provisions do not directly impose legal obligations on service suppliers, they demonstrate the possibility that the anti-competitive practices of service suppliers may nullify or impair the benefits of WTO members under the GATS and trigger a dispute under the GATS. As discussed in Section V, the GATS provides a special dispute settlement mechanism to address such disputes.

3 Intellectual Property Rights

The Agreement on Trade-Related Aspects of Intellectual Property Rights (TRIPS Agreement) has a distinctive feature in that it is closely connected with the rights of private entities. While the title of the Agreement is carefully drafted to focus on the trade-limited aspects of intellectual property rights, its rules are primarily concerned with the protection of intellectual property rights owned by private entities.[16] Although the TRIPS Agreement may not explicitly confer legal rights to private parties under WTO law, it requires their intellectual property rights to be protected through the domestic law and policy of WTO members, as implied in Article 1.1 of

[14] For example, Article 16.1.2 of the TPP Agreement, as incorporated in the CPTPP Agreement (hereinafter CPTPP Agreement), requires the contracting parties to "endeavour to apply its national competition laws to *all commercial activities* in its territory" (emphasis added).

[15] Panel Report, *Mexico – Measures Affecting Telecommunications Services*, WT/DS204/R, 2 April 2004, at para. 7.237.

[16] TRIPS Agreement, preamble, paras. 1, 4.

the TRIPS Agreement. In the TRIPS Agreement, private entities, as stakeholders, are as important as WTO members.

Disputes under the TRIPS Agreement may arise when a WTO member adopts or maintains a measure that is inconsistent with the TRIPS Agreement, thereby nullifying or impairing the interests of another member. Such disputes may be handled through the inter-governmental WTO dispute settlement process. However, disputes may more often arise between private parties under the domestic intellectual property law, which incorporates the rules under the TRIPS Agreement. In fact, the number of WTO disputes concerning the TRIPS Agreement is very limited compared to the number of domestic disputes involving domestic intellectual property law. In order to enable private entities to settle these domestic disputes and enforce their intellectual property rights, the TRIPS Agreement requires WTO members to maintain appropriate judicial and administrative procedures within their territories, as is revisited in Section V. Given the importance of private entities as stakeholders, these procedures are essential as a supplement to the inter-governmental dispute settlement procedures.

B *Stakeholders in Digital Trade*

The TREC Agreement that is under negotiation would provide for the rights and obligations of contracting parties similar to those digital trade rules under recent RTAs, which serve as important references. For example, Article 19.3.1 of the USMCA prohibits contracting parties from imposing customs duties on digital trade, and Article 19.4.1 of the USMCA requires contracting parties to accord no less favourable treatment to a digital product created by another party or by a person of another party.[17] In addition, some digital trade rules under the USMCA, such as Articles 19.5.1 and 19.7.2, require the contracting parties to adopt or maintain certain laws on digital trade within their territories.[18] Under Article 8.74 of the JEEPA, contracting parties are required to ensure that all the measures of general application affecting electronic commerce are administered in a reasonable, objective, and impartial manner.

However, many rules under the proposed TREC Agreement would also concern the rights and obligations of private entities, at least indirectly. First, the protection of the interests of consumers would be a central element in the TREC Agreement, as the existing regional trade rules on digital trade suggest. For example, Article 19.2.1 of the USMCA recognizes the importance of a framework to promote consumer confidence in digital trade. More specifically, Article 19.7.1 of the USMCA explicitly emphasizes the importance of adopting and maintaining transparent and effective measures to protect consumers from fraudulent or deceptive commercial activities.[19]

[17] See also CPTPP Agreement, Arts. 14.3.1 and 14.4.1; JEEPA, Art. 8.72.
[18] See also CPTPP Agreement, Arts. 14.5 and 14.7.2.
[19] See also CPTPP Agreement, Art. 14.7.1; JEEPA, Art. 8.78.1.

Similarly, Article 19.8.1 of the USMCA recognizes the economic and social benefits of protecting the personal information of users of digital trade, as well as the contribution this makes to enhancing consumer confidence in digital trade.[20]

Second, the conduct of enterprises and other private entities would be indirectly subject to rules under the TREC Agreement through the domestic laws of the contracting parties, since such conduct could undermine the interests of consumers protected under the TREC Agreement. For example, Article 19.7.2 of the USMCA requires contracting parties to adopt or maintain consumer protection laws to proscribe fraudulent and deceptive commercial activities that cause harm or potential harm to consumers engaged in online commercial activities.[21] Similarly, Article 19.8.2 of the USMCA requires contracting parties to adopt or maintain a legal framework that provides for the protection of personal information of the users of digital trade.[22] Most notably, Article 19.13 of the USMCA requires contracting parties to not only adopt or maintain measures regarding certain unsolicited commercial electronic communications sent to an electronic mail address, but also to provide recourse in its law against suppliers of unsolicited commercial electronic communications that do not comply with any measure adopted or maintained pursuant to this obligation.[23] Thus, consumers would be able to seek recourse against an enterprise in domestic procedures by claiming that its conduct violates the relevant domestic law incorporating rules under the TREC Agreement.

Third, enterprises and other private entities would also be beneficiaries whose interests must be protected under the TREC Agreement. For example, provisions such as Article 19.5 of the USMCA, concerning the domestic electronic transactions framework, and Article 19.6 of the USMCA, concerning electronic authentication and electronic signatures, are intended to facilitate business activities in digital trade.[24] In addition, provisions prohibiting the contracting parties from requiring localization of computing facilities,[25] or the transfer of, or access to, source codes,[26] are inserted to address one of the most urgent concerns of enterprises.

These features of the rules under the proposed TREC Agreement would characterize the nature of disputes arising under the Agreement in two ways. First, while disputes may arise between contracting parties under certain circumstances, a greater number of disputes would likely arise between a consumer and an enterprise, or between an enterprise and the government. For example, a consumer may claim that certain practices of an enterprise inappropriately use his or her personal information. Alternatively, an enterprise may claim that a regulation of the government unduly restricts its business activities in digital trade. Second, disputes would

20 See also CPTPP Agreement, Art. 14.8.1; JEEPA, Art. 8.78.3.
21 See also CPTPP Agreement, Art. 14.7.2.
22 See also CPTPP Agreement, Art. 14.8.2.
23 See also CPTPP Agreement, Art. 14.14; JEEPA, Art. 8.79.
24 See also CPTPP Agreement, Arts. 14.5 and 14.6; JEEPA, Arts. 8.76 and 8.77.
25 USMCA, Art. 19.12; CPTPP Agreement, Art. 14.13.
26 USMCA, Art. 19.16; CPTPP Agreement, Art. 14.17; JEEPA, Art. 8.73.

more often arise under domestic law rather than directly under the TREC Agreement. The TREC Agreement would presume that many of its rules are to be incorporated into the domestic laws of the contracting parties. It would be reasonable for consumers and enterprises to refer first to a relevant domestic law to determine if their benefits are legally protected under said domestic law. These characteristics must be considered when constructing dispute settlement mechanisms for digital trade disputes.

IV PROTECTION OF NON-TRADE VALUES

In accordance with the objectives and purpose under the preamble of the GATT and the Marrakesh Agreement, trade benefits need to be balanced against other non-trade values, such as the environment and human rights. To strike a proper balance, the WTO agreements provide for several exceptions to trade rules. A similar balance would be required under digital trade rules in the TREC Agreement in order to allow contracting parties to protect their legitimate objectives; however, different weighing and balancing exercises would be required because of the unique nature of conventional trade rules and digital trade rules. The following subsections A to B examine the nature of balance between trade and non-trade values under the WTO agreements, and also under the proposed TREC Agreement.

A *Non-Trade Values in Conventional Trade*

1 Trade in Goods and Services

The WTO agreements provide for several exceptions to rules on trade in goods. Most importantly, GATT Article XX provides for general exceptions for obligations, which balance trade benefits against the protection of public morals,[27] the protection of human, animal, or plant life or health,[28] and the conservation of exhaustible natural resources,[29] among others. In this regard, the Appellate Body has stated that GATT Article XX "affirm[s] the right of Members to pursue various regulatory objectives identified in the paragraphs of these provisions"[30] and "embodies the recognition on the part of WTO Members of the need to maintain a balance of rights and obligations."[31]

A similar balance is struck between the rights of members to take advantage of trade liberalization in services and the rights of members to regulate in order to pursue

[27] GATT, Art. XX(a).
[28] GATT, Art. XX(b).
[29] GATT, Art. XX(g).
[30] Appellate Body Report, *Argentina – Measures Relating to Trade in Goods and Services*, WT/DS453/AB/R, 14 April 2016, at para. 6.113.
[31] Appellate Body Report, *United States – Import Prohibition of Certain Shrimp and Shrimp Products*, WT/DS58/AB/R, 12 October 1998, at para. 156.

legitimate policy objectives. The preamble of the GATS explicitly recognizes that liberalization of trade in services shall be "aimed at promoting the interests of all participants on a mutually advantageous basis and at securing an overall balance of rights and obligations, while giving due respect to national policy objectives."[32] The Appellate Body finds that the GATS shall be interpreted "in consonance with the balance of rights and obligations that is expressly recognized in the preamble of the GATS"[33] and Article XIV "affirm[s] the right of Members to pursue various regulatory objectives identified in the paragraphs of these provisions."[34]

2 Intellectual Property Rights

It is worth noting that exceptions in the TRIPS Agreement take a different approach from trade in goods and services. Instead of providing general exceptions, the TRIPS Agreement provides for conditions, limitations, and exceptions for each category of intellectual property. For example, with respect to copyrights, Article 13 of the TRIPS Agreement provides that "Members shall confine limitations or exceptions to exclusive rights to certain special cases which do not conflict with a normal exploitation of the work and do not unreasonably prejudice the legitimate interests of the right holder." Article 30 allows members to "provide limited exceptions to the exclusive rights conferred by a patent, provided that such exceptions do not unreasonably conflict with a normal exploitation of the patent and do not unreasonably prejudice the legitimate interests of the patent owner, taking account of the legitimate interests of third parties." Additionally, Article 31 provides that "other use" without authorization of the right holder may be allowed under certain conditions.

Disputes may arise between WTO members concerning these limitations and exceptions under the TRIPS Agreement. For example, a WTO member may claim that a limitation to a certain intellectual property right imposed by another WTO member to protect legitimate non-economic interests excessively limits the right of intellectual property right holders of their nationality and thereby nullifies or impairs its own benefits under the TRIPS Agreement. Panels and the Appellate Body can settle such disputes by weighing and balancing the rights and obligations, as they do in disputes involving Article XX of the GATT.

However, disputes concerning limitations and exceptions are also likely to arise between private parties. For example, an intellectual property right holder may claim that the use of its intellectual property by a user without permission infringes upon its right, while the user may in turn contend that its use is justified as a legitimate exception. The settlement of such disputes requires consideration of the balance of interests between private parties rather than members, and the WTO dispute settlement procedures may not be an appropriate forum for such disputes for

[32] GATS, preamble, para. 3.

[33] Appellate Body Report, note 30 above, at para. 6.260.

[34] Ibid., at para. 6.113.

the following reasons. First, while the TRIPS Agreement requires WTO members to confine limitations and exceptions to certain prescribed circumstances, it does not specify what limitations and exceptions should be justified. It is left to each WTO member to decide the appropriate balance between the interests of right holders and the interests of right users within the limits of the TRIPS Agreement, and to reflect such a balance in its domestic law. Second, panels and the Appellate Body are not well suited to engage in the weighing and balancing of various private interests and judge what should be the appropriate balance within the territories of WTO members. Such judgement should be left to the domestic authorities of members that are closer to the local community. Thus, as stated in Section V, it is reasonable that disputes concerning intellectual property rights protected by the TRIPS Agreement are primarily settled through domestic tribunals.

B *Non-Trade Values in Digital Trade*

The TREC Agreement under negotiation would provide exceptions similar to Article XX of the GATT and Article XIV of the GATS, with a view towards protecting non-economic interests. In fact, digital trade rules under recently concluded RTAs provide GATT Article XX-type exceptions. For example, Article 19.11 of the USMCA provides that while no party shall prohibit or restrict the cross-border transfer of information, a party is not prevented from adopting or maintaining a measure that is inconsistent with the obligation but "necessary to achieve a legitimate public policy objective, provided that the measure is not applied in a manner which would constitute a means of arbitrary or unjustifiable discrimination or a disguised restriction on trade; and does not impose restrictions on transfers of information greater than are necessary to achieve the objective."[35] Disputes arising out of these exceptions may be settled in a manner similar to the settlement of disputes involving Article XX of the GATT, through the weighing and balancing of the right of a contracting party to invoke an exception and the substantive rights of the other contracting parties protected by the proposed TREC Agreement.

However, digital trade rules under RTAs suggest that balance between trade benefits and non-trade values would also need to be sought in different circumstances under the proposed TREC Agreement. First, a measure justified as an exception under the TREC Agreement would impact the interests of a specific private entity rather than the interests of another party. For example, Article 19.16.2 of the USMCA provides that a regulatory body or judicial authority of a party is not precluded from requiring a person of another party to preserve and make available a source code of software or an algorithm expressed in that source code to the regulatory body under certain circumstances, while Article 19.16.1 generally prohibits the parties from requiring the transfer of, or access to, such source code or algorithm as a condition of the

[35] See also CPTPP Agreement, Art. 14.11.

import, distribution, sale, or use of that software.[36] Specific circumstances under which disclosure of a source code is required would be provided in the domestic law of each contracting party. Disputes involving this exception would require the weighing and balancing of the public policy objectives of a contracting party invoking the exception against the economic interests of a private person who is required to make available its source code, which may not be properly undertaken through the WTO's inter-governmental dispute settlement procedures.

Second, in some cases, the proposed TREC Agreement would provide obligations, rather than exceptions, to take certain measures to achieve legitimate non-economic objectives. For example, Article 19.7.2 of the USMCA requires contracting parties to adopt or maintain consumer protection laws to proscribe fraudulent and deceptive commercial activities that cause harm or potential harm to consumers engaged in online commercial activities.[37] Similarly, Article 19.8.2 of the USMCA requires contracting parties to adopt or maintain a legal framework that provides for the protection of personal information of the users of digital trade.[38] Additionally, Article 19.13 of the USMCA requires each party to adopt or maintain measures to limit unsolicited commercial electronic communications.[39] These provisions require, rather than allow, contracting parties to restrict digital trade to achieve legitimate non-trade objectives.[40] It is questionable at best to assume that disputes involving such obligations can be properly regarded as "trade" disputes, and that non-trade policies can be properly examined by panels and the Appellate Body.

V DISPUTE SETTLEMENT

A *Conventional Trade Disputes*

1 Trade in Goods and Services

The WTO dispute settlement mechanism primarily seeks to redress the loss of benefits suffered by WTO members, the primary stakeholders under the covered agreements. WTO dispute settlement procedures are structured in a manner consistent with this objective. For example, participation in the WTO dispute settlement proceedings is almost[41] exclusively reserved to member governments.

36 See also CPTPP Agreement, Art. 14.17; JEEPA, Art. 8.73.
37 See also CPTPP Agreement, Art. 14.7.2.
38 See also CPTPP Agreement, Art. 14.8.2.
39 See also CPTPP Agreement, Art. 14.14; JEEPA, Art. 8.79.
40 For example, the TREC Agreement is expected to play a proactive role in protecting privacy. Compare AD Mitchell and N Mishra, "Regulating Cross-Border Data Flows in a Data-Driven World: How WTO Law Can Contribute" (2019) 22 *Journal of International Economic Law* 389, at 398–403.
41 Private parties may be allowed to participate in WTO dispute settlement proceedings as amicus curiae under limited circumstances.

According to Article XXIII:1 of the GATT, a WTO member government may bring a dispute to the WTO dispute settlement mechanism if it considers that its benefit under the WTO agreements is being nullified or impaired as a result of violations of the agreements. Moreover, remedies are granted to the complaining member government to the extent necessary to redress the nullification or impairment of its benefits. In accordance with Article 22.4 of the DSU, the level of the suspension of concessions in the case of non-implementation of a DSB recommendation is assessed by considering the level of the nullification or impairment of benefits suffered by the complaining member.

At the same time, special or additional dispute settlement procedures are also provided in the WTO agreements to complement the WTO inter-governmental dispute settlement procedures in order to settle certain disputes directly involving private parties. For example, Article 13 of the Anti-Dumping Agreement requires each member to maintain judicial, arbitral, or administrative tribunals or procedures for the purpose of the prompt review of administrative actions relating to final determinations and reviews of determinations. While anti-dumping disputes may be brought by member governments, on behalf of their exporters and producers, before the inter-governmental WTO dispute settlement procedures in accordance with Article 17 of the Anti-Dumping Agreement, anti-dumping disputes may also be brought before the domestic procedures maintained pursuant to Article 13 by exporters and producers on their own. In fact, many anti-dumping disputes are addressed in domestic proceedings between a private entity targeted by an anti-dumping measure and a member government seeking to impose said measure. The domestic procedures are made available to private entities in light of the fact that they are most directly impacted by anti-dumping investigations and measures, which means that they are de facto principal stakeholders.

The GATS provides for a special mechanism to settle disputes that are triggered by the conduct of service suppliers. More specifically, Article VIII:3 of the GATS authorizes the Council for Trade in Services to request a member establishing, maintaining, or authorizing a monopoly supplier of a service which is allegedly acting in a manner inconsistent with that member's obligations under the GATS to provide specific information concerning relevant operations at the request of another member. Moreover, Article IX:2 of the GATS provides that a "Member shall, at the request of any other Member, enter into consultations with a view to eliminating" business practices of service suppliers that may restrain competition and thereby restrict trade in services, and that it "accord full and sympathetic consideration to such a request and shall cooperate through the supply of publicly available non-confidential information of relevance to the matter in question." It "shall also provide other information available to the requesting Member, subject to its domestic law and to the conclusion of satisfactory agreement concerning the safeguarding of its confidentiality by the requesting Member." These provisions provide WTO members with a special mechanism by which to settle disputes provoked by the conduct of service suppliers rather than that of governments, in view of the fact that the conduct of service suppliers can restrict trade in services.

The special or additional procedures under the Anti-Dumping Agreement and the GATS provide useful guidance as to how digital trade disputes should be settled, as identified in the next subsection.

2 Intellectual Property Rights

Disputes involving the TRIPS Agreement may also be brought before the procedures laid out in the DSU, although the number of TRIPS disputes settled under the DSU is extremely limited. Rather, the domestic procedures within the territories of members play a central role in the implementation of the TRIPS Agreement, because disputes concerning the TRIPS Agreement often involve conflicts of interest between owners and users of intellectual property rights.

Part III of the TRIPS Agreement provides for the extensive obligations of WTO members to ensure that enforcement procedures are available under their domestic law to permit effective action against any act of infringement of intellectual property rights covered by the TRIPS Agreement. These provisions demonstrate a similarity to the Anti-Dumping Agreement, in that private entities are entitled to seek recourse to domestic procedures if their benefits, which are indirectly protected under the WTO agreements, are harmed. The enforcement procedures under the TRIPS Agreement are different from those under the Anti-Dumping Agreement, in that the former covers not only disputes between a private entity and the government, but also disputes between private entities, while the latter deals with disputes brought by a private entity against the government. It should also be noted that domestic tribunals are often better suited to make decisions regarding what limitations and conditions on intellectual property rights are justified, based on an analysis of weighing and balancing, than international tribunals. This is because domestic tribunals possess greater knowledge of the different interests of owners and users within the jurisdiction in question.

B *Digital Trade Disputes*

The previous subsections have pointed out that digital trade rules in the proposed TREC Agreement will likely differ from conventional trade rules in the WTO agreements in terms of the diversity of stakeholders and the nature of the balance between trade and non-trade values. These differences suggest that disputes arising from the TREC Agreement may take unique forms when compared with conventional trade disputes. More specifically, digital trade disputes can take six different forms, depending on the nature of the involved parties.

First, disputes may arise between contracting parties to the proposed TREC Agreement. Some provisions of the TREC Agreement may provide for the rights and obligations of the contracting parties, and violations of these provisions may trigger disputes between parties. For example, if a contracting party imposes a customs duty on digital trade in violation of the TREC Agreement, another contracting party whose digital product is subject to the duty may bring a dispute against the party imposing the duty. Alternatively, a contracting party may claim that a restriction to cross-border flows of personal data imposed by another contracting party is a violation of the Agreement, while the latter party may claim that the restriction is justified as an exception to achieve its legitimate public policy objective.[42]

Second, digital trade disputes may also be brought by a business enterprise of a contracting party against another contracting party. Some of the provisions under the proposed TREC Agreement may require contracting parties to protect the interests of enterprises engaged in digital trade. If a contracting party fails to take appropriate measures to do so, it may face a claim by an enterprise, arguing that the contracting party has violated requirements under the TREC Agreement. For example, an enterprise of a contracting party may claim that it is forced to transfer its source code to the government of another contracting party, contrary to obligations under the TREC Agreement. This type of dispute may also arise between an enterprise of a contracting party and its own government.

Third, the government of a contracting party may claim that an enterprise of another contracting party has engaged in unfair digital trade practices. For example, a contracting party may consider that an enterprise from another contracting party is abusing the personal data of its consumers and is therefore violating the obligations of its domestic law, incorporating rules of the proposed TREC Agreement. It could handle the matter pursuant to its own domestic law, but it may also seek to consult with the government of the other contracting party on the matter.

Fourth, digital trade disputes may be disputed between enterprises of different contracting parties if the conduct of an enterprise of a contracting party undermines the digital trade activities of the enterprises of another contracting party. Although many of these disputes between enterprises are commercial in nature, they may involve issues related to the interpretation and application of the proposed TREC Agreement.

Fifth, digital trade disputes may also be brought by a consumer of a contracting party against its own government. As discussed earlier, the proposed TREC Agreement requires contracting parties to protect consumer interests, such as privacy, through domestic laws and regulations. A consumer may claim that his or her government's failure to do so constitutes a violation of the TREC Agreement.

[42] Compare Mattoo and Meltzer, note 8 above, at 780–782.

Sixth, and finally, digital trade disputes may be brought by a consumer of a contracting party against an enterprise of another contracting party when the former considers that the conduct of the latter violates its interests, as indirectly protected under the TREC Agreement. In such cases, the consumer may seek to obtain remedy from the enterprise.

What would be the appropriate form of dispute settlement for such digital trade disputes arising under the TREC Agreement? The first category of disputes is similar to conventional trade disputes and could therefore be dealt with under general trade dispute settlement procedures. The TREC Agreement should provide that the rules and procedures under the DSU shall apply to disputes arising under the Agreement. Nonetheless, some special or additional rules would be needed in order to allow the contracting parties some flexibility in the implementation of the Agreement in light of the novel and evolving nature of digital trade. For example, both developing and developed parties should be given grace periods, during which a contracting party would refrain from using the dispute settlement mechanism. The use of enforcement measures, such as suspension of concessions, should be restricted.

The second category of disputes is similar to certain disputes under the Anti-Dumping Agreement. As in the case of disputes under the Anti-Dumping Agreement, this type of dispute would be best dealt with through the domestic procedures of a contracting party taking measures at issue. To effectively address this category of disputes, the TREC Agreement should require the contracting parties to establish and maintain domestic procedures that are accessible to enterprises. This type of dispute would be principally reviewed under domestic laws and regulations that have incorporated the rules under the TREC Agreement. The TREC Agreement could explicitly require domestic tribunals to apply domestic laws and regulations, in accordance with the TREC Agreement.

The third category of disputes shares some features with certain disputes under the GATS, in that the disputes are triggered by the conduct of private entities. It would be useful for the TREC Agreement to provide consultation procedures, by which the government of a contracting party can request consultations with the government of another contracting party regarding the enterprises of the latter party. The complaining party may also seek to apply its domestic law to a foreign enterprise allegedly engaged in trade-restrictive practices. A cooperative mechanism would be desirable to avoid the excessive extraterritorial application of domestic law.

The fourth category of disputes may be better dealt with outside the framework of the TREC Agreement in light of its commercial nature. Existing judicial and non-judicial procedures employed to handle commercial disputes could also be used to address this category of disputes.

It is essential that the proposed TREC Agreement would be capable of properly settling the fifth and sixth categories of disputes, given the importance of the protection of consumer interests. Principally, these types of disputes should be dealt with through domestic procedures because they are easily accessible to consumers. Domestic procedures are also desirable because domestic courts and tribunals are better suited, when compared with international mechanisms, to make decisions regarding how to weigh and balance the different interests of consumers and enterprises within the jurisdiction of a contracting party. To ensure that domestic procedures function as an effective dispute settlement mechanism for consumers, the TREC Agreement should require contracting parties to not only establish and maintain domestic procedures that are accessible to consumers, but also ensure that domestic laws and regulations are applied in accordance with the TREC Agreement.

VI CONCLUSION

Are digital trade disputes "trade disputes"? This chapter argued that digital trade disputes will differ from conventional trade disputes, particularly in terms of stakeholders and the balance between trade and non-trade values, reflecting the unique nature of digital trade rules. Effective dispute settlement mechanisms are essential to the successful enforcement of digital trade rules. WTO negotiations on trade-related aspects of electronic commerce should address not only the issue of substantive digital trade rules, but also that of special or additional dispute settlement rules and procedures required to resolve digital trade disputes.

PART III

Data Regulation as Artificial Intelligence Regulation

9

International Economic Law's Regulation of Data as a Resource for the Artificial Intelligence Economy

Thomas Streinz

I DATA AS A RESOURCE FOR THE ARTIFICIAL INTELLIGENCE ECONOMY

Business capacity to collect and process digitalized information (data) at unprecedented scale and speed is transforming economies around the globe. One aspect of this transformation is the relevance of data as a 'resource' for relatively recent advancements in artificial intelligence (AI) technology in various forms of machine learning, most notably 'deep learning'. The theoretical foundations for this kind of AI go back to the 1950s, but only the availability of novel and larger datasets led to the end of a long 'AI winter' and the dawn of an 'AI spring'.[1]

The growing but unevenly distributed ability to capture information about the world in digital form is a complex phenomenon. The public discourse surrounding data seems somewhat detached from the sophisticated ways in which scholars have theorized the relationship between data, information, knowledge, and wisdom.[2] The lack of adequate terminology to capture the phenomena caused by the gradual digitalization of economies and societies is evidenced by the vain search for metaphorical equivalents.[3] The effort to assess the effects of digitalization on the economy is severely hindered by a paradoxical lack of data about data, since the commercial value of data is reflected neither in balance sheets nor in the conventional metrics used to assess the state of the economy or trade.[4] Yet, it seems misguided to attribute this lamentable state of affairs solely to the notorious intransparency of global digital corporations or the inertia of accountants, statisticians,

1 TJ Sejnowski, *The Deep Learning Revolution* (Boston, MA, MIT Press, 2018). On the relevance of AI technology for international economic law, see also Chapter 1 in this volume.

2 R Kitchin, 'Conceptualising Data', in *The Data Revolution: Big Data, Open Data, Data Infrastructures and Their Consequences* (Los Angeles, CA, SAGE Publishing, 2014).

3 'The World's Most Valuable Resource Is No Longer Oil, but Data' (*The Economist*, 6 May 2017), https://perma.cc/YBN2-XW6D.

4 J Haskel and S Westlake, *Capitalism Without Capital: The Rise of the Intangible Economy* (Princeton, NJ, Princeton University Press, 2017); M Mazzucato, *The Value of Everything: Making and Taking in the Global Economy* (London, Penguin Books, 2017); D Ciuriak, 'Unpacking the Valuation of Data in the Data-Driven Economy' (27 April 2019), https://ssrn.com/abstract=3379133.

and policy-makers in responding to digitalization on unprecedented scales. Data's variegated characteristics pose distinct challenges for data's economic evaluation and legal conceptualization.[5] This chapter cannot resolve these questions. It treats data as an essential rent-generating productive asset in the AI economy – and therefore also a contested economic resource.[6]

The chapter builds on and expands earlier work on data-related provisions in recent instruments of international economic law (IEL) and sketches some questions for ongoing and future research about how IEL might need to be recalibrated to adapt to a global digital economy.[7] This earlier work focused on the new template of rules for a global digital economy that the United States championed in the negotiations for the Trans-Pacific Partnership (TPP), now in force as the Comprehensive and Progressive Agreement for Trans-Pacific Partnership (CPTPP),[8] followed by the US-Mexico-Canada Agreement (USMCA),[9] and the Japan-US Digital Trade Agreement (JUSDTA).[10] Negotiations on new rules for 'electronic commerce' in the World Trade Organization (WTO) seem unlikely to yield tangible outcomes in the near term,[11] but certain CPTPP members have moved ahead with TPP-plus templates for digital economy agreements, ostensibly designed for adoption by others.[12] While the tension between data governance in trade agreements and domestic data protection and privacy policies is increasingly

[5] This is one theme of the Global Data Law project launched by Guarini Global Law & Tech at NYU Law. More information and videos from the first two conferences are available at www.guariniglobal.org/global-data-law.

[6] D Ciuriak and M Ptashkina, 'The State Also Rises: The Role of the State in the Age of Data' (June 2020), https://ssrn.com/abstract=3663387; D Ciuriak, 'Data as a Contested Economic Resource: Framing the Issues' (23 November 2019), https://ssrn.com/abstract=3496281.

[7] See also T Streinz, 'Digital Megaregulation Uncontested? TPP's Model for the Global Digital Economy', in Benedict Kingsbury et al. (eds), *Megaregulation Contested: Global Economic Ordering After TPP* (Oxford, Oxford University Press, 2019) ch. 9.

[8] CPTPP entered into force for Australia, Canada, Japan, Mexico, New Zealand, and Singapore in December 2018, and for Vietnam in January 2019. Brunei, Chile, Malaysia, and Peru have signed the agreement but did not ratify it. A consolidated version of CPTPP is available at www.iilj.org/megareg/materials.

[9] Initially signed on 30 November 2018. Revised version signed on 10 December 2019. Text available at https://perma.cc/GS3J-WSTR. The agreement entered into force on 1 July 2020.

[10] Signed on 7 October 2019. Text available at https://perma.cc/UUA9-7NUD. The agreement entered into force on 1 January 2020.

[11] As of January 2020, 83 WTO members participated in plurilateral negotiations, albeit only five African countries, only three least developed countries, and no WTO members from the Caribbean or developing Pacific Island countries. See Y Ismail, 'E-commerce in the World Trade Organization: History and latest developments in the negotiations under the Joint Statement' (IISD Report, January 2020). In December 2020, a consolidated negotiating text (WTO Doc. INF/ECOM/62) was leaked, indicating both progress and continued disagreement. See also Henry Gao's Chapter 15 in this volume.

[12] The Digital Economy Partnership Agreement (DEPA) between Chile, New Zealand, and Singapore – signed electronically during the COVID-19 pandemic in June 2020 – follows a modular logic to facilitate flexible adoption. DEPA's text is available at https://perma.cc/U23E-URUS. The agreement has been in force between Singapore and New Zealand since December 2020. The Australia-Singapore Digital Economy Agreement (ASDEA) was signed in August 2020. It

better understood (despite the persistent silos and splendid isolation in which the trade and privacy communities have long operated),[13] there is surprisingly little discussion about the ways in which existing and emerging IEL constrain and shape states' policy choices for data-driven economic development.

This chapter is an attempt to contribute to this much-needed debate by exploring the extent to which IEL regulates data as a resource for the AI economy. Section II identifies regulatory interventions – open data initiatives, cross-border data transfer restrictions, and mandatory data sharing – that nation states are already enacting or at least contemplating to ensure access to data for their domestic AI economy. Section III shows how some of these regulatory interventions are in tension with existing and emerging commitments under international trade and investment law along the dimensions of data control (mainly through international intellectual property law and international investment law) and data mobility (mainly through commitments in favor of free data flows and against data localization). Section IV concludes by imagining ways through which IEL could provide more flexibility for experimental digital economy policies to confront asymmetric control over data as countries transition, asynchronously and unevenly, toward an AI economy.

II EMERGING DIGITAL ECONOMY POLICIES: REGULATING DATA AS A RESOURCE

By January 2020, twelve of the G20 countries had announced official AI strategies, with others bound to follow.[14] Virtually all of these strategies discuss the relevance of data for a future AI economy, commonly under the somewhat vague concept of 'data governance'. The emphasis is often on data protection and privacy-related concerns, which is a function of the dominant legal discourse in the digital domain and the gradual emergence and subsequent entrenchment of certain regulatory models for data protection.[15] Countries' AI strategies increasingly also recognize and address concerns about discrimination caused by algorithmic bias. In contrast, the regulatory interventions that states are considering to challenge the domination of the digital domain by US and Chinese companies, especially in AI, are relatively timid, with the notable exceptions of the European Union's (EU's) antitrust enforcement

contains novel provisions on submarine data cables and digital standard-setting; its text is available at www.dfat.gov.au/sites/default/files/australia-singapore-digital-economy-agreement.pdf.

[13] See, for example, S Yakovleva and K Irion, 'Pitching Trade Against Privacy: Reconciling EU Governance of Personal Data Flows with External Trade' (2020) *International Data Privacy Law* 1; see also Alan Hervé's Chapter 10 in this volume.

[14] See the very helpful overview by T Struett, 'G20 AI Strategies on Data Governance', https://datagovhub.org/g20-ai-strategies (https://perma.cc/FLM3-UBCW).

[15] See T Streinz, 'The Evolution of European Data Law', in P Craig and G de Burca (eds), *The Evolution of EU Law* (3rd ed., Oxford: Oxford University Press 2021) ch. 29, preprint available at https://ssrn.com/abstract=3762971.

against US companies[16] and India's emerging e-commerce policy that espouses an openly protectionist agenda to grow a domestic AI economy fueled by 'Indian data'.[17]

Countries that recognize the salience of data for the AI economy often endorse efforts to make governmental data available as 'open data'. While several countries have some form of data transfer restrictions to retain jurisdictional control over data, India stands out in its advocacy for restricting the outward transfer of data to safeguard data as a national resource, thereby challenging the anti-protectionism consensus in IEL. Some jurisdictions recognize a need for regulatory intervention to transfer data from those who have it to those who want or need it. Exploring each of these three interventions – open data, data transfer restrictions, and mandatory data sharing – as efforts to regulate data as a resource for the AI economy reveals their limited purchase in confronting pervasive data concentration – and makes apparent that alternative measures might be needed.[18]

A *Open Data Initiatives*

The open data movement has been quite successful in convincing governments that making *governmental* data publicly accessible under open data licenses is in their best interest to stimulate the domestic (or even local) AI economy. Examples include the EU's Open Data Directive[19] and Singapore's 'Smart Nation' initiative,[20] but the open data bandwagon also carries several developing countries.[21] There are many reasons for and drivers behind the push for open data, one of which is the purported value for innovation and economic growth.[22] AI development is often referenced as a use case for open data: the remarkable improvements in algorithmic image recognition technology, now widely deployed for facial recognition purposes, have been linked to the ImageNet dataset providing free and publicly available access to image data.[23]

16 See, for example, I Graef, 'When Data Evolves into Market Power: Data Concentration and Data Abuse under Competition Law', in M Moore and D Tambini (eds), *Digital Dominance: The Power of Google, Amazon, Facebook, and Apple* (Oxford, Oxford University Press, 2018), at 71.

17 'Draft National e-Commerce Policy: India's Data for India's Development' (23 February 2019), https://dipp.gov.in/sites/default/files/DraftNational_e-commerce_Policy_23February2019.pdf.

18 See A Fisher and T Streinz, *Confronting Data Inequality*, World Bank Development Report 2021 background paper (1 April 2021), https://ssrn.com/abstract=3825724.

19 Directive (EU) 2019/1024 on open data and the re-use of public sector information, OJ 2019 No. L 172, 26 June 2019, at 56.

20 See Singapore's open data resources: https://perma.cc/JAX3-55U8.

21 SG Verhulst and A Young, 'Open Data in Developing Economies' (GovLab, November 2017), https://perma.cc/W9VN-452K.

22 See J Gray, 'Towards a Genealogy of Open Data' (2014), https://ssrn.com/abstract=2605828.

23 See 'ImageNet', www.image-net.org. See also Kayu Yang et al, 'Towards fairer datasets: Filtering and balancing the distribution of the people subtree in the ImageNet hierarchy' FAT* '20 (January 2020), https://doi.org/10.1145/3351095.3375709 (detailing problems in the ImageNet dataset).

It is, however, much less clear who actually benefits from 'public' data becoming available as 'open' data. Open data might be beneficial for a wide range of reasons,[24] but it is not an effective way to counterbalance the pervasive data control asymmetries in the global digital economy. To the contrary, one might suspect that those with the capacity to collect open data and to correlate it with the 'closed data' under their (often infrastructural) control stand to gain more than those who lack such capabilities and have to rely on open data entirely. This also has geopolitical implications as those operating out of relatively closed digital economies – such as China – are able to capture open data elsewhere in addition to the data they collect domestically without much external competition.[25]

In certain cases, the local relevance of a certain dataset (for example, traffic data in Taipei) might indicate heightened relevance for a local community, which might incentivize local initiatives to use such local data for local development. But the frequency and salience of such a dynamic, while plausible, needs to be empirically established. It is equally possible that non-local actors will use local data to train algorithms for deployment locally, or indeed elsewhere. Opening up governmental data may benefit AI development, but the local or domestic development of an AI economy is highly contingent on other factors, such as research capacity, data processing ability, and so forth.

Against this backdrop, it is worth noting that the question of whether more privately held data should be made available to governments, businesses, or citizens seems comparatively underexplored.[26] Private entities are willing to share certain datasets for research purposes, but the legal technology used for such data transfers is usually contracting, not open data licenses.[27] Data contracting allows for more legal control over the conditions under which data is being shared, used, and distributed.[28] If governments wanted to make private data available, they could facilitate private–public data sharing by providing more legal certainty (for example, through model contracts, especially with a view toward mitigating liability risks) or by requiring the openness of data generated with public support (analogous to open access publishing requirements),[29] if not requiring mandatory data sharing outright, as explored further below.[30]

24 See BS Noveck, 'Rights-Based and Tech-Driven: Open Data, Freedom of Information, and the Future of Government Transparency' (2017) 19 *Yale Human Rights & Development Law Journal* 1 (claiming benefits for innovation and state–citizen collaboration more broadly).

25 I owe this insight, and many others, to Benedict Kingsbury.

26 But see A Alemanno, 'Data for Good: Unlocking Privately-Held Data to the Benefit of the Many' (2018) 9 *European Journal of Risk Regulation* 2.

27 There are exceptions; for example, Google's open image dataset of more than 9 million labeled images has been made available under a CC-BY 4.0 license: https://perma.cc/2ERW-JC4L.

28 See 'Data Sharing Agreement', www.contractstandards.com/public/contracts/data-sharing-agreement.

29 The EU requires open access publishing under Article 29.2 of the Model Grant Agreement of its Horizon 2020 research agenda: https://perma.cc/2VUD-KSUM.

30 See Section II.C.

B *Data Transfer Restrictions*

Several jurisdictions impose data transfer restrictions to secure jurisdictional control over certain categories of data.[31] The EU's General Data Protection Regulation (GDPR)[32] is routinely accused by US actors as a 'protectionist' instrument, designed to favor the European digital economy, albeit with questionable results.[33] This critique often alleges that the GDPR's intended purpose of protecting European data subjects' personal data and privacy and its underlying fundamental rights justification are false pretenses for protectionist digital industrial policy.[34] Drawing a contrast between data protection and data protectionism tacitly assumes that the economic theories in support of trade in goods and services also apply to data, despite its different and arguably unique characteristics.[35] The relationship between data protection and privacy on the one hand and data-driven innovation and economic growth on the other is more complicated than the protection/protectionism binary suggests.[36] The GDPR's predecessor – the European Data Protection Directive (DPD) – was in part motivated by concerns that disparate data protection regimes across the European single market would stymie the nascent European Internet economy.[37] Much less attention was paid, however, to the question of how European data protection law would affect the conditions under which the European digital economy operates in comparison to the rest of the world. The DPD's restriction on transfers of personal data from the EU to third countries was not designed as an instrument of economic policy but was meant to ensure that personal data would remain protected even if transferred outside the EU's territory.[38] These features contributed to the 'Brussels Effect' and the global diffusion of EU-style

[31] T Streinz, 'Data Localization as an Instrument of Jurisdictional Control' (draft paper, on file with author).

[32] Regulation (EU) 2016/679 on the protection of natural persons with regard to the processing of personal data and on the free movement of such data, OJ 2016 No. L 119, 4 May 2016, at 1.

[33] The Washington, DC-based Information Technology and Innovation Foundation (ITIF) is among the most outspoken critics of the European approach to regulating the digital economy. See, for example, E Chivot and D Castro, 'What the Evidence Shows About the Impact of the GDPR After One Year' (ITIF, 17 June 2019), https://perma.cc/TW8V-GGLW.

[34] See for a careful analysis of the competing narratives S Yakovleva, 'Privacy Protection(ism): The Latest Wave of Trade Constraints on Regulatory Autonomy' (2020) 74 *University of Miami Law Review* 416.

[35] But see SA Aaronson, 'What Are We Talking About When We Talk About Digital Protectionism?' (2019) 18 *World Trade Review* 541.

[36] Y Lev-Aretz and KJ Strandburg, 'Privacy Regulation and Innovation Policy' (2020) 22 *Yale Journal of Law and Tech* 256; M Gal and O Aviv, 'The Competitive Effects of the GDPR' (2020) *Journal of Competition Law and Economics* 349.

[37] Directive 95/46/EC on the protection of individuals with regard to the processing of personal data and on the free movement of such data, OJ 1995 No. L 281, 23 November 1995, at 31.

[38] Case C-311/18, *Data Protection Commissioner v Facebook Ireland Limited and Maximillian Schrems*, ECLI:EU:C:2020:559 (16 July 2020); on the genesis of the restriction see K Hon, *Data Localization Law and Policy* (Cheltenham, Edward Elgar Publishing, 2017), at chs 2 and 3; Paul M. Schwartz, 'European Data Protection Law and Restrictions on International Data Flows' (1995) 80 *Iowa Law Review* 471.

data protection through law.[39] The EU's new data strategy, announced with great fanfare in February 2020, conceives of data as an economic resource and seeks to reframe the GDPR as sound economic policy domestically (ensuring consumer trust in the digital economy) and globally (supposedly giving the European digital economy a competitive edge because of the EU's role as global data regulator), without mentioning the restriction on extra-EU transfers of personal data explicitly.[40]

In contrast, India has come forward with a draft 'e-commerce policy' that openly advocates for data transfer restrictions for reasons of economic policy rather than data protection concerns, whether genuine or not. The policy document – which, of course, still needs to be converted into operational law – laments the absence of a legal framework that would allow the Indian government to impose restrictions on the export of valuable data:

> Without having access to the huge trove of data that would be generated within India, the possibility of Indian business entities creating high value digital products would be almost nil. … Further, by not imposing restrictions on cross-border data flow, India would itself be shutting the doors for creation of high-value digital products in the country.[41]

This is a remarkable departure from a key tenet of the Silicon Valley Consensus according to which the uninhibited "free flow" of data is the best way to develop a digital economy. Whatever one's initial view of this policy proposal, it deserves careful legal and economic analysis, because it asks important and underexplored questions: if data is the key resource of the digital economy, especially for AI development, how to facilitate optimal allocation of this resource? Who captures its value? And how can those who do not immediately benefit from the digital transformation be supported, and by whom?

The Indian proposal assumes a strong role for the government in mediating the transition of India toward a digital economy, but this is by no means the only institutional solution imaginable. Moreover, in light of India's proposal to limit the transfer of data *from* India to ensure access to data for the domestic AI economy, one may wonder whether it might be more beneficial to incentivize the transfer of relevant data *to* India. Such ideas challenge the Silicon Valley Consensus, which holds that optimal data allocation is to be achieved through market mechanisms only – despite the digital economy's pervasive data control asymmetries and resulting market failures.[42]

39 A Bradford, *The Brussels Effect* (New York, Oxford University Press, 2020) ; P Schwartz, 'Global Data Privacy: The EU Way' (2019) 94 *NYU Law Review* 771.

40 European Commission, A European Strategy for Data, COM(2020) 66 final (hereinafter European Strategy for Data).

41 Draft National e-Commerce Policy, note 19 above, at 15.

42 D Ciuriak, 'Rethinking Industrial Policy for the Data-Driven Economy' (2018) CIGI Papers No. 192, at 6 (calling this the 'original sin' of the data-driven economy). Even those in favor of radical market solutions lament that the 'data titans' do not pay for the data on which they rely: see EA Posner and

C *Mandatory Data Sharing*

Digitalization changes the conditions under which capitalism operates.[43] Companies with superior data collection capacities benefit as they exploit the resulting information asymmetries.[44] E-commerce platforms may be able to leverage their intermediary position to gather information about commercial transactions on either side of the two-sided market they facilitate. Relying on predictive algorithms, they may be able to engineer demand through targeted advertising. The price to be paid may no longer be uniform – determined by aggregate supply and demand – but is 'personalized' (i.e., discriminatory).[45] Legally mandated data sharing has been proposed as a policy intervention to counterbalance the digital economy's tendency to create winner-takes-all dynamics and to ensure a competitive environment conducive to innovation.[46] But alternative justifications for mandatory data sharing are plausible, including data redistribution.

The EU and Australia are among the jurisdictions that have experimented with certain forms of mandatory data sharing. The EU's GDPR contains a right to data portability that requires data controllers to transmit personal data in a structured, commonly used, and machine-readable format to another data controller, at the request of the data subject.[47] The provision is supposed to enhance data protection by creating a more competitive environment (on the assumption that consumers will gravitate toward firms with higher data protection standards), but its impact has been muted.[48] In contrast, Australia's Consumer Data Right (CDR) bill was not primarily designed as a data protection law. It provides for the sharing of consumption data with consumers and accredited third parties, subject to data privacy safeguards, in certain sectors.[49]

EG Weyl, *Radical Markets: Uprooting Capitalism and Democracy for a Just Society* (Princeton, NJ, Princeton University Press, 2018), at 231.

43 Some even call into question whether Friedrich Hayek's conceptualization of the market as a superior information aggregation mechanism still holds and imagine alternative arrangements; see E Morozov, 'Digital Socialism? The Calculation Debate in the Age of Big Data' (2019) 116/117 *New Left Review* 33; P Pałka, 'Algorithmic Central Planning: Between Efficiency and Freedom' (2020) 83 *Law and Contemporary Problems* 125.

44 J Stiglitz, 'The Revolution of Information Economics: The Past and the Future' (2017) NBER Working Paper No. 23780.

45 EG Weyl, 'A Price Theory of Multi-Sided Platforms' (2010) 100 *American Economic Review* 1642.

46 V Mayer-Schönberger and T Ramge, *Reinventing Capitalism in the Age of Big Data* (New York, Basic Books, 2018); J Prüfer, 'Competition Policy and Mandatory Data Sharing on Data-Driven Markets' (2020) TILEC Policy Paper.

47 GDPR, Article 20; see also Frederike Zufall and Raphael Zingg's Chapter 11 in this volume.

48 G Nicholas and M Weinberg, 'Data Portability and Platform Competition: Is User Data Exported from Facebook Actually Useful to Competitors?' (2019), www.law.nyu.edu/centers/engelberg/pubs/2019-11-06-Data-Portability-And-Platform-Competition.

49 Treasury Laws Amendment (Consumer Data Right) Bill 2019; see J Meese et al., 'Citizen or Consumer? Contrasting Australia and Europe's Data Protection Policies' (2019) 8 *Internet Policy Review* 1.

The discussion around mandatory data sharing is most advanced in the banking sector. The EU's second payment services directive requires banks to share consumers' payment account data with third-party providers (under the condition that the consumers explicitly consented to such transfers).[50] The goal is to advance competition between traditional banks and newly emerging financial services providers, some of which rely heavily on algorithmic analysis of financial data. Banks seem to have acquiesced to these new regulatory demands by creating dedicated data transfer infrastructures in the form of web-based application programming interfaces (APIs).[51] Automotive vehicle data is another data category that is increasingly subject to mandatory data-sharing requirements. In some jurisdictions, car manufacturers must make vehicle data available to independent repair shops.[52] The EU's European data strategy contemplates further interventions in a variety of sectors, including agricultural, industrial, and health data, where other arrangements prove insufficient to facilitate data sharing.[53] The salience of data for AI development seems likely to spur further such initiatives elsewhere. As the next section explores, data holders will seek to mobilize existing and emerging commitments under IEL to oppose mandatory data sharing and data mobility restrictions.

III REGULATION OF DATA MOBILITY AND CONTROL UNDER INTERNATIONAL ECONOMIC LAW

IEL regulates data along at least two dimensions that are somewhat in tension with each other: data mobility (where does data reside and where can it move?) and data control (who has data and who decides how it can be used?). While new rules on free flows and data localization regulate data in favor of transnational data mobility, existing IEL, especially international IP and investment law, entrenches private control over data by limiting states' ability to mandate data disclosure and sharing. This chapter's focus on substantive disciplines regarding data mobility and data control is not to downplay the extent to which contemporary IEL leads to deep transformations of the regulatory state by introducing a wide range of horizontal and sectoral *procedural* requirements, which may be especially salient if new regulation is being considered in a not yet or under-regulated

50 Directive (EU) 2015/2366 on payment services in the internal market, OJ (2015) L No. 337, 23 December 2015, at 35. Australia is contemplating a comparable 'consumer data right' for banking; see Australian Competition and Consumer Commission, Competition and Consumer (Consumer Data Right) Rules 2019, accc.gov.au.

51 O Borgogno and G Colangelo, 'Data Sharing and Interoperability: Fostering Innovation and Competition through APIs' (2019) 35 *Computer Law & Security Review* 1.

52 See 'Mandatory Scheme for the Sharing of Motor Vehicle Service and Repair Information' (29 October 2019), https://treasury.gov.au/publication/p2019-30661. Vehicle data sharing with the government is under consideration: see National Transport Commission, 'Government Access to Vehicle-Generated Data Discussion Paper' (May 2020), ntc.gov.au.

53 European Strategy for Data, note 40 above.

domain.[54] Indeed, it is precisely through these procedural mechanisms that those who control data will seek to mobilize IEL to their advantage transnationally.[55] IEL is routinely invoked by lawyers representing firms, trade associations, regulatory agencies, and other actors in opposition to or support of their clients' preferred policy outcome. In this way, domestic law is to a significant extent continuously being shaped and reshaped by IEL.[56]

A *Regulation of Data Mobility*

Several disciplines in international trade law regulate data mobility in favor of cross-border transfers of data, at the expense of nation states' ability to restrict such transfers or to require the location of computing facilities (such as routers, servers, or data centers) within their territory. While established disciplines under the rules for trade in goods and trade in services in general, and telecommunication services in particular, only apply to certain categories of data, the new disciplines in "e-commerce" and "digital trade" chapters of agreements like CPTPP or USMCA apply to 'information', including personal information, generally.[57] Under the 'digital trade' framing, certain cross-border transfers of data can be conceptualized as trade in digital goods or as trade in digital services. To accommodate nonphysical goods, dedicated provisions address 'digital products'[58] that enjoy protections from discriminatory treatment.[59] However, data that is not produced for commercial sale or distribution but that is generated or assembled for machine learning purposes apparently escapes the digital product category. Similarly, if data is used to train algorithms that provide services (for example, financial services based on algorithms trained with financial market data), only the services, but not the data used to

[54] See Streinz, note 9 above. The Agreement on Technical Barriers to Trade (TBT), in particular, has emerged as a frame of reference for digital policies generally and World Trade Organization (WTO) members now routinely use the TBT committee to raise their concerns regarding new regulatory policies in the digital domain. For example, China's keystone data regulation, the Cybersecurity Law of 2017, has given rise to specific trade concerns in eleven meetings of the TBT Committee since June 2017 as members took issue with the requirement for domestic storage of personal information and the restriction on cross-border data flows, among other matters. See the WTO's dedicated TBT database at http://tbtims.wto.org and also Aik Hoe Lim's Chapter 5 in this volume.

[55] See P Mertenskötter and RB Stewart, 'Remote Control: Treaty Requirements for Regulatory Procedures' (2019) 104 *Cornell Law Review* 165.

[56] The impact of international economic law on domestic law-making outside of litigation is difficult to ascertain and requires a sophisticated social science methodology not generally used by legal scholars. But see T Dorlach and P Mertenskötter, 'Interpreters of International Economic Law: Corporations and Bureaucrats in Contest Over Chile's Nutrition Label' (2020) 54 *Law & Society Review* 571.

[57] TPP, Article 14.11; USMCA, Article 19.11; USJDTA, Article 11.

[58] Article 1 (g) of the USJDTA defines 'digital product' as a computer program, text, video, image, sound recording, or other product that is digitally encoded, produced for commercial sale or distribution, and that can be transmitted electronically. Footnote 1 clarifies that a digital product does not include a digitized representation of a financial instrument, including money, thereby excluding cryptocurrencies.

[59] USJDTA, Article 8. Note the qualified carve-out for taxation measures in Article 6.

provide the services, enjoy the protections under the General Agreement on Trade in Services (GATS) and the equivalent provisions in free trade agreements. GATS commitments apply if data is an end (data as a service) and not just a means to an end, and only if the WTO member in question has made specific commitments toward services liberalization in its schedule. Relevant categories in this regard encompass data processing services, software programming services, and various kinds of telecommunication services.[60]

Under the contested principle of technology neutrality, established commitments for services – formerly provided in analog form but now increasingly provided digitally – automatically acquire the same liberalization status as their analog counterparts.[61] In this way, the gradual digitalization of services can lead to a gradual liberalization of services economies that registered relatively liberal commitments for analog services. Conversely, some digital services escape the WTO's classification of services altogether, thereby creating new gaps within the system. It was, for example, unclear under which category Google's core business – providing search services – could be subsumed before the revised classification included a dedicated category for 'web search portal content'.[62]

If a WTO member has made specific commitments to allow for cross-border market access of digital foreign service providers, full-scale data transfer limitations that amount to a 'total prohibition' of the relevant service are principally illegal under Article XVI:2 (c) GATS (zero quotas).[63] Data transfer limitations that fall short of a 'total prohibition', as is the case under both the EU and the proposed Indian model, are not affected by this prohibition. They would need to comply, however, with the general obligation to national (that is, nondiscriminatory) treatment contained in Article XVII GATS and the requirement to administer any such limitation in a reasonable, objective, and impartial manner under Article VI GATS. The former would not apply to a situation in which both domestic and foreign service suppliers would need to comply with the data transfer limitations in question. The latter may give rise to a violation if the GATS member can show that the EU, for instance, conducted its adequacy assessment in an unreasonable, subjective, or partial manner. In this way, the GATS metaregulates the regime for personal data

60 The full list of specific commitments can be found in WTO members' GATS schedules registered as GATS/SC/135 according to the WTO's Services Sectoral Classification List (W/120).

61 See J Kelsey, 'How a TPP-Style E-commerce Outcome in the WTO Would Endanger the Development Dimension of the GATS Acquis (and Potentially the WTO)' (2018) 21 *Journal of International Economic Law* 273; see also R Baldwin, *The Globotics Upheaval: Globalisation, Robotics and the Future of Work* (Oxford, Oxford University Press, 2019).

62 Compare H Gao, 'Google's China Problem: A Case Study on Trade, Technology, and Human Rights under the GATS' (2011) 6 *Asian Journal of WTO and International Health Law and Policy* 349 (discussing several possibilities for classification under the original services classification in force when most WTO members entered their commitments); I Willemyns, 'GATS Classification of Digital Services – Does "The Cloud" Have a Silver Lining?' (2019) 53 *Journal of World Trade* 59 (arguing for comprehensive GATS application to digital services based on functionalist analysis).

63 Reasoning by analogy to WTO Appellate Body, *US – Gambling*, WT/DS285/AB/R (20 April 2005).

transfers under the EU's GDPR. While the EU is principally allowed to adopt and enforce measures to protect the privacy of individuals in relation to the processing and dissemination of personal data and the protection of confidentiality of individual records and accounts, it must not do so in a manner that would constitute an arbitrary or unjustifiable discrimination between comparable countries or a disguised restriction on trade in services.[64] In contrast, no such general exception exists for the Indian proposal to limit the transfer of Indian data for overtly protectionist purposes. This is likely inconsequential, because India made only minimal commitments toward services liberalization, but nevertheless paradigmatic for international trade law's aversion against 'protectionism' that is being carried forward in the digital domain.

Contrast the multilateral rules for trade in services under GATS – which are contingent on services classification, dependent on specific commitments by states, and not tailored toward questions of data mobility – with the newly created rules in agreements such as CPTPP, USMCA, and USJDTA that are specifically designed to protect data mobility against transnational data transfer restrictions.

These rules contain commitments to refrain from prohibiting or restricting the cross-border transfer of information, unless such measures are necessary to achieve a public policy objective and are not arbitrary, unjustifiably discriminatory, a trade restriction in disguise, or more restrictive than necessary.[65] The last clause, the trade law version of a necessity test, in particular, is reason enough for the EU to oppose these kinds of provisions in plurilateral (as in the case of the failed Trade in Services Agreement (TISA)) and bilateral negotiations (as in the case of the cratered EU-US Transatlantic Trade and Investment Partnership (TTIP)). While data and privacy protection are universally recognized as legitimate public policy objectives, at least in principle, views about what is necessary to achieve these objectives differ considerably. Accordingly, the EU carves out its data protection regime, including the data transfer restrictions, from external scrutiny in its trade agreements.[66]

The model inaugurated in TPP and subsequently used in USMCA and USJDTA also created a dedicated rule on a certain form of data localization that requires foreign businesses to use or locate computing facilities within a treaty party's territory as a condition for conducting business in that territory.[67] In contrast to the TPP, which allowed for the possibility to justify such measures in principle under the same conditions as applicable to cross-border data transfer restrictions, the USMCA and USJDTA do not preserve this option.[68] They also 'fix' the 'gap' that the TPP had

64 GATS, Article XIV.
65 USJDTA, Article 11.
66 Horizontal provisions for cross-border data flows and for personal data protection in EU trade and investment agreements: https://perma.cc/GJ8J-AUJE. In the EU-UK Trade and Cooperation Agreement (TCA), the EU deviated from this template and conceded that it would provide for data transfer arrangements under 'conditions of general application'. See TCA, Article 202.2.
67 TPP, Article 14.13.
68 USMCA, Article 19.12; USJDTA, Article 12.

created for financial data at the insistence of US financial regulators and to the disappointment of US financial services providers. While still treating financial services data differently from other information, the USA, Mexico, Canada, and Japan, respectively, agreed to refrain from mandating the use of domestic computing facilities requirements for financial services, as long as their respective financial regulatory authorities have immediate, direct, complete, and ongoing access to information processed or stored on financial services computing facilities outside their territory.[69] In this way, the USMCA and USJDTA preserve both the right of financial service providers to locate data territorially where they see fit and the right of regulators to access the data transnationally.

In sum, established rules in the multilateral trading system only protect certain kinds of data from certain kinds of restrictions. In this sense, factual data mobility – that is, the ability of data holders to decide where data resides and where it moves – exceeds the legal protection of data mobility under WTO law. For this reason, the USA and like-minded countries have been advocating for more stringent rules to preserve transnational data mobility as other countries have sought to impose data transfer restrictions.[70] The design of these provisions, in particular their reliance on categories borrowed from international investment law conducive to regulatory arbitrage by way of strategic incorporation, means that countries that sign on to the US model effectively opt for an open digital economy favoring transnational data mobility vis-à-vis everyone. The EU, and other jurisdictions interested in a more differentiated regime, are hence prudent in refraining from such commitments.[71]

B *Regulation of Data Control*

IEL regulates control over data mainly through commitments under international IP law and international investment law. International IP law – which shifted into the trade regime with the WTO's agreement on 'trade-related aspects of intellectual property rights' (TRIPS) and has since become a staple of 'free trade' agreements – regulates control over data by requiring IP protection for certain categories of data. Recent US agreements have gone further by creating new rights to data exclusivity in their IP chapters and novel protections for algorithms in 'digital trade' chapters. Yet, the entrenchment of data control under international investment law might be even more far-reaching as it lends itself to protecting data as an asset (investment), which entitles data holders (investors) to certain guarantees enforceable against nation

[69] USMCA, Article 17.18; USJDTA, Article 13.

[70] The USA considered targeted data localization measures against the Chinese-owned company TikTok before ordering its parent company, ByteDance, to divest itself from its US operations. The national security exception included in all US trade agreements – including USDTA, Article 4 – provides some cover for such measures, but they are nevertheless in tension with longstanding US policy favoring global "free flow" of data.

[71] T Streinz, 'Data Governance in International Economic Law: Non-Territoriality of Data and Multi-Nationality of Corporations' (draft paper, available at https://ssrn.com/abstract=3831743).

states by way of investor–state dispute settlement (ISDS). While ostensibly in favor of data mobility, IEL tends to entrench data control by protecting those who have data rather than those who need it or want it. The only exception are new commitments in recent agreements that encourage governments to make 'their' data available as 'open data'.[72] This encourages a shift from governmental control over data toward 'public' access, which is, in reality, often mediated by private actors such as data brokers or cloud providers.[73] No international agreement contemplates data sharing by private data holders, despite the regulatory trend toward compulsory data-sharing mechanisms in certain jurisdictions.

IEL's regulation of data control is especially salient as the question of legal ownership over data remains unsettled in domestic law.[74] The integration of international IP law into IEL has led to the gradual transformation of IP as a coordinative system of incentive governance into a commodity that can be 'traded' transnationally and an asset that enjoys investment protection.[75] While the reconceptualization of established IP rights as investments might upset the balance found under TRIPS,[76] the dynamic might be different for data where such a balance is yet to be found. Both common and civil law systems grapple with questions of whether and to what extent property rights in data should be recognized, newly established, or – where they exist – abolished. IEL may have a significant and potentially long-lasting influence on these debates. In this context, it is important to differentiate between legal rights of data ownership (property rights in data) and factual control over data. Data holders may exercise infrastructural control over data without commensurate property rights that a domestic court would recognize or enforce. Conversely, data transfer, storage, and processing infrastructures can be designed in ways that separate forms of legal or technological control over data. One example is cloud computing models in which the owner and operator of the physical and digital data infrastructure has no access to its consumer's data.[77] Another is 'safe sharing sites', which provide for differentiated access to data, while distinguishing between raw data and insights derived from them.[78] Neither of these contractual arrangements hinges on the recognition of property rights in data.

However, legal ownership claims over data can be critical when de facto control over data is being challenged. When governmental regulators require the disclosure of information or when data-sharing requirements between businesses are being

72 USMCA, Article 19.18; USJDTA, Article 20; DEPA, Article 9.4; ASDEA, Article 27.

73 See, for example, L Palk and K Muralidhar, 'A Free Ride: Data Brokers' Rent-Seeking Behavior and the Future of Data Inequality' (2018) 20 *Vanderbilt Journal of Entertainment & Technology Law* 779.

74 T Scassa, 'Data Ownership' (2018) CIGI Papers No. 187 (surveying legal bases for data ownership).

75 RC Dreyfuss and S Frankel, 'From Incentive to Commodity to Asset: How International Law Is Reconceptualizing Intellectual Property' (2015) 36 *Michigan Journal of International Law* 557.

76 RC Dreyfuss and S Frankel, 'Reconceptualizing ISDS: When Is IP an Investment and How Much Can States Regulate It?' (2019) 21 *Vanderbilt Journal of Entertainment & Technology Law* 377.

77 This is the data stewardship model as explained by P Schwartz, 'Legal Access to the Global Cloud' (2018) 118 *Columbia Law Review* 1681.

78 LM Austin and D Lie, 'Safe Sharing Sites' (2018) 94 *New York University Law Review* 581.

instituted, data controllers will claim 'data ownership' to guard their economic interests in data exploitation. Such claims under domestic law can be shaped and entrenched by commitments under IEL.

The TRIPS agreement sets a baseline for IP protection for certain categories of data, but such protection is not comprehensive and remains contested. Copyright, for example, only covers expressions (such as images, texts, videos) as data.[79] Compilations of data can be protected if they constitute intellectual creations, but such protection does not extend to the data contained therein.[80] Trade secrets might be able to fill some of these gaps. Technological shifts toward cloud computing and ML make it easier to satisfy the three-pronged test that Article 39.1 TRIPS stipulates. First, the secrecy of data can be achieved, for example, by keeping the data internal and by only allowing differentiated access. Second, the commercial value derived from secrecy may flow from competitive advantages in machine learning applications attributable to superior datasets. And third, secrecy can be maintained by way of technological safeguards such as encryption.[81] While the extent to which trade secrecy under TRIPS protects against data disclosure requirements transnationally has not yet been tested in dispute settlement proceedings,[82] companies rely routinely on trade secrecy to fight transparency domestically.[83] In light of uncertainty about the level of protection of undisclosed test data provided by Article 39.3 TRIPS, the USA has been aggressively pushing for 'data exclusivity' provisions in recent agreements.[84] While so far confined to regulatory approval for agricultural chemical and pharmaceutical products – where data exclusivity creates de facto exclusivity for the relevant product – these demands might be a precursor for future contests around data exclusivity in other contexts. Novel provisions protecting against source code disclosure that go beyond the traditional copyright protection for software are another pointer in the same direction.[85]

Meanwhile, international investment law's bearing on data control has been largely overlooked, but this might just be the calm before the storm.[86] The broad

79 TRIPS, Article 9(2).

80 TRIPS, Article 10(2).

81 See JC Fromer, 'Machines as the New Oompa-Loompas: Trade Secrecy, the Cloud, Machine Learning, and Automation' (2019) 94 *New York University Law Review* 706 (discussing the equivalent criteria under US law).

82 But see request for consultation by the EU against China regarding certain measures on the transfer of technology, WT/DS549/1 (1 June 2018) (alleging that China does not ensure effective protection of undisclosed information contrary to Article 39.1 and 39.2 TRIPS).

83 DS Levine, 'The Impact of Trade Secrecy on Public Transparency', in RC Dreyfuss and KJ Strandburg (eds), *The Law and Theory of Trade Secrecy* (Cheltenham, Edward Elgar Publishing, 2010).

84 See, for example, TPP, Article 18.47 and Article 18.50, the latter of which was suspended under CPTPP.

85 See, for example, JUSDTA, Article 17.

86 See JE Cohen, *Between Truth and Power: The Legal Constructions of Informational Capitalism* (New York, Oxford University Press, 2019), at 259–260 (predicting that ISDS disputes about states' interfering with cross-border flows of personal data will materialize).

'investment' definitions found in many agreements and the variety of approaches deployed by tribunals make it plausible that 'data' will soon be recognized as a protected asset under international investment law by at least some tribunals,[87] thereby granting property-type protection under international law where such protection under domestic law remains uncertain.[88] While the broad and relatively open-ended guarantee of fair and equitable treatment contained in many investment agreements can be leveraged against many forms of data regulation, the guarantees against indirect or even direct expropriation appear to be particularly apt to challenge the growing trend toward mandatory data sharing. To be sure, in the absence of ISDS jurisprudence, many open questions remain: does the recognition of data as an asset presuppose the recognition of IP-type rights in data (fostering convergence between international IP and investment law)?[89] Is the collection of data making a contribution to the host state economy, as required under the *Salini* test?[90] What kind of territorial nexus, if any, is required between a company's data-related activities and the host state to enjoy investment protection?[91] Answers to these question will only emerge over time. The development of ISDS jurisprudence on data control questions is likely to depend on what kind of cases are being brought against whom and on what basis. The failed attempt to challenge Australia's tobacco regulation may cause investors to tread more carefully when challenging the regulatory ambitions of developed countries (e.g., the EU's data strategy).[92] Developing countries with industrial data policies that challenge the Silicon Valley Consensus are likely targets for ISDS-backed counter pressure.

87 The threshold question of what constitutes an 'investment' is far from settled; see, for example, JD Mortenson, 'The Meaning of "Investment": ICSID's Travaux and the Domain of International Investment Law' (2010) 51 *Harvard International Law Journal* 257 (urging tribunals to recognize any activity or asset that is plausibly economic in nature); S Pahis, 'Investment Misconceived: The Investment-Commerce Distinction in International Investment Law' (2020) 45 *Yale Journal of International Law* 69 (suggesting that ordinary commercial transactions can be subject to investment protection).

88 In this regard, the dynamic is the inverse of the one identified by J Arato, 'The Private Law Critique of International Investment Law' (2019) 113 *American Journal of International Law* 1, at 10–12. Rather than displacing domestic private law, international investment law may grant property-like protections where it is not (yet) clear whether comparable protections are available under domestic law.

89 See E Horváth and S Klinkmüller, 'The Concept of "Investment" in the Digital Economy: The Case of Social Media Companies' (2019) 20 *Journal of World Investment & Trade* 577, at 608 (asserting that de facto control over data is insufficient for 'investment' status).

90 See, for example, D Tamada, 'Must Investments Contribute to the Development of the Host State? The *Salini* Test Scrutinised', in P Szwedo et al. (eds), *Law and Development: Balancing Principles and Values* (Singapore, Springer, 2018).

91 See, for example, *Abaclat and others (formerly Giovanna a Beccara and others) v. Argentine Republic*, ICSID Case No. ARB/07/5, Decision on Jurisdiction and Admissibility (4 August 2011) (holding that for investments of a purely financial nature, the relevant criteria should be where and/or for the benefit of whom the funds are ultimately used).

92 *Philip Morris Asia Limited v. Commonwealth of Australia* (PCA Case No. 2012–12).

IV ADAPTING INTERNATIONAL ECONOMIC LAW FOR THE ARTIFICIAL INTELLIGENCE ECONOMY

The picture that emerges is one in which new commitments toward data mobility under IEL enable those who have data to decide where they want to store, process, and transfer data, while international IP and investment law guard against governmentally mandated transparency about and/or re-distribution of control over data. Protections of mobility and control of capital are, of course, familiar ways in which IEL has facilitated global capitalism. Yet, data differs from other means of production and might necessitate changes to the global regulatory environment to generate societally beneficial outcomes. Developing countries appear to be in a particularly precarious position. Embracing the shift toward a data-driven economy is widely seen as the best path toward development.[93] Yet, charting this path while respecting local conditions and values such as human agency and self-determination is challenging because of the concentration of power over the relevant digital infrastructures and data that lends itself to new dependencies and carries the risk of data extractivism without adequate compensation.[94] For these reasons, contemporary IEL's tendency to apply policy prescriptions of the twentieth century to the emerging AI economy in the twenty-first century needs critical evaluation and, where necessary, reconfiguration. Future work will consider the following questions and tentative propositions.

First, how can governmental interests in local access to and/or regulatory control over data be reconciled with transnational business interests in cross-border data flows? While territorial data localization requirements are by no means the only or best way to ensure local access to data, it seems premature for governments to tie their hands when viable alternatives are not yet in place. In particular, countries that are interested in maintaining a differentiated approach to transnational data flows (or at least the possibility to institute such a regime eventually) may want to avoid the sweeping provisions that the CPTPP, USMCA, and JUSDTA have pioneered. Instead, imposing conditionalities under IEL directly on multi-national digital corporations – trading protections of free flow of data against commitments toward regulatory commands – might be a superior regulatory approach.[95]

Second, what are the implications of the fundamental differences between financial capital and data-as-capital for international investment law? As international investment law is undergoing critical re-evaluation and at least partial reform in both substance and procedure, its implications for an AI economy in

93 UNCTAD, 'Value Creation and Capture: Implications for Developing Countries' (2019), https://perma.cc/2XDY-PVZ3; World Bank, Development Report (2020), https://perma.cc/88SN-8WJK.

94 See H Farrell and AL Newman, 'Weaponized Interdependence: How Global Economic Networks Shape State Coercion' (2019) 44 *International Security* 42; N Couldry and UlA Mejias, *The Costs of Connection: How Data Is Colonizing Human Life and Appropriating It for Capitalism* (Stanford, CA, Stanford University Press, 2019).

95 Streinz, note 71 above.

which data is treated as a resource ought to be part of the agenda. Vague references to the 'right to regulate' may be insufficient to enable creative experimentation with digital economy policies without risk of 'regulatory chill'. As an ISDS moratorium for COVID-19-related measures is being considered, a comparable moratorium for certain digital economy policies should be on the table as well.

Third, is there a need to recalibrate the temporal mismatch between long-lasting obligations under IEL and the rapid pace of technological development? IEL's traditional commitment to providing 'certainty' for transnational business activity seems at odds with the rapid pace of innovation in the digital economy. The principle of technology neutrality may need to be cabined when new technologies transform the economy fundamentally.

And finally, how can IEL help to confront (rather than exacerbate) the pervasive data control asymmetries in the digital economy? A first step in this direction might lie in addressing the uncertainty about the value of data and data flows in a globalized digital economy. Existing proxies for the value of data flows (e.g., bandwidth expansion) and of data control (e.g., market capitalization) seem insufficient to inform policy-makers and treaty drafters. While the Organisation for Economic Co-operation and Development (OECD) and the WTO have gradually begun to address this challenge, their efforts so far have failed to consider proactive measures through which the data amassed by global platform companies could be leveraged to (re)assess the state of the global digital economy. As it turns out, data is a resource not just for the AI economy but also for the future development and reconfiguration of IEL.

10

Data Protection and Artificial Intelligence

The European Union's Internal Approach and Its Promotion through Trade Agreements

*Alan Hervé**

I INTRODUCTION

Europeans have only recently realized their weaknesses and the risk of remaining at the margins of the fourth industrial revolution[1] artificial intelligence (AI) is expected to bring about. Despite the existence of the single market, Europe industrial policy, including policy in the field of AI, still suffers from a lack of coordination and frequent duplications between member states. Moreover, investments in AI research and innovation remain limited when compared with Asia and North America.[2] As a result, European companies are in a weak position in terms of consumer application and online platforms, and industries are suffering from a structural disadvantage in the areas of data access, data processing and cloud-based infrastructures still essential for AI.

However, this gloomy overview calls for some nuance. The European Union (EU) and its member states are still well placed in the AI technological race, and the European economy benefits from several important assets, remaining not only an AI user but also, more critically, an AI producer. Europe[3] is still a key player in terms of research centers and innovative start-ups and is in a leading position in sectors such as robotics, service sectors, automotive, healthcare and computing infrastructure.

* I acknowledge the support of the European Commission through the European "Erasmus + Program", although all the opinions expressed in this chapter are personal. I warmly thank Thomas Streinz for his insightful comments on my preliminary draft. All mistakes that possibly remain in this final version are obviously mine.

1 For a comprehensive study on the trade impact of the fourth industrial revolution, see M Rentzhog, "The Fourth Industrial Revolution: Changing Trade as We Know It" (*WITA*, 18 October 2019), https://perma.cc/5NLX-L7VA. See also the chapters by Aik Hoe Lim (Chapter 5) and Lisa Toohey (Chapter 17) in this volume.

2 Overall, some 3.2 billion euros were invested in AI in Europe in 2016, compared with 12.1 billion in North America and 6.5 billion in Asia. European Commission, "White Paper on Artificial Intelligence: A European Approach to Excellence and Trust", 2020 (hereinafter White Paper on AI).

3 In this chapter, I will refer to "Europe" to describe the European Union and its member states.

Perhaps more importantly, there is growing awareness in Europe that competition and the technological race for AI will be a matter of great significance for the future of the old continent's economy, its recovery after the COVID-19 pandemic and, broadly speaking, the strategic autonomy of the EU and its member states.

The 2020 European Commission White Paper on Artificial Intelligence illustrates a form of European awakening.[4] This strategic document insists on the necessity of better supporting AI research and innovation in order to strengthen European competitiveness. According to the Commission, Europe should particularly seize the opportunity of the "next data wave" to better position itself in the data-agile economy and become a world leader in AI.[5] The Commission makes a plea for a balanced combination of the economic dimension of AI and a values-based approach as the development of AI-related technologies and applications raises new ethical and legal questions.[6]

Profiling[7] and automated decision-making[8] are used in a wide range of sectors, including advertising, marketing, banking, finance, insurance and healthcare. Those processes are increasingly based on AI-related technologies, and the capabilities of big data analytics and machine learning.[9] They have enormous economic potential. However, services such as books, video games, music or newsfeeds might reduce consumer choice and produce inaccurate predictions.[10] An even more serious criticism is that they also can perpetuate stereotypes and discrimination bias.[11] Studies on this crucial issue are still rare because of a lack of access, as researchers often cannot access the proprietary algorithm.[12] In several European countries, including France, the opacity of algorithms used by the administration has become a political issue and has also provoked growing case law[13] and legislative changes.[14] Finally, as the European Commission recently observed, AI increases the possibility to track and

4 See AI for Europe, COM(2018) 237 final, Brussels, 25.4.2018; and White Paper on AI, note 2 above, at 4. See also "Mission Letter: Commissioner-Designate for Internal Market" (2019), https://perma.cc/U7EW-C3MC.

5 European Commission, AI White Paper, note 2 above; see also J Manyika, "10 Imperatives for Europe in the Age of AI and Automation" (2017), https://perma.cc/R5MP-DT82.

6 FZ Borgesius, "Discrimination, Artificial Intelligence, and Algorithmic Decision Making" (2018), https://perma.cc/SHC7-WD5H.

7 GDPR, Article 4(4).

8 GDPR, Articles 15 and 22.

9 'Guidelines on Automated individual decision-making and profiling for the purpose of Regulation 2016/679, European Commission', October 2017.

10 Ibid.

11 See Z Obermeyer et al., "Dissecting Racial Bias in an Algorithm Used to Manage the Health of Populations" (2019) 336 *Science* 447.

12 H. Ledford, *Nature* 574 (2019), 608–609.

13 See, for instance, the ruling of the French constitutional court n° 2018–765 DC, "Loi relative à la protection des données personnelles", 12 June 2018. See also the Décret (executive order) n° 2017–330 du 14 mars 2017 "relatif aux droits des personnes faisant l'objet de décisions individuelles prises sur le fondement d'un traitement algorithmique", JO n° 64, 16 March 2017.

14 One of the most controversial issues was the opacity of the algorithm used for the selection process at the public university. See C Villani and G Longuet, "Les algorithmes au service de l'action publique:

analyze people's habits. For example, there is the potential risk that AI may be used for mass state surveillance and also by employers to observe how their employees behave. By analyzing large amounts of data and identifying links among them, AI may also be used to retrace and deanonymize data about persons, creating new personal data protection risks.[15]

To summarize, the official European stance regarding AI combines a regulatory and an investment-oriented approach, with a twin objective of promoting AI and addressing the possible risks associated with this disruptive technology. This is indeed crucial as the public acceptance of AI in Europe is reliant on the conviction that it may benefit not only companies and decision-makers but also society as a whole. However, so far, especially when it comes to the data economy on which AI is largely based, public intervention in Europe has occurred through laws and regulations that are based on noneconomic considerations. The General Data Protection Regulation (GDPR)[16] is essential in this respect because it reflects how a human rights-based legal instrument might interfere with data-based economic principles. This 2016 regulation aims at enforcing a high standard of personal data protection that can limit the free flow of data, which is at the heart of the development of AI technologies.

Given the worldwide economic importance of the single market, the effects of this regulation are inevitably global. Many commentators rightly emphasized the extraterritorial effect of this European regulation, as a non-European company wishing to have access to the European market has no choice but to comply with the GDPR.[17] Moreover, the most recent generation of EU free trade agreements (FTAs) contains chapters on e-commerce and digital trade, under which the parties reaffirm the right to regulate domestically in order to achieve legitimate policy objectives, such as "public morals, social or consumer protection, [and] privacy and data protection". Under the latest EU proposals, the parties would recognize cross-border data flows, but they would also be able to "adopt and maintain the safeguards [they] deem appropriate to ensure the protection of personal data and privacy, including through the adoption and application of rules for the cross-border transfer of personal data".[18]

The next section will present the growing debate on data protectionism (Section II). I will then study the EU's approach toward data protection and assess whether the set of internal and international legal provisions promoted by the EU effectively

le cas du portail admission post-bac–Rapport au nom de l'office parlementaire d'évaluation des choix scientifiques et technologiques" (2018), https://perma.cc/U9R4-ZT67.

15 See White Paper on AI, note 2 above, at 12.

16 Regulation (EU) 2016/679 of the European Parliament and of the Council of 27 April 2016 on the protection of natural persons with regard to the processing of personal data and on the free movement of such data, and repealing Directive 95/46/EC (General Data Protection Regulation), OJ L 119, 4.5.2016, 1–88.

17 GDPR, Article 83.

18 See "EU Proposal on Digital Trade for the EU-Australia FTA" (2018), https://perma.cc/2KQ8-F9HF.

translates into a meaningful balance between trade, innovation and ethical values (Section III). I will also describe the birth of European trade diplomacy in the field of digital trade, focusing the analysis on the most recent EU FTAs' provisions and proposals. I will compare them with recent US-led trade agreements, such as the Trans-Pacific Partnership (TPP) and the United States-Mexico-Canada Agreement (USMCA), to assess whether the EU's approach constitutes a model for future plurilateral or multilateral trade agreements (Section IV). In conclusion, I will assess whether the American and European approaches are reconcilable or destined to diverge given the opposing political and economic interests they translate.

II DATA PROTECTION OR DATA PROTECTIONISM?

Data has often been described as a contemporary raw material, a sort of postindustrial oil, and its free flow as the necessary condition for the convergence between globalization and digitalization. Data is at the heart of the functioning of AI, which is in turn the most important application of a data economy. The development of AI relies on the availability of data, and its value increases with detailed and precise information, including private information.[19] The availability and enhancement of data are crucial for the development of technologies, such as machine learning and deep learning, and offer a decisive competitive edge to companies involved in the global competition for AI.[20] Moreover, access to data is an absolute necessity for the emergence and development of a national and autonomous AI industry.[21] Not surprisingly, given the growing economic and political importance of data, governments and policy-makers are increasingly trying to assert control over global data flows. This makes sense as data, and in particular private data, is more and more presented as a highly political issue that has for too long been ignored in the public debate.[22]

The current move toward digital globalization could be threatened by three types of policies: new protectionist barriers, divergent standards surrounding data privacy and requirements on data localization.[23] Data localization has also been

[19] Scholars have tried to compartmentalize data into different categories such as personal data, public data, company data, business data, etc. In practice, however, it appears to be difficult to apply different legal instruments based on the nature of the data. Cross-border data transfers mostly cover personal data, which has both a private value and an economic value. See N Mishra, "Building Bridges: International Trade Law, Internet Governance, and the Regulation of Data Flows" (2019) 52 *Vanderbilt Journal of Transnational Law* 463, at 472–473; and S. Yakovleva, "Should Fundamental Rights to Privacy and Data Protection Be a Part of the EU's International Trade 'Deals'?" (2018) 17 *World Trade Review* 477.

[20] C. Villani et al., "Donner Un Sens à l'Intelligence Artificielle. Pour Une Stratégie National et Européenne" (2018), https://perma.cc/SLC9-AMNZ.

[21] European Commission, White Paper on AI, note 2 above, at 3.

[22] See S. Zuboff, "Big Other: Surveillance Capitalism and the Prospects of an Information Civilization" (2015) 30 *Journal of Information Technology* 75.

[23] See J Manyika et al., "Digital Globalization: The New Era of Global Flows" (2016), https://perma.cc/3XCW-4U86.

depicted as "data protectionism" and a new form of nationalism,[24] or even anti-Americanism,[25] whereas others have advocated for a "digital sovereignty" that would imply the state's power to regulate, limit or even prohibit the free flow of data.[26] Many countries are indeed subject to internal tensions between supporters of data openness as a catalyst for trade and technological development and those who promote comprehensive data protection in order to defend digital sovereignty as a prerequisite of national sovereignty. Old concepts and notions of international law, such as (digital) self-determination, (data) colonization, reterritorialization of data and (digital) emancipation, are also mobilized when it comes to justifying states' "right to regulate" data. However, those general concepts often appear inadequate given the intrinsic nature of data flows and Internet protocol, which tend to blur the distinction between the global and the local. Data flows somehow render obsolete the traditional considerations of geographical boundaries and cross-border control that characterize classical international law.[27]

Neha Mishra has thoroughly described different types of data-restrictive measures. State control can intervene using the physical infrastructures through which Internet traffic is exchanged, a local routing requirement and a variety of cross-border data flow restrictions, such as data localization measures or conditional restrictions imposed on the recipient country or the controller/processor.[28] Primary policy goals may justify those restrictions on the grounds of public order and moral or cultural issues. In Europe, the rationale behind the restrictions on the cross-border of data transfer and AI has been primarily addressed through the angle of data protection – that is, the defense and protection of privacy – as one of the most fundamental human rights.

This narrative extends well beyond the sole economic protection of European interests and has the enormous advantage of conciliating protectionist and nonprotectionist voices in Europe. It contrasts and conflicts with an American narrative based on freedom and technological progress, where free data flows are a prerequisite for an open and nondiscriminatory digitalized economy.

24 A Chander and UP Lê, "Data Nationalism" (2015) 64 *Emory Law Journal* 677.

25 See "The Rise of Digital Protectionism" (Council on Foreign Relations, 18 October 2017), https://perma.cc/P4H2-7BFV</int_i. The participants in this workshop considered that Chinese measures on data localization reflected China's "authoritarian" and "mercantilist" model, whereas "Europe's digital protectionism" is described as "in line with Brussels' legalistic, top-down, heavily regulated approach to economic policy".

26 This claim for sovereignty is in reality as old as the existence of a public debate on data flows. See C Kuner, "Data Nationalism and Its Discontent" (2015) 64 *Emory Law Journal* 2089. See also S Aaronson, "Why Trade Agreements Are Not Setting Information Free: The Lost History and Reinvigorated Debate Over Cross-Border Data Flows, Human Rights and National Security" (2015) 14(4) *World Trade Law Review* 671.

27 See Mishra, note 19 above, at 473.

28 Ibid., at 474–477.

III THE EUROPEAN LEGAL DATA ECOSYSTEM AND ITS IMPACTS ON ARTIFICIAL INTELLIGENCE AND INTERNATIONAL DATA FLOWS

The European Legal Framework on data, and in particular on data protection, is nothing new in the EU. It can be explained in the first place by internal European factors. European member states started to adopt their own law on the protection of personal information decades ago,[29] on the grounds of the protection of fundamental rights, and in particular the right to privacy, protected under their national Constitution, the European Convention on Human Rights and the European Charter of Human Rights, which forms part of current primary EU law. Therefore, EU institutions recognized early the need to harmonize their legislation in order to combine the unity of the single market and human rights considerations already reflected in member states' legislation. It explains why, while some international standards, namely those of the Organisation for Economic Co-operation and Development (OECD)[30] and Asia-Pacific Economic Cooperation (APEC),[31] emphasize the economic component of personal data, the EU's legal protection has been adopted and developed under a human rights-based approach toward personal data.[32]

The 1995 European Directive was the first attempt to harmonize the protection of fundamental rights and freedoms of natural persons with respect to processing activities, and to ensure the free flow of data between member states.[33] However, a growing risk of fragmentation in the implementation of data protection across the EU and legal uncertainty justified the adoption of a new instrument that took the form of a Regulation, which is supposed to provide stronger uniformity in terms of application within the twenty-seven member states.[34]

The GDPR also represents a regulatory response to a geopolitical challenge initiated by the United States and its digital economies to the rest of the world. From a political perspective, the Snowden case and the revelation of the massive surveillance organized by American agencies provoked a strong reaction among European public opinion, including within countries that had recently experimented with authoritarian regimes (such as the former East Germany and

29 For instance, the French legislation "informatique et liberté" was adopted in January 1978. See Loi n° 78–17 du 6 janvier 1978 relative à l'informatique, aux fichiers et aux libertés.

30 See "The OECD Privacy Framework" (2013), https://perma.cc/BC7W-B6VW, and also its explanatory Memorandum.

31 See "APEC Privacy Framework" (2015), https://perma.cc/VBW5-4ZCL.

32 Yakovleva, note 19 above.

33 Directive 95/46/EC of the European Parliament and of the Council of 24 October 1995 on the protection of individuals with regard to the processing of personal data and on the free movement of such data, OJ L 281, 23.11.1995 (hereinafter Data Protection Directive).

34 Despite this general assumption, one can observe that the GDPR leaves in practice some discretion to national authorities, in particular when it comes to the procedural enforcement of the substantive rights granted under this regulation.

Poland).[35] The Facebook-Cambridge Analytica scandal further demonstrated that the freedom of millions of Europeans and their democracies was at stake and could be threatened by the digital hegemony of American tech companies with commercial interests. The demand for data protection against free and uncontrolled flows of data has also been encouraged by the progressive awareness of the economic and technological consequences of free data flows, as European companies appeared to be increasingly outpaced by their American rivals, especially in the field of AI. In parallel, in a spectacular ruling in 2015, the European Court of Justice annulled a decision of the European Commission, under which the United States was until then considered to be providing a sufficient level of protection for personal data transferred to US territory (under the so-called safe harbor agreement).[36]

The GDPR has been both praised and criticized, within and outside of Europe. Still, it remains to a certain extent a legal revolution in the field of data regulation, not so much because of its content – it is not, after all, the first legal framework to deal with algorithms and data processing – but more because of the political message this legislation sends to the European public and the rest of the world.[37] Through the adoption of this Regulation in 2016, the EU has chosen to promote high standards for data protection. Every single European and non-European company that is willing to process European data, including those developing AI, must comply with the GDPR.[38]

A *European Data Protection's Regulation and Artificial Intelligence*

The GDPR regulates the processing of personal data; that is, any information relating to a directly or indirectly identified or identifiable natural person ("data subjects"). This legislation deals with AI on many levels.[39] First, it contains a very broad definition of "processing" as "any operation or set of operations which is performed on personal data or on sets of personal data, whether or not by automated means".[40]

35 The Commission proposed the first version of the future GDPR in January 2012. The discussion progressed very slowly until 2014 and the revelations of Edward Snowden in 2014. The GDPR was finally adopted in April 2016.

36 ECJ, 6 October 2015, Judgment in Case C-362/14, *Maximillian Schrems v. Data Protection Commissioner*, ECLI:EU:C:2015:650.

37 Even though Europe is not the sole region that adopted a data privacy legislation, according to the United Nations Conference on Trade and Development (UNCTAD), 66 percent of countries worldwide have a data protection law. See "Data Protection and Privacy Legislation Worldwide" (2020), https://perma.cc/BCP3-C2BA.

38 Compare GDPR Article 3(2).

39 For a comprehensive review of the GDPR, see PM Schwartz, "Global Data Privacy: The EU Way" (2019) 94 *NYU Law Review* 771.

40 GDPR, Article 4(4).

It also regulates the conditions under which "personal data"[41] can be collected, retained, processed and used by AI. The GDPR is built around the concept of lawful processing of data,[42] meaning that personal data *cannot* be processed without obtaining individual consent or without entering into a set of limited categories defined under the Regulation.[43] That is a crucial difference between current American federal and state laws, which are based on the presumption that data processing is lawful unless it is explicitly prohibited by the authorities under specific legislation.[44]

Under the GDPR, processing of personal data is subject to the lawfulness, fairness and transparency principles.[45] The Regulation also contains specific transparency requirements surrounding the use of automated decision-making, namely the obligation to inform about the existence of such decisions, and to provide meaningful information and explain its significance and the envisaged consequences of the processing to individuals.[46] The right to obtain information also covers the rationale of the algorithms, therefore limiting their opacity.[47] Individuals have the right to object to automated individual decision-making, including the use of data for marketing purposes.[48] The data subject has the right to not be subject to a decision based solely on automated decision-making when it produces legal effects that can significantly affect individuals.[49] Consent to the transfer of data is also carefully and strictly defined by the Regulation, which states that it should be given by a clear affirmative act from the natural person and establishes the principles of responsibility and liability of the controller and the processor for any processing of personal data.[50] Stringent forms of consent are required under certain specific circumstances, such as automated decision-making, where explicit consent is needed.[51]

Therefore, under the GDPR, a controller that will use data collected for profiling one of its clients and identifying its behavior (for instance, in the sector of insurance)

41 The GDPR only deals with personal data. Nonpersonal data is addressed by Regulation (EU) 2018/1807 of the European Parliament and of the Council of 14 November 2018 on a framework for the free flow of nonpersonal data in the European Union, OJ L 303, 28.11.2018, at 59–68.

42 GDPR, Article 6.

43 Compare GDPR, Article 6(1).

44 A Chander et al., "Catalyzing Privacy Law" (2019), https://scholarship.law.georgetown.edu/facpub/2190.

45 GDPR, Article 5(1)(a).

46 GDPR, Article 13.2.

47 GDPR, Article 15.1. The contours of this right are, however, controversial. Some authors argue it amounts to a right to explanation. See AD Selbst and J Powles, "Meaningful Information and the Right to Explanation" (2017) 7(4) *International Data Privacy Law*, at 233.

48 GDPR, Article 21.

49 GDPR, Article 22. Exceptions remain, for instance, if they are entering into a contract based on the data subject's explicit consent, or if they are authorized under the member states' laws. Article 22(2)(c) GDPR.

50 GDPR, Article 24.

51 GDPR, Article 22(1)(c). This is also supported by recital 71 of the GDPR.

must ensure that this type of processing relies on a lawful basis. Moreover, the controller must provide the data subject with information about the data collected. Finally, the data subject may object to the legitimacy of the profiling.

Another illustration of the interference between AI technologies and GDPR is the requirements and limitations imposed on the use of biometric data[52] for remote identification, for instance through facial recognition. The GDPR prohibits the process of biometric data "for the purpose of uniquely identifying a natural person" unless the data subject has given explicit consent.[53] Other limitations to this prohibition are exhaustively delineated, such as the "protection of the vital interests" of the data subject or other natural persons, or for reasons of "substantial public interest". Most of those limited biometric identification purposes will have to be fulfilled according to a necessity and a proportionality test and are subject to judicial law review.[54]

B *Transatlantic Regulatory Competition*

Despite its limitations and imperfections, the GDPR remains as a piece of legislation that aims to rightfully balance fundamental rights considerations with technological, economic and policy considerations in accordance with European values and standards. In contrast, US law surrounding the data privacy legal framework does not rely on human rights but, rather, on consumer protection, where the individual is supposed to benefit from a bargain with the business in exchange for its personal information (the so-called transactional approach).[55] Moreover, in contrast with Europe's unified and largely centralized legislation, the American model for data protection has primarily been based on autoregulation and a sectoral regulation approach, at least until the 2018 adoption of the California Consumer Privacy Act (CCPA).[56]

This state legislation partially resembles the GDPR. First, the CCPA is the first data protection statute that is not narrowly sectoral.[57] It defines "personal information" in a way that seems in practice equivalent to the GDPR's personal data definition.[58] Personal information is also partially relevant to AI (such as biometric data, geolocalization and Internet, or other electronic network information). It also includes a broad definition of processing, which can include automated decision-

[52] Compare the definition of biometric data in GDPR, Article 4 (14).

[53] GDPR, Article 9.1.

[54] GDPR, Article 9.2.

[55] See Chander et al., note 44 above, at 13.

[56] The CCPA entered into force in January 2020. SB-1121 California Consumer Privacy Act of 2018 (hereinafter CCPA).

[57] However, at the federal level, sensitive data that are considered noncommercial also benefit from strong protection. That is the case, in particular, for data collected by hospitals or the banking sector. See, for instance, the Health Insurance Portability and Accountability Act, 45 C.F.R. § Parts 160, 162 and 164.

[58] See CCPA SEC.9 (o).

making.[59] Echoing the GDPR's transparency requirements, the CCPA provides a right of information, under which a consumer has the right to request that a business that collects consumers' personal information disclose to that consumer the categories and specific pieces of personal information collected.[60] This right of disclosure is particularly significant.[61] The CCPA also contains a right to opt out and deny the possibility for a business to use its personal information.[62]

Despite those similarities, important differences remain between the two statutes. Concretely, under the CCPA's transactional approach, the right to opt out cannot be opposed if it is necessary to business or service providers to complete the transaction for which the personal information was collected or to enable solely internal uses that are reasonably aligned with the expectations of the consumer's relationship with the business.[63] Moreover, whereas the GDPR rests on the principle of the "lawful processing of data",[64] the CCPA does not require processing to be lawful, implying that data collection, use and disclosure is allowed unless it is explicitly forbidden. Whereas the GDPR requires some specific forms of consent related to sensitive data and limits individual automated decision-making, the CCPA "does nothing to enable individuals to refuse to give companies their data in the first place".[65] Another striking difference is related to the consumer's right not to be discriminated against under the CCPA if he or she decides to exercise the right to seek information or the right to opt out. The effect of this nondiscrimination principle seems tenuous as, in those circumstances, a business is not prohibited from charging a consumer a different price or rate, or from providing a different level or quality of goods or services to the consumer.[66] This is typically the result of a consumer protection-based approach, which in reality tolerates and admits discrimination (here, the price or the quality of the service provided), and a human rights-based approach that is much more reluctant to admit economic differentiations among individuals to whom those fundamental rights are addressed.

This brief comparison between the GDPR and the CCPA is not meant to suggest that one legislative model is intrinsically superior, more efficient, more legitimate or more progressive than the other. Both statutes merely translate ontological discrepancies between the European and American legal conceptions and policy choices. However, the conflict between those two models is inevitable when considering the current state of cross-border data flows. Not surprisingly, the question of extraterritoriality was crucial during the GDPR's drafting.[67] Even though the Regulation is based on the necessity of establishing a single digital market, under which data

59 See CCPA SEC.9 (q).
60 CCPA SEC.1A. See further Chander et al., note 44 above, at 14–16.
61 CCPA SEC.3 (a).
62 CCPA SEC.2 (a).
63 CCPA SEC.2 (d). Compare GDPR Article 22(2)(a).
64 GDPR Article 6(1). Chander et al., note 44 above, at 19.
65 Ibid., at 20.
66 CCPA SEC.6 (a)(2).
67 See in particular D. Bernet's insightful documentary *Democracy: Im Rausch der Daten* (2015).

protection and fundamental EU rights are equally guaranteed, its extraterritorial effects are expressly recognized as the GDPR applies "in the context of the activities of an establishment of a controller or a processor in the Union, *regardless of whether the processing takes place in the Union or not*" and "to the processing of personal data subjects who are in the Union by a controller or processor *not established in the Union*".[68] The extraterritorial effects of the GDPR and, more broadly, of the EU's legal framework are undeniable given the importance of the single EU market.[69] Extraterritoriality should be understood as a kind of "effet utile" of the Regulation, as most of the data processors and controllers are currently located outside the EU's territory. The EU's effort would in practice be doomed if personal data protection were to be limited to the EU borders.[70]

The European legislator admits that flows of personal data to and from countries outside the EU are necessary for the expansion of international trade.[71] Yet, international data transfers must not undermine the level of data protection and are consequently subject to the Regulation's provisions. Data transfer to third countries is expressly prohibited under the GDPR unless it is expressly authorized thanks to one of the legal bases established under the Regulation.[72] The European Commission may decide under the GDPR that a third country offers an adequate level of data protection and allow transfers of personal data to that third country without the need to obtain specific authorization.[73] However, such a decision can also be revoked.[74] In the absence of an adequacy decision, the transfer may be authorized when it is accompanied by "appropriate safeguards", which can take the form of binding corporate rules[75] or a contract between the exporter and the importer of the data, containing standard protection clauses adopted by the European Commission.[76] Even in the absence of an adequacy decision or appropriate safeguards, data transfer to third countries is allowed under the GDPR, in particular on the consent of the data subject, and if the transfer is necessary for the performance of a contract.[77]

68 GDPR, Article 3.

69 See A Bradford, *The Brussels Effect: How the European Union Rules the World* (New York, Oxford University Press, 2020). For a distinction between the so-called Delaware Effect, California Effect and Brussels Effect, see Chander et al., note 44 above.

70 Schwartz, note 39 above, at 11. For a discussion of the GDPR's limits see ECJ, 24 September 2018, Judgment in Case C-507/17, *Google LLC, v. Commission nationale de l'informatique et des libertés (CNIL)*, ECLI:EU:C:2019:772.

71 GDPR, Recital 201.

72 GDPR, Article 44.

73 This adequacy requirement of the data protection level in the foreign jurisdiction was already in place in the Data Protection Directive, note 33 above. Before its adoption, member states had their own adequacy requirements. Schwartz, note 39 above, at 11–12.

74 GDPR, Articles 44 and 45.

75 Defined as internal corporate rules for data transfers within multinational organizations.

76 GDPR Articles 46 and 47.

77 GDPR Article 49.

Under the current regime, the EU Commission adopted a set of adequacy findings with select third countries, such as Japan, in February 2019.[78] The European Commission also commenced adequacy negotiations with Latin American countries (Chile and Brazil) and Asiatic countries (Korea, India, Indonesia, Taiwan), as well as the European Eastern and Southern neighborhoods, and is actively promoting the creation of national instruments similar to the GDPR.[79] Moreover, in July 2016, the European Commission found that the EU-US Privacy Shield ensures an adequate level of protection for personal data that has been transferred from the EU to organizations in the USA, demonstrating regard for, inter alia, safeguards surrounding access to the transferred data by the United States' intelligence services.[80] More than 5,300 companies have been certified by the US Department of Commerce in charge of monitoring compliance with a set of common data privacy principles under the Privacy Shield, which is annually and publicly reviewed by the Commission.[81] The Privacy Shield seemed to demonstrate that despite profound divergence between European and American approaches to data protection, there was still room for transatlantic cooperation and mutual recognition. However, in mid-July 2020, the European Court of Justice (ECJ) concluded that the Commission's Privacy Shield decision was invalid as it disregarded European fundamental rights.[82] As the Court recalled, the Commission must only authorize the transfer of personal data to a third country if it provides "a level of protection of fundamental rights and freedoms essentially equivalent to that guaranteed within the European".[83] The ECJ found lacunae in judicial protections for European data subjects against several US intelligence programs.[84]

The question of data transfer between the EU and UK after Brexit is one of the many hot topics that should be dealt with in a future EU/UK trade agreement, and it is a perfect example of the problematic nature of the GDPR's application to EU third countries with closed economic ties. The October 2019 political declaration setting out the framework for the future relationship between the two parties contains a specific paragraph on digital trade that addresses the question of data

78 The European adequacy decision came after Japanese internal reforms on data privacy law, in particular the extensive 2015 amendment to Japan's Act on the Protection of Personal Information (APPI). See Schwartz, note 39 above, at 14–16. See the Commission Implementing Decision (EU) 2019/419 of 23 January 2019, OJ L 76, 19.3.2019. This decision scrutinizes the Japanese legal framework concerning data protection.

79 Data protection rules as a trust-enabler in the EU and beyond – taking stock, COM(2019) 374 final, July 2019. See also the list of adequacy decisions at https://perma.cc/VA6X-ZQ3T.

80 The Privacy Shield had to be negotiated after the European Court of Justice found that a former EU-US safe harbor arrangement was incompatible with EU law. See *Maximillian Schrems v. Data Protection Commissioner*, note 35 above.

81 "Privacy Shield Framework", https://perma.cc/RTZ2-UAT5.

82 Case C-311/18, *Data Protection Commissioner v. Facebook Ireland Limited, Maximilian Schrems*, 16.07.2020.

83 Ibid., at part 94.

84 The adequacy decision being annulled, future data transfer will, however, remain possible under GDPR Article 49.

protection. It says that future provisions on digital trade "should ... facilitate cross-border data flows and address unjustified data localisation requirements, noting that this facilitation will not affect the Parties' personal data protection rules".[85] However, in June 2020, six months after Brexit, the Commission was still uncertain regarding a future UK adequacy assessment because of a lack of specific data protection commitment in the UK. Moreover, the British government indicated that it wanted to develop a separate and independent data protection policy.[86] One of the EU's main concerns is that through bilateral agreements concluded between the UK and the USA, data belonging to EU citizens could be "siphoned off" to the United States.[87]

The issue of compatibility between European privacy rules and the Chinese legal framework is also a growing matter of concern for Europeans. China applies much stricter data border control on the grounds of national security interests. For instance, the 2017 Chinese law on cybersecurity provides that companies dealing with critical infrastructures of information, such as communications services, transport, water, finances, public services energy and others, have an obligation to store their data in the Chinese territory. Such a broad definition can potentially affect all companies, depending on the will of Chinese authorities, who also have broad access to personal information content on the grounds of national security.[88] However, Chinese attitudes regarding privacy protection are not monolithic. According to Samm Sacks, "[t]here is a tug of war within China between those advocating for greater data privacy protections and those pushing for the development of fields like AI and big data, with no accompanying limits on how data is used". This expert even describes a growing convergence between the European and Chinese approaches in data protection regimes, leading the USA to be more isolated and American companies to be more reactive.[89] However, based on the model of the recent conflict between European data privacy rules and US tech companies' practices, emerging cases that shed new light on data protection regulatory divergence between China and the EU are inevitable.[90]

Fragmentation and market barriers are emerging around requirements for privacy and data flows across borders. Can this fragmentation be limited through international

85 See "Revised Political Declaration Setting Out Setting Out the Framework for the Future Relationship Between the European Union and the United Kingdom as Agreed at Negotiators' Level" (17 October 2019), https://perma.cc/5Y4S-XBQU.

86 See Boris Johnson's Government written statement on the UK/EU relationship made on 3 February 2020.

87 See, for instance, the Access to Electronic Data for the Purpose of Countering Serious Crime Agreement signed between the UK and the USA in October 2019.

88 S Livingstone, "China Sets to Expand Data Localization and Security Services Requirements" (IAPP, 25 April 2017), https://perma.cc/3R5N-CL4A.

89 See S Sacks, "New China Data Privacy Standard Looks More Far-Reaching Than GDPR" (Center for Strategic and International Studies, 29 January 2018), https://perma.cc/A6AH-8EYX.

90 See German Labour Court ruling concerning Huawei, "Arbeitsgericht Düsseldorf, 9 Ca 6557/18" (Justiz-Online, 5 March 2020), https://perma.cc/9FEV-2TGX.

trade law? What is the EU's position on international data flows and data protection in the context of its trade policy? Can and should European trade agreements become an efficient way to promote the GDPR's privacy approach?

IV THE BIRTH OF EUROPEAN DIGITAL TRADE DIPLOMACY

Not surprisingly, given its imprecise nature, AI is not covered as such by trade agreements, although AI technologies that combine data, algorithms and computing power can be affected by trade commitments in the field of goods and services. In this section, I will focus on the issue of the trade dimension of cross-border data flows, given its strategic relevance to AI applications. Although data cannot be assimilated to traditional goods or services, trade rules matter with regard to data in multiple ways.[91] As I have already noted, even though regulating data flows on national boundaries might seem counterintuitive and inefficient,[92] states and public authorities are tempted to regain or maintain control of data flows for many reasons, ranging from national security to data protection to economic protectionism. A trade agreement is one international public law instrument that might constitute a legal basis to promote cross-border data control or, on the contrary, the free flow of data principle.

A *A Limited Multilateral Framework*

Despite recent developments, digital trade rules currently remain limited, both at the multilateral and the bilateral level. World Trade Organization (WTO) disciplines do not directly confront the problematic nature of digital trade or AI, even though the WTO officially recognizes that AI, together with blockchain and the Internet of Things, is one of the new disruptive technologies that could have a major impact on trade costs and international trade.[93] Mira Burri has, however, described how WTO general nondiscrimination principles – Most Favorable Nation Treatment and National Treatment – could potentially have an impact on the members' rules and practices regarding digital trade, as well as more specific WTO agreements, especially the General Agreement on Trade in Services (GATS).[94] She notes that WTO members have made far-reaching commitments under the GATS. The EU in particular has committed to data processing services,

[91] See Mishra, note 19 above; M Burri, "The Regulation of Data Flows Through Trade Agreements" (2017) 51 *UC Davis Law Review* 407, at 468.

[92] Mishra, note 19 above.

[93] See World Trade Organization, "World Trade Report 2018: The Future of World Trade – How Digital Technologies Are Transforming Global Commerce" (2018), https://perma.cc/S9AM-A26P; D Mitchell and N Mishra, "Regulating Cross-Border Data Flows in a Data-Driven World: How WTO Law Can Contribute" (2019) 22(3) *Journal of International Economic Law* 389.

[94] M Burri, "The Governance of Data and Data Flows in Trade Agreements: The Pitfalls of Legal Adaptation" (2017) 51 *UC Davis Law Review* 65.

database services and other computing services.[95] These commitments might prohibit new measures with regard to search engines that limit market access or discriminate against foreign companies, as they should be considered data processing services. Localization requirements with regard to computer and related services would also be prima facie GATS-inconsistent, but could well be justified under the agreement's general exceptions.[96]

Despite a few updates, such as the Information Technology Agreement, WTO members have failed, as in other fields, to renovate and adapt proper WTO disciplines to strategic issues, such as digital trade and AI. The current plurilateral negotiations on e-commerce, which involve seventy-nine members including China, Japan, the USA and the EU and its member states, might represent a new opportunity to address these issues.[97] However, given the current state of the WTO, such evolution remains, at present, hazardous.[98] So far, the most relevant provisions on digital trade are those negotiated within the bilateral or plurilateral trade deals, beginning with the TPP.[99]

Recent developments in EU digital trade diplomacy can be seen as a reaction to the United States' willingness to develop an offensive normative strategy whose basic aim is to serve its big tech companies' economic interests and to limit cross-border restrictions based on data privacy protection as much as possible.

B *The US Approach to Digital Trade Diplomacy*

The United States' free trade agreement (FTA) provisions on digital trade are the result of the Digital Agenda that was endorsed in the early 2000s. Several US trade agreements containing provisions on e-commerce have been concluded by different American administrations over the last two decades.[100] In 2015, the United States Trade Representative described the TPP as "the most ambitious and visionary

95 Ibid., at 84.

96 Ibid. See also the way the WTO Appellate Body interpreted GATS article XIV in *US – Gambling* (WT/DS285/ABR, 7 April 2005).

97 See the WTO Joint Statement on Electronic Commerce, WT/L/1056, 25 January 2019. See also Henry Gao's Chapter 15 in this volume.

98 It can even be traced back to the Clinton administration's framework for global electronic commerce. See T Streinz, "Digital Megaregulation Uncontested? TPP's Model for the Global Digital Economy," in B Kingsbury et al. (eds), *Megaregulation Contested Global Economic Ordering After TPP* (Oxford, Oxford University Press, 2019).

99 Ibid.

100 See the FTAs concluded with Australia (2002), Singapore (2003), Bahrain (2004), Chile (2004), the central American countries (2004), Morocco (2006), Oman (2009), Peru (2009), Panama (2012), Colombia (2012) and especially Korea (2012), which was, until the TPP, the most advanced FTA on digital trade. See S Wunsch-Vincent and A Hold, "Toward Coherent Rules for Digital Trade: Building on Efforts in Multilateral versus Preferential Trade Agreements", in M Burri and T Cottier (eds), *Trade Governance in the Digital Age* (Cambridge, Cambridge University Press, 2011).

internet agreement ever attempted".[101] The TPP provisions relate to digital trade[102] in various respects, including, inter alia, nondiscriminatory treatment of digital products,[103] a specific ban of custom duties on electronic transmission[104] and free supply of cross-border digital services.[105] More specifically, despite recognizing the rights of the parties to develop their own regulatory requirements concerning the transfer of information by electronic means, the agreement prohibits the limitation of cross-border transfer of information by electronic means, including personal information.[106] Additionally, under the TPP, "no Party shall require a covered person to use or locate computing facilities in that Party's territory as a condition for conducting business in that territory".[107] US tech companies were deeply satisfied with the content of the agreement.[108]

However, the TPP drafters did not ignore the problematic nature of personal information protections. Indeed, the text of this agreement recognized the economic and social benefits of protecting the personal information of users of electronic commerce.[109] It even indicated that each party *shall* adopt or maintain a legal framework that provides for the protection of the personal information of the users of electronic commerce, therefore admitting the possibility of following different legal approaches. However, each party should adopt instruments to promote compatibility between the different legal frameworks,[110] and the agreement's wording is relatively strong on the nondiscriminatory practices in terms of user protections.

The GDPR was still under discussion when the TPP was concluded. However, there is room for debate concerning the possible compatibility of the European legislation and this US trade treaty. As with the WTO compatibility test, the main issue concerns the possible discriminatory nature of the GDPR, which in practice is arguable. This doubt certainly constituted an incentive for the EU to elaborate upon and promote its own template on digital trade, in order to ensure that its new

101 The Bipartisan Congressional Trade Priorities and Accountability Act of 2015, P.L. 114–26 sec. 102 (b) (6) adopted by the US Congress included precise negotiations objectives for digital trade in goods and services and cross-border data flows.

102 See TPP chapter 14 on "Electronic Commerce".

103 TPP, Article 14.4.

104 TPP, Article 14.3.

105 Cross-border service provisions of US FTAs have always been very liberal as they rely on a negative approach, meaning that a cross-border service should be liberalized unless the contracting parties expressly restrict it. See TPP, Article 14.2.4.

106 TPP, Article 14.11.2.

107 TPP, Article 14.13. However, such a provision is subject to limitations on the grounds of legitimate public policy objectives, provided that they are not applied in a discriminatory and disproportionate manner. TPP, Article 14.8.

108 See "IBM Comments on U.S. Review of Trade Agreements" (THINKPolicy Blog, 31 July 2017), https://perma.cc/4GGR-YZVC.

109 TPP, Article 14.8.1.

110 Both autonomous instruments and mutually agreed-upon solutions are permitted, which seems to echo the GDPR mechanisms described.

legislation wouldn't be legally challenged by its trade partners, including the US administration.

Just like the TPP, the USMCA contains several provisions that address digital trade, including a specific chapter on this issue.[111] It also prohibits custom duties in connection with digital products[112] and protects source code.[113] The prohibition of any cross-border transfer or information restriction is subject to strong wording, as the agreement explicitly provides that "[n]o Party *shall* prohibit or restrict the cross border transfer of information, including personal information, by electronic means if this activity is for the conduct of the business of a covered person".[114] Yet, the USMCA admits the economic and social benefits of protecting the personal information of users of digital trade and the relevance of an internal legal framework for the protection of this information.[115] However, the conventional compatibility of internal regulations that would limit data collection relies on a necessity and proportionality test and a nondiscrimination requirement. In any case, the burden of proving compatibility will undoubtedly fall on the party that limited data transfer in the first place, even though it did so on the grounds of legitimate policy objectives. Under these circumstances, the legality of GDPR-style legislation would probably be even harder to argue than under the former TPP.

C *The European Union's Response to the American Trade Regulatory Challenge*

Before studying the precise content of existing EU agreements and proposals on digital trade, one should bear in mind that European trade policy is currently subject to strong internal tensions. Trade topics have become increasingly politicized in recent years, especially in the context of the Comprehensive Economic and Trade Agreement (CETA) and Transatlantic Trade and Investment Partnership (TTIP) negotiations. It is not only member states, through the Council, and the European Parliament – which has obtained, after the Lisbon Treaty, the power to conclude trade agreements together with the Council – that have placed pressure on the Commission. Pressure has also come from European civil society, with movements organized at the state and the EU level.[116] As a result, the idea that trade deals should no longer be a topic for specialists and be subject to close political scrutiny is gaining ground in Europe. As a response, the capacity of trade agreements to better regulate international trade is now part of the current Commission's narrative to advocate for

111 The name of the USMCA chapter is now "digital trade", which may sound more precise than the TPP's "electronic commerce" language.
112 USMCA, Article 19.3.
113 USMCA, Article 19.16.1.
114 USMCA, Article 19.11.1.
115 USMCA, Article 19.8.
116 See Stop-TTIP European Citizens' Initiative, registered in July 2017, Commission registration number: ECI(2017)000008.

the necessity of its new FTA generation,[117] in line with European primary law provisions that connect trade with nontrade policy objectives.[118] The most recent generation of EU FTAs incorporate a right to regulate, which is reflected in several provisions, in particular in the context of the sustainable development[119] and investment chapters.[120] More recently, the EU also showed a willingness to include a right to regulate in the digital chapter's provisions.[121] Paradoxically, the recall of the state power to regulate is the prerequisite of stronger trade liberalization[122] and, more broadly, a way in which to legitimize the extension of trade rules.

Older trade agreements, meaning those concluded before 2009, when the Lisbon Treaty entered into force, remained practically silent on the issue of digital trade or electronic commerce. The EU-Chile (2002) trade agreement is probably the first FTA that contains references to e-commerce, probably under the influence of the US-Chile FTA concluded during the same period. However, the commitments were limited as they refer to vague cooperation in this domain.[123] Moreover, the service liberalization was strictly contained within the limits of the positive list-based approach of the former generation of European FTAs.[124] The EU-Korea FTA of 2011 contains more precise provisions on data flows, yet it is limited to specific sectors.[125] For instance, Article 7.43 of this agreement, titled "data processing", is part of a broader subsection of the agreement addressing financial services. The provision encourages free movement of data. Yet, it also contains a safeguard justified by the protection of privacy. Moreover, the parties "agree that the development of electronic commerce must be fully compatible with the international standards of data protection, in order to ensure the confidence of users of electronic commerce". Finally, under this agreement, the cross-border flow of supplies can be limited by the necessity to secure compliance with (internal) laws or regulations, among which is

117 See, for instance, the Commission's Communication *Trade for All*, COM (2015) 497 final, 14.10 and A Hervé, "The European Union and Its Model to Regulate International Trade Relations" (2020) Schuman Foundation Paper, European Issue n° 554, https://perma.cc/B43D-37P2.

118 Compare TFEU Article 207.

119 See JEFTA (Japan/EU FTA, OJ L 330, 27.12.2018, 3–899), Article 16.2.

120 See CETA, Article 8.9 (in the context of the investment protection's chapter); see also the EU-Canada Joint Interpretative Instrument where both parties "recognise the importance of the right to regulate in the public interest" (OJ L 11, 14.1.2017, 3–8).

121 See the recently concluded EU/Mexico FTA chapter on digital trade.

122 This paradox of a deeper liberalization accompanied by measures involving a stronger state and administrative control has been famously pictured by Michel Foucault through his concept of "biopower" and "biopolitics". See M Foucault, *The Birth of Biopolitics: Lectures at the College de France* 1978–1979 (New York, Palgrave Macmillan, 2008).

123 Compare Article 104 of the EU-Chile Association Agreement, OJ L 352, 30.12.2002, 3–1450.

124 See Burri, note 91 above, at 426. However, after CETA, the EU accepted to conclude FTAs based on a negative service liberalization approach. That is the case of the JEFTA, although the liberalization remains subject to a long list of exceptions.

125 This evolution might be explained by the existence of commitments on e-commerce in the KORUS FTA, signed in 2007 (see KORUS chapter 15 on Electronic Commerce). However, KORUS Article 15.8 uses soft wording regarding free data flows ("the Parties *shall endeavor to refrain* from imposing or maintaining unnecessary barriers to electronic information flows across borders").

the protection of the privacy of individuals.[126] Although limited to specific sectors, those provisions demonstrate that the EU was aware of the potential effect of data protection on trade long before the adoption of the GDPR.[127]

This sectoral approach has been followed by the EU and its partners in more recent trade agreements, such as the CETA between the EU and Canada, which was concluded in 2014.[128] Chapter 16 of the CETA agreement deals expressly with e-commerce. It prohibits the imposition of customs duties, fees or charges on deliveries transmitted by electronic means.[129] It also states that "[e]ach Party *should* adopt or maintain laws, regulations or administrative measures for the protection of *personal information of users* engaged in electronic commerce and, when doing so, *shall* take into due consideration international standards of data protection of relevant international organizations of which both Parties are a member".[130] However, the CETA also contains another innovative and broader exception clause based on data protection. Article 28.3 addresses the general exception to the agreement, and provides that several chapters of the agreement (on services and investment, for instance) can be subject to limitation based on the necessity to "secure compliance with laws or regulations which are not inconsistent with the provisions of this Agreement including those relating to . . . the protection of the privacy of individuals in relation to the processing and dissemination of personal data". Finally, the CETA agreement, unlike the US model, does not contain a general free data flow provision and only promotes specific forms of data transfer, consistent with European economic interests, such as financial transfers for data processing in the course of business.[131]

The current European strategy regarding trade and data protection appears more clearly in the negotiations after the adoption of the GDPR. In 2018, the European Commission made public proposals on horizontal provisions for cross-border data flows, and for personal data protection in EU trade and investment agreements.[132] This template is an attempt to reconcile diverging regulatory goals, in particular human rights considerations and economic considerations.[133] This conciliation is also symbolized by the internal conflict, inside the Commission, between the

126 EU-Korea FTA, Article 7.50 (e) (ii), OJ L 127, 14.5.2011, 1–1426.

127 At the time, data protection was regulated under the 1995 Data Protection Directive; note 33 above.

128 Only the investment chapter of the CETA was renegotiated after 2014. The agreement has been provisionally in force since September 2017.

129 CETA, Article 16.3. However, Article 16.3 clarifies the possibility to submit electronic commerce to internal taxes.

130 CETA, Article 16.4. Both the 2005 APEC and 2013 OECD privacy frameworks are therefore relevant to justify the parties' regulations.

131 CETA, Article 13.15.1. However, the following paragraph immediately outlines that the parties are allowed "to maintain adequate safeguards to protect privacy, in particular with regard to the transfer of personal information".

132 "Horizontal Provisions for Cross-Border Data Flows and for Personal Data Protection", https://perma.cc/P6YB-7M9N.

133 See Yakovleva, note 19 above.

Directorate General for Trade (DG Trade), traditionally in charge of trade negotiations, and the Directorate General for Justice and Consumers (DG JUST). DG Trade has shown greater sensitivity toward cross-border data flows, whereas DG JUST conceived trade law as an instrument to expand Europe's privacy protections.[134] As a result, this template supports cross-border data flows while also immediately recognizing that the protection of data and privacy is a fundamental right. Therefore, the protection of data privacy is exempted from any scrutiny.[135] This privacy safeguard uses the wording from a clause to the national security exceptions and contrasts with the necessity and proportionality tests put in place under the TPP and USMCA. Not surprisingly, this privacy carve-out was immediately criticized by tech business lobbyists in Brussels.[136]

However, the EU proposals formulated in late 2018, under the framework of the negotiation of two new FTAs with Australia and New Zealand (initiated in 2017), largely confirmed the template's approach. First, the EU's proposed texts refer to the right of the parties to regulate within their territories to achieve legitimate objectives, such as privacy and data protections.[137] These proposals also further cross-border data flows in order to facilitate trade in the digital economy and expressly prohibit a set of restrictions, among which are requirements relating to data localization for storage and processing, or the prohibition of storage or processing in the other party's territory. Moreover, the proposals protect the source code, providing that, in principle, the parties cannot require the transfer of, or access to, the source code of software owned by a natural or juridical person of the other party.[138] A review clause on the implementation of the latter provision, in order to tackle possible new prohibitions of cross-border data flows, is included. Additionally, the European proposals allow the parties to adopt and maintain safeguards they deem appropriate to ensure personal data and privacy provisions. The definition of personal data is similar to the GDPR's conception.[139] This approach is also in line with the EU's proposal, formulated within the context of the plurilateral negotiations regarding e-commerce, which took place at the WTO in April 2019.[140]

The ability of the EU to persuade its trading partners to endorse its vision on digital trade remains uncertain. In this context, the content of the Digital Chapter of

134 See Streinz, note 98 above, at 334–335.

135 See Article B.2 of the European Template.

136 This includes "Digital Europe", which represents the largest European, but also non-European, tech companies (such as Google, Microsoft, Amazon and Huawei). See "DIGITALEUROPE Comments on the European Commission's Draft Provisions for Cross-Border Data Flows" (DIGITALEUROPE, 3 May 2018), https://perma.cc/RPB6-XGUM.

137 Article 2 of the proposals.

138 Article 11 of the proposals. However, this provision is potentially subject to the general exception clause of the agreement.

139 Articles 5 and 6 of the proposals. Under Article 6.4 "personal data means any information relating to an identified or identifiable natural person".

140 EU proposal for WTO disciplines and commitments related to e-commerce, INF/ECOM/22, 26 April 2019.

the recently concluded FTA between the EU and Japan is not very different from the CETA,[141] demonstrating the absence of real common ground and Japanese support on this issue. Whereas the JEFTA is an ambitious text in a wide range of sensitive trade matters (such as geographical indications, service liberalization and the link between trade and the environment), it only refers to a vague review clause regarding digital trade and free data flows.[142] However, as mentioned earlier, the question of cross-border data flows between Japan and the EU has been dealt with through the formal process that led Japan to reform its legal framework on data protection, which in turn led to the Commission's 2019 adequacy decision.[143] Unilateral instruments remain, for the EU, the de facto most efficient tools when it comes to the promotion of its conception of data protection.[144]

V CONCLUSION

The entry into force of the GDPR coincides with a new era of international trade tensions, which might be interpreted as a new symbol of the European "New, New Sovereigntism" envisioned by Mark Pollack.[145] The European way of addressing the issue of data processing and AI is, in reality, illustrative of the limits of the current European integration process. European industrial policies in this field have been fragmented among the member states, which have not achieved the promise of a single digital market and, even more problematically, have not faced strong international competition. So far, the EU's response to this challenge has been mostly legal and defensive in nature. Yet, such a strategy is not in itself sufficient to address the challenges raised by AI. Smart protectionism might be a temporary way for Europe to catch up with the United States and China, but any legal shield will in itself prove useless without a real industrial policy that necessitates not only an efficient regulatory environment but also public investment and, more broadly, public support. The post-COVID-19 European reaction and the capacity of the EU and its member states to coordinate their capacities, modeled on what has been done in other sectors such as the aeronautic industry, will be crucial. After all, the basis of the European project is solidarity and the development of mutual capacity in

[141] See JEFTA, Article 8.63 (promoting data transfers in the field of financial services) and JEFTA Article 8.78.3 (recognizing the importance of personal data protection for electronic commerce users).

[142] JEFTA, Article 8.81. Similarly, the new digital trade chapter of the renovated EU-Mexico FTA is limited to a three-year review clause when it comes to cross-border data flows. See EU-Mexico renovated FTA Article XX (a provisional version of the text was made public in May 2020 and is available at https://perma.cc/7TAZ-J8F9).

[143] See the Commission's Implementing Decision (EU) 2019/419 of 23 January 2019 on the adequate protection of personal data by Japan under the Act on the Protection of Personal Information, OJ L 76, 19.3.2019, 1–58.

[144] This unilateralism does not preclude political dialogue with the partner.

[145] MA Pollack, "The New, New Sovereigntism (Or, How the Europe Union Became Disenchanted with International Law and Defiantly Protective of Its Domestic Legal Order)", in C Giorgetti and G Verdirame (eds), *Concepts of International Law in Europe and the United States* (forthcoming).

strategic economic areas, such as coal and steel in the 1950s, and a context of crisis and the risk of a decline of the "old continent" may serve as a strong catalyst for an efficient European AI policy.

On a more global and general level, the analysis of the GDPR and the European trade position on data flows and AI illustrates that this new and disruptive sector has not escaped the existing tensions between free trade and protectionism. Unsurprisingly, the new digital trade diplomacy is subject to an old rule: negotiators' positions are largely influenced by economic realities and the necessity to promote a competitive industry or to protect an emerging sector, respectively. Fundamental rights protection considerations that led to a form of "data protectionism" in the EU are certainly also influenced by its economic agenda. On the other hand, the US promotion of free flows of data essentially responds to the interest of its hegemonic companies and their leadership on the Internet and AI. The admission of the free data flows principle from the EU might correspond to the growing presence of data centers in the EU's territory, which followed the entry into force of the GDPR, given the necessity to comply with this regulation.[146] It can also be interpreted as a hand up to its trade partner, in exchange for the admission of a large data privacy carve-out that would legally secure the GDPR under international trade law. However, unless extremely hypothetical political changes occur and a willingness to forge a transatlantic resolution or a multilateral agreement on these questions materializes, the fragmentation of the digital rules on data transfer will likely remain a long-term reality.

[146] See Mishra, note 19 above, at 477.

11

Data Portability in a Data-Driven World

Frederike Zufall and Raphael Zingg

Today's technology giants have won market dominance through the collection, analysis, and synthesis of data. With the increasing dependence on digital technology, and increasing data dependency of said technology, data can be seen as a precondition to economic participation. Exploiting the steep economies of scale and network externalities of data, firms such as Google, Facebook, and Amazon are in positions of near monopoly. When such service providers disallow users from transferring their data to competing services, they can lock in users and markets, limiting the entry of market competition. Providing users with rights to both retrieve their data and transmit it to other firms potentially serves as a counterbalance, easing the acquisition of users for new market entrants. As such, data portability legislation has been claimed to have far-reaching implications for the private sector, reducing or hindering tools of forced tenancy. With users no longer married to a single firm, inroads for new technology are paved, with the average user more likely to have the ability and resource to change provider and adopt a solution that better suits their individual needs.

This chapter explores the concept of data portability in a world driven by artificial intelligence (AI). Section I maps out the journey that data takes in a data economy and investigates the valuation and cost of data. It posits that, because of data analytics and machine learning models, "generated" data, as data that has been derived or inferred from "raw" data, is of higher value in the data market, and carries a higher cost of production. Section II discusses what is required for the free flow of data in competitive datacentric markets: regulations on data tradability and portability. Our analysis leads to doubt that the newly introduced, hotly debated rules regarding portability of data under European Union (EU) law will adequately provide these prerequisites. The chapter concludes by suggesting an alternative model for data portability that distinguishes on a value basis rather than between personal and nonpersonal data.

I THE JOURNEY AND VALUE OF DATA

This first section reviews the journey of data from collection to classification: the path from its moment of provision by a data subject to its subsequent transformation into inferred data. We present a categorization model that distinguishes data according to its origin, primarily distinguishing between raw and generated data. Utilizing these categories, we illustrate how data generated by machine learning models is being created at an exponential rate in today's data-driven economy. Lastly, a data valuation model is introduced, holding that the value of generated data is higher than raw data, and that the value of generated data scales exponentially in aggregation. We claim that the added value of generated data is created by firms that carry the costs of providing big data analytics, including machine learning.

A *Origin of Data*

Data can be classified according to a variety of parameters. A classification model can rely on the sensitivity of the subject, purpose of use, context of procession, degree of identifiability, or method of collection of data. We build on a categorization model of data that was introduced by a roundtable of Organisation for Economic Co-operation and Development (OECD) privacy experts in 2014,[1] and expanded by Malgieri.[2] The taxonomy categorizes data according to its origin – that is, the manner in which it originated – and distinguishes between raw data (provided and observed data) and generated data (derived and inferred data).

Raw data ("user-generated data") encompasses provided and observed data. Provided data is data originating from the direct actions of individuals (e.g., registration form filing, product purchases with credit card, social media post, etc.). Observed data is data recorded by the data controller (e.g., data from online cookies, geolocation data, or data collected by sensors).

Generated data ("data controller-generated data") consists of derived and inferred data. Derived data is data generated from other data, created in a "mechanical" manner using simple, non-probabilistic reasoning and basic mathematics for pattern recognition and classification creation (e.g., customer profitability as a ratio of visits and purchases, common attributes among profitable customers). Inferred data is data generated from other data either by using probabilistic statistical models for

1 "Protecting Privacy in a Data-Driven Economy: Taking Stock of Current Thinking" (OECD, 21 March 2014), https://perma.cc/AFH5-MZF9 refers to provided, observed, derived, and inferred data – inferred data being defined as the "product of probability-based analytic processes".

2 G Malgieri, "Property and (Intellectual) Ownership of Consumers' Information: A New Taxonomy for Personal Data" (2016) 4 *Privacy in Germany* 133; G Malgieri and G Comandé, "Sensitive-by-Distance: Quasi-Health Data in the Algorithmic Era" (2017) 26 *Information & Communications Technology Law* 229; Boston Consulting Group, "The Value of Our Digital Identity" (2012), distinguishes between volunteered, required, tracked, and mined data; World Economic Forum, "Personal Data: The Emergency of a New Asset Class" (2011), distinguishes between volunteered, observed, and inferred data.

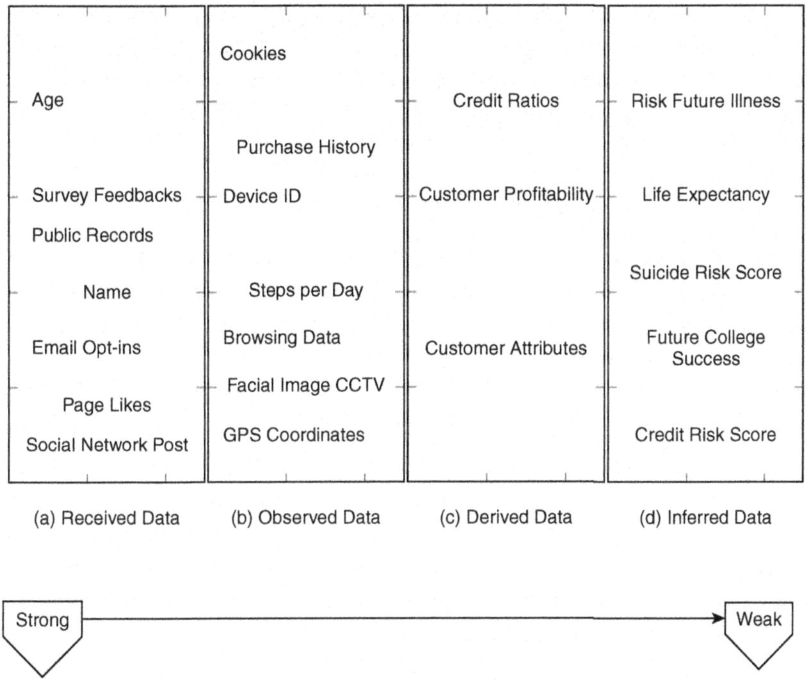

FIGURE 11.1 Data types and examples

testing causal explanation ("causal inferences") or by using machine learning models for predicting output values for new observations given their input values ("predictive inferences").[3]

The relationship between information and the data subject can be classified as either strong (provided data), intermediate (observed and derived data), or weak (inferred data). The stronger the relationship, the more individuals are involved in the creation of the data. Illustratively, a Facebook user has a strong relationship with their registration data and their posts. An example of a weaker relationship would exist when Facebook, based on its algorithmic models, assigns a liberal or conservative political score to this user. The user's age, geographic location, and posts are all data provided by the user, and eventually included as independent variables in the model. But it is Facebook's model that will ultimately predict the likelihood the user belongs to either group.

The evolving relationship from provided to inferred data, or from a weak to strong relationship between the data subject and the data, is illustrated in Figure 11.1. Although the delimitation of data types is crucial, a number of gray areas exist. Take the example of a data subject that does not upload data themself, but actively selects which sets of data and their conditions the data controller may access. It is unclear

3 G Shmueli, "To Explain or to Predict" (2010) 25(3) *Statistical Science* 289.

whether these datasets are received or observed by the controller.[4] Note that inferred data is created not only by the analysis of a specific user's data, but also by the analysis – via statistical learning and automatic techniques to elicit patterns – of all data available to the data generator, including personal data provided by other users.[5]

B *Artificial Intelligence and Data*

With the rise of AI, generated data is expected to proliferate at an exponential rate. As more and more institutions take advantage of increasingly broad datasets, computing power, and mathematical processes,[6] the amount of generated data will expand and the costs of prediction decrease.[7] As pointed out by a recent report ordered by the House of Commons of the United Kingdom, protecting data helps to secure the past, but protecting inferences is what will be needed to protect the future.[8] Inferential data generated by machine learning techniques has already been used (with varying success)[9] to predict sexual orientation based upon facial recognition; emotions of individuals based on voice, text, images, and video; a neighborhood's political leanings by its cars; and physical and mental predictions, to name but a few.[10] With the advancement of the technology and the availability of large training sets, the accuracy of inferred predictions will increase as well.

The predictive potential of machine learning is not confined to academic use cases, as commercial applications abound. Recent patent applications in the USA include methods for predicting personality types from social media messages,[11] predicting user behavior based on location data,[12] predicting user interests based on image or video metadata,[13] or inferring the user's sleep schedule based on smartphone and communication data.[14] In all these instances, raw user data is collected on mobile devices

4 G Malgieri, "'User-Provided Personal Content' in the EU: Digital Currency Between Data Protection and Intellectual Property" (2018) 32(1) *International Review of Law, Computers & Technology* 118.

5 R Accorsi and G Müller, "Preventive Inference Control in Data-centric Business Models" (2013), https://perma.cc/T722-JM47.

6 "Analytics Comes of Age" (2018), https://perma.cc/MV8Y-3M5B; M Abrahams, "The Origins of Personal Data and Its Implications for Governance" (2014), https://papers.ssrn.com/sol3/papers.cfm?abstract_id=2510927.

7 J O'Callaghan, "Inferential Privacy and Artificial Intelligence: A New Frontier?" (2018) 11(2) *Journal of Law & Economic Regulation* 72.

8 "Disinformation and 'Fake News': Final Report" (2018) Eighth Report of Session 2017–19, HC 1791, https://perma.cc/ZPK4-WB9J.

9 O Etzioni, "No, the Experts Don't Think Superintelligent AI Is a Threat to Humanity" (*MIT Technology Review*, 20 September 2016), https://perma.cc/B543-HZZ5.

10 See O'Callaghan, note 7 above.

11 US10013659, "Methods and Systems for Creating a Classifier Capable of Predicting Personality Type of Users", granted 3 July 2018.

12 US20170255868, "Systems and Methods for Predicting User Behavior Based on Location Data", filed 3 March 2017.

13 US9798980, "Method for Inferring Latent User Interests Based on Image Metadata", granted 24 October 2017.

14 US20160292584, "Inferring User Sleep Patterns", filed 31 March 2015.

(e.g., smartphones, tablets, etc.) to build and train the predictive model, and then used to predict individual user characteristics and behaviors (as generated data). This generated data is of value to marketing and advertising firms or organizations more generally to identify target users for their products and services.

C *Valuation of Data*

In general, the valuation of data is difficult, as it varies widely by type, scale, and industry sector. We make two assumptions that underly this chapter, and that support our position that generated data is of higher value than raw data. We claim that the higher value of generated data derives from the investment of firms in development, and subsequent use of statistical and machine learning models.

Our first assumption is that at the single datapoint level, raw data is on average of lower value than generated data. Our explanation for this assumption is as follows: raw data (such as the age of a data subject) is assumed to be, on average, of lower value to companies than generated data (such as future health predictions). In fact, in the marketplace, the price for general information, such as age, gender, and location, can be purchased for as little as $0.0005 or $0.50 per 1,000 people.[15] We assume that the price for creation of and access to generated data is higher.[16] The value of the datapoint integrates the value-added created by the respective algorithm. This is a generalizable claim despite specific and highly contextual differences. To provide a counterexample, data relating to diseases directly provided by a patient might be of higher value to an insurance company than a prediction based on that data.[17]

Our second assumption is that, on a large scale, the value of raw data increases linearly, whereas the value of generated data increases exponentially. We make this assumption for the following reasons: for statistical or machine learning approaches, received and observed data will need to be purchased on a large scale in order to

15 E Steel et al., "How Much Is Your Personal Data Worth?" (*Financial Times*, 12 June 2013), https://perma.cc/EDY4-7G6U. On the cryptocurrency marketplace, where the user can monetize their data directly, selling GPS location data (to Datum), Apple Health data (to Doc.ai), and biographical Facebook information and Strava running routes (to Wibson) will yield an estimated $0.3; see G Barber, "I Sold My Data for Crypto. Here's How Much I Made" (*WIRED*, 17 December 2018), https://perma.cc/AV2V-B9G2.

16 B Ehrenberg, "How Much Is Your Personal Data Worth?" (*The Guardian*, 22 April 2014), https://perma.cc/MS7V-5R3W ("[t]he inferred data is the type with real practical value, and the first two, unsurprisingly, don't cost much; they just help to build a picture of the third"). D Ciuriak, "Unpacking the Valuation of Data in the Data-Driven Economy" (2019), https://papers.ssrn.com/sol3/papers.cfm?abstract_id=3379133 (contending that "[t]he major share of the market value of these firms is comprised of IP [intellectual property] and data – arguably, mostly data, although there is no empirical basis for venturing a specific point estimate").

17 With a price point at $0.3 per name for a list with names of individuals suffering from a particular disease, see P Glikman and N Glady, "What's the Value of Your Data?" (*TechCrunch*, 14 October 2015), https://perma.cc/M3GB-BA78.

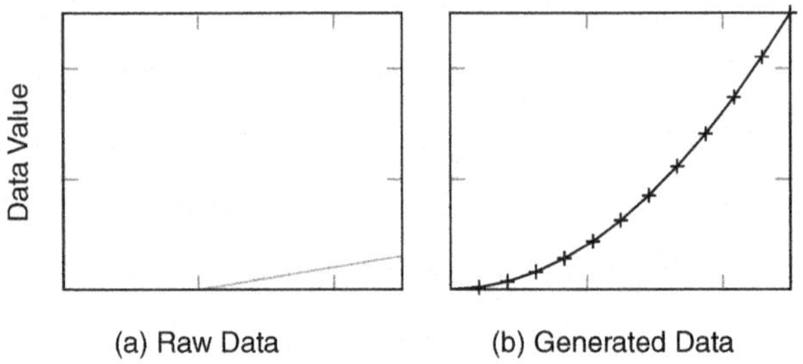

FIGURE 11.2 Data value of raw data and generated data

build models that will create inferred data. Since the accuracy of predictions is largely a function of the size of training datasets, we can assume that the value of received and observed data is close to zero for small-scale datasets. On the other hand, past acquisitions of datacentric companies reveal a significantly higher value per user, varying between $15 and $40. For instance, Facebook acquired WhatsApp and Instagram for $30 per user.[18] These per-user valuations reflect both the quality and scope of the information collected, as well as the expectation of continued platform engagement, and subsequent additional data creation by each acquired user.[19] In short, these acquisitions aim at exploiting trends and patterns in large groups with high confidence in the quality of the data. The process of value creation directly depends on investment in machine learning models needed to convert data into predictions.[20] These include direct operating costs, such as the employment costs of engineers, the licensing costs for software programs, the costs for obtaining more computer power and storage, and the costs of integrating systems with the implementation platform, as well as indirect costs such as training and change management costs or cybersecurity monitoring costs.[21] Therefore, the valuation of datacentric companies reflects the value of aggregated generated data or the potential for firms to create aggregated generated data.[22] We represent the respective value of raw data and generated data in Figure 11.2: with more data, the value of raw data increases linearly (a), whereas the value of generated data increases exponentially (b).

18 G Sterling, "What's the Most Expensive (Per User) Acquisition? Hint: Not WhatsApp" (Marketing Land, 26 February 2014), https://perma.cc/KR3D-DWMQ.

19 Glikman and Glady, note 17 above.

20 DQ Chen et al., "How the Use of Big Data Analytics Affects Value Creation in Supply Chain Management" (2015) 32 *Journal of Management Information Systems* 4 (showing that the use of big data analytics explained 8.5 percent of the variance in asset productivity and 9.2 percent of the variance in business growth).

21 N Cicchitto, "What Is the Cost of Implementing AI Today?" (Avatier, 9 May 2019), https://perma.cc/G8ML-WF8Q.

22 See D Ciuriak, note 16 above (contending that the only comprehensive way to data valuation is to infer it from the market capitalization of data-driven firms).

II PORTABILITY OF DATA

This second section analyzes the newly introduced regulation of data portability in Europe. With the goal of moving toward a single market for data, the EU has sought to remove obstacles to the free movement of data via two regulations regarding personal and non-personal data. We evaluate the newly introduced right to data portability under the General Data Protection Regulation (GDPR)[23] and the porting of data regime under the Non-Personal Data Regulation (NPDR).[24] Our analysis of both data portability concepts suggests that the current separation between personal and non-personal data does not provide for a comprehensive and coherent data portability regime.

A *Free Flow of Data*

EU law has a long tradition of shaping regulation to create a single market for goods, services, people, and capital. In recent years, the European Commission has emphasized the need for a data ecosystem built on trust, data availability, and infrastructure.[25] Ensuring the free flow of data is part of this effort to establish a "digital single market".[26] Data is increasingly seen as a tradable commodity.[27] While the framework for trading data can be found in the traditional civil law rules for purchase contracts, the contract performance – that is, the actual transfer of the data – largely depends on the existence of data portability as a legal institution.[28] We are interested in how a regulatory framework for the market may level the playing field, challenging large incumbents with a vested interest in not transferring potentially valuable data to competitors.[29]

The more data is concentrated in the hands of a provider, the more likely it will be considered to hold a dominant position under EU competition law.[30] Although the

23 Regulation (EU) 2016/679 of the European Parliament and of the Council of 27 April 2016 on the protection of natural persons with regard to the processing of personal data and on the free movement of such data, and repealing Directive 95/46/EC (hereinafter GDPR), OJ L 119, 4.5.2016, 1–88.

24 Regulation (EU) 2018/1807 of the European Parliament and of the Council of 14 November 2018 on a framework for the free flow of non-personal data in the European Union (hereinafter NPDR), OJ L 303, 28.11.2018, 59–68.

25 "The Single Market in a changing world: A unique asset in need of renewed political commitment", COM/2018/772 final.

26 F Zufall, "Digitalisation as a Catalyst for Legal Harmonisation: The EU Digital Single Market" (2017) 10 *WIAS Research Bulletin* 103.

27 D Ciuriak, note 16 above.

28 There is an ongoing debate surrounding the tradability of digital goods, and whether a resale is admissible or not; see H Zech, "Data as a Tradeable Commodity", in A De Franceschi (ed.), *European Contract Law and the Digital Single Market: The Implications of the Digital Revolution* (Cambridge, Intersentia, 2017).

29 M Peritz and H Schweitzer, "Ein Neuer Europäischer Ordnungsrahmen für Datenmärkte?" (2018) 71 *Neue Juristische Wochenschrift* 275, at 277–278.

30 Treaty on the Functioning of the European Union (TFEU), Article 102. Traditionally, the European Court of Justice considered the threshold to be at 40 percent or more market share; see Judgment of 13 February 1979 (*Hoffmann-La Roche & Co. AG v. Commission of the European Communities*), Case 85/76, ECLI:EU:C:1979:36.

dominant competition law test is based on market share, not data concentration, said concentration is likely to lead to large market shares in data-driven markets.[31] The European Data Protection Supervisor has discussed how portability of data can foster a functioning market by preventing the abuse of dominance and the lock-in of consumers.[32] EU competition law, however, can generally be characterized as an *ex post* regulation: in fact, the European Commission only intervenes once a dominant position has been abused in already existing markets.[33]

As digital markets are especially prone to winner-takes-all (or -most) outcomes,[34] additional *ex ante* regulations are key. The EU has set up a number of these *ex ante* mechanisms, in particular in sector-specific regulation. A prominent example of this is the telecommunications sector: the Universal Service Directive established a right to number portability, considered a predecessor to the right to data portability under EU law.[35] The portability of telephone numbers and of data facilitates effective competition and can be considered a form of *ex ante* regulation as it creates the prerequisites for establishing a functioning telecommunication market.

The free movement of data is further addressed in Art. 16(2)1 of the Treaty on the Functioning of the European Union (TFEU), which gives the EU legislator the power to establish rules regarding the protection and free movement of personal data. The GDPR confirms the free movement of data as a subject-matter of the regulation and postulates that the free movement of personal data within the EU shall not be restricted or prohibited for the protection of personal data.[36] These affirmations refer once more to the foundation of the EU: free movement of goods, services, people, capital, and now data in a single market. Since May 2019, the regime is complemented by the NPDR.[37] Targeting non-personal data, the NPDR is entirely based on the ideal of the free flow of data. According to the NPDR, the two regulations provide a coherent set of rules that cater for free movement of different types of data.[38]

31 See the recent decision of the German Federal Court of Justice: BGH, 23.06.2020 (KVR 69/19) confirming the assessment of the German Federal Cartel Authority, BKartAmt, 06.02.2019 (B6-22/16).

32 "Preliminary Opinion of the European Data Protection Supervisor, Privacy and competitiveness in the age of big data: The interplay between data protection, competition law and consumer protection in the Digital Economy", March 2014 (hereinafter EDPO, Opinion 2014), paragraph 82–83 with reference to K Coates, *Competition Law and Regulation of Technology Markets* (Oxford, Oxford University Press, 2011).

33 Although competition law, on the flipside, creates incentives for firms to adjust their behavior under threat of enforcement.

34 E Brynjolfsson and A McAfee, *The Second Machine Age: Work, Progress, and Prosperity in a Time of Brilliant Technologies* (New York, W.W. Norton & Company, 2014).

35 Universal Service Directive (2002/22/EC), Article 30. EDPO, Opinion 2014, note 32 above, paragraph 83.

36 GDPR, Article 1(1) and 1(3).

37 NPDR, note 24 above.

38 NPDR, Recital (10).

B *Regimes for Data Portability*

The portability of data is explicitly covered by both the GDPR and the NPDR. The former only applies to "personal data", the latter to "non-personal data".[39] EU law therefore clearly delineates personal from non-personal data.

Personal data is defined as "any information relating to an identified or identifiable natural person ('data subject')".[40] The notion of personal data is broad, as it only requires that a natural person can be identified directly or indirectly. It is sufficient, for instance, that the link to the natural person can be established using other reasonably accessible information – such as a combination of specific browser settings used to track behavior for personalized advertising.[41]

Non-personal data, by contrast, is any information that does not relate to an identified or identifiable natural person. Firstly, this encompasses data that originally does not relate to an identified or identifiable natural person, such as weather information or data relating to the operation of machines. Secondly, properly anonymized data cannot be attributed to a specific person and is therefore non-personal.[42] However, if non-personal data can be linked to an individual, the data must be considered personal.[43]

1 Portability of Personal Data

The newly introduced right to data portability in Art. 20 GDPR gives the data subject the "right to receive the personal data concerning him or her, which he or she has provided to a controller, in a structured, commonly used and machine-readable format and have the right to transmit those data to another controller without hindrance from the controller to which the personal data have been provided". Data subjects shall have the right to receive the personal data concerning them and transmit that data to other controllers.

The provision mirrors the GDPR's dual purpose: both the protection of personal data and the free flow of personal data. The right to the protection of personal data is intertwined with a market-centered economic approach to personal data.[44]

[39] GDPR, Article 2(1).

[40] GDPR, Article 4(1).

[41] See for IP addresses: ECJ, Judgment of 24.11.2011 – C-70/10 – Scarlet/SABAM; ECJ, Judgment of 19.10.2016 – C-582/14 – Breyer/BRD.

[42] "Guidance on the Regulation on a framework for the free flow of non-personal data in the European Union, May 29, 2019", COM (2019) 250 final (hereinafter Guidance on NPDR). See further subsection C.

[43] See M Finck and F Pallas, "They Who Must Not Be Identified: Distinguishing Personal from Non-Personal Data under the GDPR" (2020) 10 *International Data Privacy Law* 11; and I Graef et al., "Towards a Holistic Regulatory Approach for the European Data Economy: Why the Illusive Notion of Non-Personal Data Is Counterproductive to Data Innovation" (2019) 44 *European Law Review* 605.

[44] GDPR, Article 1(1); see P De Hert et al., "The Right to Data Portability in the GDPR: Towards User-centric Interoperability of Digital Services" (2018) 34 *Computer Law & Security Review* 193;

Not all personal data is subject to the right of portability. Only personal data for which the processing is based on consent or a contractual relationship is covered by the norm.[45] This limitation largely corresponds to the requirement that the personal data in question was provided by the data subject.[46] Accordingly, raw personal data is covered by portability because provided data is, by definition, directly provided by the data subject and observed data is (by most accounts) considered as such.[47] Generated data, however, whether derived or inferred, is not considered as being provided by the data subject.[48] Therefore, a large share of personal data is not subject to portability as it is not provided by the data subject.[49]

The GDPR provides a relatively strong right to data portability for the data subject. Data portability is seen from the data subject's perspective, with a focus on data protection. Creating a comprehensive regime for the portability of all kinds of personal data was not the priority of the EU legislator, as shown by the exclusion of generated personal data. Although the norm is often discussed as being situated in the area of competition law – with its aim of facilitating the free flow of data – data portability under the GDPR is still being considered closer to genuine data protection law than to regulatory competition law.[50]

2 Portability of Non-personal Data

With the NPDR, the EU encourages the porting of non-personal data.[51] The Internet of Things or industrial settings are major sources of non-personal data, as exemplified by aggregate and anonymized datasets used for big data analytics, data on precision farming, or data on maintenance needs for industrial machines.[52] The Regulation addresses two obstacles to non-personal data mobility: data localization

T Jülicher et al., "Das Recht auf Datenübertragbarkeit – Ein datenschutzrechtliches Novum" (2016) *Zeitschrift für Datenschutz* 358.

45 Typical cases are the creation of a social media profile based on personal data or providing shipping and billing information to an online shop (GDPR, Art. 6(1)(a) and (b)). Besides the data subject's right to data portability, the GDPR also takes into consideration the rights and protection of third parties as a limiting factor in case the datasets contain their personal data (GDPR, Art. 20(4)).

46 As the GDPR uses different phrasing for "personal data" and for "data provided by the data subject", the latter must be a part of the former.

47 "Guidelines on the right to data portability 16/EN/WP242rev.01" (hereinafter Guidelines on DP).

48 Ibid.

49 S Wachter and B Mittelstadt, "A Right to Reasonable Inferences: Re-Thinking Data Protection Law in the Age of Big Data and AI" (2018) 2 *Columbia Business Law Review* 494. For the practical challenge of porting Facebook data, see G Nicholas and M Weinberg, "Data Portability and Platform Competition: Is User Data Exported from Facebook Actually Useful to Competitors?" (2019), https://perma.cc/54RV-3G6G.

50 In this sense, Guidelines on DP, note 47 above, at 4. See further EDPO, Opinion 2014, note 32 above, paras 26, 83; W Kerber, "Digital Markets, Data, and Privacy: Competition Law, Consumer Law and Data Protection" (2016) *GRUR International* 639; Jülicher/Röttgen/v. Schönfeld, note 44 above; Peritz and Schweitzer, note 29 above, at 275, 277, 278.

51 NPDR, Article 6.

52 NPDR, Recital (9).

requirements imposed by the public sector and private vendor lock-in practices.[53] Such a lock-in effect might exist if cloud services like data storage or cloud-based data applications do not ensure the portability of the respective data.

While the GDPR provides for an enforceable right of the data subject, the NPDR approaches portability differently. The regulation encourages self-regulatory codes of conducts; that is, legally nonbinding instruments. The norm expressively refers to best practices that should facilitate the porting of data through "structured, commonly used and machine-readable formats including open standard formats where required or requested by the service provider receiving the data".[54] Meanwhile, codes of conduct on the porting of data and switching between cloud service providers have been developed by the cloud switching and porting data working group (SWIPO) for Infrastructure-as-a-Service (IaaS) and Software-as-a-Service (SaaS) cloud services.[55] These codes require, inter alia, the use of application programming interfaces (APIs),[56] open standards, and open protocols by cloud service providers.

C *Analysis: The Concept of Data Portability*

Our analysis depicts the limitations of existing EU law in providing for the free movement of data via a comprehensive and effective portability regime. In particular, we discuss how the distinction between personal versus non-personal data and raw versus generated data may impact the concept of data portability.

1 Distinction between Personal and Non-personal Data

The EU framework separates data into two types: personal and non-personal. This separation subjects data to different regulatory regimes – with a number of consequences in terms of portability. The distinction between personal and non-personal data is meant to preserve a high level of protection for data that can be related to an individual. The GDPR accordingly sets forth a right to access available for all type of personal data, whether raw or generated.[57] The NPDR targets data that is not related to an identifiable natural person. The interests of datacentric businesses stand in the center of the regulation. The free flow of data is therefore targeted from the data subject's perspective as well as from the perspective of market regulation.

53 Compare NPDR Article 4 and Article 6.

54 NPDR, Article 6(1)(a).

55 See "Presentation of Codes of Conduct on Cloud Switching and Data Portability" (European Commission, 9 December 2019), https://perma.cc/H46G-33WN. Platform-as-a-Service might be considered at a later stage: "Cloud Stakeholder Working Groups Start Their Work on Cloud Switching and Cloud Security Certification" (European Commission, 16 April 2018), https://perma.cc/K2TT-DJKN.

56 See, on the role of APIs, O Borgogno and G Colangelo, "Data Sharing and Interoperability Through APIs: Insights from European Regulatory Strategy" (2018) European Union Law Working Paper No. 38, https://ssrn.com/abstract=3288460.

57 GDPR, Article 15.

In theory, the distinction between personal and non-personal data appears straightforward. In practice, this is often not the case. For instance, large datasets where personal and non-personal data are mixed up (so-called mixed datasets) make it hard to identify the applicable legal regime. The NPDR recognizes this situation and addresses it by splitting up the application of both legal regimes to the respective type of data.[58] In cases where both types are inextricably linked, the application of the GDPR takes precedence (even if personal data represents a small part of the set only).[59] Addressing the complexity of GDPR compliance for mixed datasets can have a large impact on technology firms' associated costs. Uncertainty still prevails in the field on how to avoid falling under the GDPR.

This lack of legal certainty provides an incentive to anonymize data. The underlying belief is that personal data can be turned into non-personal data by anonymization, as anonymization destroys the link to an identifiable person. Consequently, the NPDR takes into consideration future technological developments making it possible to turn anonymized data into personal data, with the consequence of then having to treat such data as personal data and to apply the GDPR to it.[60] Recent studies, however, have challenged the common understanding of anonymization. The European Commission itself has addressed these concerns, but remains committed to the belief that anonymization can be achieved in practice.[61] In an influential study, Rocher, Hendrickx, and de Montjoye showed that 99.98 percent of Americans would be correctly reidentified in any dataset using fifteen demographic attributes.[62] A range of additional studies have supported this point, with reidentification of supposedly anonymous datasets in healthcare, ride-sharing, subway, mobile phone, and credit card datasets.[63] All this raises doubts about whether the distinction between personal and non-personal data can be upheld in the future.

2 Distinction between Raw and Generated Data

The right to data portability under the GDPR only applies to personal data provided by the data subject. From the viewpoint of providing access to the market of social media services, the portability of raw data alone is considered sufficient to prevent customer lock-in. Although the controller uses raw data (provided and observed) to generate derived and inferred data, generated data is not considered as "provided by the data subject" in the sense of Art. 20(1) GDPR. As such, generated data does not fall under the right to data portability. However, if it qualifies as personal data,

58 NPDR, Article 2(2).
59 Guidance on NPDR, note 42 above, at 8–10.
60 NPDR, Recital (9).
61 Guidance on NPDR, note 42 above.
62 L Rocher et al., "Estimating the Success of Re-identifications in Incomplete Datasets Using Generative Models" (2019) 10 *Nature Communications* 1; see also C Blackman and S Forge, "Data Flows: Future Scenarios" (2017), https://perma.cc/QN7C-YRPZ at 22, box 2.
63 For a summary, see Rocher et al., note 62 above; see further Finck and Pallas, note 43 above.

generated data is still subject to the right of access or the right to not be subject to automated individual decision-making.[64] Consequently, the GDPR offers the data subject access to its personal data and protection regardless of whether the data is raw or generated.[65]

A reason why the right to data portability under the GDPR does not cover data created by the controller (i.e., generated data) might be that portability would here grant a strong advantage to competitors. Porting generated data would grant companies access to especially valuable data (Assumption 1), whose aggregation scales exponentially (Assumption 2).[66] The GDPR envisages a model where the data subject provides raw data to social media providers and leaves the additional value of the data to these providers as a compensation of their costs. But this is only justified in instances like Facebook, where the user "pays" with their data in exchange for the free use of the service. The service provider bears the cost of providing the social network and may recoup their investments by gaining profit from the added value the raw data gains through inferential information, illustratively via advertising. If the data subject, however, pays for a service, be it social networking or an analysis of their personal data, the situation is entirely different: the service provider's costs are being compensated by monetary payment. The added value of the derived or inferred data should then remain with the data subject and fall under the scope of the right to data portability.[67]

This situation is similar to the one envisaged by the NPDR: one between a customer and a service provider. When the customer provides raw data to the data service provider who conducts statistical analysis or prediction through machine learning on this data on behalf of the customer, the customer bears the cost of transformation of the data. As the costs are assigned to them, they should be able to obtain the value of the resultant generated data, to transfer it and switch providers. This right would in general already be subject to a civil law contract by which the relationship between service provider and customer is governed. The role and task of regulation would then only be to enforce portability in cases where service providers have market power to the extent that such portability and its conditions (portable file format, interfaces, etc.) is not subject to the service agreement. For this reason, the data porting rules under the NPDR may be insufficient as they are nonbinding and limited to self-regulatory measures. The European Commission or the respective member state authorities would need to take competition law measures based on abuse of dominant position, which have the limitation of being *ex post* in nature.

64 GDPR, Articles 15 and 22.

65 Compare the Opinion of the Committee on Legal Affairs for the Committee on Civil Liberties, Justice and Home Affairs, A7-0402/2013, PE501.927v05-00, at 520 ("This new right [to data portability] included in the proposal for a directive brings no added value to citizens concerning right of access").

66 See Section I, subsection C.

67 All the more if the service provider in these cases might not be a controller in the sense of Art. 4 (7) GDPR anymore, if the decision-making power is assigned to the data subject.

An already binding obligation of non-personal data portability can be seen in Art. 16(4) Digital Content Directive,[68] albeit limited to the area of digital content and digital services: the consumer is granted the right to request "any content other than personal data, which was provided or created by the consumer when using the digital content or digital service supplied by the trader". This stipulation affirms our position: the value of digital content – that is, the data – created by the customer is assigned to the customer, leading to a right to retrieve that data in a commonly used and machine-readable format, as the second subparagraph states.

D *Data Portability beyond the European Union*

The EU has taken the lead in shaping the way the world thinks about data protection, privacy, and other areas of digital market regulation.[69] Its data protection standards in particular have been diffused globally.[70] Firstly, the ideas and concepts of the GDPR – in our case of data portability – have influenced a number of jurisdictions to enact data portability norms themselves. Secondly, international firms are bound directly by the GDPR's and the NPDR's extraterritorial scope, even without being established in the EU. Thirdly, because of the "Brussels Effect" foreign corporations often prefer to respect EU law even without a legal obligation to do so. Fourthly, international soft law has been and can be deployed to integrate data privacy principles from the EU, playing thereby a key role in the international governance of portability regimes. Fifthly, data privacy obligations have been stipulated in international treaties, requiring the implementation of data portability norms within the national law of ratifying states. In this regard, international economic law can help to diffuse data portability rules across the world.

1 Adoption by Third Countries

Numerous data protection laws around the world have emulated the GDPR, including its right to data portability.[71] A prominent example is the California Consumer Privacy Act, signed a month after the GDPR came into effect. The legislation incorporates portability in the context of the right to access as

68 Directive (EU) 2019/770 of the European Parliament and of the Council of 20 May 2019 on certain aspects concerning contracts for the supply of digital content and digital services, OJ L 136, 22.5.2019, 1–27.

69 See, on the idea of a "digital single market", "Communication from the Commission to the European Parliament, the Council, the European Economic and Social Committee and the Committee of the Regions: A Digital Single Market Strategy for Europe", COM (2015) 192 final; and Zufall, note 26 above, at 103–110.

70 A Bradford, *The Brussels Effect: How the EU Rules the World* (New York, Oxford University Press, 2020).

71 G Greenleaf, "The Influence of European Data Privacy Standards Outside Europe: Implications for Globalization of Convention 108" (2012) 2 *International Data Privacy Law* 68, at 77.

a modality of how electronic access should be provided; that is, in a portable format.[72] In comparison to the GDPR, the stipulation has an arguably broader scope, as all personal data is portable, and not only the personal data provided by the data subject. On the other hand, the norm is weaker as the businesses collecting personal information can provide access nonelectronically by simple mail, even if the data is stored digitally. Businesses are thus offered a way to circumvent portability, unless they do not mind the additional costs of mail delivery (which might be less than investing in interoperability).

Other examples of adoption include Benin, which enacted a GDPR-like legislation with its *Code du numérique* and included a right to data portability.[73] Brazil has adopted a new General Data Protection Law that introduces a right to the portability of data.[74] A possible codification of data portability is further vividly discussed by a number of countries.[75] Japan, for instance, has initiated a study to assess the merits and demerits of data portability, taking into consideration the costs for firms to establish portability.[76]

2 Extraterritorial Application

EU law imposes itself on foreign entities by extending its scope of application beyond EU territory. Inspired by the famous Google Spain judgment of the European Court of Justice,[77] Art. 3(2) GDPR introduces a remarkably broad territorial scope: GDPR applies to controllers or processors not established in the EU if the processing activities are related to the offering of goods or services to data subjects in the EU or to the monitoring of their behavior within the EU.[78] Data portability can therefore be requested by an EU citizen or resident from a foreign – for instance, US – firm, if the activities of the firm fall under the GDPR.

72 The California Consumer Privacy Act (CCPA) of 2018 (Assembly Bill No. 375), Division 3, Part 4, Section 1798.100 (c) of the Civil Code ("The information may be delivered by mail or electronically, and if provided electronically, the information shall be in a portable and, to the extent technically feasible, in a readily useable format that allows the consumer to transmit this information to another entity without hindrance").

73 G Greenleaf, "Global Data Privacy Laws 2019: 132 National Laws and Many Bills" (2019) 157 *Privacy Laws & Business International Report* 14.

74 Federal Law No. 13,709 of 14 August 2018 (General Law for the Protection of Personal Data).

75 "OECD Expert Workshop on Enhanced Access to Data: Reconciling Risks and Benefits of Data Re-Use" (2018), https://perma.cc/R673-W629; "Key Issues for Digital Transformation in the G-20" (2017), https://perma.cc/WJK5-PVU8.

76 https://perma.cc/NG7U-K649; Japan's Ministry of Economy, Trade and Industry (METI) (2017), "Future Vision towards 2030s", full text in Japanese: https://perma.cc/AQK8-JLP2, at 204.

77 Judgment of the Court (Grand Chamber), 13 May 2014, Case C-131/12 – *Google Spain SL, Google Inc v. AEPD, Mario Costeja González* [2014] EU:C:2014:317.

78 See on the extraterritorial application of the GDPR: EDPB, Guidelines 3/2018 on the territorial scope of the GDPR (Art. 3), 2018; M Brkan, "Data Protection and Conflict-of-Laws: A Challenging Relationship" (2016) *European Data Protection Law Review* 324; DS Villa, "The Concept of Establishment and Data Protection Law" (2017) 4 *European Law Review* 491.

Similarly, the NPDR applies in cases where the processing of electronic non-personal data in the EU is provided as a service to users residing or having an establishment in the EU, regardless of whether the service provider is established in the EU (Art. 2(1)(a) NPDR). However, since data portability under the NPDR is of a nonbinding nature, abiding is voluntary. As we suggest, a comprehensive data portability regime for personal and nonpersonal data would therefore be desirable at an international level.

3 Unilateral Power

The EU has been able to externalize its laws beyond its borders via the so-called unilateral power of the EU. While foreign firms are only bound by their national laws, they increasingly have been following EU data protection law.[79] This can, on the one hand, be explained by the advantages of international firms following a single rule, and preferring to harmonize their process and services for cost mitigation purposes.[80] In other words, it might be cheaper for a company to develop a single framework (that follows European data protection law), rather than two or more different ones (one following a stricter European regime, one a more lenient one). In the past, large technology companies like Facebook and Google have often made their data portability tools available to all their customers, independently of their location.[81] On the other hand, Apple took a staged approach and introduced its portability tool for users in Europe only in 2019 and made it available to US and Canadian users in 2020.[82] Apple, Facebook, Google, Microsoft, and Twitter are further contributing to the creation of an open-source framework connecting providers by translating provider specific APIs into common "data models" that can be transferred.[83]

4 International Soft Law

In the past, a number of guiding documents from the EU, such as the Article 29 Working Party Guidelines on the right to data portability in particular, already had a major impact on the interpretation of data portability concepts.[84] The guidelines, set by this former advisory board that has been replaced by the European Data Protection Board (EDPB) representing the data protection authorities of the EU

79 PM Schwartz, "Global Data Privacy: The EU Way" (2019) 94 *New York University Law Review* 778.
80 Ibid., further referring to the difficulties of firms to screen out EU customers.
81 "How Do I Download a Copy of Facebook?", https://perma.cc/7ULQ-AW3K; "Takeout", https://takeout.google.com/settings/takeout.
82 C Fisher, "Facebook Lets Users in the US and Canada Move Media to Google Photos" (Engadget, 30 April 2020), https://perma.cc/MRB5-7JKK.
83 "Data Transfer Project", https://perma.cc/PF9J-XL9L.
84 Guidelines on DP, note 47 above.

member states, have been subject to extensive academic discussion and scrutiny by corporations.[85]

International soft law has long served as inspiration for national privacy codification, beginning with the OECD Privacy Guidelines of 1980, which were revised in 2013.[86] The Guidelines explicitly refer to personal data as an "increasingly valuable asset". Their aim has been to foster the free flow of information by preventing unjustified obstacles to economic development, namely by setting a minimum standard for national legal frameworks on privacy. The original 1980 OECD Privacy Guidelines were influential at first, encouraging the adoption of data protection laws in eight countries outside Europe (including Canada and Japan), but their impact diminished when the EU adopted its Data Protection Directive in 1995,[87] which went beyond the OECD Guidelines.[88] The OECD Guidelines also influenced the Asia-Pacific Economic Cooperation (APEC) Privacy Framework.[89]

As the OECD is reviewing its Guidelines, it could include a data portability norm in a future revision. However, as the OECD Guidelines only cover personal data, a right to data portability in the OECD Guidelines (alone) would not match its (optimal) scope.[90] Data portability should, in our view, rather be added to other international soft law instruments and encompass both personal and non-personal data.

5 International Hard Law

European portability concepts have been reflected in international treaties. This may be exemplified by the inclusion of a clause regarding the portability of telephone numbers in the Comprehensive and Progressive Agreement for Trans-Pacific Partnership (CPTPP), a trade agreement between Australia, Brunei, Canada, Chile, Japan, Malaysia, Mexico, New Zealand, Peru, Singapore, and Vietnam.[91] As mentioned in subsection B, the right to telephone number portability in the former Art.

85 See PN Yannella and O Kagan, "Analysis: Article 29 Working Party Guidelines on Automated Decision Making Under GDPR" (CyberAdviser, 16 January 2018), https://perma.cc/L34H-PNYQ. See for an overview on instruments of transnational exchange on data protection: F Zufall, Art 50 DSGVO Rn. 13, in Eßer/Kramer/von Lewinski (eds), *DSGVO/BDSG – Kommentar*, 7th ed. 2020.

86 Recommendation of the Council concerning Guidelines governing the Protection of Privacy and Transborder Flows of Personal Data – Annex [C(80)58/FINAL, as amended on 11 July 2013 by C (2013)79].

87 Directive 95/46/EC of the European Parliament and of the Council of 24 October 1995 on the protection of individuals with regard to the processing of personal data and on the free movement of such data. OJ L 281, 23.11.1995, 31–50; G Greenleaf, "It's Nearly 2020, so What Fate Awaits the 1980 OECD Privacy Guidelines?" (2019) 159 *Privacy Laws & Business International Report* 18.

88 Greenleaf, note 87 above.

89 See "APEC Privacy Framework (2015)", https://perma.cc/Z6LT-57X5.

90 The same applies for the APEC Privacy Framework of 2005.

91 CPTPP, Article 13.5.4 ("Each Party shall ensure that suppliers of public telecommunications services in its territory provide number portability without impairment to quality and reliability, on a timely basis, and on reasonable and non-discriminatory terms and conditions").

30 Universal Services Directive[92] can be seen as a predecessor to data portability. Furthermore, the Eastern Caribbean Telecommunications Authority is planning to codify number portability in its new Electronic Communications Bill.[93]

Against this backdrop, the question arises whether international trade agreements should include data portability provisions going forward – either in competition chapters or in dedicated electronic commerce or digital trade chapters. Regulation on an international level, however, would require a supranational understanding of the modalities of data portability. Because data flows cross-countries, the need for a coherent regulation of portability is strong. Nonetheless, views on the modalities of a portability regime differ across states. The type of data it should cover, the concrete definition of "portability", the extent of interoperability required, the kinds of standardization of formats and interfaces, and whether retrieval "in a commonly used and machine-readable format" suffices are some of the many questions on which consensus should be reached. In this regard, the first experiences with the GDPR and NPDR will be crucial in determining the future of portability.

III CONCLUSION: TOWARD AN ALTERNATIVE CONCEPT OF DATA PORTABILITY

The EU regulations regarding data portability have an ambitious aim: to contribute to the creation of an effective data ecosystem characterized by the free flow of data. Both regimes, however, were designed to address very specific situations – the GDPR regime for users and their free-of-charge social media provider; the NPDR regime for business customers and their big data analytics providers. Both regimes find application beyond the use cases they were designed for. Instead of distinguishing between personal and non-personal data, a better regime for data portability could hinge on whether the value of generated data serves as compensation for the respective service providers' costs.

Ultimately, the distinction between personal and non-personal data can be challenged as inappropriate for data portability. Data portability is a concept that primarily serves the free flow of data rather than the protection of personal data. A classification distinguishing between raw and generated data has its advantages, particularly when it factors in the value of data. Competition law could rely more heavily on the value of data and its role in providing cost compensation, instead of using a terminology inherited from data protection law. Future data portability regimes may be better designed once they are removed from the realm of data protection. This assumes that the data subject is sufficiently protected by the remaining rights under the GDPR, especially via the right of access. Guaranteeing an effective right of access for raw and generated data is key.

92 European Electronic Communications Code (Directive (EU) 2018/1972) OJ L 321, 17.12.2018, 36–214, Art. 106.

93 "Electronic Communications Bill Revised 16 October 2019", https://perma.cc/AP3V-Z64E.

Consequently, we propose that the difference in choice of the regulatory regime for data portability should be made with a view to the value of data and depending on whether it provides compensation for cost-bearing. Raw data, being assigned to the customer or the data subject, would be portable, while generated data would require a more refined regime depending on whether it serves as a means of compensation.

PART IV

International Economic Law Limits to Artificial Intelligence Regulation

12

Public Morals, Trade Secrets, and the Dilemma of Regulating Automated Driving Systems

*Ching-Fu Lin**

I INTRODUCTION

The market for automated driving systems (ADSs, commonly referred to as automated vehicles, autonomous cars, or self-driving cars)[1] is predicted to grow from US$54.2 billion in 2019 to US$556.6 billion in 2026.[2] Around 21 million in sales of vehicles equipped with ADSs globally in 2035, and 76 million in sales through 2035,[3] are expected in an inextricably connected global market of automobiles, information and communication technology (ICT), and artificial intelligence (AI) platforms and services, along a massive value chain that transcends borders. Indeed, ADSs – one of the most promising AI applications – build on software infrastructure that works with sensing technologies such as Light Detection and Ranging (LiDAR), radar, and high-resolution cameras to perform part or all of the dynamic driving tasks.[4] The ADS industry landscape is complex and dynamic, including not only automobile companies and suppliers (e.g., Daimler AG, Ford Motor Company, BMW AG, Tesla Inc., and Denso Corporation), but also ICT giants (e.g., Waymo, Intel Corporation, Apple Inc., NVIDIA Corporation, Samsung, and Baidu) and

* The author would like to thank Chia-Chi Chen, I-Ching Chen, Mao-wei Lo, and Si-Wei Lu for their research assistance. Any remaining errors are the author's sole responsibility.

1 Various terms are used to refer to vehicles equipped with different levels of driving automation systems (a generic term that covers all levels of automation), such as self-driving cars, unmanned vehicles, and automated vehicles. However, as explained in Section II, the inconsistent and sometimes confusing use of terms may lead to regulatory misconceptions. This chapter uses "automated driving systems" to cover level 3–5 systems according to the most widely recognized classification by SAE International. See also Peng's Chapter 6 in this volume.

2 "Autonomous Vehicle Market Outlook – 2026' (2018), https://perma.cc/9B5S-GYRE.

3 "IHS Clarifies Autonomous Vehicle Sales Forecast – Expects 21 Million Sales Globally in the Year 2035 and Nearly 76 Million Sold Globally Through 2035' (*IHS Markit*, 9 June 2016), https://perma.cc/77J7-VQ56.

4 More specifically, AI algorithms and sensing technologies help to draw a real-time, three-dimensional map of the environment (a 60-meter range around the vehicle), monitor surrounding activities, navigate and operate (e.g., speed, brake, steer, and change gear selection) the vehicle. See Autonomous Vehicle Market Outlook – 2026, note 2 above. See also HY Lim, *Autonomous Vehicles and the Law: Technology, Algorithms and Ethics* (Cheltenham, Edward Elgar Publishing, 2019), at 5–19.

novel service providers (e.g., Uber, Lyft, and China's Didi Chuxing) in different parts of the world. There have also been an increasing number of cross-sectoral collaborative initiatives between such companies, including the partnership between Uber and Toyota to expand the ride-sharing market,[5] or General Motor's investment in Lyft, undertaken with the goal of developing self-driving taxis.[6]

While governments around the world have been promoting ADS development and relevant industries,[7] they have also been contemplating rules and standards in response to its legal, economic, and social ramifications. Apart from road safety and economic development,[8] ADSs promise to transform the ways in which people commute between places and connect with one another, which will further alter the conventional division of labor, social interactions, and the provision of services. Regulatory requirements for testing and safety, as well as technical standards on cybersecurity and connectivity, are necessary for vehicles with ADSs to be allowed on roadways, but governments worldwide have not established comprehensive and consistent policy frameworks within their jurisdictions because of the experimental nature of related technologies, not to mention multilateral consensus or harmonization. Furthermore, liability rules, insurance policies, and new law enforcement tools are also relevant issues, if not prerequisites. Last but not least, ethical challenges posed by ADSs play a key role in building trust and confidence among consumers, societies, and governments to support the wide and full-scale application. How to align ADS research and development with fundamental ethical principles embedded in a given society – with its own values and cultural contexts – remains a difficult policy question. The "Trolley Problem" aptly demonstrates such tension.[9] As will be discussed, such challenges not only touch upon substantive norms, such as morality, equality, and justice, but also call for procedural safeguards, such as algorithmic transparency and explainability.

Faced with such challenges, governments are designing and constructing legal and policy infrastructures with diverse forms and substances to facilitate the future of connected transportation. Major players along the global ADS value chain have yet to agree upon a common set of rules and standards to forge regulatory governance on a global scale, partly because of different political agendas and strategic positions.[10]

5 See K Kokalitcheva, "Toyota Becomes Uber's Latest Investor and Business Partner" (*Fortune*, 24 May 2016), https://perma.cc/254A-7HSX.

6 See K Korosec, "Autonomous Car Sales Will Hit 21 Million by 2035, IHS Says" (*Fortune*, 7 June 2016), https://perma.cc/4HEX-MHJT.

7 For example, the United States government announced in 2016 its $4 billion investment in automated vehicles. See B Vlasic, "U.S. Proposes Spending $4 Billion on Self-Driving Cars" (*New York Times*, 14 January 2016), https://perma.cc/36DJ-QKMQ.

8 See A Taeihagh and HSM Lim, "Governing Autonomous Vehicles: Emerging Responses for Safety, Liability, Privacy, Cybersecurity, and Industry Risks" (2018) 39(1) *Transport Reviews* 103, at 107–109; S Nyholm and J Smids, "The Ethics of Accident-Algorithms for Self-Driving Cars: An Applied Trolley Problem?" (2016) 19(5) *Ethical Theory & Moral Practice* 1275, at 1275–1289.

9 See the discussion in Section II.

10 In addition, the respective regulatory governance strategies of these countries may change and adapt in light of ongoing economic growth, national security, and business competition issues. Their

While it seems essential to have rules and standards that reflect local values and contexts, potential conflicts and duplication may have serious World Trade Organization (WTO) implications. In Section II, this chapter examines key regulatory issues of ADSs along the global supply chain. Regulatory efforts and standard-setting processes among WTO members and international (public and private) organizations also evidence both the convergence and divergence in different issues. While regulatory issues such as liability, cybersecurity, data flow, and infrastructure are multifaceted, complex, and fluid, and certainly merit scholarly investigation, this chapter cannot and does not intend to cover them all. Rather, in Section III, this chapter uses the most controversial (but not futuristic) issue – the ethical dimension of ADSs, which raises tensions between the protection of public morals and trade secrets – to demonstrate the regulatory dilemma faced by regulators and its WTO implications. It points out three levels of key challenges that may translate into a regulatory dilemma in light of WTO members' rights and obligations, including those in the General Agreement on Tariffs and Trade (GATT), the Agreement on Technical Barriers to Trade (TBT Agreement), and the Agreement on Trade-Related Aspects of Intellectual Property Rights (TRIPS Agreement).[11] Section IV concludes.

II AUTOMATED DRIVING SYSTEMS: MAPPING KEY REGULATORY ISSUES

A *Regulatory Challenges Facing Automated Driving Systems and the "Moral Machine" Dilemma*

At the outset, the use of terminology and taxonomy must be clarified. There exist various terms that are used to refer to vehicles equipped with different levels of driving automation systems (a generic term that covers all levels of automation), such as self-driving cars, unmanned vehicles, autonomous cars, and automated vehicles. However, for reasons to be elaborated later, this chapter consciously uses

regulatory endeavors, as well as competition (or cooperation), may also lead to a more coherent global standard-setting process in international arenas. See generally H-W Liu, "International Standards in Flux: A Balkanized ICT Standard-Setting Paradigm and Its Implications for the WTO" (2014) 17(3) *Journal of International Economic Law* 551; M Du, "WTO Regulation of Transnational Private Authority in Global Governance" (2018) 67(4) *International and Comparative Law Quarterly* 867.

[11] In some cases, the General Agreement on Trade in Services (GATS) may come into play, especially when most ADSs do not fall squarely into either "goods" or "services" in light of the increasing "servitization" of modern manufacturing. See E Lafuente et al., "Territorial Servitization and the Manufacturing Renaissance in Knowledge-Based Economies" (2019) 53(3) *Regional Studies* 313; T Baines et al., "Servitization of the Manufacturing Firm: Exploring the Operations Practices and Technologies That Deliver Advanced Services" (2014) 34(1) *International Journal of Operations & Production Management* 2; G Lay (ed.), *Servitization in Industry* (New York, Springer, 2014). The discussion on service under the GATS is beyond the scope of this chapter, the primary focus of which lies in product-oriented standards and rules.

"ADSs" – namely, level 3–5 systems as defined by the SAE International's taxonomy and definitions[12] – to refer to the kinds of driving automation that require only limited human intervention and that more appropriately denote the essence of commonly known terms such as "self-driving cars" or "autonomous vehicles." Indeed, the inconsistent and sometimes confusing use of terms such as "self-driving cars" or "autonomous vehicles" may lead to problems not only related to misleading marketing practices, mistaken consumer perceptions, and information asymmetry, but also insufficient and ineffective regulatory design. For instance, in the robotics and AI literature, the term "autonomous" has been used to denote systems capable of making decisions and acting "independently and self-sufficiently,"[13] but the use of such terms "obscures the question of whether a so-called 'autonomous vehicle' depends on communication and/or cooperation with outside entities for critical functionality (such as data acquisition and collection)."[14] Some products may be fully autonomous as long as their functions are executed entirely independently and self-sufficiently to the extent entailed in level 5, while others may depend on external cooperation and connection to work (which may fall under the scope of level 3 or level 4). Yet when the term "autonomous vehicle" is commonly used to refer to level 5, levels 3 and 4, or even all levels of driving automation as defined in various legislation enacted in different states,[15] regulatory confusion ensues. Comparable conceptual and practical problems can also be found with the use of "self-driving," "automated," or "unmanned" in regulatory discourse.

While ADSs offer many benefits to road safety, economic growth, and transportation modernization,[16] myriad regulatory issues – such as safety, testing and certification, liability and insurance, cybersecurity, data flow, ethics, connectivity, infrastructure, and service – must be appropriately addressed.[17] First, reducing

[12] See SAE International, J3016_201806: *Surface Vehicle Recommended Practice: (R) Taxonomy and Definitions for Terms Related to Driving Automation Systems for On-Road Motor Vehicles* (first issued in January 2014, and revised in June 2018 to supersede J3016, adopted in September 2016) (hereinafter SAE International J3016_201806). This definition and taxonomy is embraced by the United States Department of Transportation (US DoT) and the National Highway Traffic Safety Administration (NHTSA); see US DoT, "Preparing for the Future of Transportation: Automated Vehicles 3.0' (2018), https://perma.cc/E4WY-AMN3, at 45.

[13] Ibid., at 28.

[14] Ibid.

[15] Ibid.

[16] According to the US DoT and NHTSA's estimation, around 90 percent of car accidents are the result of human error. See US DoT and NHTSA, "Traffic Safety Facts: A Brief Statistical Summary – Critical Reasons for Crashes Investigated in the National Motor Vehicle Crash Causation Survey" (2015), https://perma.cc/JV6M-TC3M. The advent of ADSs may help reduce or even eliminate this human error factor, as these systems promise to outperform human drivers. See Taeihagh and Lim, note 8 above, at 107–109. See also Y Sun et al., "Road to Autonomous Vehicles in Australia: An Exploratory Literature Review" (2017) 26(1) *Road and Transport Research: A Journal of Australian and New Zealand Research and Practice* 34, at 34–47.

[17] See, for example, A von Ungern-Sternberg, "Autonomous Driving: Regulatory Challenges Raised by Artificial Decision-Making and Tragic Choices," in W Barfield and U Pagallo (eds), *Research*

human errors does not mean that ADSs are free from machine error, especially when the technology continues to grow in complexity.[18] A review of recent incidents involving Tesla and Volvo-Uber systems suggests that ADSs may be subject to different standards of care, considering the many new safety threats and consumer expectations for the technology.[19] Other commentators also point to cybersecurity and industry risks related to ADSs, given their reliance on data collection, processing, and transmission through vehicle-to-vehicle and vehicle-to-infrastructure communications.[20] The multifaceted yet under-addressed issues of privacy and personal freedom also call for clearer rules and standards.[21] Issues including the Internet of Things (IoT), 5G networks, and smart city development – which are beyond the scope of this chapter – also play a crucial role in the regulatory discourse surrounding ADSs.[22] The different risks posed by ADSs and IoT and their consequential interactions with the physical world may have crucial ramifications for international trade and investment law.[23]

This chapter will not exhaust all of these regulatory issues, but rather focuses on the most controversial, ethical dimension of ADSs. There are concerns about the "crash algorithms" of ADSs, which are the programs that decide how to respond at the time of unavoidable accidents.[24] Ethical issues stem from the infamous "Trolley Problem," a classic thought experiment of utilitarianism vis-à-vis deontological

Handbook on the Law of Artificial Intelligence (Cheltenham, Edward Elgar Publishing, 2018), at 253–254; and Taeihagh and Lim, note 8 above, at 107–109.

18 "After all, humans can be amazing drivers, the performance of advanced automation systems is still unclear . . . and automation shifts some errors from driver to designer." BW Smith, "Human Error as a Cause of Vehicle Crashes" (Centre for Internet and Society, 18 December 2013), https://perma.cc/VN5B-SST4.

19 See generally Lim, note 4 above.

20 See, for example, DM West, "Moving Forward: Self-Driving Vehicles in China, Europe, Japan, Korea, and the United States" (2016), https://perma.cc/8SWG-GX2Y; V Dhar, "Equity, Safety, and Privacy in the Autonomous Vehicle Era" (2016) 49(11) *Computer* 80, at 80–83; JM Anderson et al., "Autonomous Vehicle Technology: A Guide for Policymakers" (2014), https://perma.cc/5FBA-UVRQ; FD Page and NM Krayem, "Are You Ready for Self-Driving Vehicles?" (2017) 29(4) *Intellectual Property and Technology Law Journal* 14.

21 See J Boeglin, "The Costs of Self-Driving Cars: Reconciling Freedom and Privacy with Tort Liability in Autonomous Vehicle Regulation" (2015) 17(1) *Yale Journal of Law and Technology* 171, at 176–185; M Gillespie, "Shifting Automotive Landscapes: Privacy and the Right to Travel in the Era of Autonomous Motor Vehicles" (2016) 50 *Washington University Journal of Law and Policy* 147, at 147–169. See also DJ Glancy, "Privacy in Autonomous Vehicles" (2012) 52(4) *Santa Clara Law Review* 1171; J Schoonmaker, "Proactive Privacy for a Driverless Age" (2016) 25(2) *Information & Communications Technology Law* 96; S Gambs et al., "De-anonymization Attack on Geolocated Data" (2014) 80(8) *Journal of Computer and System Sciences* 1597.

22 See SA Bhatti, "Automated Vehicles: Challenges to Full Scale Deployment" (Wavelength, 26 September 2019), https://perma.cc/5J8G-3B4V.

23 See JP Trachtman, "The Internet of Things Cybersecurity Challenge to Trade and Investment: Trust and Verify?" (2019), https://papers.ssrn.com/sol3/papers.cfm?abstract_id=3374542.

24 See, for example, I Coca-Vila, "Self-Driving Cars in Dilemmatic Situations: An Approach Based on the Theory of Justification in Criminal Law" (2018) 12(1) *Criminology Law & Philosophy* 59; see also FS de Sio, "Killing by Autonomous Vehicles and the Legal Doctrine of Necessity" (2017) 20(2) *Ethical Theory and Moral Practice* 411.

ethics introduced in 1967 by Philippa Foot.[25] It involves a runaway, out-of-control trolley moving toward five people who are tied up and lying on the main track. You are standing next to a lever that can switch the trolley to a side track, on which only one tied-up person is lying. The problem? Would you pull the lever to save five and kill one? What is the right thing to do? In modern times, the advent of ADSs makes the Trolley Problem, once an exercise of applied philosophy, a real-world challenge rather than an ethical thought experiment.[26] Should ADSs prioritize the lives of the vehicle's passengers over those of pedestrians? Should ADSs kill the baby, the doctor, the mayor, the jaywalker, or the grandma? Or should ADSs be programmed to reach a decision that is most beneficial to society as a whole, taking into account a massive range of factors? Researchers at the Massachusetts Institute of Technology (MIT) designed scenarios representing ethical dilemmas that call upon people to identify preferences for males, females, the young, the elderly, low-status individuals, high-status individuals, law-abiding individuals, law-breaking individuals, and even fit or obese pedestrians in a fictional, unavoidable car crash.[27] They collected and consolidated around 40 million responses provided by millions of individuals from 233 jurisdictions and published their results in an article titled "The Moral Machine Experiment."[28] How does the world respond to the Trolley Problem? While a general, global moral preference can be found, there exist strong and diverse demographic variations specifically associated with "modern institutions" and "deep cultural traits."[29] For instance, respondents from China, Japan, Taiwan, South Korea, and other East Asian countries prefer saving the elderly over the young, while those in North America and Europe are the opposite.[30]

As ADSs cannot be subjectively assessed *ex post* for blame or moral responsibility, it seems necessary – yet it is unclear how – to design rules to regulate the reactions of ADSs when faced with moral dilemmas.[31] Presumably, ethics as well as cultural, demographic, and institutional factors may play a role in likely heterogeneous regulatory measures that could increase frictions in international trade. From a practical, legalist perspective, different tort systems in varying jurisdictions may also have an anchoring effect on ADS designs.[32] While the decision at the time of

[25] See generally Philippa Foot, "The Problem of Abortion and the Doctrine of the Double Effect," in *Virtues and Vices* (Oxford, Basil Blackwell, 1978) (originally appeared in *Oxford Review* 5, 1967).

[26] See K Hao, "Should a Self-Driving Car Kill the Baby or the Grandma? Depends on Where You're from" (*MIT Technology Review*, 2018), https://perma.cc/K69S-V8H6.

[27] E Awad et al., "The Moral Machine Experiment" (2018) 563 *Nature* 59.

[28] Ibid.

[29] Ibid., at 62–63.

[30] Ibid.

[31] See Coca-Vila, note 24 above, at 62–66.

[32] One commentator also notes that the Trolley Problem and ethical principles might play a less decisive role than predictive legal liabilities that readily translate into monetary constraints on ADS manufacturers that are driven by profits. See B Casey, "Amoral Machines, or: How Roboticists Can Learn to Stop Worrying and Love the Law" (2017) 111 *Northwestern University Law Review* 231.

unavoidable accidents has immense legal, economic, and moral consequences, it is *predetermined* when the algorithms are written and built into ADSs. Algorithms are not objective. Rather, they carry the existing biases and discriminations against minority groups in human society, which are reflected and reinforced by the training data used to power the algorithms.[33] Further, algorithms do not build themselves, so they may carry the values and preferences of people who write or train them.[34] Therefore, ADS manufacturers are increasing exposed to legal and reputational risks associated with these moral challenges.[35] Governments have not yet addressed these ethical puzzles posed by ADS algorithms.

B *Regulatory Initiatives at National and Transnational Levels*

One may ask whether there are existing or emerging international standards that can serve as a reference for domestic regulations. What approaches are regulators in different jurisdictions taking to address these issues? This chapter maps out some representative regulatory initiatives that have taken place at both the national and the transnational level and are respectively backed by public, private, and hybrid institutions – without concrete harmonization.[36]

What are the relevant positions of the governments of these countries in the global value chain of automated vehicles? What are their respective regulatory governance strategies in light of concerns related to economic growth, national security, and business competition?[37] To what extent are these countries competing (or cooperating) with one another to lead the global standard-setting process in various international arenas?[38] At the national level, crucial questions have largely been left unaddressed. A leader in regulating ADSs, the United States Department of Transportation (US DoT) has been stocktaking and monitoring current ADS standards development activities, including those led by, inter alia, the SAE International, the International Organization for Standardization (ISO), the Institute of Electrical and Electronics Engineers (IEEE), the Federal Highway Administration (FHWA), the American Association of Motor Vehicle Administrators (AAMVA), and the National Highway Traffic Safety Administration (NHTSA), in relation to issues such as cybersecurity framework, data sharing, functional safety, event data recorders, vehicle interaction, encrypted communications, infrastructure signage and traffic, and

33 See J Kleinberg et al., "Discrimination in the Age of Algorithms" (2018) 10 *Journal of Legal Analysis* 1, at 4.

34 Ibid.

35 See A Hevelke and J Nida-Rümelin, "Responsibility for Crashes of Autonomous Vehicles: An Ethical Analysis" (2015) 21(3) *Science and Engineering Ethics* 619, at 619–630; and JM Tien, "The Sputnik of Servgoods: Autonomous Vehicles" (2017) 26(2) *Journal of Systems Science and Systems Engineering* 133, at 133–162.

36 See generally H-W Liu and C-F Lin, "Artificial Intelligence and Global Trade Governance: Towards A Pluralist Agenda" (2020) 61 *Harvard International Law Journal* 407 .

37 See, for example, Liu, note 10 above.

38 See generally Du, note 10 above.

testing approaches.[39] While a couple of initiatives might partly touch upon some issues with ethical implications,[40] nothing concrete has been designated to address ADSs' ethical issues. In the United Kingdom, the British Standard Institution published a prestandardization document based on relevant guidelines developed by the UK Department for Transport and Centre for the Protection of National Infrastructure to facilitate further standardization on cybersecurity.[41] Taiwan also set up a sandbox scheme for the development and testing of vehicles equipped with ADSs,[42] and the sandbox is open to a broadly defined scope of experimentation, including automobiles, aircraft, and ships, and even a combination of these forms.[43]

Again, none has been initiated to specifically address the ethical issues of ADSs. The world's first[44] concrete government initiative specifically on ADS ethical issues at the moment is the report with twenty ethical rules issued by the Ethics Commission for Automated and Connected Driving, a special body appointed by Germany's Federal Ministry of Transport and Digital Infrastructure.[45] The report consists of twenty ethical rules for ADSs.[46] Of importance are the ethical rules, which ask that "[t]he protection of individuals takes precedence over all other utilitarian considerations,"[47] that "[t]he personal responsibility of individuals for taking decisions is an expression of a society centred on individual human beings,"[48] and that "[i]n hazardous situations that prove to be unavoidable, the protection of human life enjoys top priority in a balancing of legally protected interests."[49] In particular, Ethical Rule 8 provides that:

> Genuine dilemmatic decisions, such as a decision between one human life and another . . . can thus not be clearly standardized, nor can they be programmed such that they are ethically unquestionable . . .. Such legal judgements, made in retrospect and taking special circumstances into account, cannot readily be transformed

[39] See US DoT, note 12 above, at 57–63.
[40] Ibid., at 60.
[41] See British Standard Institution, *PAS 1885:2018: The Fundamental Principles of Automotive Cyber Security* (December 2018); see also United Kingdom Department for Transport, Centre for Connected and Autonomous Vehicles, and Centre for the Protection of National Infrastructure, "The Key Principles of Cyber Security for Connected and Automated Vehicles" (2017), www.gov.uk/government/publications/principles-of-cyber-security-for-connected-and-automated-vehicles/the-key-principles-of-vehicle-cyber-security-for-connected-and-automated-vehicles.
[42] Unmanned Vehicles Technology Innovative Experimentation Act (Taiwan) (UV Act). The UV Act was promulgated on 19 December 2018.
[43] UV Act, Art. 3.
[44] See Taeihagh and Lim, note 8 above, at 10.
[45] See "Federal Ministry of Transport and Digital Infrastructure, Ethics Commission: Automated and Connected Driving" (2017), https://perma.cc/YQ8S-KTE9 (hereinafter 2017 Germany Ethical Commission Report); see also C Lütge, "The German Ethics Code for Automated and Connected Driving" (2017) 30(4) *Philosophy and Technology* 547.
[46] 2017 Germany Ethical Commission Report, note 45 above.
[47] 2017 Germany Ethical Commission Report, at 6–9 ("Ethical Rules for Automated and Connected Vehicular Traffic"), Rule 2.
[48] Ibid., Rule 4.
[49] Ibid., Rule 7.

> into abstract/general ex ante appraisals and thus also not into corresponding programming activities.[50]

Ethical Rule 9 further prescribes that "[i]n the event of unavoidable accident situations, any distinction based on personal features," such as age, gender, and physical or mental conditions, "is strictly prohibited."[51] While the ethical rules are not mandatory, they certainly mark the first step toward addressing ADSs' ethical challenges.[52] It remains to be seen how these ethics rules will be translated into future legislations and regulations in Germany and beyond.[53]

Other relevant initiatives, while not specifically addressing ADS ethical issues, include algorithmic accountability rules (generally applicable to data protection and AI applications) that may inform future regulations. For instance, the European Union's General Data Protection Regulation (GDPR) sets out rights and obligations in relation to algorithmic explainability and accountability in automated individual decision-making.[54] The European Commission also established the High-Level Expert Group on Artificial Intelligence in 2018, which published the final version of its Ethics Guidelines for Trustworthy Artificial Intelligence in April 2019.[55] At the same time, lawmakers in the United States recently tabled a new bill, the Algorithmic Accountability Act of 2019, which intends to require companies to audit systems based on machine learning algorithms, to examine instances of potential bias and discrimination therein, and to fix any issues found in a timely manner.[56]

There have been active and dynamic regulatory initiatives at the transnational level.[57] The United Nations Economic Council for Europe (UNECE)[58] and the 1968 Vienna Convention on Road Traffic[59] have struggled to change the formal rules under their existing framework, given the complexity of the issues, high negotiation costs, and institutional inflexibility.[60] The Vienna Convention was

50 Ibid., Rule 8.

51 Ibid., Rule 9.

52 See Taeihagh and Lim, note 8 above, at 10.

53 See Lütge, note 45 above, at 557.

54 Regulation (EU) 2016/679 of the European Parliament and of the Council of 27 April 2016 on the protection of natural persons with regard to the processing of personal data and on the free movement of such data, and repealing Directive 95/46/EC (General Data Protection Regulation, GDPR), Arts. 21 and 22.

55 European Commission, "Building Trust in Human-Centric AI, Ethics Guidelines for Trustworthy AI," https://perma.cc/M2WL-NL24.

56 Algorithmic Accountability Act of 2019, OLL19293, 116th Congress (2019).

57 For a review of such transnational regulatory initiatives and their normative ramifications, see Liu and Lin, note 36 above, at 440–450.

58 United Nations Economic Council for Europe (hereinafter UNECE), Economic and Social Council, Inland Transportation Committee, Working Party on Road Traffic Safety, U.N. Doc. ECE/TRANS/WP.1/145 (24–26 March 2014); UNECE, "UNECE Paves the Way for Automated Driving by Updating UN International Convention" (23 March 2016), https://perma.cc/7PNX-2GA4.

59 1968 Vienna Convention on Road Traffic (78 Parties) and the March 2014 Amendment, https://perma.cc/5C8K-Y3ST.

60 See Liu and Lin, note 36 above, at 410–411.

somewhat passive in the development of driving automated systems until an amendment to its Articles 8 and 39 entered into force in March 2016.[61] The amendment allows for the transfer of driving tasks from humans to vehicles under certain conditions, lifting the formalistic requirement that a "human" must be in charge of driving tasks.[62] In September 2018, the UNECE's Global Forum on Road Traffic Safety (WP.1) adopted a resolution to promote the deployment of vehicles equipped with ADSs in road traffic.[63] This resolution is rather soft and represents an informal approach to guiding Contracting Parties to the 1968 Vienna Conventions on the safe deployment of ADSs in road traffic.[64] In any case, because major ADS players like the United States, China, and Japan are not contracting parties to the Vienna Convention, what will be done under the treaty body may not readily generate direct policy relevance and normative influence at the national level (at least for the moment). A few additional private and hybrid organizations have also been engaging in ADS standard-setting, including the SAE International,[65] the ISO,[66] and the IEEE.[67] Among such standard-setting bodies, the SAE International and the ISO are the most comprehensive, cited, and embraced references. Given the complex and dynamic nature of ADS technologies, the SAE International and the ISO, as informal, private/hybrid bodies with more institutional flexibility, have been able to incorporate their members' expertise to work together in developing common standards – SAE/ISO standards on road vehicle and intelligent transportation systems.[68] The SAE International further offers the ISO a Secretariat function and services for ISO's TC204 Intelligent Transport System work.[69] With its transnational scope, domain expertise, and industry support, the SAE International's standards, especially the recent clarification and definition of the J3016 standard's six levels of driving automation, serve as the "most-cited reference" for the ADS industry and governance.[70] While there has been progress at the transnational level, these

61 Ibid.

62 UNECE, "Report of the Sixty-Eighth Session of the Working Party on Road Traffic Safety" (2014), https://perma.cc/JZ3Q-PM62.

63 UNECE, "Report of the Global Forum for Road Traffic Safety on Its Sixty-Seventh Session" (2014), https://perma.cc/RC99-WAXQ (Annex 1, Global Forum for Road Traffic Safety (WP.1) Resolution on the Deployment of Highly and Fully Automated Vehicles in Road Traffic).

64 See Liu and Lin, note 36 above, at 427–428.

65 SAE International J3016_201806, note 12 above.

66 International Organization for Standardization, "ISO 26262 Road Vehicles Functional Safety," https://perma.cc/L4DL-4V97; ISO, "Intelligent Transport Systems–Taxonomy and Definitions for Terms Related to Driving Automation Systems for On-Road Motor Vehicles, ISO/SAE NP PAS 22736" (hereinafter ISO/SAE NP PAS 22736), https://perma.cc/BW2M-SVQK.

67 IEEE Global Initiative on Ethics of Autonomous and Intelligent Systems (IEEE Global Initiative) has launched "Ethically Aligned Design: A Vision for Prioritizing Human Well-Being with Autonomous and Intelligent Systems," https://perma.cc/BQH5-HGHN.

68 ISO/SAE NP PAS 22736, note 66 above.

69 See J Pokrzywa, "SAE Global Ground Vehicle Standards" (2019), https://perma.cc/9BV6-LBVQ.

70 See J Shuttleworth, "SAE Standards News: J3016 Automated-Driving Graphic Update" (2019), https://perma.cc/6STW-BXJF. See also Liu and Lin, note 36 above, at 427.

regulatory initiatives have yet to touch upon contentious ethical issues that extend beyond the narrower understanding of road safety of ADS.[71]

III REGULATORY AUTONOMY UNDER THE WORLD TRADE ORGANIZATION: TECHNICAL STANDARDS, PUBLIC MORALS, AND TRADE SECRETS

As noted, the complex ethical questions, algorithmic designs, and cultural, demographic, and institutional factors may readily be translated into heterogeneous regulatory measures that could increase frictions in international trade and bring about highly contentious issues under the GATT, TBT Agreement, and TRIPS Agreement. These potential frictions beg the questions: How much room in terms of regulatory autonomy will WTO members enjoy in addressing relevant public and moral challenges by conditioning the import and sale of fully autonomous vehicles and dictating the design of ADS algorithms to reflect and respect their local values? What are the normative boundaries set by the relevant covered agreements? Bearing this in mind, this chapter uses the ethical dimensions of ADSs as an example to identify three levels of challenges, in terms of the substance, form, and manner of regulation, for WTO members in regulating this evolving technology.

As the MIT research demonstrated, while a general sense of global moral preference may be identified, there are salient diversities in terms of demographic variations, modern institutions, and cultural underpinnings.[72] It is therefore likely that some regulators in East Asian countries may adopt technical standards that uphold collective public moral and communal values in their efforts to regulate ADSs. Such technical standards may in turn prevent vehicles whose ADS algorithms (which may be trained with data collected from Western societies or written by programmers who do not embrace similar preferences) do not reflect such local ethics and values from entering the market. For instance, if China requires that ADS algorithms built into fully autonomous vehicles must make decisions about unavoidable crashes based on pedestrians' "social status" or even their "social credit scores,"[73] and vehicles that do not run on compliant algorithms will not be allowed in the market, what are the legal and policy implications under the GATT and TBT Agreement? To achieve similar regulatory objectives, WTO members may require ADS manufacturers to disclose their algorithm designs (including source code and training data) to verify and ensure conformity to

[71] At this moment, it appears challenging to reach multilateral consensus on controversial issues of ADS ethics. As some regulatory initiatives will likely be designed to pursue diverse policy objectives reflecting local values and moral preferences, there may be growing competition among countries.

[72] Awad et al., note 27 above, at 62–63.

[73] For an in-depth discussion of China's social credit system and its impact on social and economic activities, see generally Y-J Chen et al., "'Rule of Trust': The Power and Perils of China's Social Credit Megaproject" (2018) 32(1) *Columbia Journal of Asian Law* 1.

applicable technical standards. In this case, what boundaries are established in the TRIPS Agreement that may prohibit WTO members from forcing disclosure of trade secrets (or other forms of intellectual property)?

A *Public Moral Exception, Technical Regulations, and International Standards*

First, import bans on vehicles equipped with ADSs because they are designed and manufactured in a jurisdiction and a manner that reflect a different value set, even if they are reasonable, could violate the national treatment or most favored nation obligations under the GATT. Certainly it would be interesting to see whether vehicles equipped with ADS algorithms that are trained with different data reflecting different cultural and ethical preferences are "like products,"[74] or whether ADSs with "pet-friendly," "kids-friendly," and "elderly-friendly" algorithms are like products. How would diverse consumer morals in a given market influence the determination of likeness? The determination of likeness is "about the nature and extent of a competitive relationship between and among the products at issue,"[75] and underlying regulatory concerns "may play a role" only if "they are relevant to the examination of certain 'likeness' criteria and are reflected in the products' competitive relationship."[76] Given the compliance costs and the distributional role of the global value chain, "even-handed regulation would be found to treat like products less favorably."[77] Furthermore, to discipline algorithm designs in terms of how source codes are written and what/how training data are fed, WTO members would need to regulate not only the end product, but also the process and production methods, which remain controversial issues in WTO jurisprudence.[78] Nevertheless, even if a violation of Article I or III is found, such measures may well be justified under GATT Article XX(a), namely when they are "necessary to protect public morals" and "not applied in a manner which would constitute a means of arbitrary or unjustifiable discrimination between countries where the same conditions prevail, or a disguised restriction on international trade" – the so-called two-tier test.[79] Most other free trade agreements also contain such a standard

[74] Appellate Body Report, *European Communities – Measures Affecting Asbestos and Asbestos-Containing Products*, WT/DS135/AB/R (5 April 2001) [*EC–Asbestos*], para. 99.

[75] Ibid. See also Appellate Body Report, *United States – Measures Affecting the Production and Sale of Clove Cigarettes*, WT/DS406/AB/R (24 April 2012) [*US–Clove Cigarettes*], para. 120.

[76] Ibid. Arguably, this market-oriented approach systematically excludes the bases for regulatory distinctions. See JP Trachtman, "WTO Trade and Environment Jurisprudence: Avoiding Environmental Catastrophe" (2017) 58(2) *Harvard International Law Journal* 273, at 277–281.

[77] See Trachtman, note 23 above, at 20.

[78] Ibid.

[79] GATT, art. XX(a) and chapeau. See Appellate Body Report, *United States – Standards for Reformulated and Conventional Gasoline*, WT/DS2/AB/R (20 May 1996) [*US–Gasoline*], at 22; see also Appellate Body Report, *United States – Import Prohibition of Certain Shrimp and Shrimp Products*, WT/DS58/AB/R (6 November 1998) [*US–Shrimp*], paras. 119–120; Appellate Body Report,

exception, allowing parties to derogate from their obligations to protect public morals. Similar clauses can also be found in GATS Article XIV(a)[80] and TBT Agreement Article 2.2. Further examinations include whether the measures are "designed to protect public morals,"[81] and whether they are "necessary" based on a weighing and balancing process.[82] Such a process has been the yardstick of the GATT Article XX necessity test, which is, as reaffirmed by the Appellate Body in *China – Publications and Audiovisual Products*, "a sequential process of weighing and balancing a series of factors," including assessing the relative importance of the values or interests pursued by the measure at issue, considering other relevant factors, and comparing the measure at issue with possible alternatives in terms of reasonable availability and trade restrictiveness.[83] Most importantly, the definition and scope of "public morals" can be highly contentious, and WTO adjudicators have embraced a deferential interpretation:

> [T]he term "public morals" denotes standards of right and wrong conduct maintained by or on behalf of a community or nation ... the content of these concepts for Members can vary in time and space, depending upon a range of factors, including prevailing social, cultural, ethical and religious values ... Members, in applying this and other similar societal concepts, should be given some scope to define and apply for themselves the concepts of "public morals" ... in their respective territories, according to their own systems and scales of values.[84]

More recently, the Appellate Body in *EC–Seal Products* also emphasized that WTO members must be given some scope to define and apply the idea of "public morals" pursuant to their own systems and values.[85] Given this deferential approach, WTO members appear to enjoy ample leeway in defining and applying public moral-based measures according to their own unique social systems and communal values.

Brazil – Measures Affecting Imports of Retreaded Tyres, WT/DS332/AB/R (17 December 2017) [*Brazil–Retreaded Tyres*], para. 139.

80 As noted, however, the discussion on service under the GATS is beyond the scope of this chapter.

81 Appellate Body Report, *Colombia – Measures Relating to the Importation of Textiles, Apparel and Footwear*, WT/DS461/AB/R (22 June 2016) [*Colombia–Textiles*], paras. 5.67–5.70.

82 Appellate Body Report, *China – Measures Affecting Trading Rights and Distribution Services for Certain Publications and Audiovisual Entertainment Products*, WT/DS363/AB/R (19 January 2010) [*China–Publications and Audiovisual Products*], paras. 239 and 242.

83 Ibid., paras. 300–311, 326–327.

84 Panel Report, *China – Publications and Audiovisual Products*, WT/DS363/R (19 January 2010), paras. 7.759 and 7.763; see also Panel Report, *United States – Measures Affecting the Cross-Border Supply of Gambling and Betting Services*, WT/DS285/R (7 April 2005) [*US–Gambling*], paras. 6.461 and 6.465.

85 See Appellate Body Report, *European Communities – Measures Prohibiting the Importation and Marketing of Seal Products*, WT/DS401/AB/R (18 June 2014) [*EC–Seal Products*], paras. 5.200–5.201. Indeed, WTO members and their societies "are not homogenous, either in their domestic political structures or in their ethical, moral, or religious beliefs." R Howse et al., "Pluralism in Practice: Moral Legislation and the Law of the WTO After Seal Products" (2015) 48 *George Washington International Law Review* 81, at 85.

Further, because the TBT Agreement cumulatively applies in conjunction with the GATT, an ADS regulatory measure that is justified may still violate the TBT Agreement, which similarly contains nondiscrimination obligations but lacks public moral exceptions. According to Trachtman, "the scope of the TBT national treatment requirement has been interpreted somewhat narrowly compared to that of GATT, excluding from violation measures that 'stem exclusively from a legitimate regulatory distinction,' in order to avoid invalidating a broader scope of national technical regulations than the GATT."[86] Under Articles 2.1 and 2.2 of the TBT Agreement, ADS regulatory measures are required to be sufficiently "calibrated" to different conditions in different areas, and to not be "more trade-restrictive than necessary to fulfill a legitimate objective, taking account of the risks non-fulfillment would create."[87] That is, similarly to the jurisprudence in the GATT, a holistic weighing and balancing process taking into account the degree of contribution, levels of trade restrictiveness, and the risks of non-fulfillment of the stated objectives as well as a comparison with possible alternatives are mandated.[88] As will be demonstrated next, the necessity of regulatory measures that focus on mandatory disclosure of source codes and training data (both the substance and form of the regulation) may be fiercely challenged; at the same time, locating a reasonably available alternative can be equally problematic.

Given the transnational regulatory initiatives, Article 2.4 of the TBT Agreement also plays a crucial role here. WTO members are required to use the standards developed by the SAE/ISO and UNECE (so long as they are "relevant international standards") as the bases for domestic regulations unless such standards cannot effectively or appropriately fulfill the legitimate objective of protecting public morals in the ADS issue area.[89] While this may impose certain (albeit weak) restrictions on the regulatory autonomy and flexibility of WTO members when designing and imposing their ADS algorithm rules and standards in the ethical dimension,[90] the implausible (if not impossible) global consensus on ethical decision-making means that such international standards remain far out of reach. In the long run, there might be more and more initiatives of international standards in this regard, potentially resulting in concerns over the structure, process, and participation in a standard-setting body as well as political confrontations at the TBT Committee.[91]

[86] Trachtman, note 23 above, at 21 (citing Appellate Body Report, *United States – Measures Affecting the Production and Sale of Clove Cigarettes*, WT/DS406/AB/R (24 April 2012), paras. 96–102).

[87] TBT Agreement, Arts. 2.1 and 2.2. See Appellate Body Report, *United States – Measures Concerning the Importation, Marketing and Sale of Tuna and Tuna Products, Recourse to Article 21.5 of the DSU by Mexico*, WT/DS381/AB/RW (3 December 2015), para. 284.

[88] Appellate Body Report, *United States – Measures Concerning the Importation, Marketing and Sale of Tuna and Tuna Products*, WT/DS381/AB/R (13 June 2012) [*US–Tuna*], at 320, 322.

[89] TBT Agreement, Art. 2.4.

[90] See Trachtman, note 23 above, at 22.

[91] See Liu and Lin, note 36 above, at 411, 429–430, 446–447.

B *Automated Driving System Algorithms, Source Codes, and Training Data as "Undisclosed Information" under the TRIPS Agreement*

Even if the substance of ADS regulatory measures does not violate existing obligations under the GATT and TBT Agreement, WTO members may require ADS manufacturers to disclose their algorithms designs, source code, and training data to verify compliance and achieve their regulatory objectives. If WTO members force ADS vehicle manufacturers or programmers to disclose their trade secrets – proprietary algorithm designs, source codes, and training data – can they survive the test of the TRIPS Agreement? To be sure, entities that own ADS algorithms can seek protection via various channels including patents, copyrights, and trade secrets.[92] However, the commercial practice in the ADS field (and many other AI applications) has been to hold both source code and training data as trade secrets to maximize the protection of interests and to remain competitive in the market.[93]

Article 39.1 of the TRIPS Agreement requires members, when "ensuring effective protection against unfair competition as provided in Article 10bis of the Paris Convention (1967)," to "protect undisclosed information in accordance with paragraph 2."[94] Article 39.2 further provides that information – when it is secret (not "generally known among or readily accessible to persons within the circles that normally deal with the kind of information in question"), has commercial value, and is controlled by the lawful custodian – shall be protected "from being disclosed to, acquired by, or used by others without their consent in a manner contrary to honest commercial practices."[95] This requires WTO members to provide minimum protections for undisclosed information, recognized in Article 1.2 as a category of intellectual property,[96] in accordance with the conditions and criteria provided in Article 39.2.[97]

Article 39 does not explicitly prohibit members from promulgating laws, consistent with other provisions of the TRIPS Agreement, to allow lawful disclosure or create exceptions where trade secrets may lawfully be forced to be disclosed. Yet what may constitute a lawful disclosure under the TRIPS Agreement can also be controversial. Can members promulgate any law that requires disclosure of trade secrets to serve certain regulatory objectives? Are all measures regulating ADSs and requiring disclosure of source code and training data for conformity assessment

92 See generally SK Katyal, "The Paradox of Source Code Secrecy" (2019) 104 *Cornell Law Review* 101.

93 Ibid., at 145–146.

94 TRIPS Agreement, Art. 39.1.

95 TRIPS Agreement, Art. 39.2.

96 TRIPS Agreement, Art. 1.2. See World Intellectual Property Organization (WIPO), *Introduction to Intellectual Property: Theory and Practice* (2nd ed., Alphen aan den Rijn,Wolters Kluwer, 2017), at 243–246. See NP de Carvalho, *The TRIPS Regime of Antitrust and Undisclosed Information* (Alphen aan den Rijn, Kluwer Law International, 2008), at 189–190.

97 See J Malbon et al., *The WTO Agreement on Trade-Related Aspects of Intellectual Property Rights: A Commentary* (Cheltenham, Edward Elgar Publishing, 2014), at 577.

lawful and consistent with the TRIPS Agreement? There has been no case law related to Article 39, but the fact that the United States' proposal to include "theft, bribery, [and] espionage" of secrets in "a manner contrary to honest commercial practices"[98] was rejected in the negotiation process indicates that what may constitute a lawful disclosure can also prove contentious.[99] A contextual reading of TRIPS Agreement Articles 7 and 8 suggests that "Members may . . . adopt measures necessary to . . . promote the public interest in sectors of vital importance to their socio-economic and technological development,"[100] and "a balance of rights and obligations"[101] is called for, but such measures cannot "unreasonably restrain trade."[102] The scope of disclosure, the regulated entities, the manner of disclosure, and enforcement and safeguard may therefore be crucial factors in determining consistency. In this sense, in China's social credit scenario, a *limited* approach that requires essential source code and training data (from companies that program the algorithms making ethical decisions, instead of all of the actors along the global ADS supply chain) to be disclosed to an expert committee (or similar institutional designs)[103] for review and certification, rather than a wholesale, systematic forced disclosure, may appear to be more TRIPS-consistent. Additional safeguards that prohibit government agencies from sharing disclosed proprietary information with others may also help to avoid inappropriate forced technology transfers, unfair competition, and unfair commercial use.[104] Relatedly, some recent megaregional free trade agreements (mega-FTAs) have included provisions that explicitly prevent governments from demanding access to an enterprise's proprietary software source code.[105] Demands for stronger protection of source code and training data and limitations on governments' regulatory room for maneuver are likely to grow in the age of AI.

98 Negotiating Group on Trade-Related Aspects of Intellectual Property Rights, including Trade in Counterfeit Goods (1990), *Status of Work in the Negotiating Group: Chairman's Report to the GNG*, MTN.GNG/NG11/W/76, Part III, s. 7. 1 A.2.

99 Malbon et al., note 97 above, at 579.

100 TRIPS Agreement, Art. 8.1.

101 TRIPS Agreement, Art. 7.

102 TRIPS Agreement, Art. 8.2.

103 See F Pasquale, *The Black Box Society: The Secret Algorithms That Control Money and Information* (Cambridge, MA, Harvard University Press, 2015), at 160–161; see also F Pasquale, "Beyond Innovation and Competition: The Need for Qualified Transparency in Internet Intermediaries" (2010) 104 *Northwestern University Law Review* 105.

104 For instance, China has been accused of forcing foreign companies to disclose sensitive technical data and proprietary source code via a series of administrative processes as a necessary step for market entry, and such data and source code could be passed to domestic competitors. See L Wei and B Davis, "How China Systematically Pries Technology from U.S. Companies" (*Wall Street Journal*, 26 September 2018), https://perma.cc/ZCV4-DHTK; JY Qin, "Forced Technology Transfer and the US-China Trade War: Implications for International Economic Law," Wayne State University Law School Research Paper No. 201961 (5 October 2019), 3–4.

105 See, for example, Comprehensive and Progressive Agreement for Trans-Pacific Partnership (CPTPP), Art. 14.17.

C "*Algorithmic Black Box*" *and the Limits of Regulatory Measures*

An additional layer of regulatory challenge that may prevent the effectiveness (therefore necessity) of these measures stems from the technological nature of machine/deep learning algorithms – its opaque characteristic, or as criticized by a leading commentator, the "black box" problem.[106] This problem refers to the complexity and secrecy of algorithm-based (especially deep learning-based) decision-making processes, which frustrates meaningful scrutiny and regulation. Without understanding and addressing the black box challenge, it may be unrealistic to rely on disclosure or source codes as a regulatory approach. The black box problem can further be disentangled into "legal black box" and "technical black box."[107] The "legal black box" is opaque because of the proprietary status of complex statistical models or source codes, as they are legally protected by trade secret laws.[108] Regulatory measures focusing on forced disclosure are one way to fix such black box problems by unpacking the algorithms therein to secure a certain level of compliance.

However, the "technical black box," which arises in applications based on machine/deep learning algorithms, is much more problematic.[109] A technically inherent lack of transparency persists as decisions and classifications emerge automatically in ways that no one – even the programmers themselves – can adequately explain in human-intelligible terms why and how certain decisions and classifications are reached.[110] There exists "no well-defined method to easily interpret the relative strength of each input and to each output in the network" due to the highly nonlinear technological characteristic.[111] Therefore, the measures that are limited to legally forced disclosure can hardly address this technical black box problem. Even if the regulator forces ADS manufacturers to disclose source codes and algorithm designs, the level of compliance may not be effectively ascertained and evaluated. Because of this technical black box problem, regulatory measures designed to disclose source codes and ensure compliance with ethical

106 See generally Pasquale, note 104 above; and F Pasquale, "Secret Algorithms Threaten the Rule of Law" (*MIT Technology Review*, 1 July 2017), https://perma.cc/6UYB-86VD.

107 See generally H-W Liu et al., "Beyond State v. Loomis: Artificial Intelligence, Government Algorithmization, and Accountability" (2019) 27(2) *International Journal of Law and Information Technology* 122.

108 Ibid.

109 Ibid.

110 See ibid. See JV Tu, "Advantages and Disadvantages of Using Artificial Neural Networks versus Logistic Regressions for Predicting Medical Outcomes" (1996) 49 (11) *Journal of Clinical Epidemiology* 1225; M Aikenhead, "The Uses and Misuses of Neural Networks in Law" (1996) 12(1) *Santa Clara Computer and High Technology Law Journal* 31, at 33; and P Margulies, "Surveillance by Algorithms: The NSA, Computerized Intelligence Collection, and Human Rights" (2016) 68 *Florida Law Review* 1045, at 1069.

111 See L Zhou et al., "A Comparison of Classification Methods for Predicting Deception in Computer-Mediated Communication" (2004) 20(4) *Journal of Management Information Systems* 139, at 150–151.

rules on ADSs (hence the rational nexus between regulatory means and objectives) may be significantly frustrated.

IV CONCLUSION

ADSs promise to transform modern transportation, conventional division of labor, social interactions, and provision of services. However, when vehicles equipped with different levels of ADSs enter the market, a range of regulatory issues should be addressed. In particular, the ethical puzzles pose formidable and multifaceted challenges to governments to act individually and collectively in delivering good ADS governance. As analyzed by this chapter, complex ethical questions, algorithmic designs, and cultural, demographic, and institutional factors may readily be translated into heterogeneous regulatory measures that could increase frictions in international trade and bring about highly contentious issues in the WTO. This chapter used ADS ethics as a vantage point to identify and unpack three levels of challenges WTO members may face in addressing public moral issues by conditioning the import and sale and dictating the design of ADS to reflect and respect their local values. These challenges may well translate into a regulatory dilemma for WTO members. Premised upon a review of regulatory initiatives at national and transnational levels, this chapter not only identified the normative boundaries set by the relevant WTO-covered agreements but also highlighted the inherent limitations of potential regulatory measures due to the technological nature of AI,[112] which call for a reconceptualization of the forms and substances of regulations on such evolving technology.

[112] See generally MU Scherer, "Regulating Artificial Intelligence Systems: Risks, Challenges, Competencies, and Strategies" (2016) 29(2) *Harvard Journal of Law & Technology* 353.

13

International Trade Law and Data Ethics

Possibilities and Challenges

Neha Mishra

I INTRODUCTION

The global economy is constantly being reshaped because of the rapid growth of data-driven services and technologies. The complementary relationship of big data analytics and artificial intelligence (AI)[1] holds the potential to generate significant economic and social benefits.[2] However, such data-driven services can also be misused by companies, governments and cyber-criminals in different ways, resulting in increased privacy and security breaches; disinformation campaigns; and biased algorithmic decision-making that disempower users of such technologies/services.[3] These misuses often result because of deficiencies/loopholes in how data-driven services collect, process, transfer and share data, as well as the technical design of their algorithms or computer programs, thereby raising strong concerns regarding the ethics of data management and data-driven technologies. In response to these concerns, several governments and private initiatives have formulated data ethics frameworks that regulate data-driven technologies.[4] Similarly, scholars have started evaluating how data ethics principles can act as a 'moral compass' in determining 'good' digital regulation and

[1] J Yeung, 'What Is Big Data and What Can Artificial Intelligence Do?' (Towards Data Science, 30 January 2020), perma.cc/Z7CS-JZQ3.

[2] T Philbeck et al., 'Values, Ethics and Innovation Rethinking Technological Development in the Fourth Industrial Revolution' (White Paper, World Economic Forum, August 2018), at 4; Organisation for Economic Co-operation and Development (OECD), 'Data-Driven Innovation for Growth and Well-Being' (2015), www.oecd.org/sti/ieconomy/data-driven-innovation.htm; World Health Organization, 'Big Data and Artificial Intelligence', www.who.int/ethics/topics/big-data-artificial-intelligence/en; NITI Aayog, 'National Strategy for Artificial Intelligence' (2018), https://niti.gov.in/national-strategy-artificial-intelligence, at 24–45.

[3] D Leslie, 'Understanding Artificial Intelligence Ethics and Safety' (Alan Turing Institute, 2019), https://perma.cc/7V82-JRNR, at 4. See also M Brundage et al., 'The Malicious Use of Artificial Intelligence: Forecasting, Prevention, and Mitigation' (Future of Humanity Institute and others, February 2018), https://perma.cc/46NB-8HS2.

[4] See generally J Fjeld et al., 'Principled Artificial Intelligence: Mapping Consensus in Ethical and Rights-Based Approaches to Principles for AI' (Berkman Klein Center for Internet & Society, 2020).

governance.[5] Some governments have translated these ethical frameworks applicable to data-driven services and technologies into binding laws and regulations (or 'data ethics-related measures').

In some cases, data ethics-related measures can have a trade-restrictive impact. For instance, in order to protect personal privacy, governments could restrict the cross-border transfer and processing of personal data that could be burdensome and inefficient, especially for foreign companies. Governments may also demand mandatory access to vital technical information of companies such as the source code and algorithms of their data-driven technologies so as to ensure they are robust, fair and non-discriminatory. Further, as platforms increasingly use automated processes to moderate online content,[6] governments might desire to scrutinise these algorithms to ensure compliance with domestic censorship laws. Such measures may be more burdensome for foreign companies, especially if they prejudice the safety and integrity of their proprietary technologies. Governments may also prescribe specific domestic standards for data-driven services, which may or may not be compatible with global standards.[7] Such measures can interfere with the cross-border supply of digital services and technologies and thus act as trade barriers.[8] However, to date, neither scholars nor policy experts have examined the interface of international trade law and data ethics. For instance, the World Trade Report 2018 of the World Trade Organization (WTO), which focused on AI, mentioned the word 'ethics' only once.[9]

Given these gaps in the existing literature, this chapter addresses whether international trade agreements, such as the WTO's General Agreement on Trade in Services (GATS), provide sufficient policy space to governments to implement data ethics-related measures, despite their possible trade-restrictive effect. More specifically, this chapter explores the role of general exceptions in GATS (art. XIV) in delineating WTO members'[10] policy space to implement data ethics-related measures. Section II discusses the key principles of data ethics common to various policy frameworks, including the protection of human rights; algorithmic accountability; and ethical design. Further, this section highlights examples of government measures intended to implement these data ethics principles, and if and when such measures have a trade-restrictive impact.

5 L Floridi and M Taddeo, 'What Is Data Ethics?' (2018) 374 *Philosophical Transactions* 1, at 1.

6 See Ofcom/Cambridge Consultants, 'Use of AI in Content Moderation' (2019), https://perma.cc/4WA4-NKVA.

7 See Department for Promotion of Industry and Internal Trade (Government of India), 'Draft Electronic Commerce Policy' (2019), https://dipp.gov.in/sites/default/files/DraftNational_e-commerce_Policy_23February2019.pdf, at 30; N Wilson, 'China Standards 2035 and the Plan for World Domination – Don't Believe China's Hype' (CFR, 3 June 2020), https://perma.cc/K5LX-PDXQ; A Gross et al., 'Chinese Tech Groups Shaping UN Facial Recognition Standards' (*The Financial Times*, 2 December 2019), https://perma.cc/T4VD-A8MD.

8 See subsection B in Section II.

9 World Trade Organization, 'World Trade Report 2018: The Future of World Trade: How Digital Technologies are Transforming Global Commerce' (2018), https://perma.cc/7NHM-BCU7, at 32.

10 Henceforth referred to as 'members'.

Section III examines the interface of international trade law and data ethics in light of the general exceptions in GATS art. XIV. This section argues that GATS art. XIV contains relevant defences for data ethics-related measures. For instance, members may argue that their measures are necessary to achieve compliance with domestic laws, including privacy laws (GATS art. XIV(c)(ii)) or to protect public morals or maintain public order (GATS art. XIV(a)). An evolutionary interpretation of GATS art. XIV can cover several data ethics concerns. However, regulatory diversity across countries and the evolving nature of data ethics frameworks set out a difficult test for assessing the limits of GATS art. XIV, especially examining the core rationale underlying data ethics-related measures, and identifying the least burdensome and trade-restrictive means to realise policy goals enshrined in data ethics frameworks.

Ultimately, applying international trade agreements to data ethics-related measures offers both possibilities and challenges. For instance, WTO panels[11] can meaningfully apply GATS art. XIV to accommodate data ethics principles within the WTO framework, including by referring to relevant private/transnational technical standards on data-driven services and international/multi-stakeholder norms on data ethics and governance. Similarly, using both technological and legal evidence, panels can apply the necessity test in GATS art. XIV to curtail protectionist measures that governments have disguised as being necessary for implementing data ethics principles. However, panels also face the challenge of balancing dynamic domestic and transnational interests related to ethical data governance. In order to better engage with these possibilities and challenges, this chapter recommends that the WTO should open itself to policy developments in data governance as well as remain abreast of technological advances, especially in the designing and verification of digital technologies and services.

II IMPLEMENTING DATA ETHICS PRINCIPLES AND THEIR TRADE REPERCUSSIONS

Across the world, governments are developing frameworks and high-level principles on data ethics, particularly for AI-driven sectors.[12] Subsection A of this section discusses certain key principles common to these frameworks such as protection of human rights, including individual privacy; algorithmic accountability; and ethical design. It also provides examples of measures that governments impose when

[11] Henceforth referred to as 'panels'.

[12] See Authority of the House of Lords, 'Regulating in a Digital World' (2019), https://perma.cc/YM3H-FG6B; European Parliament, A *Comprehensive European Industrial Policy on Artificial Intelligence and Robotics*, Doc no. P8_TA-PROV(2019)0081 (12 February 2019); European Commission, 'Ethics Guidelines for Trustworthy AI' (2019), https://perma.cc/37YZ-2E59; OECD, *Recommendation of the Council on Artificial Intelligence*, Doc no. OECD/LEGAL/0449 (22 May 2019); NIST, 'US Leadership in AI: A Plan for Federal Engagement in Developing Technical Standards and Related Tools' (2019), https://perma.cc/Z4G7-TUKJ.

intending to realise these principles. Subsection B then highlights the potential trade-restrictive impact of certain data ethics-related measures.

A *Key Principles of Data Ethics*

The fundamental component of all data ethics frameworks is the protection of human rights.[13] Several international and regional instruments highlight the importance of a human rights-centric approach in data governance.[14] Similarly, individual governments specifically recognise the importance of protecting human rights in the use of data-driven technologies.[15] The essence of a human rights-centric approach involves increasing individual control over personal data, and ensuring that all data is used, processed and shared in a manner compliant with fundamental human rights.

In this regard, the human rights-centric approach entails protecting individuals against discrimination, promoting digital access and inclusion, and safeguarding individual privacy.[16] From the perspective of data ethics, privacy is essential at all stages of data management, from ensuring informed consent of individuals in the collection of their personal data to increasing human control over all aspects of data processing, including the choice not to be subject to profiling and automated decision-making. The emergence of big data analytics also raises concerns around group privacy (although it remains debatable if this falls within the scope of personal privacy).[17] Unsurprisingly, various domestic laws and regulations now deal with privacy concerns, including data protection laws.[18]

Data-driven technologies can be used to breach human rights other than the right to privacy in various ways. For example, AI algorithms using training data with sensitive variables such as gender and race often generate biased outcomes or

[13] C Cath and L Floridi, 'The Design of the Internet's Architecture by the Internet Engineering Task Force (IETF) and Human Rights' (2017) 23(2) *Science and Engineering Ethics* 449, at 455; IEEE, 'Ethically Aligned Design – First Edition' (2019), https://perma.cc/6VZ2-EXNC, at 10. In the specific context of AI, see Fjeld et al., note 4 above.

[14] *Progress Report of the United Nations High Commissioner for Human Rights on Legal Options and Practical Measures to Improve Access to Remedy for Victims of Business-Related Human Rights Abuses*, UN Doc A/HRC/29/39 (May 2015); *Montreal Declaration for Responsible Development of Artificial Intelligence* (2018); OECD, note 12 above.

[15] Personal Data Protection Commission Singapore, 'A Proposed Model for Artificial Intelligence Governance Framework' (January 2019), at 6; Department of Industry, Innovation and Science (Government of Australia), 'AI Ethics Principles' (2019), www.industry.gov.au/data-and-publications/building-australias-artificial-intelligence-capability/ai-ethics-framework/ai-ethics-principles; European Commission, note 12 above.

[16] United Nations, 'A Human-Rights Based Approach to Data' (2018), https://perma.cc/AX88-85VN.

[17] L Taylor, 'Group Privacy: Big Data and the Collective' (MyData 2017, 24 September 2017), www.youtube.com/watch?v=BsZ05MVFXLU.

[18] For further details, see UNCTAD, 'Summary of Adoption of E-Commerce Legislation Worldwide', https://perma.cc/M7MS-E8AF.

decisions that adversely affect the fundamental rights of minority groups.[19] Big data analytics can be used to identify and then persecute political minorities or dissidents.[20] Further, governments increasingly use automated algorithms to filter content online, potentially harming the right to freedom of expression and access to information.[21]

A human rights-centric approach in data governance has implications for both governments and the private sector. For instance, governments are required to respect, protect and fulfil human rights[22] by ensuring fair and non-discriminatory use of data-driven technologies for public functions; protecting individuals from potential harms and misuses of data-driven technologies by private sector entities, including enforcement of regulations requiring transparent and non-discriminatory data practices by private entities; and ensuring that private companies provide appropriate remedies to affected individuals. Governments may also require businesses to change specific practices in data management and processing to ensure compliance with a human rights-centric approach in data governance. However, the structural mechanisms by which governments hold the private sector accountable for complying with human rights norms may vary across countries. This difference is attributable to varying perceptions among countries regarding how human rights should be formulated and enforced domestically.

A human rights-centric approach in the governance of data-driven technologies necessitates algorithmic accountability. This means that companies should be held responsible for how their algorithms function, including the decisions taken using them. For instance, in AI-driven technologies, huge datasets (known as training data) are used for predictive analytics and generating decisions in various areas including healthcare, credit reporting, law enforcement, retail and marketing. Several experts argue that increasing algorithmic accountability requires data-driven technologies to be transparent and explainable (i.e. the computer programmers must be able to explain how their algorithms/designs use and process data to generate certain results).[23] This can facilitate rectifying algorithms that generate unfair or discriminatory outcomes.[24] Algorithms can be explained at a systemic level

19 Fjeld et al., note 4 above, 49; JA Kroll et al., 'Accountable Algorithms' (2017) 165 *University of Pennsylvania Law Review* 633, at 681.

20 See Human Rights Watch, 'China: Big Data Fuels Crackdown in Minority Region' (HRW, 26 February 2018), https://perma.cc/76QL-RTGK.

21 L Yuan, 'Learning China's Forbidden History, So They Can Censor It', (*The New York Times*, 2 January 2019), https://perma.cc/3G2D-DUNH.

22 See generally Committee on Economic, Social and Cultural Rights, *General Comment No 24 on State Obligations under the International Covenant on Economic, Social and Cultural Rights in the Context of Business Activities*, UN Doc E/C.12/GC/24 (10 August 2017).

23 See AD Selbst and S Barocas, 'The Intuitive Appeal of Explainable Mechanisms' (2018) 87 *Fordham Law Review* 1085, at 1100 – 1120 (on the rationales for explainability of algorithms); Centre for Data Innovation, 'Re: Competition and Consumer Protection in the 21st Century Hearings', Project Number P181201, 15 February 2019.

24 Ibid.

(i.e. the logic of an algorithm) or at an individual level (i.e. how the algorithm decides in a specific case),[25] although this distinction remains debatable.[26]

Significant debate exists regarding the extent to which algorithms are or can be explainable and what regulatory mechanisms are needed to achieve the same. Certain experts argue that the transparency of source code/algorithms allows understanding the decision-making rule of the algorithms, but not their functionality in every random set of circumstances.[27] Therefore, they suggest that alternative technological mechanisms must be explored to achieve stronger algorithmic accountability such as verification programs that *ex ante* check if algorithms meet certain specifications (e.g. if they comply with the rule of law), and holding designers/technology companies accountable if and when a program fails to meet those specifications.[28] Others argue that explainability can be achieved through transparency and adequate regulatory inspection of algorithms.[29] On a different note, some experts emphasise that policymakers must be concerned about how data scientists build their datasets and the possible deficiencies in that process rather than solely concentrating on algorithmic accountability.[30]

While it is outside the scope of this chapter to explore these arguments in detail, the diversity of perspectives on algorithmic accountability, including transparency, leads to differing regulatory approaches across countries. This is important because governments are increasingly advocating that transparency and explainability of algorithms is a means to achieving accountability in data-driven technologies.[31] However, certain governments also acknowledge the limitations of transparency and explainability mechanisms in ensuring algorithmic accountability.[32] Separately,

25 S Wachter et al., 'Why a Right to Explanation of Automated Decision-Making Does Not Exist in the General Data Protection Regulation' (2017) 7(2) *International Data Privacy Law* 76, at 78.

26 AD Selbst and J Powles, 'Meaningful Information and the Right to Explanation' (2017) 7(4) *International Data Privacy Law* 233, at 239.

27 M Perel and N Elkin-Koren, 'Black Box Tinkering: Beyond Disclosure in Algorithmic Enforcement' (2017) 69 *Florida Law Review* 181, at 184–185, 188; Kroll et al., note 19 above, at 657, 660 (several technologies employ deep learning AI, which constantly self-learns and improvises its design, increasing the difficulty for engineers to explain the outputs of its algorithms).

28 Kroll et al., note 19 above, at 642. Similarly, see K Martin, 'Ethical Implications and Accountability of Algorithms' (2019) 160 *Journal of Business Ethics* 835, at 844.

29 DK Citron and F Pasquale, 'The Scored Society: The Due Process for Automation' (2014) 89 *Washington Law Review* 1, 25–30.

30 D Lehr and P Ohm, 'Playing with the Data: What Legal Scholars Should Learn about Machine Learning' (2017) 51 *UC Davis Law Review* 653, at 663–664.

31 Personal Data Protection Commission Singapore, note 15 above; Department of Industry, Innovation and Science, note 15 above; European Commission, *Policy and Investment Recommendations for Trustworthy AI* (26 June 2019); European Commission, *Structure for a White Paper on Artificial Intelligence – A European Approach* (2020) (leaked draft), https://perma.cc/M7QH-UEQV, at 16–17; UK House of Lords (Select Committee on Artificial Intelligence), *AI in the UK: Ready, Willing and Able?* (16 April 2018).

32 UK House of Lords, ibid., 128; Personal Data Protection Commission Singapore, note 15 above, at 6; Department of Industry, Innovation and Science, note 15 above.

governments may be concerned about the potential trade-offs between transparency and accuracy of algorithms.

The General Data Protection Regulation (GDPR) of the European Union (EU) arguably incorporates important elements of data ethics.[33] GDPR arts 44 and 45 limit data transfers to outside the EU to ensure that all personal data of EU residents is processed according to the highest data protection standards. GDPR art. 12 imposes an obligation on the data controllers to provide concise, transparent, easily understandable and accessible information to individuals regarding how they use personal data, including the extent to which they may use or rely upon personal data for automated decision-making.[34] GDPR art. 22 provides an individual the right not to be subjected to a decision solely based on automated decision-making or profiling,[35] if such a decision has 'legal effects' or 'significantly affects' the concerned individuals. However, significant debate exists regarding whether GDPR art. 22 incorporates a right to explainability of algorithms, for instance, those used in AI technologies.[36]

More recently, other domestic laws have started focusing on data ethics. For instance, the Digital Republic Act in France requires that all algorithmic decision-making by governments should be fully explainable.[37] In the USA, certain senators have proposed an Algorithmic Accountability Act, requiring companies to scrutinise their algorithms for potential risks and biases, thereby enabling greater algorithmic accountability.[38] Finally, certain regional trade agreements include provisions requiring the parties to adopt basic frameworks on data protection.[39] The recently concluded Digital Economy Partnership Agreement between New Zealand, Singapore and Chile includes a specific provision requiring the parties to endeavour to adopt ethical AI governance frameworks, although it only vaguely refers to 'internationally recognised principles or guidelines'.[40]

Another key element in data ethics is ethical design, which is an extension of a human rights-centric approach in data governance. In practice, ethical design requires that all suppliers of data-driven technologies devise and implement technical designs and standards compliant with human rights. For example, privacy-by-

33 European Commission, 'Ethics and Data Protection' (2018), https://perma.cc/V2C4-8KBK.

34 See Article 29 Data Protection Working Party, *Guidelines on Automated Individual Decision-Making and Profiling for the Purposes of Regulation 2016/679* (6 February 2018), at 10.

35 Profiling is defined to include any form of automated processing that considers an individual's personal information to analyse their lives. See GDPR art. 4(4).

36 See Wachter et al., note 25 above; Selbst and Powles, note 26 above; L Edwards and M Veale, 'Slave to the Algorithm? Why a "Right to Explanation" Is Probably Not the Remedy You're Looking For' (2017) 16 *Duke Law & Technology Review* 18.

37 See L Edwards and M Veale, 'Enslaving the Algorithm: From a "Right to an Explanation" to a "Right to Better Decisions"?' (May/June 2018) *AI Ethics* 46, at 48.

38 See Algorithmic Accountability Act of 2019 (Proposed Bill), https://perma.cc/V5UQ-LZ53.

39 See M Wu, 'Digital Trade-Related Provisions in Regional Trade Agreements: Existing Models and Lessons for the Multilateral Trade System' (2017) ICTSD, at 25.

40 Digital Economy Partnership Agreement (DEPA), art. 8.2.

design and security-by-design measures require digital service suppliers to use digital technologies and implement corporate policies that, by default, ensure data privacy and security. This can be instrumental in protecting personal data and increasing trust in data-driven technologies. Further, as ethical design focuses on technologically robust solutions, it promotes more reliable and sustainable outcomes in comparison to prescriptive data localisation measures or mandatory use of indigenous technical standards. GDPR art. 25 requires all digital service suppliers in the EU to adopt EU data protection principles by design and by default.

In practice, however, implementing ethical design is difficult. This challenge arises as the appropriate standards and benchmarks in the digital sector remain controversial, both in terms of regulatory practices and industry practices. For instance, with respect to privacy, considerable debate exists regarding whether the GDPR should be considered a global standard.[41] Similarly, technical standards developed by leading digital powers such as the USA and China are often market competitors, especially for AI-driven services.[42] Further, while laws and regulations tend to be ambiguous in their meaning (e.g. what is personally identifiable information in a privacy law), engineering models are highly dependent on precision of definitions in designing robust and reliable technologies.[43]

B *Trade Implications of Data Ethics-Related Measures*

As discussed in Section I, certain data ethics-related measures may be trade-restrictive as they hinder the cross-border supply of digital services, thereby breaching members' obligations in WTO agreements. Some examples include: (i) restrictions on data processing or transfers; (ii) prescribing specific technical standards for digital services and products; and (iii) requiring digital technology providers to submit their algorithms, source code and other vital technical information for government scrutiny/audit.

Governments may impose restrictions on cross-border data flows/processing or even require local storage and processing of data in sensitive sectors, to safeguard individual privacy rights. Some data protection laws even restrict the use of personal data for profiling. In other cases, regulatory approvals may be required to process sensitive data outside of the borders of a country. These measures typically increase costs, especially for foreign companies, lacking local data storage or processing capabilities.[44] When the regulatory requirements for trans-border data transfers/

41 See generally C Ryngaert and M Taylor, 'The GDPR as Global Data Protection Regulation?' (2020) 114 *AJIL Unbound* 5.

42 A Roberts et al., 'Toward a Geoeconomic Order in International Trade and Investment' (2019) 22(4) *Journal of International Economic Law* 655, at 673–675.

43 See K Nissim et al., 'Bridging the Gaps Between Computer Science and Legal Approaches to Privacy' (2018) 31(2) *Harvard Journal of Law & Technology* 689.

44 N Mishra, 'Privacy, Cybersecurity, and GATS Article XIV: A New Frontier for Trade and Internet Regulation?' (2020) 19 *World Trade Review* 341, at 344–346.

processing are administered in an unfair or unreasonable manner, they may be inconsistent with domestic regulation provision in GATS art. VI. Further, data processing restrictions may affect the development and accuracy of AI technologies as they prevent data accumulation on a global scale, especially affecting foreign, multi-national suppliers. Such measures may be considered discriminatory against foreign services or service suppliers, potentially breaching national treatment obligation in GATS art. XVII. Under the GDPR, digital service suppliers in the EU face several restrictions in transferring and processing personal data of EU residents abroad (except for a select group of countries that the EU identifies as having an adequate framework of data protection).[45] This restriction on the transfer of personal data to non-EU countries may be inconsistent with the most favoured nation obligation in GATS art. II.

As data-driven services have become common, several governments have started prescribing domestic technical standards, especially in AI-related sectors. These technical standards may be imposed for a variety of reasons, including ensuring that digital technologies are robust and secure, thereby reducing the chances of misuse of data. In the future, governments may prescribe standards that they consider compliant with ethical design requirements. However, if such prescribed standards are incompatible with competitive global standards or extremely onerous to implement, they create barriers for foreign services and service suppliers. In such scenarios, domestic technical standards may violate disciplines on domestic regulation under GATS art. VI.

Requirements imposed on digital technology providers to submit their algorithms and source code for government scrutiny/audit could have an underlying data ethics rationale, but such measures could also be trade-restrictive.[46] For instance, such measures may restrict entry of foreign competitors in domestic markets, thereby breaching national treatment obligation contained in GATS art. XVII. Additionally, such measures can prejudice the security/reputation of global data operations of digital suppliers, thereby violating obligations on domestic regulation in GATS art. VI. For instance, governments can implement such measures unreasonably or unfairly to deliberately harm the commercial interests of foreign players, including sharing their vital technical information with domestic competitors.[47]

45 GDPR, arts. 44–45. See also 'Adequacy Decisions' (*European Commission*), https://ec.europa.eu/info/law/law-topic/data-protection/international-dimension-data-protection/adequacy-decisions_en.

46 See J Vainan, 'Microsoft Just Built a Special Version of Windows for China' (*Fortune*, 23 May 2017), https://perma.cc/WG34-F7FK; B Darrow, 'IBM Gives China Sneak Peek of Software Source Code: Report' (*Fortune*, 16 October 2015), https://perma.cc/F2N5-6MRE.

47 Such a measure could also violate the Agreement on Trade-Related Aspects of Intellectual Property Rights (TRIPS) art. 39, for example, if the measure affects vital commercial interests of foreign companies by increasing the chances of trade secret theft. However, this chapter does not cover justifications of data ethics-related measures under TRIPS. See White House, 'How China's Economic Aggression Threatens the Technologies and Intellectual Property of the United States and the World' (June 2018), https://perma.cc/4ZE6-FQ89. See also JY Qin, 'Forced Technology Transfer and the US–China Trade War: Implications for International Economic Law' (2019) 22(4) *Journal of International Economic Law* 743, at 745–746.

Additionally, in rare scenarios, countries may implement extreme measures banning a certain kind of data-driven technology to prevent abuse of human rights. For example, given the potential dangers and abuses of facial recognition technology, a government could potentially ban commercial software facilitating facial recognition, especially from foreign companies. Such measures may be in conflict with obligations on market access and non-discrimination under GATS.

III DEFENDING DATA ETHICS-RELATED MEASURES UNDER GATS GENERAL EXCEPTION

Although data ethics-related measures can violate obligations contained in WTO treaties, governments can argue that they protect vital public interests, including protecting privacy and addressing other ethical concerns regarding the processing and sharing of data, under the general exceptions contained in GATS art. XIV. While a significant amount of scholarship has discussed the justification of privacy laws under GATS art. XIV(c)(ii),[48] the role of GATS art. XIV(a) (the public morals/public order exception) in facilitating other public interests related to data ethics such as protecting against discrimination, facilitating technical robustness and security of technologies, and ensuring appropriate online content moderation remains unexplored. Therefore, after highlighting the relevance of GATS art. XIV(c)(ii) and GATS art. XIV(a) in justifying data ethics-related measures in subsection A of this section, subsection B focuses on how GATS art. XIV(a) applies to data ethics-related measures. Finally, subsection C discusses the various possibilities and challenges involved in accommodating data ethics-related measures within the WTO/GATS framework.

This section argues that GATS art. XIV can play a role in preserving the policy space necessary for members to impose data ethics-related measures. For instance, under GATS art. XIV(c)(ii), members may argue that certain data ethics-related measures are necessary to achieve compliance with domestic laws, especially data protection/privacy laws. Similarly, under the public morals/public order exception in GATS art. XIV(a), panels have generally interpreted 'public morals' broadly in line with domestic values/culture; thus, data ethics-related measures can generally qualify under GATS art. XIV(a). However, to ensure a holistic assessment under GATS art. XIV, panels must adopt a cautious, well-reasoned and coherent standard of review in evaluating the necessity of data ethics-related measures under GATS art. XIV. This would entail panels considering both the possibility of accommodating data ethics principles within the GATS framework (e.g. through a meaningful interpretation and application of the exception) and the challenge of balancing

[48] See RH Weber, 'Regulatory Autonomy and Privacy Standards under the GATS' (2012) 7 *Asian Journal of WTO and International Health Law & Policy* 25; S Yakovleva and K Irion, 'The Best of Both Worlds: Free Trade in Services and EU Law on Privacy and Data Protection' (2016) 2(2) *European Data Protection Law Review* 191.

(often conflicting) domestic and international perspectives on data governance (e.g. in conducting a holistic weighing and balancing test on the various regulatory means adopted to achieve a data ethics-related policy objective). The ability of the WTO to remain open to relevant policy and technological developments related to data-driven technologies (including relevant multi-stakeholder/transnational norms and standards) will be crucial in ensuring that the GATS framework can support genuine and legitimate data ethics-related measures.

A *Applying General Exceptions to Justify Data Ethics-Related Measures*

1 Relevance of GATS Art. XIV(c)(ii)

GATS art. XIV(c)(ii) is likely to be relevant in justifying data ethics-related measures aimed at protecting individual privacy. Under GATS XIV(c)(ii), a measure violating GATS obligations can be justified if: (a) it is implemented to secure compliance with domestic 'laws and regulations',[49] including those 'relat[ing] to' (ii) the protection of the privacy of individuals in relation to the processing and dissemination of personal data and the protection of confidentiality of individual records and accounts; (b) the above 'laws and regulations' are consistent with WTO law; and (c) the measure is necessary to secure compliance with these laws and regulations.[50]

GATS art. XIV(c)(ii) can be interpreted in an evolutionary manner to cover privacy concerns.[51] For instance, 'protection of privacy of individuals' in GATS art. XIV(c)(ii) could potentially cover measures preventing unauthorised online surveillance of individuals or indiscriminate use of personal data by companies without informed user content. Similarly, data processing outside one's borders may be restricted to prohibit illegal third-party use of personal data. Under GATS art. XIV(c)(ii), members must also demonstrate that the domestic law the measure seeks to achieve compliance with should be consistent with WTO law. While privacy laws are not per se inconsistent with WTO law, certain elements such as discriminatory or ambiguous conditions for cross-border data transfers may violate WTO law.[52] Group privacy concerns arguably do not fall under this exception as deidentified/anonymised data is not generally considered 'personal data', although this data can be used to discriminate against specific groups of individuals. These concerns are more likely to be addressed under GATS art. XIV(a), as discussed next.

[49] See AB Report, *Mexico – Taxes on Soft Drinks* [79] ('laws and regulations' refers to domestic laws and regulation, and not international law, unless it is incorporated into domestic law).

[50] Panel Report, *Colombia – Ports of Entry* [7.514]; AB Report, *US – Shrimp (Thailand)* [7.174]. See also AB Report, *Korea – Various Measures on Beef* [157]; AB Report, *Thailand – Cigarettes (Philippines)* [177]; AB Report, *US – Gambling*, [6.536] – [6.537].

[51] For evolutionary interpretation, see AB Report, *US – Shrimp* [129].

[52] For a more detailed analysis, see Mishra, note 44 above, at 352.

2 Relevance of GATS Art. XIV(a)

When data ethics-related measures do not specifically relate to personal privacy or achieving compliance with other domestic laws, they are more likely to be justified under GATS art. XIV(a) that allows measures: (a) necessary to protect public morals or to maintain public order. The public order exception may be invoked only where a genuine and sufficiently serious threat is posed to one of the fundamental interests of society. Further, members may rely on GATS art. XIV(a) in addition to GATS art. XIV(c)(ii) in justifying their data ethics-related measures.

The terms 'public morals' and 'public order' are distinct. However, panels have generally taken the view that 'to the extent that both concepts seek to protect largely similar values, some overlap may exist'.[53] 'Public order' is defined as 'a genuine and sufficiently serious threat' to 'one of the fundamental interests of society'.[54] Public morals is an undefined term; therefore, panels could theoretically interpret public morals with reference to international norms or the domestic values/culture of the country or both. Although this conflict between international/universal values and domestic values remains debatable,[55] WTO tribunals have generally shown an inclination to consider local values in determining the meaning of 'public morals'. In fact, in the *US – Gambling* dispute, the panel held that 'public morals' in GATS art. XIV(a) 'denotes standards of right and wrong conduct maintained by or on behalf of a community or nation', and such standards 'can vary in time and space, depending upon a range of factors, including prevailing social, cultural, ethical and religious values'.[56]

The WTO tribunals have generally applied GATS art. XIV(a) in a broad, flexible and evolutionary manner.[57] For instance, in *China – Publications and Audiovisual Products*, the Appellate Body (AB) held that censorship of printed and digital content fell within the scope of 'public morals' in GATS art. XIV(a).[58] In *US – Gambling*, 'public morals' was interpreted to cover public morals and public order concerns related to online gambling (including money laundering).[59] In *EC – Seals*, the AB held that the term 'public morals' covered animal welfare concerns.[60] In *Brazil – Taxation*, the panel held that a measure imposed to bridge the digital divide and

53 See Panel Report, *US – Gambling* [6.648].

54 GATS, art. XIV(a), note 5.

55 M Wu, 'Free Trade and the Protection of Public Morals: An Analysis of the Newly Emerging Public Morals Clause Doctrine' (2008) 33 *Yale Journal of International Law* 215; S Charnovitz, 'The Moral Exception in Trade Policy' (1998) 38 *Vanderbilt Journal of International Law* 689, at 743.

56 Panel Report, *US – Gambling* [6.461].

57 See generally G Marceau, 'Evolutive Interpretation by the WTO Adjudicator' (2018) 21(4) *Journal of International Economic Law* 791. For a discussion of WTO disputes on public morals, see RY Simo, 'Trade and Morality: Balancing Between the Pursuit of Non-Trade Concerns and the Fear of Opening the Floodgates' (2019) 51 *George Washington International Law Review* 407.

58 Panel Report, *China – Publications and Audiovisual Products* [7.759].

59 AB Report, *US – Gambling* [296].

60 AB Reports, *EC – Seal Products* [5.199].

promote social inclusion in Brazil fell within the scope of 'public morals'.[61] In *Colombia – Textiles*, the panel held that a domestic tariff intended to combat money laundering in Colombia fell within the scope of 'public morals'.[62]

Governments have significant freedom in deciding how to define and achieve public morality and public order. In *EC – Seals*, the panel identified two steps in assessing measures under the public morals exception: first, if the stated policy concern actually existed in the society and, second, if it fell within the scope of 'public morals'.[63] However, in the same dispute, the AB held that it is not necessary for the tribunal to identify the existence of a specific risk to public morals[64] or identify the exact content of public morals at issue (thus implying that variations of public morals exist depending on the member's values).[65] Further, members have the right to set different levels of protection to address identical moral concerns.[66] Arguably, a similar standard of review may apply when members impose measures necessary for maintaining public order. Although the requirement of a genuine and serious threat is a high threshold, members are likely to have sufficient discretion in determining the fundamental interest of their society. For instance, a member desiring to control the domestic internet activities of their residents could argue that restricting data transfers/processing is required for maintaining 'public order'.

Given the flexible interpretation of GATS art. XIV(a), data ethics-related measures are likely to fall within the scope of this provision. First, governments could argue that algorithmic accountability and ethical design are important elements of domestic public policy such as protecting social order and protecting consumers from harm. Second, the adoption of a human rights-centric approach can be a defining element of a society's public morals and constitute a fundamental public interest. For example, in order to protect minority groups from algorithmic discrimination, a government must be able to scrutinise the algorithms/source code, thereby qualifying under 'public morals' and 'public order'. Third, privacy is considered to be a 'moral' issue in many societies because of its connection with socio-cultural and religious values.[67] For example, sexual preferences and religious affiliation are considered highly intimate information in many societies. Finally, certain governments may argue that their data ethics-related measures are connected to human rights recognised in international instruments and declarations of the international policy community on data governance.[68] While panels are unlikely to accept public

[61] Panel Report, *Brazil – Taxation* [7.591]–[7.592].

[62] Panel Report, *Colombia – Textiles* [7.338]–[7.339]; AB Report, *Colombia – Textiles* [5.105].

[63] Panel Report, *EC – Seal Products* [7.381]–[7.383].

[64] AB Report, *EC – Seal Products* [5.198].

[65] AB Report, *EC – Seal Products* [5.199].

[66] AB Report, *EC – Seal Products* [5.200].

[67] See JQ Whitman, 'The Two Western Cultures of Privacy: Dignity Versus Liberty' (2004) 113 *Yale Law Journal* 1151.

[68] Scholars have generally advocated that 'public morals' could include universal human rights. See C Glinski, 'CSR and the Law of the WTO: The Impact of *Tuna Dolphin II* and *EC–Seal Product*' (2017) 1 *Nordic Journal of Commercial Law* 121, at 133.

morals or public order exception as a basis for enforcing international human rights,[69] they are likely to attempt to interpret GATS art. XIV(a) in a manner that respects human rights and international public policy.

B *Applying the Public Morals/Public Order Exception to Data Ethics-Related Measures*

If a data ethics-related measure qualifies under GATS art. XIV(a) or GATS art. XIV(c)(ii), the panel must examine its necessity to achieve the underlying policy objective under a 'weighing and balancing test'. This subsection focuses on the necessity of data ethics-related measures to protect public morals or maintain public order in accordance with the 'weighing and balancing test'.

The first step in this test is assessing the contribution of the measure to the policy objective under GATS art. XIV – that is, the nexus between the measure and the policy objective under GATS art. XIV[70] – for instance, by looking at the design, content, structure and expected operation of the data ethics-related measure.[71] For example, if a member requires companies to provide their source code or algorithms to verify them for bias (e.g. discriminating against minorities) or other privacy loopholes (particularly, group privacy concerns), the panel will examine if this requirement contributes to protecting public morals or maintaining public order under GATS art. XIV(a). From a technological perspective, this assessment can be difficult as the efficacy of transparency/disclosure of algorithms and source code to understand the underlying logic and discriminatory outcomes in algorithmic decision-making remains debatable.[72] For complex AI, such disclosure requirements can also be counterproductive; for example, in autonomous vehicles, requiring access to the algorithms could compromise the security of the digital technologies. As explainability of algorithms improves with technological developments (especially the development of explainable AI or XAI), panels can make better assessments by seeking additional expert technical evidence on relevant issues.

Similarly, questions may arise regarding whether restrictions on cross-border data flows contribute to achieving the key principles of data ethics. Several studies indicate that severe restrictions on data flows are generally ineffective in enhancing the privacy or security of data-driven technologies.[73] Similarly, locating data within

[69] G Marceau, 'WTO Dispute Settlement and Human Rights' (2002) 13(4) *European Journal of International Law* 753, at 761, 777, 813–814; SM Zonaid, 'Trading in Human Rights: Questioning the Advance of Human Rights into the World Trade Organization' (2015) 27 *Florida Journal of International Law* 261, at 286.

[70] AB Report, *US – Gambling* [292].

[71] AB Report, *EC – Seal Products* [5.302].

[72] See discussion in subsection A, Section II.

[73] See T Maurer et al., 'Technological Sovereignty: Missing the Point?', in M Maybaum et al. (eds), *Architectures in Cyberspace* (Tallinn, NATO CCD COE Publications, 2015), at 53, 61–62; K Komaitis, 'The "Wicked Problem" of Data Localization' (2017) 3(2) *Journal of Cyber Policy* 355, at 361–362.

one's borders does not automatically increase control or access to data. To the contrary, such measures increase the possibility of unauthorised surveillance and violation of human rights as well as interfering with the development of a healthy and competitive domestic digital market, especially when few companies (potentially state-controlled) own all the domestic data centres. However, easy access to local data servers may facilitate easier regulatory enforcement (e.g. pursuing action against companies that fail to comply with data ethics-related measures).

To facilitate a higher standard of data ethics, members may impose domestic regulations requiring technology companies to comply with internationally recognised technical standards, or adopt designs that protect privacy and security by default and/or use certification mechanisms to verify compliance with these ethical design requirements.[74] In comparison to blatant cross-border data transfer restrictions, these requirements appear more effective in facilitating digital inclusion, preventing disinformation campaigns and ensuring technologically robust solutions. Therefore, such measures are more likely to contribute to protecting public morals and maintaining public order.

The next step under the weighing and balancing test is assessing the trade-restrictiveness of the data ethics-related measure; that is, the restrictive impact of the measure on international commerce.[75] This step involves an assessment not only of the sector affected directly by the measure but also other sectors. For example, as data-driven services are used across several industries, restrictions on cloud computing services (e.g. mandatory compliance with domestic technical standards or data/security certifications) can potentially impact several sectors.[76]

Finally, in applying the weighing and balancing test, panels will take into account any alternative less trade-restrictive measures proposed by the complainant. The key factors examined are whether such alternatives are reasonably available to and feasible to implement.[77] Further, any proposed alternatives must achieve an equivalent level of protection of the stated policy objective as the imposed measure.[78] With regard to regulating certain aspects of the digital sector, self-regulatory (or market-driven) approaches may be more effective and efficient than highly prescriptive laws and regulations.[79] For example, rather than imposing specific technical standards, competitive standards developed by the industry in sectors such as AI are more likely

74 IEEE, note 13 above, at 28.

75 AB Report, *China – Publications and Audiovisual Products* [306].

76 See JP Meltzer, 'The Impact of Artificial Intelligence on International Trade' (2018), https://perma.cc/A3H7-FXVB (in the context of AI-driven technologies); A Goldfarb and D Trefler, 'AI and International Trade' (2017), https://perma.cc/5Z9K-29EK, at 24–29.

77 AB Report, *US – Gambling*, [308]; AB Report, *China – Publications and Audiovisual Products* [326]–[327]; AB Report, *EC – Seal Products* [5.279].

78 See AB Report, *Brazil – Retreaded Tyres* [156]; AB Report, *China – Publications and Audiovisual Products* [246].

79 See S-Y Peng, 'The Rule of Law in Times of Technological Uncertainty: Is International Economic Law Ready for Emerging Supervisory Trends?' (2019) 22 *Journal of International Economic Law* 1, at 13–15.

to be transparent and secure. Similarly, instead of restricting data-driven technologies through unreasonable regulations on data processing, countries could recognise market-driven verification mechanisms that certify compliance with robust standards on ethical design.

Despite the growing popularity of these market-driven mechanisms, panels are likely to consider them as, at best, complementary measures rather than alternatives to prescriptive laws and regulations.[80] This is because countries may be concerned about the robustness of the representativeness of private/multi-stakeholder standards, especially when developed without sufficient government oversight.[81] This would be the case even if the private/multi-stakeholder standards are robust and generally considered industry best practices. Further, verification/certification mechanisms could be very difficult and expensive for developing countries to adopt and monitor and thus not feasible. Therefore, at least in the current scenario, most market-driven or self-regulatory alternatives to data ethics-related measures are likely to fail to satisfy the threshold in GATS art. XIV. The same argument could also be made for technological mechanisms to ensure greater algorithmic accountability (as discussed in subsection A, Section II). In such cases, panels are likely to find more prescriptive measures such as mandatory disclosure of source code/algorithms compliant with GATS art. XIV.

If a trade-restrictive measure provisionally satisfies the necessity test under GATS art. XIV(a), it must further be consistent with the chapeau:

> Subject to the requirement that such measures are not applied in a manner which would constitute a means of arbitrary or unjustifiable discrimination between countries where like conditions prevail, or a disguised restriction on international trade in services, nothing in this Agreement shall be construed to prevent the adoption or enforcement by any Member of measures.

The chapeau prevents members from abusing exceptions contained in the subsections of GATS art. XIV and ensures that members implement all measures in good faith.[82] It requires an enquiry into the 'design, architecture, and revealing structure of a measure'[83] to assess if the measure violates the GATS art. XIV chapeau in 'its actual or expected application'.[84] For example, if a measure deliberately prohibits foreign service suppliers from obtaining licences or authorisations to provide their services on grounds that their algorithms or technical standards do not meet the adequate threshold (irrespective of the quality and robustness of the standard/algorithms), then it might be inconsistent with the GATS art. XIV

80 See AB Report, *Brazil – Retreaded Tyres* [151], [211]; Panel Report, *China – Rare Earths* [7.186]; Panel Report, *Australia – Plain Packaging* [7.1384]–[7.1391].

81 L DeNardis and M Raymond, 'The Internet of Things as a Global Policy Frontier' (2017) 15 *UC Davis Law Review* 475, at 493.

82 AB Report, *US – Shrimp* [158].

83 AB Report, *EC – Seal Products* [5.302].

84 Ibid.

chapeau. Another example of a potential violation is, when governments illegally share vital technical information regarding foreign digital technologies with domestic competitors, making it harder for foreign companies to compete in that market and further causing potential intellectual property losses.

C *Data Ethics and International Trade Law: Possibilities and Challenges*

The previous subsections indicate that although GATS art. XIV can justify data ethics-related measures, several questions remain unanswered regarding the extent to which GATS art. XIV provides sufficient policy space for members to impose data ethics-related measures. For instance, should panels place any limits in defining 'public morals' or 'public order' under GATS art. XIV(a) in accommodating data ethics concerns? Given the technological and policy uncertainty, what standard of review should panels adopt under GATS art. XIV in reviewing data ethics-related measures? Should panels be completely deferential to the risk assessment made by governments in relation to their data ethics-related measures or should they conduct a more substantive assessment? What tools should the panels use in this assessment? How will the growth of new technological mechanisms such as XAI or market-driven standards and verification mechanisms impact the assessment of data ethics-related measures under GATS art. XIV?

Data ethics-related measures are typically nuanced in nature. To understand these measures holistically, governments must focus on both their legal/policy implications and technological impact. Thus, in assessing data ethics-related measures under GATS, panels must follow a well-reasoned, cautious and coherent standard of review that looks at both the technological and legal evidence. However, given the limited technical expertise of panels, they should refrain from engaging in a de novo review of data ethics-related measures and cautiously use technical expert opinions.

In applying this standard of review, two routes are possible. First, in assessing whether certain data ethics-related measures relate to GATS art. XIV, panels can, in addition to considering local values and policy preferences of members, pay regard to developments in the international/multi-stakeholder policy community on data governance. This route is not entirely unrealistic given that data ethics issues implicate several transnational policy concerns and not just domestic concerns. Further, such an approach is also helpful given the critical role of multi-stakeholder institutions in promoting data ethics, as discussed in subsection A, Section II. In *Brazil – Taxation*, for instance, the panel considered not only the importance of the digital divide as a domestic policy objective within Brazil, but also discussed its relationship with the Millennium Development Goals.[85] However, this route is

[85] G Moon, 'A "Fundamental Moral Imperative": Social Inclusion, the Sustainable Development Goals and International Trade Law After Brazil- Taxation' (2018) 52(6) *Journal of World Trade* 995, at 1004.

politically and legally challenging in circumstances where local values conflict with international/multi-stakeholder norms. WTO tribunals do not have the capacity or mandate to determine the appropriate data ethics frameworks for individual members. Therefore, if a country considers that certain international/multi-stakeholder norms are not aligned with its policy preferences, trade tribunals must not interfere, even when those international/multi-stakeholder norms can lead to better outcomes for data ethics. This limitation, however, may lead to scepticism towards the WTO; that is, the panels cannot make decisions that clearly support a human rights-centric approach in data governance.

The second route is adopting a more stringent weighing and balancing test in assessing data ethics-related measures under GATS art. XIV(a).[86] The necessity test can be effective in detecting discriminatory or unnecessarily trade-restrictive measures.[87] For example, looking at the technical aspect of the measure (i.e. inviting expert evidence on whether a data ethics-related measure is actually capable of achieving important policy goals) is less controversial than examining the moral elements of the measure, which often implicates sensitive political or cultural questions. This approach, however, does not necessarily allow panels to consider innovations in the digital sector such as the potential role of technological mechanisms in the verification of data-driven technologies. For instance, engineers and computer scientists designing data-driven services can build *ex ante* verification mechanisms that ensure that the program/algorithm meets the specifications in domestic laws and processes.[88] Panels are unlikely to consider such mechanisms as a viable less trade-restrictive alternative under GATS art. XIV, especially when the defendant governments do not consider them as effective as regulatory access to source code/algorithms. Similarly, panels are unlikely to consider strict scrutiny/audits of training data by the private companies themselves a fool-proof mechanism to ensure fair and transparent outcomes in algorithmic decision-making, especially when governments restrict automated decision-making in risky and sensitive sectors.[89] However, as such market-based, technological mechanisms become more fit-for-purpose and reliable, they could be considered as more viable and qualify as potential candidates as less trade-restrictive alternatives under GATS art. XIV. Such mechanisms are also likely to be considered credible if they are developed and implemented by the private sector in collaboration with regulatory bodies, especially for countries with sufficient resources to hold private companies accountable for their poor data ethics practices.[90]

86 S Nuzzo, 'Tackling Diversity Inside WTO: GATT Moral Clause After Colombia – Textiles' (2017) 10 (1) *European Journal of Legal Studies* 267, at 290–292; JC Marwell, 'Trade and Morality: The WTO Public Morals Exception After Gambling' (2006) 81 *New York University Law Review* 802, 805.

87 See generally Mishra, note 44 above.

88 Kroll et al., note 19 above, at 642.

89 Wachter et al., note 25 above, at 99.

90 See C Sabel et al., 'Regulation under Uncertainty: The Coevolution of Industry and Regulation' (2018) 12 *Regulation and Governance* 371, at 373, 375 (arguing that uncertainties can prompt coordination among firms and between firms and regulatory bodies).

In the long run, the WTO needs to respond to the predominantly decentralised nature of data governance. For example, the WTO needs to adopt new rules and institutional mechanisms that allow collaboration between governments, technology companies and relevant multi-stakeholder or transnational organisations dealing with data governance. An important example in this regard is the development of technical standards on AI software by the private sector. Currently, GATS does not provide sufficient room for such standards for services.[91] However, at domestic/regional levels, several governments are coordinating with the private sector on certain aspects of data governance such as development of AI standards. These multi-stakeholder mechanisms could eventually grow transnationally (especially among like-minded countries) and can be facilitated through WTO committees. Eventually, such a broad-based approach could ensure that the WTO plays a more meaningful role in promoting good global data ethics practices and robust digital technologies.

IV CONCLUSION

This chapter investigated whether the general exceptions in GATS provide adequate policy space to governments to impose data ethics-related measures. In evaluating data ethics-related measures under GATS art. XIV, panels can take into account both international norms and best practices as well as local values or socio-cultural preferences, especially if they are aligned with each other. This chapter also demonstrates that panels can adopt a well-reasoned, cautious and coherent standard of review in assessing the necessity of data ethics-related measures under GATS art. XIV by holistically looking at both legal and technological evidence in each step of the weighing and balancing test. However, the possibility of panels considering a wider range of private sector-driven or multi-stakeholder mechanisms as alternatives to prescriptive data ethics-related measures, especially new verification technologies and technical standards, currently remains limited. Therefore, moving forward, the WTO framework must better co-opt international/multi-stakeholder norms and standards applicable to data-driven services so as to remain more open and responsive to the dynamic policy developments in data governance.

[91] GATS art. VI:4 read with art. VI:5 allows panels to only take into account technical standards of multilateral institutions. A possible route is exploring technical barrier to trade-like provisions for trade in services.

14

Disciplining Artificial Intelligence Policies

World Trade Organization Law as a Sword and a Shield

Kelly K. Shang and Rachel R. Du[*]

I INTRODUCTION

The rapid development of artificial intelligence (AI) technology has brought to humanity benefits and challenges. The potential risk for AI technology to be used for controversial purposes, and the need for the international community to develop disciplines on the use of AI, are noticed by many. For example, in May 2019, the Secretary-General of the United Nations (UN) denounced AI-powered "lethal autonomous weapons" as "politically unacceptable [and] morally repugnant", and called for such weapons to be "prohibited by international law".[1] In November 2019, a US Congressional Research Service (CRS) report identified the risks of AI applications being used in surveillance and reconnaissance applications, in autonomous weapon systems,[2] or to serve "dual-use" purposes.[3] In February 2020, a European Union (EU) White Paper on AI identified that the use of AI could affect, inter alia, "fundamental rights, including the rights to freedom of expression[,] non-discrimination ... [and the] protection of personal data".[4]

In addition to national security or fundamental rights concerns, the theme of "fair competition" in developing of AI products causes further controversies. For

* An earlier version of this chapter received the Young Scholar Award from the Asian International Economic Law Network (AIELN) in 2019. The authors give thanks to Peter Van den Bossche, Ching-Fu Lin, Shin-yi Peng, Thomas Streinz and Rolf H. Weber for their comments.

1 "Secretary-General's Message for Third Artificial Intelligence for Good Summit" (United Nations, 28 May 2019), https://perma.cc/B5HW-RV5U (hereinafter SG Message for AI).

2 Congressional Research Service (CRS), "Artificial Intelligence and National Security" (2019), https://perma.cc/B5TC-J2U9</int_i, at 10.

3 Ibid., at 3. For discussions on the dual use of AI technologies, see M Brundage et al., "The Malicious Use of Artificial Intelligence: Forecasting, Prevention, and Mitigation" (2018), https://perma.cc/Z2KJ-WYJ3, at 79.

4 "Commission White Paper on Artificial Intelligence: A European Approach to Excellence and Trust" (2020), https://perma.cc/24AE-UJGM, at 10; see also J Purshouse and L Campbell, "Privacy, Crime Control and Police Use of Automated Facial Recognition Technology" (2019) 3 *Criminal Law Review* 188 (arguing that England and Wales should adopt a "narrower and more prescribed legal framework" in their use of facial recognition to comply with international law).

example, the 2019 CRS report on AI, while alluding to China's Military-Civil Fusion policy, cautioned that some "US competitors may have fewer moral, legal, or ethical qualms" about the development of certain AI applications.

Suggestions and proposals have been made by entities including the EU, the G-20[5] and the Organisation for Economic Co-operation and Development (OECD)[6] for the international community to develop new disciplines in regulating the development and use of AI technologies.[7] However, no *binding* rules seem to have been reached on an international level at this stage.[8]

In certain areas, states are bound by their existing international law obligations when shaping their AI policies. For instance, AI policies concerning face-recognition cameras need to comply with the various international obligations prescribed in (inter alia) the International Covenant on Civil and Political Rights (ICCPR). Similarly, AI policies seeking to undermine the national security of other states also must comply with (inter alia) the principle of non-intervention in internal affairs as a general principle of international law.

At present, the primary deterrence for trade powers from abusing AI technology is perhaps the unilateral economic sanctions[9] taken by states in an individual or collective manner (AI sanctions). Occasionally, such sanctions are criticised for breaching the sanctioners' commitments under the World Trade Organization (WTO).[10]

This chapter aims to examine the relationship between the current WTO law and the controversial use of AI policies. In particular, it examines the following questions: (a) whether WTO law can sufficiently regulate "data-sharing" policies that seek to promote the development of AI technologies; and (b) whether WTO law can justify sanctions against other WTO members for their controversial use of AI technologies, especially those seeking to undermine fundamental rights or national security.

A preliminary comment needs to be made at this stage: this chapter does not seek to set out legal or ethical "tests" to judge what kind of AI policies are "controversial",

5 "G20 Ministerial Statement on Trade and Digital Economy" (2019), https://perma.cc/WCC2-J32P.

6 OECD, "Recommendation of the Council on Artificial Intelligence" (2019) OECD/LEGAL/0449, https://perma.cc/DV5K-B6A3.

7 See M Risse, "Human Rights and Artificial Intelligence: An Urgently Needed Agenda" (2018), https://perma.cc/SX67-78YE; and Beijing Academy of Artificial Intelligence, "Beijing AI Principles" (2019), https://perma.cc/GB28-8J6A. For comments concerning the "Beijing Principles", see W Knight, "Why Does Beijing Suddenly Care about AI Ethics?" (*MIT Technology Review*, 31 May 2019), https://perma.cc/3KDH-QHJJ.

8 See J Thornhill, "Formulating Values for AI Is Hard When Humans Do Not Agree" (*Financial Times*, 22 July 2019), https://perma.cc/5XAG-JQXC.

9 Such instruments are commonly referred to as "autonomous sanctions" by Australia and the United States. Shaw convincingly argued that non-military sanctions are "legitimate method[s] of showing displeasure" and do not contravene general public international law. MN Shaw, *International Law* (8th ed., Cambridge, Cambridge University Press, 2017), 859.

10 See subsection C in Section II for detailed examples.

nor does it seek to pronounce any *specific* AI policy as such. No universal legal or ethical guideline concerning the development or use of AI seems to have been reached so far, possibly because of the significant cultural and ideological differences among major AI powers.

The structure of this chapter is as follows. Section II reviews major types of controversial AI policies among the trade powers, and provides an overview of the international responses to such controversial uses. Section III considers whether current WTO disciplines can sufficiently regulate "data-sharing" policies for the development of AI technologies. Section IV turns to examine whether WTO law can justify sanctions against other WTO members for their controversial use of AI technologies. Section V summarises and concludes this chapter.

II CURRENT USE AND INTERNATIONAL RESPONSE TO CONTROVERSIAL ARTIFICIAL INTELLIGENCE POLICIES

A *Major Controversies Concerning Artificial Intelligence Policies*

Major controversies among trade powers on AI policies are manifested in two ways. The first way concerns the *development* of AI systems. Specifically, a country may use state power to collect personal data and "feed" them to their AI industry, or alternatively encourage the "shared use" of personal data across government and private sectors.[11] For example, China's "military-civil fusion" policy seeks to promote (if not require) data-sharing between its commercial companies and its government,[12] apparently with the aim of "creating [at a lower cost] the large databases on which AI systems train".[13]

The second way concerns the *use* of AI systems. Specifically, AI policies can be used to undermine fundamental rights, either within the WTO member in question itself or within other members,[14] in order to pursue such policy objectives including domestic surveillance, legal enforcement or international espionage. Further, AI policies can be pursued to undermine the national security of other members, including espionage and manipulation of another member's domestic politics such as elections.[15]

[11] See Notice of the State Council on Issuing the Development Plan on the New Generation of Artificial Intelligence (PRC), which sets out a strategy of "civil–military integration" in the PRC's AI development plan, *and* seeks to promote the "sharing and joint use" of AI innovation platforms including data resources, and cloud service platform etc.

[12] See CRS, note 2 above, at 21. See also "Military-Civil Fusion and the People's Republic of China", https://perma.cc/4DMR-B2K9.

[13] CRS, note 2 above, at 20.

[14] See M Wang, *China's Algorithms of Repression: Reverse Engineering a Xinjiang Police Mass Surveillance App* (New York, Human Rights Watch, 2019); Purshouse and Campbell, note 4 above.

[15] See A Polyakova, "Weapons of the Weak: Russia and AI-Driven Asymmetric Warfare" (Brookings, November 2001), https://perma.cc/CG8V-U4QA (arguing that Russian institutions interfered with the 2016 US presidential elections by AI-powered propaganda), and "The Propaganda Tools Used by

B *International Response to Predatory Artificial Intelligence Policies*

The potential risks of AI policies have, in recent years, attracted increasing international attention. For example, in 2019, the UN Secretary-General called for international collaborations to "address the risks [of AI and] to develop the frameworks and systems that enable responsible innovation".[16]

In achieving such a goal, the Secretary-General called for an international regulatory system to be developed for the "responsible innovation" on AI, with "binding laws and instruments" in place.[17] In addition to this suggested path, WTO members may also decide to take collective or individual countermeasures as a deterrence against other states which, under their judgement, maintain problematic AI policies.

In practice, the primary deterrence against problematic AI policies appears to be unilateral economic sanctions. Such uses are piecemeal: as an example of AI sanctions targeted against human rights abuses, consider the USA's imposition of Magnitsky sanctions in July 2020 against certain Chinese government individuals and entities that (according to the USA) used AI platforms "for racial profiling" and "data-driven surveillance" against ethnic minorities.[18] Also, consider the call in June 2020 by the European Parliament for "the EU … and the international community … [to impose] appropriate export control mechanisms including cyber surveillance items to deny China, and in particular Hong Kong, access to technologies used to violate basic rights".[19]

Sanctions may also be used to restrict AI-powered computer programs that act as surveillance and propaganda instruments for foreign countries. The US Secretary of State's statement in July 2020 for a possible ban on China's TikTok app, which apparently uses an AI-powered algorithm for "censorship and surveillance", can serve as an example.[20]

Russians to Influence the 2016 Election" (*New York Times*, 16 February 2018), https://perma.cc/CP7C-BV4L.

16 SG Message for AI, note 1 above.

17 Ibid.

18 "Treasury Sanctions Chinese Entity and Officials Pursuant to Global Magnitsky Human Rights Accountability Act" (U.S. Department of the Treasury, 9 July 2020), https://perma.cc/8ZFE-9XK8. For background information, see "Xinjiang Supply Chain Business Advisory" (2020), https://perma.cc/G53R-D66W. Also see Wang, note 14 above.

19 "European Parliament Resolution on the PRC National Security Law for Hong Kong and the Need for the EU to Defend Hong Kong's High Degree of Autonomy" (2020) 2020/2665, at para. 13. For an earlier resolution, see "European Parliament Resolution of 18 July 2019 on the Situation in Hong Kong" (2019) 2019/2732(RSP), at para. 11.

20 "Secretary Michael R. Pompeo with Laura Ingraham of Fox News" (US Department of State, 6 July 2020), https://perma.cc/HLN9-UVUN; F Ryan et al., "Mapping More of China's Technology Giants: AI and Surveillance" (2019) ASPI Issues Paper Report No. 24 (proposing that TikTok is a "vector for censorship and surveillance", empowered by an AI-powered algorithm).

C Sanctions on Artificial Intelligence-Powered Goods/Services and World Trade Organization Law

From the perspective of international trade law, it appears that AI sanctions can take at least two forms. First, a sanction may take the form of an *import* restriction, possibly with the aim of preventing the sanctionee's problematic AI technology from being in contact with the sanctioner: the USA's proposed restriction against TikTok being installed on US mobile phones could be an example.

Second, a sanction may also take the form of an *export* barrier: examples of these measures include the USA's restriction against China over its use of AI for "racial profiling" and "data-driven surveillance", and the European Parliament's proposed sanctions against China and Hong Kong. Specifically, such sanctions can either be used *aggressively* with the aim of terminating a (perceived) predatory AI policy (such as by cutting off the "raw materials" supply), or *defensively* as a measure to protect the sentiment of the invoking member's own citizens as "abetters" of the problematic policy in question.

Sanctionees frequently argue that the sanctions they encounter are against WTO rules.[21] Some scholars seem to hold similar views: Lester and Zhu questioned the WTO consistency of the Trump administration's expansive use of trade barriers on national security grounds.[22] In the context of trade restrictions to address data security or foreign influence concerns, Zhou and Kong argued that Australia's Huawei ban is "unjustifiable under the WTO".[23] Similarly, Voon argued that Australia would "face significant challenges" if China were to lodge a WTO complaint against Australia's Huawei ban.[24] While the Huawei controversies primarily involve national security concerns on 5G networks, it would seem that similar arguments could be advanced against sanctions on AI products that threaten national security.

Can the trade liberalisation commitments undertaken by WTO members restrict their ability to impose AI sanctions to safeguard fundamental rights or national security? Indeed, it would seem that if a member were to impose "sanctions" in the forms of import or export restrictions on goods or services, it might prima facie contravene its obligations to offer most favoured nation (MFN) treatment (General Agreement on Tariffs and Trade (GATT) Art. I, General Agreement on Trade in Services (GATS) Art. II) and national treatment (NT)

21 See "China: India's Ban on Chinese Apps May Violate WTO Rules" (*China Global Television Network*, 1 July 2020), https://perma.cc/7EEA-HVE8 (reporting that Ji Rong, spokesperson for the Chinese embassy in New Delhi, said that India's ban of certain Chinese mobile apps including TikTok and WeChat "runs against fair and transparent procedure requirements, abuses national security exceptions and (is suspected of) violating WTO rules").

22 S Lester and H Zhu, "A Proposal for 'Rebalancing' to Deal with 'National Security' Trade Restrictions" (2019) 42 *Fordham International Law Journal* 1451.

23 W Zhou and Q Kong, "Why Australia's Huawei Ban Is Unjustifiable under WTO" (*China Global Television Network*, 29 April 2019), https://perma.cc/A4DW-3YB5.

24 J Fernyhough, "Australia's Huawei ban on shaky ground at WTO" (Australian Financial Review, 15 April 2019), https://perma.cc/EH2L-U3NT

(GATT Art. III:1, GATS Art. XVII – provided specific commitments were made), as well as the general obligations to eliminate quantitative restrictions on goods (GATT Art. XI) or the market access obligations for services (GATS Art. XVI – provided specific commitments were made). Accordingly, the centre of the argument concerning the WTO consistency of AI-related sanctions would be the availability of justifications.

This chapter uses the following roadmap in assessing the relationship between predatory AI policies and WTO law. First, it considers whether certain AI policies, especially those promoting "data-sharing" mechanisms between government and private AI firms, can be challenged under WTO law. Second, it considers whether sanctions against controversial AI policies are consistent with WTO law. In doing so, this chapter examines in turn: (a) whether such sanctions contravene non-discriminatory obligations under WTO law; (b) whether "public morals" exceptions are available to such sanctions; (c) whether security exceptions are available to such sanctions; and (d) whether "international peace and security" exceptions are available to such sanctions.

III DISCIPLINING "DATA-SHARING" MECHANISMS: WORLD TRADE ORGANIZATION LAW AS A SWORD?

As stated earlier, state-operated "data-sharing" mechanisms, through which a government "feeds" data to its private entities for their development of AI products, is potentially controversial for distorting fair competition. This chapter now turns to examine whether such mechanisms can constitute an actionable subsidy under the Agreement on Subsidies and Countervailing Measures (SCM Agreement).

A *Are "Data-Sharing" Mechanisms Subsidies?*

The general principle in determining actionable subsidies is well established. A measure constitutes an actionable subsidy if (a) it is a subsidy, (b) it is "specific" and (c) its use causes "adverse effects".[25] A subsidy exists when (a) there is a *financial contribution* provided by a government or any public body and (b) such a financial contribution *confers a benefit*.[26]

1 Do "Data-Sharing" Mechanisms Provide a "Financial Contribution"?

First, the Appellate Body in *US–Softwood Lumber IV (2004)* observed that "the term of 'financial contribution' has a wide definition as the transfer of something of economic value".[27] Scholars further argued that data is a "substantial intangible

[25] Panel Report, *US–Offset Act (Byrd Amendment) (2002)*, para. 7.106.
[26] Appellate Body Report, *US–Carbon Steel (India) (2014)*, para. 4.8; Article 1.1 of the SCM Agreement.
[27] Appellate Body Report, *US–Softwood Lumber IV (2004)*, para. 52.

asset"[28] that can "itself be traded",[29] or alternatively be seen as capital "for value creation".[30] In practice, data is sold by some governments for profits.[31] Accordingly, the provision of data would clearly constitute a "financial contribution".

Furthermore, in determining the existence of a "financial contribution", a government conduct must fall under one of the four types of manifestations described in subparagraphs (i)–(iv) of Art. 1.1(a)(1) of the SCM Agreement.[32] Most notably, Art. 1.1(a)(1)(iii) stipulates that:

> [A subsidy shall be deemed to exist if . . .] a government provides goods or services other than general infrastructure, or purchases goods[.]

Accordingly, a "financial contribution" falling under Art. 1.1(a)(1)(iii) exists if (a) there is a "good or service" (b) "provided" by a government and (c) the goods/services provided are "other than general infrastructure".

WTO jurisprudence appears to construe the concept "goods or services" broadly to include all non-monetary resources. In *US–Softwood Lumber IV (2004)*, the Appellate Body ruled that Art. 1.1(a)(1)(iii) aims to prevent the circumvention of subsidy disciplines in cases of financial contributions granted in a form *other than money*.[33]

Case law further shows that the "goods or services" requirement would be satisfied if the resource provided is non-monetary, without requiring a panel or the Appellate Body to distinguish whether the resources in question are "goods" or "services". For instance, in *US–Large Civil Aircraft (2nd complaint)*, the Appellate Body commented that shared "scientific information" and "rights over data" are provisions of "non-monetary resources",[34] without specifying whether they are goods or services. Similarly, the Appellate Body in the same dispute ruled that the grant of access to NASA employees constitutes the provision of "goods or services".[35]

Turning to consider the meaning of "provides", the Appellate Body ruled that the ordinary meaning of such a term is "supply or furnish for use; make available",[36] and that "provide" does not necessarily need to be gratuitous.[37]

28 A Boerding et al., "Data Ownership: A Property Rights Approach from a European Perspective" (2018) 11 *Journal of Civil Law Studies* 330; M Burri, "The Regulation of Data Flows through Trade Agreements" (2017) 48 *Georgetown Journal of International Law* 446.

29 F Casalini and JL González, "Trade and Cross-Border Data Flows" (2019) OECD Trade Policy Papers, No. 220.

30 J Sadowski, "When Data Is Capital: Datafication, Accumulation, and Extraction" (2019) 6 *Big Data & Society* 1.

31 See N Lindsey, "State DMVs Selling Personal Data for Millions of Dollars in Profit" (*CPO Magazine*, 18 September 2019), https://perma.cc/7SBW-KRF3.

32 See Appellate Body Report, *US–Large Civil Aircraft (2nd complaint) (2012)*, para. 613.

33 Appellate Body Report, *US–Softwood Lumber IV (2004)*, para. 64.

34 Appellate Body Report, *US–Large Civil Aircraft (2nd complaint) (2012)*, paras 608–609.

35 Ibid., at para. 624.

36 Appellate Body Report, *US–Softwood Lumber IV (2004)*, para. 69.

37 Appellate Body Report, *US–Large Civil Aircraft (2nd complaint) (2012)*, para. 618.

As for the meaning of "other than general infrastructure", the panel in *EC and Certain Member States–Large Civil Aircraft (2011)* defined "general infrastructure" as "[i]nfrastructure that is not provided to or for the advantage of only a single entity or limited group of entities, but rather is available to all or nearly all entities".[38] The panel in the same case further held that such an assessment is stringent, involving any related factors including "the circumstances surrounding the creation of the infrastructure in question … the recipients or beneficiaries of the infrastructure".[39]

Applying the case law summarised here to the present enquiry, the following observations can be made: first, even assuming that data may not be easily categorised as "goods" or "services", the fact that data is a non-monetary resource is already sufficient to ensure that it falls under the general scope of "goods or services".[40] Second, even if a data-sharing mechanism may involve a bilateral exchange of data between a government and its private sector, such a mechanism still involves the *provision* of data, as a part of such a mechanism involves the "supply or furnish" of data by a government to its private sectors. Third, such a data-"sharing" mechanism will not qualify as general infrastructure if such a mechanism is created and designed specifically for AI firms, which are usually a small number of monopolies;[41] the beneficiaries are therefore quite limited. Moreover, some data is not likely to fall within the scope of so-called public information/data, whereas it is useful for AI training, for example, medical records and ID photos. If these kinds of data are shared, the data-sharing mechanism also cannot be justified as "general infrastructure". Accordingly, it is likely that a "data-sharing" AI policy will constitute a "financial contribution" that falls within the scope of Art. 1.1(a)(1)(iii) of the SCM Agreement.

2 Does the Financial Contribution Confer a Benefit?

Case law stipulates that the conferral of benefit "should be determined by assessing whether the recipient has received a 'financial contribution' on terms more favourable than those available to the recipient in the market".[42]

Turning to the present issue of data-sharing mechanisms, note that a government operating a data-sharing mechanism is highly likely to have access to a larger pool of data than private enterprises can obtain by themselves under market conditions. Furthermore, certain governments may have access to confidential data that they have extracted through state power. Accordingly, the provision of such a data pool

38 Panel Report, *EC and Certain Member States–Large Civil Aircraft (2011)*, para. 7.1036.

39 Ibid., at para. 7.1039.

40 The panel in *US–Large Civil Aircraft (2nd complaint) (Recourse to Article 21.5) (2019)* ruled that patents and right to data cannot be treated as "goods" within the meaning of Article 1.1(a)(1)(iii) since they are intangible (para. 8.832); such a ruling was rejected in the appeal (paras 5.70–5.77).

41 This is because of the high-tech nature of the AI industry and economies of scale.

42 Appellate Body Report, *Canada–Renewable Energy (2013)*, para. 5.163; see also Appellate Body Report, *Canada–Aircraft (1999)*, para. 157.

can confer the recipients crucial "raw materials" that cannot be easily obtained, and thereby confers them a stronger position in the market. Accordingly, such a financial contribution would confer a benefit under the meaning of SCM Art. 1.1(b); assuming that a granting authority is a "government or any public body",[43] a data-sharing mechanism would constitute a subsidy.

B *Do "Data-Sharing" Mechanisms Meet the Standard of "Specificity"?*

The examination of "specificity" largely depends on the facts of a particular case; it is difficult to make general pronunciations in abstract. However, a shared "data pool", being a highly technical mechanism, perhaps can only be meaningfully used by the AI industry. If this is so, then it is likely that a data-sharing mechanism would be specific to "certain enterprises" and not "broadly available and widely used *throughout an economy*".[44]

Further, considering that fact that a data-sharing platform designed for development of AI constitutes "a subsidy programme which is mainly used by certain enterprises",[45] it is likely that a "data-sharing" mechanism can (at least)[46] constitute de facto specificity under the meaning of SCM Art 2.1(c).

In the light of this analysis, a "data subsidy" is highly like to meet the standard of specificity pursuant to the SCM Agreement.

C *Do "Data-Sharing" Mechanisms Have Adverse Effects?*

An examination of the adverse effects of a subsidy largely depends on the specific facts of an actual case; it is difficult to make general pronouncements concerning "data-sharing" mechanisms in abstract. However, a "data subsidy" has the potential of reducing the cost of collecting data for "training" AI systems, thus allowing commercial firms to cut the price of their AI products for exportation. This is likely to constitute "significant price undercutting" under the meaning of SCM Art. 6.3(c). As such, it is possible that a "data subsidy" will have adverse effects pursuant to Arts 5 (c) and 6.3 of the SCM Agreement.

Summarising these discussions, it can be concluded that an AI policy involving a "data-sharing" mechanism is likely to constitute an actionable subsidy, under the meaning of the SCM Agreement. Consequently, injured members would be entitled to impose countervailing duties against AI products (such as AI-powered robots or vehicles) that are subsidised by "data-sharing" mechanisms.

43 Such a determination would necessarily depend on the facts of actual cases.

44 Panel Report, *US–Upland Cotton* (2004), para. 7.1143; see also Appellate Body Report, *EC and Certain Member States–Large Civil Aircraft* (2011), para. 949.

45 Panel Report, *EC and Certain Member States–Large Civil Aircraft* (2011), para. 7.974.

46 In an actual case where the legislation in question is available, it is even possible that an assessment of the legislation will lead one to conclude that such a mechanism constitutes de jure specificity.

IV DISCIPLINING ARTIFICIAL INTELLIGENCE POLICIES: WORLD TRADE ORGANIZATION RULES AS A SHIELD?

This chapter now proceeds to consider whether an AI sanction, being an import or export restriction aimed to address other members' AI policies that undermine fundamental rights or national security (such as the proposed EU export control for cyber surveillance items against Hong Kong), would be consistent with WTO law. At the outset, it should be noted that some AI sanctions may not contravene the non-discriminatory obligations under the WTO law in the first place, since AI products that "do" and "do not" undermine such values may not satisfy the "likeness test" because of different consumer habits and preferences.

A *Availability of a "Public Moral" Defence*

Assuming that an AI sanction does prima facie contravene WTO rules (such as MFN/NT, general elimination of quantitative restrictions or market access obligations), this chapter now proceeds to consider whether such a sanction may be justified under the "public moral exceptions", especially Art. XX(a) of the GATT 1994 and Art. XIV(a) of the GATS.

1 Summary of Existing Case Law

The law pertaining to public moral exceptions is well settled. Using Art. XX(a) of the GATT 1994 as an example (as the position of GATS Art. XIV(a) is similar), the invocation of such a justification involves a two-tier test: a measure must "first be provisionally justified under [Art. XX(a)], before it is subsequently appraised under the chapeau of Article XX".[47] In satisfying Art. XX(a), a member must demonstrate that its measure (a) was adopted or enforced[48] "to protect public morals", and (b) is "necessary" to protect such public morals.[49] The enquiry then proceeds to the chapeau of Art. XX, which probes whether the *application* of a measure constitutes "arbitrary or unjustifiable discrimination" or "disguised restriction of international trade".

It is well settled that "public morals" is defined as "standards of right and wrong conduct maintained by or on behalf of a community or nation".[50] Panels and the

[47] Appellate Body Report, *EC–Seal Products (2014)*, para. 5.169, referring to Appellate Body Report, *US–Gasoline (1996)*, 22.

[48] Appellate Body Report, *EC–Seal Products (2014)*, para. 5.168.

[49] Appellate Body Report, *EC–Seal Products (2014)*, para. 5.169, referring to Panel Report, *US–Gambling (2005)*, para. 6.455.

[50] *Panel Report, US–Gambling (2005)*, para. 6.465. Note that *US–Gambling (2005)* is a case concerning Art. XIV(a) of the GATS. The interpretation in *US–Gambling (2005)* was subsequently adopted in the context of Article XX(a) of the GATT 1994 by the panels in *China–Publications and Audiovisual Products (2009)* (in para. 7.759) and *EC–Seal Products (2014)* (in para. 7.380). None of these interpretations was appealed.

Appellate Body have further given a considerable degree of deference to the members to "define and apply for themselves the concept of public morals according to their own systems and scales of values".[51]

The constituent test of "public morals" in GATT Art. XX(a) is represented by the panel report in *EC–Seal Products (2014)*, in which a two-tier test was prescribed to examine:[52]

> first, whether the [public morals] concern ... indeed exists in that society; and, second, whether such concern falls within the scope of "public morals" as "defined and applied" by a regulating Member "in its territory, according to its own systems and scales of values".

With regard to the first element, the panel considered the EU measure's text,[53] legislative history,[54] and structure and design; it also considered (although to a limited extent) the result of a public survey.[55]

With regard to the second element, the panel considered the legislative history of the EU measure under challenge,[56] the ethical/moral references concerning seal welfare in EU law,[57] the domestic law of certain EU countries[58] and certain recommendations from international organisations.[59]

2 Availability of the Defence

Applying the law summarised in the previous subsection to the present discussion on AI sanctions, the following observations can be made. First, concerns relating to fundamental rights or national security are very likely to exist in the sanctioner's society, and indeed perhaps in any major society in the world. Second, fundamental rights or national security are very likely to fall within the scope of "public morals" within the sanctioner's society; in practice, the sanctioner may refer to documents such as its constitutional legislations or parliamentary records to show that its concerns are genuinely held.

Accordingly, assuming that other requirements for a "public morals" defence (such as the "necessity" test and the tests under the GATT Art. XX/GATS Art. XIV chapeau) are satisfied, an AI sanction would be successfully defended under the "public morals" exceptions. In sum, it appears that the "public morals" exceptions are, perhaps in a way similar to that in *EC–Seal Products (2014)*, capable of

51 Ibid., at para. 6.461. This was followed in Panel Report, *EC–Seal Products (2014)*, para. 7.380 and confirmed in Appellate Body Report, *EC–Seal Products (2014)*, paras 5.199–200.
52 Panel Report, *EC–Seal Products (2014)*, para. 7.383.
53 Ibid.
54 Ibid.
55 Ibid.
56 Ibid.
57 Ibid.
58 Ibid.
59 Ibid.

justifying AI sanctions genuinely held to address a concern of national security *or* fundamental rights.

B *Availability of a Defence under the "Security Exception"*

This chapter now proceeds to consider whether a WTO member may seek to justify an AI sanction relating to the protection of national security of fundamental rights under the "security exception", especially Art. XXI(b)(iii) of the GATT 1994 or Art. XIV bis of the GATS.

1 Summary of Existing Case Law

The panel report in *Russia–Traffic in Transit (2019)*[60] is currently the leading case law concerning security exceptions. In essence, it ruled (in the context of Art. XXI(b)(iii) of the GATT 1994) that (a) in general, it is left to every member to define, on its own *subjective* standards, what *it considers* to be its essential security interests,[61] although the exercise of such a liberty must be subject to the "obligation of good faith";[62] and (b) it is for the panels and the Appellate Body to determine *objectively* whether an action taken in time of an *emergency in international relations* is "subject to objective determination".[63]

Given that the subjective tests set out here are relatively easily met, it would appear that, in determining the availability of a security exception, the core of the enquiry would be the objective determination of whether there exists an "emergency in international relations" (the "subparagraph (iii) test").

In *Russia–Traffic in Transit (2019)*, the panel went to some lengths in considering what would constitute an "emergency in international relations". For the purpose of the present discussion, it is perhaps sufficient to notice the following points. First, the panel appeared to interpret "emergency in international relations" liberally; it held that such an expression includes "war"[64] and "[a]rmed conflict ... between governmental forces and private armed groups ... (non-international armed conflict)".[65]

Second, the panel ruled that an "emergency in international relations" must be understood as "eliciting the same type of interests as those arising from the other matters addressed in the enumerated subparagraphs of Article XXI(b)",[66] and that such interests are "all defence and military interests, as well as maintenance of law

60 This chapter assumes that the panel report in *Russia–Traffic in Transit (2019)*, which was not appealed by either party, represents good law.
61 Panel Report, *Russia–Traffic in Transit (2019)*, para. 7.131.
62 Ibid., at para. 7.133.
63 Ibid., at para. 7.77; also see para. 7.82.
64 Ibid., at para. 7.72.
65 Ibid.
66 Ibid., at para. 7.74.

and public order interests".[67] According to the panel, while it is "normal to expect that Members will ... encounter political or economic conflicts with other Members or states",[68] such conflicts "will not be "emergencies in international relations ... unless they give rise to defence and military interests, or maintenance of law and public order interests".[69]

Third, the panel suggested a definition for the expression "emergency in international relations", which must be reproduced in full:

> An emergency in international relations would, therefore, appear to refer generally to a situation of armed conflict, or of latent armed conflict, or of heightened tension or crisis, or of general instability engulfing or surrounding a state. Such situations give rise to particular types of interests for the Member in question, i.e. defence or military interests, or maintenance of law and public order interests.[70]

Summarising this, it appears that the subparagraph (iii) test involves a two-pronged examination[71] in determining whether an "emergency in international relations" exists, namely: (a) whether there exists a "situation" of conflict, tension or crisis; and (b) whether such a "situation" gives rise to interests of "defence or military interests, or maintenance of law and public order interests".[72]

With regard to element (a), case law seems to require that although a "situation" needs to have some degree of seriousness (recall that the panel used the expressions "*heightened* tension" and "*general* instability" in the paragraph cited earlier),[73] such a "situation" does not necessarily need to involve armed conflict[74] or international conflict. With regard to element (b), recall that the expression "public order" was interpreted in the jurisprudence relating to Art. XIV(a) of the GATS to include a broad range of interests, such as the prevention of gambling.

Returning to the application of the law pertaining to the determination of "emergency in international relations", the panel report in *Russia–Traffic in Transit (2019)* cited approvingly the following headings of evidence adduced by Russia, and considered them "sufficient":[75]

> (a) the time-period in which it arose and continues to exist, (b) that the situation involves Ukraine, (c) that it affects the security of Russia's border with Ukraine in

67 Ibid.

68 Ibid., at para. 7.75.

69 Ibid.

70 Ibid., at para. 7.76.

71 However, note the somewhat cautious language used in the panel report: "An emergency in international relations would, therefore, appear to refer generally" (para. 7.76).

72 It appears that *Russia–Traffic in Transit (2019)* considers this to be a closed list: paras 7.74 and 7.76.

73 Panel Report, *Russia–Traffic in Transit (2019)*, at para. 7.76.

74 Recall that the panel in *Russia–Traffic in Transit (2019)* ruled that "latent armed conflict, or of heightened tension or crisis, or of general instability engulfing or surrounding a state" would constitute "emergency in international relations".

75 Panel Report, *Russia–Traffic in Transit* (2019), at para. 7.119.

various ways, (d) that it has resulted in other countries imposing sanctions against Russia, and (e) that the situation in question is publicly known.[76]

In considering such evidence, the panel referred to at least two resolutions of the UN General Assembly (UNGA), one of which "ma[de] explicit reference to the Geneva Conventions of 1949",[77] as well as several Russian domestic decrees.

Summarising this, it can be concluded that, in examining the existence of an "emergency in international relations", it is "not relevant"[78] for a panel or the Appellate Body to determine which actor bears international responsibility for the "situation", or how the "situation" should be "characterize[d] … under international law in general".[79] Instead, a panel or the Appellate Body needs to be persuaded as to the existence of a "situation" (or "element (a)" identified earlier); in doing so, it may consider the following evidence:

(a) whether the international relations in question have "deteriorated to such a degree" that they have become "a matter of concern to the international community"
(b) whether the "situation" was "recognized internationally" or "publicly known"[80]
(c) whether the "situation" "continued to exist"[81] for some period
(d) whether other countries have imposed sanctions or countersanctions in connection with this "situation".

2 Availability of the Defence

In applying this jurisprudence to the current question of AI sanctions, it appears that sanctions for the protection of fundamental rights or for the protection of national security will satisfy the requirement of "emergency in international relations", provided the "situations" involved have the required degree of seriousness.

The determination of the degree of "seriousness" largely depends on the facts of particular cases. Nevertheless, using as an example the EU's potential ban on China's "access to technologies used to violate basic rights" due to the instabilities in Hong Kong, it would appear that the Hong Kong "situation", which involves worldwide controversies with trade powers such as Australia, Canada, China, the EU, New Zealand, the UK and the USA, is likely to have the required degree of "heightened tension or crisis" and seriousness to satisfy element (a) of the "subparagraph (iii) test".

76 Ibid., at para. 7.119.
77 Ibid., at footnote 204.
78 Ibid., at para. 7.121.
79 Ibid.
80 Ibid., at para. 7.119.
81 Ibid.

Turning to element (b) of the subparagraph (iii) test, it is obvious that a "situation" concerning fundamental rights, such as the situation in Hong Kong, would (at least) give rise to interests in public order and possibly security interests. This is especially so when considering the close relationship (elaborated in subsection 1 of Section IV) between the fundamental rights of individual citizens, on the one hand, and international peace and security, on the other. Moreover, a "situation" concerning national security (such as spying) would clearly give rise to interests of defence, military and public order, consequently satisfying element (b) of the test.

As stated earlier, other requirements under Art. XXI(b)(iii) of the GATT 1994 or Art. XIV bis of the GATS are, under the current case law, subjective tests that do not present difficult hurdles to an invoking WTO member (although subject to the "obligation of good faith" requirement).[82] Assuming that such tests are satisfied, it would appear that if an AI sanction serves the purpose of protecting national security or fundamental rights protection, such a sanction will be eligible for the "security exception" justification.

C *Availability of a Defence under the "International Peace and Security" Exceptions*

It is also possible that an AI sanction can be justified under the "international peace and security" exceptions, especially Art. XXI(c) of the GATT 1994 and Art. XIV bis (c) of the GATS, both of which allow a member to justify "any action in pursuance of its obligations under the United Nations Charter for the maintenance of international peace and security". Again, the EU's proposed export control mechanisms on cyber surveillance items against China and Hong Kong can serve as an example.

The exact ambit of GATT Art. XXI(c) and GATS Art. XIV bis(c) remain uncertain at present, since none of the two provisions have been invoked before any WTO or GATT panel so far. However, using GATT Art. XXI(c) as an example, it appears that the text of this provision entails the following constituent tests: (a) the measure is imposed "in pursuance of" (b) "[the invoking member's] obligations under the United Nations Charter", (c) "for the maintenance of international peace and security".

Moreover, the broad expression "any action", read together with the lack of any "chapeau" similar to that in GATT Art. XX, seems to indicate that Art. XXI(c) entails less stringent tests than those under Art. XX. Nevertheless, the "obligation of good faith" requirement,[83] which was first introduced to eliminate members' "re-label [ling of] trade interests" as "essential security interests" under GATT Art. XXI(b)(iii), might play a similar role in preventing the abuse of Art. XXI(c) justifications.

[82] Panel Report, *Russia–Traffic in Transit* (2019), para. 7.133.
[83] Ibid.

1 "For the Maintenance of International Peace and Security"

A close examination of the Charter of the United Nations (UN Charter) and the ICCPR shows that it is a well-recognised principle of international law that the protection of fundamental rights for individuals also serves the purpose of maintaining international peace and security. To start with, recall that the preamble of the UN Charter provides, inter alia, that:

> We the peoples of the United Nations determined ... to reaffirm faith in fundamental human rights, in the dignity and worth of the human person, in the equal rights of men and women[.]

Art. 55(c) of the UN Charter provides that:

> With a view to the creation of conditions of stability and well-being which are necessary for peaceful and friendly relations among nations ... the United Nations shall promote ... universal respect for, and observance of, human rights and fundamental freedoms for all[.]

A collective reading of the UN Charter's preamble and Art. 55(c), especially the expression "with a view" in Art. 55, shows that the promotion of universal human rights and fundamental freedoms *does* serve for the maintenance of "peaceful ... relations among nations". Further, Art. 1.3 of the UN Charter states that "promoting and encouraging respect for human rights and for fundamental freedoms" is one of the purposes of the UN.[84]

In addition, the preamble of the ICCPR provides, inter alia, that:

> The States Parties ... [c]onsider that, in accordance with the principles proclaimed in the Charter of the United Nations, recognition of the inherent dignity and of the equal and inalienable rights of all members of the human family is the foundation of freedom, justice and peace in the world[.]
>
> [The States Parties recognise that] the ideal of free human beings enjoying civil and political freedom and freedom from fear and want can only be achieved if conditions are created whereby everyone may enjoy his [sic] civil and political rights[.]

These provisions reinforce a close causal relationship between the protection of the rights of "all members of the human family" and the achievement of international peace. The expression "in accordance with the principles proclaimed in the [UN] Charter" further confirms the close relationship between the obligations under the ICCPR and the UN Charter. Summarising this, it would appear that

[84] See also K Kenny, "Fulfilling the Promise of the UN Charter: Transformative Integration of Human Rights" (1999) 10 *Irish Studies in International Affairs* 44 (arguing that international conflicts in the 1990s confirmed that human rights violations could lead to the escalation of international conflict, thus the promotion of "respect for human rights" is crucial for the UN's purpose of "the maintenance of international peace and security").

the policy aim of protecting fundamental rights is likely to fall within the scope of "for the maintenance of international peace and security".

2 "Obligations under the UN Charter"

Turning to examine whether the protection of fundamental rights for individuals is an "obligation" under the UN Charter,[85] one could again be assisted by the earlier-cited UN Charter and ICCPR provisions to find a positive answer to such an enquiry. Further, the preamble of the ICCPR unequivocally recognises an "obligation of States under the [UN Charter] to promote universal respect for, and observance of, human rights and freedoms"; this confirms that the protection of fundamental rights is a Charter obligation.

3 "In Pursuance of . . ."

Finally, turning to examine whether an AI sanction imposed to protect fundamental rights can satisfy the "in pursuance of" element of such a policy aim, it is perhaps prudent to say that such a determination should only be made in the context of the actual cases. However, note that the term "pursuance" is defined under the *Shorter Oxford Dictionary* as (inter alia) "[t]he action of trying to attain or accomplish something", and nothing (in the context, the objective and purpose, etc.) seems to indicate that the ordinary meaning of such a term should depart from its dictionary meaning. As "trying to . . ." clearly denotes a much weaker causal link than "relating to", "necessary to" or "essential to", it would appear that the "in pursuance of" element would, in practice, be relatively easy to satisfy.

4 Availability of the Defence

As the discussions in subsection C of Section IV demonstrate, it is possible for an AI sanction imposed to protect fundamental rights to be justified under the "international peace and security" exceptions, especially Art. XXI(c) of the GATT 1994 and Art. XIV bis of the GATS. In particular, an examination of the UN Charter and the ICCPR provisions can show that the protection of fundamental rights does satisfy the "for the maintenance of international peace and security" requirement. Further, the protection of fundamental rights is also an obligation under the UN Charter. Whether an AI sanction can satisfy the "in pursuance of" requirement necessarily depends on the actual circumstances of a case, but the ordinary meaning of "in pursuance of" does not seem to demand a test as stringent as, for example, the

[85] It is obvious that the general "maintenance of international peace and security" is an UN Charter obligation. For example, Art. 43(1) of the Charter provides that "All Members ... in order to contribute to the maintenance of international peace and security, undertake to make available to the Security Council, on its call".

"necessary to" test under "general exceptions". Accordingly, it is likely that an AI sanction imposed to protect fundamental rights can be justified under the "international peace and security" exceptions.

V CONCLUSION

AI technologies have brought to humanity benefits and challenges. However, some AI products may be used to threaten non-trade values including fundamental rights and national security.[86] This is especially so when a trade power pursues controversial AI policies, such as developing AI systems through means that undermine fundamental rights or national security, or using AI systems for purposes of diminishing such values.

AI policies can become controversial among the international community if they (a) undermine fundamental rights, and by doing so threaten international peace and security; (b) threaten national security; and (c) raise fair competition concerns by allowing certain AI developers an unfair advantage under "data-sharing" mechanisms in accessing data to "train" their AI. Suggestions have been made for the international community to develop new disciplines in ensuring that AI technologies are used for the benefit of humanity. Yet at present, economic sanctions taken by trade powers are currently the main deterrence against the adoption of controversial AI policies.

In this chapter, it is argued that WTO law can provide some assistance in controlling controversial AI policies. First, AI policies that promote "data-sharing" mechanisms between government and private AI firms can be challenged as actionable subsidies which transfer data as "raw materials" to the private sector for the latter's development of AI products.

Second, economic sanctions against WTO members for controversial AI policies, if genuinely held to combat threats to fundamental rights or national security, are likely to be consistent with WTO law: accordingly, WTO law allows liberty for the international community to promote fundamental rights and national security by sanctioning the controversial AI policies that undermine such values. Specifically, some AI sanctions may not contravene non-discriminatory obligations under WTO law, since there might be no "likeness" between AI products that "do" and "do not" attract controversies (such as between mobile "apps" that collect data for racial profiling and those that do not). Assuming that AI sanctions are prima facie inconsistent with WTO rules on trade liberalisation, they may be justified under "public morals exceptions", "security exceptions" and/or "international peace and security" exceptions or under the GATT 1994 and/or the GATS.

It might be asked whether the WTO law, especially the various exceptions discussed here, can be used to harbour protectionist measures under the guise of

[86] See Brundage et al., note 3 above, at 3.

fundamental rights or national security concerns. This is unlikely to be so. First, a member may find it difficult to argue that a protectionist measure does not contravene WTO principles of non-discrimination, since the products involved will be "like". Second, a member would also face difficulties in invoking the "public morals" defence for a protectionist measure, since doing so would involve the stringent "necessity" test and the tests under GATT Art. XX/GATS Art. XIV chapeau. Third, a protectionist measure is unlikely to be defended under security exceptions: as *Russia–Traffic in Transit (2019)* shows, such a measure would face difficulties in satisfying the "emergency in international relations" requirement and the "good faith" requirement.

Finally, a protectionist measure also cannot be defended under the "international peace and security" exceptions, since it is difficult to establish how a protectionist measure could contribute to the maintenance of international peace and security.

Accordingly, although WTO rules cannot be seen as a "magic pill" that instantly heals the deep divisions of humankind that were perhaps ultimately caused by ideological differences, one should be confident in their contribution to non-trade values such as security and fundamental rights.

PART V

Reconfiguration of International Economic Law

15

Across the Great Wall

E-commerce Joint Statement Initiative Negotiation and China

*Henry Gao**

On 13 December 2017, seventy-one members of the World Trade Organization (WTO) led by the USA, European Union (EU) and Japan issued a "Joint Statement on Electronic Commerce" at the 11th WTO Ministerial Conference in Buenos Aires, Argentina. In the Joint Statement, the members announced that they would "initiate exploratory work together toward future WTO negotiations on trade-related aspects of electronic commerce". At the World Economic Forum on 25 January 2019, seventy-six WTO members issued another Joint Statement, which announced their intention to "commence WTO negotiations on trade-related aspects of electronic commerce". The most notable new participant in the second Joint Statement is China, which has so far resisted the electronic commerce initiative.

Why was China reluctant to participate in the e-commerce negotiation at first? Why did it change position in 2019? What will be the main issues in the negotiation? What are the positions of China and how will its participation shape the negotiation? By answering these questions, this chapter provides a critical analysis of the data regulation of China, a world leader in the artificial intelligence (AI) and data-driven economy.

This chapter will proceed in four parts. Section I reviews the development of the Internet and e-commerce in China, as well as China's experiences with e-commerce issues in the WTO and beyond, especially in free trade agreements (FTAs). Section II discusses the history of the e-commerce negotiations in the WTO, from the 1998 e-commerce Declaration and the Doha Declaration to the Joint Statement in 2017 and the launch of the plurilateral Joint Statement Initiative (JSI) negotiations in 2019, with China joining at the last minute. Section III analyses in detail China's three submissions in the negotiations, as well as the most problematic issues for China. In Section IV, the chapter concludes with reflections on how the

* This research is supported by the National Research Foundation, Singapore under its Emerging Areas Research Projects (EARP) Funding Initiative. Any opinions, findings and conclusions or recommendations expressed in this material are those of the author(s) and do not reflect the views of National Research Foundation, Singapore. All data in the paper are current as of 2 April 2021.

negotiations will unfold, especially how the main sticking points in China's Internet and data regulatory regime could be addressed.

I CHINA AND E-COMMERCE

"Across the Great Wall we can reach every corner of the world". Such is the prescient message in the very first email from China, sent on 20 September 1987 by a group of researchers at the Institute for Computer Science of China's State Commission of Machine Industry to the University of Karlsruhe in Germany.[1] However, it was not until 20 April 1994 that the first connection to the international network was established by the China Education and Research Network, which marked the launch of the Internet in China.[2]

Since then, the Chinese Internet has grown by leaps and bounds, despite occasional hiccups such as Google's exit from China in 2009.[3] In 2013, China's e-commerce volume exceeded 10 trillion RMB and it overtook the USA as the largest e-commerce market in the world.[4] Nowadays, Chinese e-commerce giants like Alibaba are among the biggest online retailers in the world and Chinese online shopping festivals such as the Singles Day (11.11) Sale have gained loyal followings all around the world.[5]

Notwithstanding the phenomenal growth in the e-commerce sector, the Internet remains under tight regulation in China.[6] This started with hardware regulations in the early days of the Chinese Internet, which required that all internet connections must go through official gateways sanctioned by the Chinese government. Then the government moved to software regulation and started to require that software used for internet access must be sanctioned by the government. The latest iteration is content and data regulation, which culminated in the introduction of Cybersecurity Law in 2016, elevating internet regulation to a matter of national security.

1 W Li, "In the Beginning . . ." (*China Daily*, 17 March 2008), https://perma.cc/VG6T-CBXT.

2 Guowuyuan Xinwen Bangongshi [State Council Information Office] "《中国互联网状况》白皮书 [China's White Paper on the State of the Internet]" (*SCIO*, 8 June 2010), www.scio.gov.cn/tt/Document/1011194/1011194.htm.

3 For a review of the background of the case and the trade law issues it raised, see H Gao, "Google's China Problem: A Case Study on Trade, Technology and Human Rights Under the GATS" (2011) 6 *Asian Journal of WTO & International Health Law and Policy* 347, at 347–385.

4 "我国大宗电子商务交易额已超10万亿元 [China's Bulk E-commerce Transaction Value Exceeds 10 Trillion]" (*Zhongguo Caijing Bao* [*China Financial and Economic News*], 7 August 2014), https://perma.cc/3ZCE-P4MX. See also "中国电子商务报告 (2013) [China E-commerce Report of 2013]" (MOFCOM, 23 September 2014), https://perma.cc/UB9Y-C3YA.

5 See M Smith, "Australian Brands Woo Shoppers at China's Singles' Day Sales" (*Financial Review*, 12 November 2018), https://perma.cc/V3KA-9UBE; J Lim, "Singles' Day Sales in S[inga]pore Doubled from a Year Before: ShopBack's Data" (*Today Singapore*, 12 November 2018), www.todayonline.com/singapore/singles-day-sales-spore-doubled-year-shopbacks-data.

6 For a detailed analysis of the evolution of internet regulation in China, see H Gao, "Data Regulation with Chinese Characteristics", in M Burri (ed.), *Big Data and Global Trade Law* (Cambridge, Cambridge University Press, 2021), at 245–267, https://ssrn.com/abstract=3430284.

Internationally, China has engaged with e-commerce regulation at both the multilateral and regional levels. In the WTO, China's first encounter with data regulation started on the wrong foot as it concerned a sensitive area: China's regulation of publications and audio-visual products.[7] In that case, the USA complained that China had failed to grant foreign firms the right to import and distribute publication and audio-visual products. One of the key issues in the case is whether China's commitments on "sound recording distribution services" covers "electronic distribution of sound recordings" as alleged by the USA.[8] China disagreed with the US approach and argued instead that such electronic distribution "in fact corresponds to network music services",[9] which only emerged in 2001 and were totally different in kind from the "sound recording distribution services". According to China, the most fundamental difference between the two is that, unlike "traditional" sound recording distribution services, network music services "do not supply the users with sound recordings in physical form, but supply them with the right to use a musical content".[10] In response, the USA cited the panel's statement in *US–Gambling*[11] that "the GATS [General Agreement on Trade in Services] does not limit the various technologically possible means of delivery under mode 1", as well as the principle of "technological neutrality" mentioned in the Work Programme on Electronic Commerce – Progress Report to the General Council,[12] and argued that electronic distribution is merely a means of delivery rather than a new type of service.[13] Furthermore, the USA argued that the term "distribution" encompasses not only the distribution of goods, but also distribution of services.[14] After a lengthy discussion canvassing the ordinary meaning, the context, the provisions of the GATS, the object and purpose and various supplementary means of interpretation, the panel concluded that the term "sound recording distribution services" does extend to distribution of sound recording through electronic means.[15] China appealed the panel's findings, but they were upheld by the Appellate Body, which largely adopted the panel's reasoning.[16]

7 Panel Report, *China – Measures Affecting Trading Rights and Distribution Services for Certain Publications and Audiovisual Entertainment Products*, WT/DS363/R and Corr.1, adopted 19 January 2010, as modified by Appellate Body Report WT/DS363/AB/R, DSR 2010:II, 261 [hereinafter *Panel Report: China – Publications and Audiovisual Products*].

8 Ibid., at paras. 4.49–4.71.

9 Ibid., at para. 4.147.

10 Ibid., at para. 4.149.

11 Panel Report, *United States – Measures Affecting the Cross-Border Supply of Gambling and Betting Services*, WT/DS285/R, adopted 20 April 2005, as modified by Appellate Body Report, WT/DS285/AB/R, DSR 2005:XII, 5797.

12 Work Programme on Electronic Commerce, *Progress Report to the General Council*, adopted by the 230 Council for the Trade in Services on 19 July 1999, S/L/74, circulated 27 July 1999, at para. 4.

13 Ibid., at para. 4.69.

14 Ibid., at para. 7.1156.

15 Ibid., at paras. 7.1168–1265.

16 Appellate Body Report, *China – Measures Affecting Trading Rights and Distribution Services for Certain Publications and Audiovisual Entertainment Products*, WT/DS363/AB/R, adopted

The case was also the first WTO case concerning China's censorship regime. It is interesting to note, however, that the USA did not challenge the censorship regime per se.[17] Instead, the USA only challenged the alleged discrimination in the operation of the regime, where imported products were subject to more burdensome content review requirements.[18] Ironically, the USA even proposed, as the solution to the alleged discrimination, that the Chinese government itself should shoulder the sole responsibility for conducting content review, rather than outsourcing it to importing firms.[19]

With such an unpleasant experience, China took a cautious approach on the inclusion of internet or data regulation in other forums, such as FTAs. While it has signed more than a dozen FTAs so far, most of them have not included provisions on such regulations. Until China signed the Regional Comprehensive Economic Partnership (RCEP) in November 2020, the only ones with included stand-alone chapters on e-commerce are the two FTAs China signed with Korea and Australia in 2015,[20] the FTA signed with Mauritius and Cambodia in 2019 and in 2020, respectively, as well as the recently upgraded FTAs with Chile[21] and Singapore.[22] However, unlike the US FTAs, which often include provisions on free flow of data and bans on data localization requirements,[23] these six pre-RCEP FTA chapters only address e-commerce-related issues such as a moratorium on customs duties on electronic transmission; electronic authentication and electronic signatures; protection of personal information in e-commerce; and paperless trading.[24]

Over the past five years, capitalizing on the enormous success of the Chinese e-commerce market, China has been pushing for wider adoption of its e-commerce model beyond its own shore. At the regional level, China has been building the electronic silk road, which provides online e-commerce platforms to facilitate both the exports of Chinese products abroad and the imports of foreign products into

19 January 2010, DSR 2010:I, 3, at paras. 338–413 [hereinafter *ABR, China – Publications and Audiovisual Products*].

17 Ibid., at para. 20.

18 *Panel Report: China – Publications and Audiovisual Products*, note 7 above, paras. 4.72–4.85.

19 Ibid., at para. 7.875; *ABR, China – Publications and Audiovisual Products*, note 16 above, at para. 72.

20 See H Gao, "E-Commerce in ChAFTA: New Wine in Old Wineskins?", in C Piker et al. (eds), *The China Australia Free Trade Agreement: A 21st-Century Model* (Oxford, Hart Publishing, 2018).

21 "Protocol to Amend the Free Trade Agreement and the Supplementary Agreement on Trade in Services of the Free Trade Agreement between the Government of the People's Republic of China and the Government of the Republic of Chile" (2017), https://perma.cc/8PGG-HNVF, at chapter 4.

22 "Protocol to Upgrade the Free Trade Agreement between the Government of the People's Republic of China and the Government of the Republic of Singapore" (2018), https://perma.cc/8DKV-UUB8, at appendix 6, new chapter 15.

23 See H Gao, "Regulation of Digital Trade in US Free Trade Agreements: From Trade Regulation to Digital Regulation" (2018) 45 *Legal Issues of Economic Integration* 47; M Wu, "Digital Trade Related Provisions in Regional Trade Agreements: Existing Models and Lessons for the Multilateral Trade System" (2017), RTA Exchange, https://perma.cc/C2JJ-UKWP; RF Fefer et al., "Digital Trade and U.S. Trade Policy" (2019), CRS Report for Congress R44565, https://perma.cc/SHH7-7MKF.

24 See H Gao, "Digital or Trade? The Contrasting Approaches of China and US to Digital Trade" (2018) 21 *Journal of International Economic Law* 297.

China.[25] At the multilateral level, Alibaba, with the support of the Chinese government, has been aggressively promoting its Electronic World Trade Platform (eWTP) concept, which led to the launch of the "Enabling e-commerce" initiative along with the WTO and the World Economic Forum in late 2017.[26] As discussed later in the chapter, these initiatives have also found their way into China's e-commerce proposals in the JSI.

II CHINA AND THE JOINT STATEMENT INITIATIVE: RESISTANCE AND ACCEPTANCE

Recognizing the growing importance of e-commerce, WTO members adopted the Declaration on Global Electronic Commerce at the second Ministerial Conference in 1998.[27] In addition to establishing a temporary moratorium on customs duties on digital transmission, the Declaration also calls on WTO members to "examine all trade-related issues relating to global electronic commerce". Pursuant to the Declaration, the General Council adopted the Work Programme on Electronic Commerce,[28] which divided up the work among several WTO bodies such as the Council for Trade in Services, the Council for Trade in Goods, the Council for Trade-Related Aspects of Intellectual Property Rights and the Committee on Trade and Development. While the division of work among the different bodies provided an opportunity for in-depth discussions on the impact of e-commerce in different areas, such a compartmentalized approach was not really conducive to the negotiations because of the inherent complexity of e-commerce, which does not fit neatly into the pigeonholes of goods, service and intellectual property rights. Thus, by July 1999, the bodies had reached an impasse in their respective discussions and the discussions were suspended.

As WTO members started to grasp the cross-cutting nature of e-commerce issues, the General Council decided on 8 May 2001 to have dedicated sessions to discussions cross-cutting issues in e-commerce, with the first held on 15 June 2001.[29] Since then, a total of twelve dedicated session have been held, with the last one on 18 October 2016.[30] However, other than agreeing to continue the moratorium on customs duties on electronic transmission periodically, these cross-cutting discussions have failed to produce substantive results and the members remain divided on

[25] "跨境电商连接网上丝绸之路 [Cross-Border E-commerce Connects Cyber Silk Road]" (*People's Daily*, 12 June 2018), https://perma.cc/K4H9-A47U.

[26] See Gao, note 24 above, at 308–310.

[27] WTO, *Declaration on Global Electronic Commerce*, adopted on 20 May 1998 at the Second WTO Ministerial Conference in Geneva, WT/MIN(98)/DEC/2, 25 May 1998.

[28] WTO, *Work Programme on Electronic Commerce: Ministerial Decision of 13 December 2017*, Ministerial Conference, Eleventh Session, Buenos Aires, 10–13 December 2017, WT/MIN(17)/65, WT/L/1032, 18 December 2017.

[29] *Dedicated Discussion on Electronic Commerce under the Auspices of the General Council on 15 June 2001*, Summary by the Secretariat of the Issues Raised, WT/GC/W/436, 6 July 2001.

[30] "Electronic Commerce" (WTO), https://perma.cc/7ZKN-KVSD.

even the most basic issues such as the mode of supply and classification of e-commerce. Indeed, the division among the members was so wide that no substantive discussion was held at the twelfth dedicated session because of the procedural concerns raised by some members.[31] Because of the opposition, discussions have only been held in informal, open-ended meetings convened by the General Council Chair since then and the process has basically stalled.

In view of the lack of progress under the formal Work Programme, the proponents of the e-commerce negotiation started to explore alternative ways to advance the negotiation. This was recognized by the Ministerial Declaration at the Nairobi Ministerial Conference in December 2015, which acknowledged that some members "believe new approaches are necessary to achieve meaningful outcomes in multilateral negotiations".[32] The USA was even more explicit in its statement, with the then United States Trade Representative (USTR) Michael Froman declaring the Nairobi Ministerial would begin "the road to a new era for the WTO" and stating that "[a]s WTO members start work next year, they will be freed to consider new approaches to pressing unresolved issues and begin evaluating new issues for the organization to consider".[33]

After Nairobi, e-commerce gained "renewed interest" among WTO members.[34] On 1 July 2016, the first post-Nairobi submission was made by the USA. Likely in anticipation of the strong resistance from developing countries, the USA took a rather cautious approach and labelled its submission a "non-paper" that is "intended solely to contribute to constructive discussion among Members" rather than to advance "specific negotiating proposals".[35] While the non-paper repeatedly emphasizes that the USA has "no preconceived views on best approaches, or on whether negotiations on specific aspects of e-commerce should be pursued, and if so on what bases",[36] many of the examples raised in the paper reiterated the US proposals in the negotiations of the Trade in Services Agreement (TiSA) and Trans-Pacific Partnership Agreement (TPP) and brought into the WTO new issues such as free flow of data, bans on data localization and forced transfer of source code for the first time.[37]

The US submission spurred a new wave of activity from other members, with major players such as Japan, the EU, Brazil, Canada and Singapore all making

31 General Council, 7 December 2016, Item 6 – Work Programme on Electronic Commerce: Progress Report by the Chairman, WT/GC/W/728, 8 December 2016.

32 "Nairobi Ministerial Declaration" (WTO), https://perma.cc/3NP6-YGUF, at para. 30.

33 "Statement by Ambassador Michael Froman at the Conclusion of the 10th World Trade Organization Ministerial Conference" (Office of the United States Trade Representative (USTR), 19 December 2015), https://perma.cc/JAN3-2EE9.

34 WTO General Council, "Item 4 – Work Program on Electronic Commerce – Review of Progress: Report by Ambassador Alfredo Suescum – Friend of the Chair", WT/GC/W/721, 1 August 2016.

35 WTO, *Work Program on Electronic Commerce: Non-paper from the United States*, JOB/GC/94, 4 July 2016, at para. 1.3.

36 Ibid., at para. 1.2.

37 Gao, note 24 above, at 307–308.

submissions within the same month.[38] The work intensified over the next sixteen months, and at the 11th Ministerial Conference held in December 2017 in Buenos Aires, seventy-one members led by three co-conveners – Australia, Japan and Singapore – launched a joint statement to "initiate exploratory work together toward future WTO negotiations" on e-commerce.[39] Nine meetings were held in 2018, and the negotiations were finally launched by seventy-six members at the side-lines of the World Economic Forum Annual Meeting in Davos on 25 January 2019.[40]

Initially, China was quite reluctant to support the launch of e-commerce negotiations. In its first submission on e-commerce at the WTO, China tried to pre-empt the upcoming e-commerce negotiation in several ways.[41] First, reflecting its long-standing position that only goods-related e-commerce issues should be discussed, China proposed, at the outset, that the scope of e-commerce discussions should "focus on promotion and facilitation of cross-border trade in goods enabled by internet, together with services directly supporting such trade in goods, such as payment and logistics services".[42] Second, China also indicated that it was not ready to negotiate new rules for e-commerce by stating that e-commerce discussions are "to clarify and to improve the application of existing multilateral trading rules", which are normally understood not to include issues such as free flow of data, data localization, etc.[43] Third, China also tried to prevent e-commerce negotiations from being used as a Trojan horse for "new market access commitments including tariff reductions".[44] By taking out new rules and new tariff concessions, the Chinese submission then spelt out the only issues China might be willing to consider: trade facilitation, transparency, digital certificates, electronic signatures, electronic authentication and consumer protection and privacy.[45] The same elements were reiterated in China's submission to the General Council and the three subsidiary councils on the General Agreement on Tariffs and Trade (GATT), GATS and Development in October 2017, which deemed these issues as "elements acceptable to Members".[46]

38 JOB/GC/96 (Japan et al.); JOB/GC/97 (EU et al.); JOB/GC/98 (Brazil); JOB/GC/99 (MIKTA countries); JOB/GC/100 (Japan); JOB/GC/101/Rev.1 (Singapore et al.).

39 WTO, *Joint Statement on Electronic Commerce, Ministerial Conference*, Eleventh Session, Buenos Aires, 10–13 December 2017, WT/MIN(17)/60, 13 December 2017.

40 WTO, *Joint Statement on Electronic Commerce*, WT/L/1056, 25 January 2019.

41 WTO General Council, Council for Trade in Goods, Council for Trade in Services, Committee on Trade and Development, *Work Programme on Electronic Commerce: Aiming at the 11th Ministerial Conference*, Communication from the People's Republic of China and Pakistan, Revision, JOB/GC/110/Rev.1, JOB/CTG/2/Rev.1, JOB/SERV/243/Rev.1, JOB/DEV/39/Rev.1, 16 November 2016.

42 Ibid., introduction. For a detailed explanation of the meaning of "trade in goods enabled by internet", see Gao, note 24 above, at 314.

43 Ibid., introduction.

44 Ibid.

45 See Gao, note 24 above, at 314–315.

46 *E-Commerce Elements for MC11*, Communication from China, JOB/GC/142, JOB/CTG/9, JOB/SERV/271, JOB/DEV/49, 19 October 2017.

Trying to steer the course on e-commerce negotiations at the Ministerial Conference, China even submitted a draft Ministerial Decision on Electronic Commerce, which suggested continuing the work under the Work Programme on Electronic Commerce in the General Council, while raising the possibility of reinvigorating the dedicated discussions on "elements acceptable to Members" such as "facilitating cross-border e-commerce; promoting paperless trading; transparency; as well as development and cooperation".[47] Most of the draft made its way into the final Ministerial Decision,[48] prompting Chinese Ministry of Commerce (MOFCOM) Vice Minister Wang Shouwen to boast that "China has become a participant and even leader in rule-making".[49] However, by abandoning the consensus-based approach and launching the JSI via the plurilateral route, the USA and the other seventy members have turned China's success into a pyrrhic victory.

In a way, the e-commerce Joint Statement caught China by surprise. For China, the most important issue at the 11th Ministerial Conference was investment facilitation, which China has been pushing for at the WTO since 2014 as the coordinator of the group on "friends of investment facilitation for development".[50] Designed to provide support for its Belt and Road Initiative, China successfully persuaded seventy WTO members to co-sponsor a Joint Statement on the issue.[51] While China was also interested in e-commerce, its main task at the 11th Ministerial Conference was to push the WTO and World Economic Forum to officially endorse the "Enabling e-commerce" initiative – the brainchild of the Alibaba-backed eWTP – a mission that was also accomplished.[52] In contrast, the e-commerce Joint Statement, as a US-led initiative, made China quite wary.

Thus, many observers were surprised by China's "last-minute" decision to join the 2nd e-commerce Joint Statement on 25 January 2019.[53] However, a careful reading of the events in 2018 still reveals many hints explaining China's shift. After the 11th Ministerial, the sponsors of the e-commerce Joint Statement did not waste any time in getting to business and held nine meetings over the short span of one year. Such a frenzy of activities was unheard of in the WTO and proves that they are quite

47 *Work Programme on Electronic-Commerce*, Communication from China, JOB/GC/150, 10 November 2017.

48 *Work Programme on Electronic Commerce*, Ministerial Decision of 13 December 2017, WT/MIN(17)/65, WT/L/1032, 18 December 2017.

49 "热点问答：世贸组织第11届部长级会议中国怎么看 [Hot Questions Q&A: China's Opinion on the 11th WTO Ministerial Meeting]" (*Xinhua News*, 14 December 2017), https://perma.cc/GWY9-7UK8.

50 "Investment Facilitation for Development", https://perma.cc/8LKD-LPCV.

51 *Joint Ministerial Statement on Investment, Facilitation for Development*, WT/MIN(17)/59, 13 December 2017.

52 "WTO, World Economic Forum and eWTP Launch Joint Public-Private Dialogue to Open up E-commerce for Small Business" (WTO, 11 December 2017), https://perma.cc/W97H-SQ5F.

53 B Baschuk and S Donnan, "China to Join Talks on $25 Trillion E-Commerce Market at Last Minute" (*Bloomberg*, 25 January 2019), https://perma.cc/273Y-EEHK.

serious. Moreover, the key players in the e-commerce Joint Statement – the USA, the EU and Japan – kept referring to e-commerce in the three trilateral statements on WTO reform they issued in 2018.[54] In the last one issued in September 2018, they further agreed to "intensify and accelerate this process" to achieve "the timely launch of negotiations of a high standard agreement with the participation of as many members as possible". Three more trilateral statement were issued after 2018, with the latest one being issued on 14 January 2020.[55] All these developments reminded China that the e-commerce Joint Statement parties are taking the issue very seriously and China could not just ignore it. Indeed, China learned its lesson the hard way when its attempt to join the TiSA negotiations was blocked by the USA, making it impossible for China to shape the rules on services trade, where e-commerce was a major issue.[56] The first indication of the policy change can be detected when China released its position paper on WTO reform on 23 November 2018.[57] While the position paper took the cautious approach and did not explicitly mention e-commerce, at the press conference held on the same day, Vice Minister Wang made a direct reference to e-commerce in response to a question from a journalist for examples on how to "keep the WTO rules relevant", a key objective for China in WTO reform.[58]

After China joined the 2nd e-commerce Joint Statement on 25 January 2019, Chinese WTO Ambassador Dr Zhang Xiangchen also gave an official explanation for the shift in position.[59] First, referring to the critical juncture the WTO was at, Zhang pointed to the special significance the launch of the e-commerce negotiation could have in reinvigorating the negotiation function of the WTO and boosting people's confidence in the multilateral trading system and economic globalization. Second, Zhang also regarded China's participation as a good opportunity for it to play an active role in the negotiations, especially in reflecting the participation of

54 The three statements are: "Joint Readout from Meeting of the United States, European Union and Japan in Brussels" (USTR, 10 March 2018), https://perma.cc/9WUC-S7MU; "Joint Statement on Trilateral Meeting of the Trade Ministers of the United States, Japan, and the European Union" (USTR, 31 May 2018), https://perma.cc/UG6U-GDHV; "Joint Statement on Trilateral Meeting of the Trade Ministers of the United States, Japan, and the European Union" (USTR, 25 September 2018), https://perma.cc/ZL3Q-UTEL.

55 The three statements are: "Joint Statement of the Trilateral Meeting of the Trade Ministers of the European Union, Japan and the United States" (USTR, 9 January 2019), https://perma.cc/D9PS-UWS5; "Joint Statement of the Trilateral Meeting of the Trade Ministers of the United States, European Union, and Japan" (USTR, 23 May 2019), https://perma.cc/LGD4-GDP2; "Joint Statement of the Trilateral Meeting of the Trade Ministers of Japan, the United States and the European Union" (USTR, 14 January 2020), https://perma.cc/43M8-VYLC.

56 Gao, note 24 above, 301–304.

57 MOFCOM, "中国关于世贸组织改革的立场文件 [China's Position Paper on WTO Reform]", https://perma.cc/K9S4-JN2F.

58 "商务部召开世贸组织改革有关问题新闻吹风会 [China's Ministry of Commerce Opens News Conference for Response to WTO-Related Reforms]" (PRC Gov, 23 November 2018), https://perma.cc/RS6E-C32Q.

59 "世贸组织成员在达沃斯签署电子商务联合声明 [WTO Members Sign Joint Statement on E-commerce at Davos]" (*Xinhua News*, 25 January 2019), https://perma.cc/CT5U-4L9J.

developing countries and designing a flexible framework to reflect the reasonable demands of different parties.

For long-time observers of China's trade policy, such shifts in position are not unprecedented. For example, in the early stages of the Doha Round negotiations, China sided with developing countries. Before the Cancun Ministerial Conference in September 2003, China and sixteen other developing countries formed the "Core Group", which resisted the push by the "Colorado Group" of developed countries to start negotiations on the Singapore issues including trade facilitation.[60] However, when the General Council decided to start negotiations on trade facilitations on 1 August 2004, China became an active participant.[61] This makes sense because China, as one of the top exporters in the world, would benefit from more efficient and cheaper customs processes.[62] Like trade facilitation, China's decision to join the e-commerce negotiations demonstrated once again its flexibility when it comes to specific trade issues and its willingness "to take up commitments commensurate with its level of development and economic capability", as stated in its position paper on WTO reform.[63]

III THE CHINESE PROPOSALS

From an initial group of seventy-six members in January 2019, the JSI has grown to include eighty-six members as of 1 April 2021, with Ecuador the newest participant. Together, they represent more than 90 per cent of global trade and over half of the WTO's membership. In addition, the JSI also remains open for participation by non-members, which include Senegal, the LDC signatory of the Osaka Declaration on e-commerce, which has yet to join the JSI as a formal member.[64]

Before January 2019, the JSI was framed around four themes: (1) enabling digital trade/e-commerce; (2) openness and digital trade/e-commerce; (3) trust and digital trade/e-commerce; and (4) cross-cutting issues, including development, transparency and cooperation.[65] During the exploratory discussions held in 2018, each theme was further divided into several sub-themes, resulting in thirteen sub-themes in total. Selected issues and topics were further identified under each sub-theme, resulting in over forty issues in total.[66]

60 Z Sun (ed.), *WTO多哈回合谈判中期回顾 [Mid-Term Review of the WTO Doha Round Negotiations]* (Beijing, People's Publishing House [Renmin Chubanshe] 2005), at 178–181.

61 Ibid., 194–195.

62 H. Gao, "China's Ascent in Global Trade Governance: From Rule Taker to Rule Shaker, and Maybe Rule Maker?", in C. Deere-Birkbeck (ed.), *Making Global Trade Governance Work for Development* (Cambridge, Cambridge University Press, 2001), at 166.

63 MOFCOM, note 57 above, at 4.

64 IDEAS, "WTO Joint Statement on Electronic Commerce: Advancing the Search for Convergence" (IDEAS), https://perma.cc/6EQJ-YTHY.

65 Ibid.

66 Ibid.

Since January 2019, the group has moved on to the plurilateral negotiations phase and the themes were also expanded to include two new ones: (5) telecommunications; and (6) market access.[67] The six themes were further divided into fifteen subthemes and thirty-five selected issues/topics.[68] In the negotiation process, China has emerged as one of the most active participants with four submissions out of a total of fifty-two substantive submissions so far.[69] As China's last submission is restricted and only has one page,[70] this section will examine the first three submissions, which provide a detailed account of China's position.

A *The First Submission*

The first submission was submitted by China on 23 April 2019[71] and reiterated its general positions made on prior occasions leading to China's participation in the JSI. The first part sets out China's overall approach to the JSI negotiation, which covers four areas: the objective, the relationship with the WTO, the negotiation process, and its direction and focus. It started by noting that development should be the objective of the JSI and calling on participates to help "Members, particularly developing Members and LDCs, to integrate into global value chains, bridge the digital divide, seize development opportunities and benefit from inclusive trade, and hence better participating in the economic globalization". Consistent with the developing country position, China also stated that the JSI negotiation "should be complementary to the electronic commerce discussion in relevant subsidiary bodies of the WTO" and "ultimately achieve a multilateral outcome". This approach is also reflected in China's proposal for the negotiation process, where it noted that the JSI negotiation "should be open, inclusive and transparent" with "well-designed frameworks and flexible approaches on the implementation of negotiation outcomes". This point probably reflects China's unhappy experience with the TiSA negotiations, when the USA reportedly blocked its request to participate in the closed, exclusive and non-transparent negotiation. The mentioning of "flexible approaches on the implementation of negotiation outcomes", on the other hand, indicates that China might not accept all obligations but prefers a tiered approach on commitments, which again

67 Ibid.

68 Ibid.

69 A search on WTO's Documents Online system on 1 April 2021 using the document symbol for the e-commerce JSI "INF/ECOM/*" generated seventy submissions, but four of them are consolidated or stockpile texts; six of them are revisions or addenda to original submissions, while the other eight are just communications from new participants informing their decisions to participate, which include, for example, INF/ECOM/18 by Benin; INF/ECOM/37 by Kenya; INF/ECOM/38 by Côte D'Ivoire; INF/ECOM/48 by Cameroon; INF/ECOM/50 by the Philippines; INF/ECOM/53 by Burkina Faso; INF/ECOM/56 by Guatemala; INF/ECOM/56 by Ecuador.

70 *Joint Statement on Electronic Commerce*, Communication from China, INF/ECOM/60, 28 October 2020.

71 *Joint Statement on Electronic Commerce*, Communication from China, INF/ECOM/19, 24 April 2019.

affirms its willingness to "take up commitments commensurate with its level of development and economic capability".[72] With regard to the scope of the JSI negotiation, China further emphasized that it should "focus on the discussion of cross-border trade in goods enabled by the internet, together with relevant payment and logistics services while paying attention to the digitalization trend of trade in services, and explore the way to develop international rules for electronic commerce centering on a sound transaction environment and a safe and trust-worthy market environment." This is again unsurprising given China's strong interests in trade in goods and the relevant trade facilitation and electronic payment issues,[73] as evidenced by the enormous success of its homegrown e-commerce model with Alibaba as the e-commerce platform, Alipay as the payment gateway and the many courier services companies as distributors of goods.

The next four subsections further elaborate the focus of the negotiation by listing China's priority issues, which are grouped into four action areas.

1 Definition and Clarification

China calls on members to define terms such as trade-related aspects of electronic commerce and electronic transmission, and to clarify the relationship between future electronic commerce rules and existing WTO Agreements.

Both tasks appear innocuous, but as the history of the e-commerce Work Programme has shown, even such mundane discussions could become contentious, especially given the open hostility some WTO members have displayed towards the JSI. Thus, it seems that the more sensible approach is to adopt the "constructive ambiguity" approach and leave these issues undisturbed.

2 Trade Facilitation Measures

China also calls on members to "establish a sound environment for electronic commerce transaction", which includes two types of measures. The first are measures to facilitate customs process, such as the improvement of customs procedures, electronic payment of customs fees and electronic customs documentation, establishment of free zones and customs warehouses, and a moratorium on customs duties. The second is mainly the establishment of the necessary legal framework to enable the recognition of electronic signatures, electronic authentication and electronic contracts.

These measures are mostly uncontroversial as they largely copy from the provisions under the Agreement on Trade Facilitation, of which China is a main proponent. The only exception is the moratorium on customs duties on e-commerce, which

72 MOFCOM, note 57 above, at 4.
73 Gao, note 24 above.

became a contentious issue in 2019 because of the opposition of India and South Africa to extend.[74] While a decision to extend the moratorium until the 12th Ministerial Conference was finally made by the General Council on 10 December 2019, there is still a possibility for the revocation of the moratorium because of the growing interest among WTO members in collecting tax on digital services and e-commerce. Thus, instead of a permanent moratorium, China only suggested to maintain the practice "until the next Ministerial Conference". This implies that China has yet to decide where its interests lie on the issue and wants to have more time to study the issue.

3 Safety and Security

This part of the submission focuses on measures to "create a safe and trust-worthy market environment for electronic commerce", which mainly includes consumer safety regulations, such as measures for online consumer protection, personal information protection and fighting spam or unsolicited electronic commercial messages. Interestingly, the submission also includes a paragraph on "cyber security", which, in addition to language on enhancing e-commerce security and safeguarding cyber security, also calls on members to "respect the Internet sovereignty".

As I discussed in another paper, "Internet sovereignty" has been a favourite slogan for the Chinese government, which elevated internet regulation to the level of national security or even sovereignty to justify its draconian laws.[75] As shown by the latter parts of the submission discussed next, the reference to "Internet sovereignty" is more than empty propaganda; it does reflect the seriousness China attaches to certain issues and is indicative of China's position on these issues.

4 Development

The submission also encourages members to "promote pragmatic and inclusive development cooperation", including measures to help developing countries to improve the e-commerce infrastructure and bridge the digital divide, to share best practices on e-commerce development and help them build up their capacity, and also to "establish an Electronic Commerce for Development Program under the WTO framework".

These initiatives, if successfully implemented, will definitely help developing countries to boost their e-commerce development, which, in turn, could also facilitate the expansion of Chinese e-commerce giants like Alibaba in these countries, especially in regions covered by the Belt and Road Initiative.

[74] B Reinsch et al., "Ongoing Goings On: A News Update on WTO" (2020), https://perma.cc/ZQ5Q-V5PD.

[75] Gao, note 6 above.

In the final part titled "Other Issues", China also discussed the main demands of the USA in the JSI; that is, data flow, data storage, treatment of digital products, etc. By addressing them directly and acknowledging them as issues of concern for some members, China has broken from its traditional approach of simply ignoring them. This itself is a positive sign, as it indicates China's willingness to engage on these issues.

At the same time, China also indicated that it was not ready to discuss these issues, at least not in the early stages of the negotiation. Citing the "complexity and sensitivity" of these issues, as well as "the vastly divergent views among the Members", China stated that "more exploratory discussions are needed before bringing such issues to the WTO negotiation, so as to allow Members to fully understand their implications and impacts, as well as related challenges and opportunities". Such an approach is all too familiar to those who follow WTO negotiations closely, as it is basically a polite way of saying "we don't want to discuss these issues now".

In particular, China singled out the issue of cross-border data flow, by stating that "[i]t's undeniable that trade-related aspects of data flow are of great importance to trade development". It is interesting to note, however, what China did and did not say in this sentence. It did not, for example, use "free flow of data", which is how the USA has always referred to the issue in its submissions.[76] On the other hand, it qualified "data flow" with "trade-related aspects". This implies that China is not willing to address all kinds of data flows, just those related to trade. In other words, to the extent that some data flows do not have a trade nexus, they could be legitimately excluded. This qualification could have wide implications as it could be employed to justify restrictions on data flows in sectors where China has not made a commitment,[77] or even for those covered by existing commitments but are provided free of charge (such as Google's search engine services) as they are not technically "traded".

Moreover, in an effort to turn the table, China also prefaced the discussion on these "other issues" with the affirmation of "the legitimate right" by members "to adopt regulatory measures in order to achieve reasonable public policy objectives". This language is reminiscent of the calls for more "policy space", a term often employed in trade negotiations to justify special and differential treatment and resort to exceptions clauses. As the *China – Publications and Audiovisual* case mentioned earlier illustrated, China will, most likely, invoke the public order exception contained in the General Exceptions clauses of both the GATT and GATS to justify its online censorship regime. In particular, on data flow, China emphasized that it

76 See *Work Programme on Electronic Commerce*, Non-paper from the United States, JOB/GC/94, which refers to "free flow of information" in para. 2.3; and *Joint Statement on Electronic Commerce Initiative*, Communication from the United States, INF/ECOM/5, which refers to "free flows of information" in section 2.

77 Gao, note 3 above.

"should be subject to the precondition of security",[78] and should "flow orderly in compliance with Members' respective laws and regulations".[79] This extends China's domestic narrative of cybersecurity to the international level, which is made complete with the earlier reference for all members to "respect the Internet sovereignty" of other members. By elevating the issue to one of "sovereignty", China has shown the seriousness it attaches to the issue of regulating data flow.

In summary, China has made it clear that it is not yet ready to discuss these sensitive issues, at least not in the early stages of the negotiations. There is a possibility that it will consider some of the issues further down the road, but such negotiations will not be easy given China's guarded position on these issues.

B *The Second Submission*

In its second submission dated 8 May 2019,[80] China spelt out its detailed proposals on its priority issues. As China's first substantive proposal, the twelve draft articles in the submission largely corresponds to three of the four main action areas mentioned in section 3 of its first submission; that is, section 3.1 on definition and clarification, section 3.2 on trade facilitation and section 3.3 on safety and security.

The first draft article is titled "scope", but actually dealt with the definition issue by proposing that the agreement "apply to measures affecting the production, distribution, marketing, sale or delivery of goods and services by electronic means". This language copies verbatim the language from the 1998 e-commerce declaration[81] and confirms China's position that the JSI should "support the multilateral trading system" and "keep WTO rules relevant". In the alternative, China suggests that the agreement "apply to measures adopted or maintained by Members that affect trade by electronic means", which mirrors the language in its FTAs.[82]

The next draft article addresses the relationship with existing WTO Agreements by noting first that in the event of conflicts between the new agreement and the WTO Agreements, those in Annex 1 to the Marrakesh Agreement shall prevail. The next paragraph explicitly states that the new agreement "shall not be construed to have changed or modified Members' market access commitments made under the [GATT or GATS]". This partly reflects China's sour experience in the *China–Publications* case discussed earlier, where the USA used the technology neutrality principle to persuade the panel that China's services schedule also includes commitments on electronic distribution of audio-visual products. Thus, this article was

78 Communication from China, note 71 above, at para. 4.3.

79 Ibid.

80 *Joint Statement on Electronic Commerce*, Communication from China, INF/ECOM/32, 9 May 2019.

81 *Work Programme on Electronic Commerce*, WT/L/274, adopted by the General Council on 25 September 1998.

82 China-Singapore Free Trade Agreement (CSFTA), in chapter 15 at Art. 2.2.

proposed in an attempt to seal the loophole and ensure that China would not inadvertently modify its commitments by participating in the JSI.

The third draft article deals with exceptions, and starts by explicitly noting that Article XX of the GATT 1994 and Article XIV of the GATS "shall apply to this Agreement to the extent applicable" and their provisions "shall be incorporated into and made an integral part of this Agreement, mutatis mutandis". Again, like the previous article, this provision is partly the result of the hard lessons China has learned in the *China–Raw Materials*[83] and *China–Rare Earth*[84] cases, where because of the lack of explicit reference to the general exception clause of the GATT, China was denied the right to justify its export restrictions under GATT Article XX. In addition, China also specifically pointed out that the new agreement

> shall not prevent Members from adopting or maintaining any measures for the purposes of guaranteeing cybersecurity, safeguarding cyberspace sovereignty, protecting the lawful rights and interests of its citizens, juridical persons and other organizations and achieving other legitimate public policy objectives, provided that such measures are not applied in a manner which would constitute a means of arbitrary or unjustifiable discrimination or a disguised restriction on trade, and are no more than necessary to achieve the objectives.

This strong language confirms once again China's obsession with cybersecurity, which is elevated to the level of sovereignty and thus non-negotiable. The second part of the article focuses on "Security Exceptions", where China proposes that the agreement shall not be construed "to require any Member to furnish any information, the disclosure of which it considers contrary to its essential security interests" or "to prevent any Member from taking any action which it considers necessary for the protection of its essential security interest". Again, it is probably not unreasonable to surmise that cybersecurity would be considered a matter of "essential security interest".

The rest of the proposals are mostly unexciting, as they either deal with the issue of trade facilitation, with four articles on electronic authentication and electronic signatures, electronic contracts, electronic invoices and maintaining domestic legal frameworks governing electronic transactions; or the issue of e-commerce safety, with three clauses on unsolicited commercial electronic messages, personal information protection and online consumer protection. Then there are two articles on good governance, with one focusing on transparency and calls for publication of

[83] Panel Reports, *China – Measures Related to the Exportation of Various Raw Materials*, WT/DS394/R, Add.1 and Corr.1 / WT/DS395/R, Add.1 and Corr.1 / WT/DS398/R, Add.1 and Corr.1, adopted 22 February 2012, as modified by Appellate Body Reports WT/DS394/AB/R / WT/DS395/AB/R / WT/DS398/AB/R, DSR 2012:VII, at 3501.

[84] Panel Reports, *China – Measures Related to the Exportation of Rare Earths, Tungsten, and Molybdenum*, WT/DS431/R and Add.1 / WT/DS432/R and Add.1 / WT/DS433/R and Add.1, adopted 29 August 2014, upheld by Appellate Body Reports WT/DS431/AB/R / WT/DS432/AB/R / WT/DS433/AB/R, DSR 2014:IV, at 1127.

"all measures of general application which pertain to electronic commerce" and "all measures relating to public telecommunications networks or services", while the other is on domestic regulation. The last draft article is particularly interesting, as it, in addition to incorporating GATS Article VI, also specifically states that "[n]othing in this Agreement shall be construed to affect any Member's right to conduct a content review for the purposes of achieving legitimate public policy objectives". Again, the inspiration for this clause comes from the *China–Publications* case. Even though China's right to conduct content review was explicitly affirmed by the Appellate Body in that case, China's inclusion of this draft clause indicates that it is not taking any chances and attaches high importance to its censorship regime, which is another non-negotiable item.

C *The Third Submission*

Compared to the second submission, China's third submission,[85] made on 20 September 2019, has fewer draft articles – eight instead of twelve – but at a greater length – six instead of five pages. This is because the draft articles are more detailed in the third submission, indicating that China has probably put more effort into drafting these articles.

With the exception of the last article, the third submission mainly focuses on trade facilitation measures. These include three articles on streamlining customs administration, such as transparency and non-discrimination of trade policy, paperless trading and various measures to enhance trade facilitation, including implementation of a trade facilitation agreement, advance electronic data for customs clearance, electronic payment of duties, bounded warehouse and free zones, regional distribution centres, and expedited clearance for low-risk cargo and collective clearance. Three other articles call on members to improve their e-commerce-related services commitments, such as online trade facilitating and supporting services like those provided by Alibaba, logistics services like those provided by SF Express and electronic payment services like those provided by Alipay. Together, they help to solve three common problems faced by developing countries when they try to develop e-commerce: lack of a good e-commerce platform, a slow or non-existent logistics network and the inability to transfer payments between buyers and sellers. Of course, all these are likely to be achieved with the help of Chinese firms, which are now the world leaders in providing e-commerce solutions on platform, logistics and payment. Even though such services are mainly provided online, they might need the physical presence of e-commerce-related personnel to set up, maintain and repair. Thus, another article suggests members facilitate the temporary entry and sojourn of such

85 WTO, *Joint Statement on Electronic Commerce*, Communication from China, INF/ECOM/40, 23 September 2019.

personnel. This is similar to the GATS visa proposal by India, albeit further limiting the beneficiaries to e-commerce-related personnel.

The last draft article in the submission is on "Electronic Commerce-Related Network Equipment and Products". Ostensibly, it can be said to be related to trade facilitation in e-commerce, but it is quite obvious that such equipment and products are capable of much wider use in the telecom sector, especially in view of the expansive definition provided in the article, which covers "all hardware and related software and services that can be used to support transactions done by electronic means, including telecommunication network equipment, products, resources, and related services such as installation, trial operation, testing, optimization, maintenance and repair services and etc., and other related equipment, products, resources and related services". The article calls on members to not discriminate against "network equipment and products of any other Member", which are further elaborated in three successive substantive paragraphs to mean not to exclude such network equipment and products, not to prevent public telecommunications networks or their services suppliers from choosing them and not to "block the supply chains of electronic commerce-related network equipment and products, in particular those based on long-term commercial cooperation, including cutting or prohibiting the supply to enterprises of any other Member of necessary raw materials, components, parts, software, technologies and their updates for electronic commerce-related network equipment and products".

As this proposal was submitted after the widely reported exclusion of Huawei in the 5G network in Europe and Australia, and the ban on the sales of chips and the licence of the Android system to Huawei by the USA, the inclusion of the article on network equipment and products is probably far from mere coincidence. It reflects China's attempt to fight what it perceives as "technology protectionism" using trade rules, which along with the "Made in China 2025" plan is another key component of China's quest for technological supremacy. But for two reasons, China might see its initiative thwarted.

First, this is more of a telecom issue, which is arguably beyond the scope of e-commerce negotiation. Even though telecommunication has been added as one of the focus groups of discussion, past experiences in GATS negotiations such as the Reference Paper have shown that the members are more concerned with services regulatory issues such as competitive safeguards, licensing and regulatory requirements rather than hardware-related issues.[86] Instead, technical issues on hardware and software have traditionally been dealt with at the International Telecommunication Union (ITU). This is also confirmed by the recent discussions of the issue in the JSI, where several members noted either that "the JSI was

[86] See H Gao, "Telecommunications Services: Reference Paper", in R. Wolfrum et al. (eds), *Max Planck Commentary on World Trade Law, Volume VI: Trade in Services* (Leiden, Martinus Nijhoff Publishers, 2008), at 718–747.

not the appropriate forum to discuss this topic" or "some topics were more appropriate to be discussed at the ITU".[87]

Second, even if JSI participants agree to engage in discussions on the issue, it would not be hard for them to justify any restrictions they might introduce or maintain with the security exception, which, ironically, also features prominently in China's second submission discussed earlier, where China advocates broad leeway for members to take "any action which it considers necessary for the protection of its essential security interest".

Interestingly, even though China addresses – albeit in a negative manner – the issues of data flow and localization in its first submission, neither the second nor the third submission contain language on these issues. Nor was the moratorium on customs duty mentioned.

IV ACROSS THE GREAT WALL

Initially reluctant to join the JSI negotiation on e-commerce over concerns about it being a US plot, China has finally jumped on the JSI bandwagon at its launch in Davos in January 2019 and emerged as one of the most active participants. Such a policy shift is the result of China's realization that it is important to enhance its rule-making power in e-commerce and cyberspace, as noted by President Xi in his speech at the 36th Collective Study Session of the Politburo.[88]

Despite being a world leader in e-commerce, or in China's own words, "trade in goods facilitated by the internet", China's draconian approach to cybersecurity has made people question whether it would make a positive contribution to global e-commerce governance, with some even calling for "disqualifying" China from participation in the JSI negotiation.[89] Indeed, as reviewed earlier in this chapter, while many of China's detailed proposals, especially those on trade facilitation and consumer protection, seem rather innocuous or even benevolent as they do offer good lessons for developing countries eager to catch the e-commerce train, its proposals on security exception and content review do raise concerns on whether China would be willing to accept the main demands of the USA and other Western countries; that is, free flow of information across border; free and open internet; and prohibition of localization requirements, forced technology transfer and transfer of source code.[90]

87 *Joint Statement on Electronic Commerce, 11–14 February 2020*, Facilitator's Reports, Seventh Negotiating Round, INF/ECOM/R/7, 25 February 2020.

88 "习近平：加快推进网络信息技术自主创新　朝着建设网络强国目标不懈努力 [Xi Jinping: Accelerate the Promotion of Indigenous Innovation on Internet Information Technology, Strive Unrelentingly Towards the Objective of Building the Internet Power]" (*Xinhua News*, 9 October 2016), https://perma.cc/S3Z9-33ZD.

89 N Cory, "Why China Should Be Disqualified from Participating in WTO Negotiations on Digital Trade Rules" (2019), https://perma.cc/A9LM-3SZT.

90 WTO, *Work Program on Electronic Commerce*, Non-paper from the United States, JOB/GC/94, 4 July 2016. Also affirmed in *Joint Statement on Electronic Commerce*, Communication from the United States, INF/ECOM/23, 26 April 2019.

However, all these considerations do not necessarily have to spell the end of China's participation in the JSI, especially if one takes a closer look at the nuances of the contrasting positions between China and the West. Here I will illustrate the potential for compromises with a few key examples.

A *Free Flow of Information*

Many commentators, especially those with a technology or internet background, tend to believe that the free flow of data should be absolute; that is, it should apply to all data. While this could be a laudable ultimate goal, at present this is far from how the principle is understood in trade agreements. Take, for example, the relevant provisions in the Comprehensive and Progressive Agreement for Trans-Pacific Partnership (CPTPP) and the United States-Mexico-Canada Agreement (USMCA), both of which are regarded as providing the "gold standard for digital trade", at least in the eyes of the USA, the main drafter of the rules.[91] Instead of calling for a blanket free flow of information, both agreements only require the parties to allow the cross-border transfer of information by electronic means "when this activity is for the conduct of the business of a covered person".[92] This is entirely understandable because trade agreements, at the end of the day, are not human rights agreements. Instead, they are designed to facilitate cross-border trade, which means data flow is protected only when it contributes to the trade flow. Thus, to the extent that China does not wish to allow data flow for a specific type of service activity, it can simply carve out an exception for that specific sector. Indeed, this is probably why Google, despite the loud noises it made when it was forced to pull out of China in 2009, never successfully persuaded the USTR to bring a WTO case against China. As I analysed in the case study of the merits of such a case in 2011, such a complaint would be doomed as China has not made any commitments on the search engine services provided by Google.[93]

Moreover, both agreements also provide, in the same article, an exception clause that allows parties to adopt or maintain inconsistent measures "to achieve a legitimate public policy objective" so long as they do not constitute "arbitrary or unjustifiable discrimination or a disguised restriction on trade" and fulfil the necessity requirement. Thus, if needed, China could also invoke the exception clause to justify its data flow restrictions, as it did in the *China–Publications* case. Moreover, as shown by the case, the USA does not have a problem with the exception per se; instead, its main concern is that it is discriminatory and not necessary.

[91] J Garber, "USMCA Is 'Gold Standard for Digital Trade': Trade Chief Robert Lighthizer" (*Fox News*, 17 December 2019), https://perma.cc/LTA6-KGRZ.

[92] USMCA, Art. 19.11; CPTPP, Art. 14.11.

[93] See Gao, note 3 above.

B *Data Localization*

Another oft-mentioned concern is data localization, where people believed that China requires the localization of all data. Again, this is another misconception as the provision in question, Article 37 of China's Cyber Security Law, only requires local storage for "personal information and important data collected and generated by operators of critical information infrastructure from its operations within the people's Republic of China".[94] Thus, there are important qualifiers on the types of data (only personal information and important data); types of operators (only operators of critical information infrastructure); and geographical scope (only data generated from its operations in China). Moreover, the final version of the law already improves previous drafts. For example, the first draft of the law applies the localization requirement to all such data generated by such operators from its operation all over the world,[95] and the final text greatly reduces the impact by limiting the geographical scope to those generated within China.

Of course, the final provision on data localization is far from perfect for several reasons. First, in addition to the commonly used concept of "personal information", the law also includes "important data", a concept that has yet to be defined by Chinese law. Second is what constitutes "critical information infrastructure". Article 31 of the Cyber Security Law defines it as those in "important industries and fields such as public communications and information services, energy, transport, water conservancy, finance, public services and e-government affairs", as well as those "that will result in serious damage to state security, the national economy and the people's livelihood and public interest if it is destroyed, loses functions or encounters data leakage". Such a broad definition could potentially capture everything and is not really helpful, which is why the same Article also directed the State Council to develop the "specific scope of critical information infrastructure". In 2016, the Cyberspace Administration of China issued the National Network Security Inspection Operation Manual[96] and the Guide on the Determination of Critical Information Infrastructure,[97] which clarified the scope of critical information infrastructure by grouping them into three categories: websites, which includes the websites of government and party organizations, enterprises and public institutions, and news media; platforms, which includes internet service platforms for instant

94 "中华人民共和国网络安全法 [Cyber Security Law of the People's Republic of China]", 7 November 2016, https://perma.cc/NZ2C-ET2X.

95 Article 31 of the first draft dated 6 July 2015; see 网络安全法（草案）全文 [Cyber Security Law (Draft) Full Text], 6 July 2015, https://perma.cc/49LT-3ZKF.

96 Central Leading Group on Cyber Security and Informatisation General Office, "国家网络安全检查操作指南 [Network Security Coordination Bureau, National Network Security Inspection Operation Manual]", June 2016 (on file with author).

97 关键信息基础设施确定指南（试行）[Guide on the Determination of Critical Information Infrastructure (Trial)], under 关于开展关键信息基础设施网络安全检查的通知 [Notice on Conducting Network Security Inspections of Key Information Infrastructure], Zhongwangban Fawen [2006] #3, Annex 1, July 2016, https://perma.cc/E3PF-H6RD.

messaging, online shopping, online payment, search engines, emails, online forums, maps and audio video; and production operations, which includes office and business systems, industrial control systems, big data centres, cloud computing and TV broadcasting systems. They also laid down three steps in determining the critical information infrastructure, which starts with the identification of the critical operation, then continues with the determination of the information system or industrial control system supporting such a critical operation, and concludes with the final determination based on the level of the critical operations' reliance on such systems and possible damages resulting from security breaches in these systems. More specifically, they listed eleven sectors, which include energy, finance, transportation, hydraulic, medical, environmental protection, industrial manufacturing, utilities, telecom and internet, radio and TV, and government agencies. The detailed criteria include both quantitative and qualitative criteria. For example, critical information infrastructure includes websites with a daily visitor count of more than 1 million people and platforms with more than 10 million registered users or more than 1 million daily active users, or a daily transaction value of 10 million RMB. On the other hand, even those that do not meet the quantitative criterion could be deemed to be critical information infrastructure if there are risks of security breaches that would lead to leakage of lots of sensitive information about firms or enterprises, or leakage of fundamental national data on geology, population and resources, seriously harming the image of the government or social order, or national security. The potentially wide reach of the criteria was well illustrated by the case of the BGI Group, which was fined by the Ministry of Science and Technology in October 2018 for exporting certain human genome information abroad via the Internet without authorization.[98] Given the nature of their business, the BGI case could fall under the category of "leakage of fundamental national data on … population", as mentioned earlier.

The last problem with China's data localization policy is that, according to Article 37, only the export of personal information and important data requires security review, while there is no such requirement for domestic use. This could be interpreted as discriminatory and arbitrary, and constitute disguised restrictions in international trade.

Of course, this does not mean that all hope is lost on a potential deal on data localization. Instead, as I explained in another article,[99] the key to understanding China's data regulation is national security, which translates into the ability to maintain its censorship regime. So long as the Chinese regulators can continue to conduct content view and block foreign websites on security grounds, where the data is stored would be much less important. Actually, given the sophistication of the Great Firewall, data stored in offshore servers would be easier to block and filter.

98 S An, "数据出境如何"安检 [How to Conduct a 'Safety Check' for Exporting Data]" (*Zhihu*), https://perma.cc/V6VZ-P8TM.

99 Gao, note 6 above.

In this regard, it is instructive to study the evolution of the US approach on data localization for financial services. In the TPP negotiation, the USA carved out the entire financial services sector from the scope of its e-commerce chapter, including prohibition of data localization requirements.[100] In the new USMCA, however, the USA explicitly brought over the ban to the financial services sector by stating that data localization should not be required "so long as the Party's financial regulatory authorities, for regulatory and supervisory purposes, have immediate, direct, complete, and ongoing access to information processed or stored on computing facilities that the covered person uses or locates outside the Party's territory".[101] If such language can successfully overcome the grave concerns of the US Federal Reserve, then the Chinese regulators would probably also have less reason to insist on local storage instead of having "immediate, direct, complete, and ongoing access to information processed or stored on computing facilities outside the Party's territory".[102]

To conclude, while China's participation in the JSI would make the negotiations difficult, it also provides an opportunity to understand better the policy rationale of China's data regulation, so that avenues for convergence and compromise can be found.

C *Postscript*

When I first raised the possibility of China agreeing to provisions on the free flow of data and a ban on data localization in trade agreements at the Biennial Conference of the Asian International Economic Law Network hosted by Prof. Shin-yi Peng in October 2019, few if any scholars took the idea seriously. However, barely a year later, my prediction was confirmed when China signed the RCEP, which includes provisions disallowing its members from "requir[ing] a covered person to use or locate computing facilities in that Party's territory as a condition for conducting business in that Party's territory"[103] or "prevent[ing] cross-border transfer of information by electronic means where such activity is for the conduct of the business of a covered person".[104] While both Articles are subject to exceptions allowing a Party to adopt or maintain measures that such a Party considers necessary "to achieve a legitimate public policy objective" or "for the protection of its essential security interests", the very fact that China is willing to accept such obligations is encouraging. Moreover, unlike four of the fifteen RCEP members,[105] China did not seek

100 TPP, Art. 14.1.
101 USMCA, Art. 17.18.2.
102 Ibid.
103 RCEP, Art. 12.14.
104 Ibid., Art. 12.15.
105 For the implementation of both obligations, Cambodia, Lao PDR and Myanmar were granted a transition period of up to eight years, while Viet Nam was granted five years. See footnotes 11 and 13 in chapter 12 of the RCEP.

any transition period for both obligations to take effect. While the chapter on e-commerce is not subject to the normal dispute settlement procedure under the RCEP, the importance China attaches to the RCEP and the peer pressure under the consultation and Joint Committee procedures could provide some incentive for China to implement the obligations in good faith. This is partially confirmed by MOFCOM, which announced in March 2021 that China has ratified the RCEP and finished the preparatory work to implement 613 of the total 701 obligations China has assumed under the RCEP, with the rest ready to implement when the agreement comes into effect.[106] Presumably, the 701 obligations would include the twin obligations on free flow of data and prohibition of data localization requirements.

If we can learn anything from the RCEP, it is that actively engaging China in e-commerce negotiations is much better than leaving China in its own cyber enclave. The Internet was built to transcend walls. International negotiations on the Internet and e-commerce should also help people reach across walls, no matter how great they might be.

106 "积极推动RCEP生效，我国已完成协定核准工作 [Actively Pushing for the Coming into Force of the RCEP, China Has Finished the Ratification of the Agreement]" (*People's Daily*, 26 March 2021), http://paper.people.com.cn/rmrb/html/2021-03/26/nw.D110000renmrb_20210326_6-02.htm.

16

The Next Great Global Knowledge Infrastructure Land Rush Has Begun

Will the USA or China Prevail?

Jane K. Winn and Yi-Shyuan Chiang

I INTRODUCTION: COULD CHINA PREVAIL AS ARCHITECT OF THE EMERGING GLOBAL KNOWLEDGE INFRASTRUCTURE?

[China] should pursue innovation-driven development and intensify cooperation in frontier areas such as digital economy, artificial intelligence, nanotechnology and quantum computing, and advance the development of big data, cloud computing and smart cities so as to turn them into a digital silk road of the 21st century.[1]

[The USA] must continue to advance innovation that's ingrained with our approach to human rights, civil liberties and privacy. It is critically important in this age, when so many of our adversaries [such as the Chinese Communist Party] are twisting these technologies against American values.[2]

By 2020, there was no denying that the USA and China were engaged in a full-fledged trade war. A long, slow narrative arc that began with the rise of Japan, followed by South Korea, Taiwan, Hong Kong, Singapore and finally China as export-oriented economies with the support of the USA and other Western nations, appeared to be winding up for good. With the loss of this narrative, the likely future trajectory of global economic activity will become more difficult to predict. A nation's progress from economic backwardness through late development or catch-up industrialization strategies to middle-income or beyond could be mapped out relatively easily. The foundation of comparative advantage appears to be shifting from Industrial Revolution business strategies to business strategies emerging from the crucible of "digital transformation," but the winning formula for success in the new global information economy is not yet clear. The world trade system itself, so painstakingly assembled in the decades following World War II, appears to be

[1] "President Xi Jinping's Speech at Opening of Belt and Road Forum" (*Xinhua*, 15 May 2017), https://perma.cc/E6V5-YFHR.

[2] Brooke Singman, "US Technology Chief Warns China 'Twisting' Artificial Intelligence to Target Critics, as America Joins Global Pact" (*Fox News*, 28 May 2020), https://perma.cc/YP22-YYA6.

unraveling, making it even harder for individual nations or enterprises to pinpoint future sources of global competitive advantage with any certainty.

Where some commentators might have seen an "Information Revolution" following the Industrial Revolution, others now believe they can discern a "Knowledge Revolution" gaining momentum. In 2003, the neoliberal international relations theorist Joseph Nye observed, "The current information revolution is based on rapid technological advances in computers, communications, and software that in turn have led to dramatic decreases in the cost of processing and transmitting information."[3] A few years earlier, however, the so-called Father of Post-War Management Thinking[4] Peter Drucker suggested the transformation was more radical than that:

> What we call the Information Revolution is actually a Knowledge Revolution. What has made it possible to routinize processes is not machinery; the computer is only the trigger. Software is the reorganization of traditional work, based on centuries of experience, through the application of knowledge and especially of systematic, logical analysis. The key is not electronics; it is cognitive science. This means that the key to maintaining leadership in the economy and the technology that are about to emerge is likely to be the social position of knowledge professionals and social acceptance of their values.[5]

Technological advances including advances in data science, artificial intelligence (AI), machine learning, cloud computing, the Internet of Things, mobile computing and social production are all fueling this Knowledge Revolution. The consulting firm Gartner has grouped these advances together and labeled the bundle a "nexus of forces" that is transforming the "infrastructure of civilization."[6] While the economic rivalry between the USA and China is intensifying across many industries, it may be most intense in the struggle for control over the emerging global information architecture emerging out of this "Knowledge Revolution."

In order to distinguish a Knowledge Revolution from an Information Revolution, it is first necessary to distinguish knowledge from information. Data is generally thought of as records of simple factual observations, while information is data that has been organized and combined within structures to create meaning, with knowledge arising when meaningful information is contextualized in a form that can be used to solve problems. Knowledge viewed from this perspective may be thought of as the "strategic competence" of being able to discern "what one needs to know and

[3] JS Nye, *The Paradox of American Power: Why the World's Only Superpower Can't Go It Alone* (New York, Oxford University Press, 2003), at 42.

[4] "Peter Drucker," https://perma.cc/CT9X-9FQK.

[5] Peter Drucker, "Beyond the Information Revolution," *The Atlantic* (1999), https://perma.cc/P4WX-4X2N.

[6] C Howard, "The Nexus of Forces Is Creating the Digital Business" (2014), https://perma.cc/Z5B9-EP2K; J Lopez, "Digital Business Success Depends on Civilization Infrastructure: A Gartner Trend Report" (2017), https://perma.cc/E3L2-DVMZ.

remember what one ought to remember" through the application of a sense-making framework.[7]

On the question of whether a Western nation such as the USA or a non-Western rival such as the China would most likely prevail in the contest to lead the Knowledge Revolution now unfolding, the conventional wisdom among most Western observers seems to be that the odds are stacked in favor of the West. Western nations can claim to be the source of the Enlightenment's Scientific Revolution as well as liberal institutions such as free markets, representative democracy and the rule of law. Far from being perceived as a hotbed of innovation and entrepreneurship with the capacity to rival the USA in the production of knowledge, China is frequently viewed in the West as "totalitarian," which is the antithesis of a liberal society. In 2020, a conservative American think-tank asked, "Is China Totalitarian?" and answered in the affirmative:

> By any reasonable measure, the PRC [People's Republic of China] is becoming a totalitarian state whose actions are dictated and determined by Xi Jinping and the Communist Party he heads . . . . To say otherwise is to ignore the totalitarian behavior of Communist China for the past four decades and to doubt that a despot like Xi will do whatever is necessary to maintain his power and control.[8]

In its World Report 2020, Human Rights Watch reached a similar conclusion.[9] Even more neutral commentators feel justified in making oblique references to China's totalitarian character:

> Great struggles between great powers tend to have a tipping point. It's the moment when the irreconcilability of differences becomes obvious to nearly everyone . . . the curtailment of freedom that awaits Hong Kong is nothing like the totalitarian tyranny that Joseph Stalin imposed on Warsaw, Budapest and other cities. But the analogies aren't inapt, either.[10]

Given that authoritarianism generally refers to the harsh rule of a strong state that is not accountable to its citizens while totalitarianism generally refers to the use of political terror and an all-embracing ideology to politicize all aspects of life and subordinate all citizens to the state,[11] China's critics might more accurately characterize it as authoritarian rather than totalitarian.

7 P Porrini and WH Starbuck, "Organizational Information and Knowledge," in JD Wright (ed.), *International Encyclopedia of the Social & Behavioral Sciences* (2nd ed., Amsterdam, Elsevier, 2015), at 72–76.

8 L Edwards, "Is China Totalitarian?" (The Heritage Foundation, 26 February 2020), https://perma.cc/TF25-SJ56.

9 Human Rights Watch, "World Report 2020" (2020), https://perma.cc/S79K-ZK7Y, at 4–5.

10 B Stephens, "China and the Rhineland Moment: America and Its Allies Must Not Simply Accept Beijing's Aggression" (*New York Times*, 29 May 2020), https://perma.cc/RR4Z-HXT5.

11 L Holmes, "Totalitarianism," in JD Wright (ed.), *International Encyclopedia of the Social & Behavioral Sciences* (2nd ed., Amsterdam, Elsevier, 2015), at 448–452.

Whichever nation can foster the greatest "strategic knowledge competence" among the largest number of its citizens is likely to emerge as the leader of the global Knowledge Revolution. Whether it is more accurate to characterize China today as totalitarian or merely authoritarian, few China watchers appear convinced China will be able to overtake the West in the production of knowledge. In 1945, Frederick von Hayek contrasted the kind of formal, scientific knowledge that technocrats could centralize and control with the decentralized, unorganized kind of "knowledge of particular circumstances of time and place" that technocrats cannot easily control but that individuals actually use to solve the concrete problems they face.[12] Societies controlled by unaccountable elites might be able to surpass more democratic societies in the production of technocratic knowledge, but more democratic societies seem more likely to produce more of the kind of practical knowledge Hayek believed would translate into greater market competitiveness. For example, firms in China with more than fifty employees are required to have a Chinese Communist Party (CCP) representative, while companies with more than a hundred employees are required to have a CCP cell.[13] Individuals who know these representatives and cells are being used to monitor their words and conduct may curtail their efforts to produce "knowledge of particular circumstances" in order to reduce the risk they might suffer negative consequences for inadvertently violating some CCP norm. The use of highly pejorative terms such as totalitarian when less pejorative terms such as authoritarian might be more accurate suggests how deeply some of China's Western critics are discounting the possibility that China might prevail over the West by cultivating greater "strategic knowledge competence" among its citizens.

Some other China watchers in the West, however, have detected evidence that the number of Chinese citizens and enterprises developing knowledge as a strategic competence may be growing rapidly. Taiwan-born entrepreneur and research scientist Lee Kai-Fu has described the emergence in China of many unique and highly forms of disruptive innovation that are enjoying phenomenal success in China and around the world.[14] For example, because digital entrepreneurs in China face the same threat of software piracy as foreign firms, they quickly learned that any competitive advantage gained on the basis of the kind of "pure play" Internet business model favored by Western technology entrepreneurs was unlikely to be sustainable. So they responded to local market conditions by developing the "online-to-offline" (O2O) business model in order to mitigate intellectual property piracy risks. The "O2O Revolution" in China is made up of firms that invest in physical assets such as delivery vehicles and staff such as drivers to provide more than a digital experience to their users, which in turn creates barriers to market entry.

12 F von Hayek, "The Use of Knowledge in Society" (1945) 35 *American Economic Review* 519.

13 RM Abrami et al., "Why China Can't Innovate" (2014) 92 *Harvard Business Review* 107–111.

14 K-F Lee, *AI Superpowers: China, Silicon Valley and the New World Order* (Boston, MA, Houghton Mifflin Harcourt, 2018).

Management consultant Edward Tse highlights the resilience of many Chinese entrepreneurs in a legal environment for business that provides them with considerably less predictability than their Western counterparts enjoy.[15] Tse believes that China's domestic disruptors such as Alibaba, Tencent, Xiaomi, Haier and Huawei often triumph over their foreign rivals not because they are sheltered by protectionist government policies, but because they are better than their foreign rivals at accelerating decision-making, increasing flexibility and continually updating products and capabilities. Political scientist Douglas Fuller has identified a "global hybrid" model of innovation that outperforms purely foreign or purely domestic firms by combining overseas Chinese management talent and foreign financial capital with responsiveness to domestic government policy and global market conditions.

This chapter will consider how nations' pursuit of competitive advantage might unfold within the context of a global Knowledge Revolution, and how China might triumph in a contest among nations to foster the greatest "strategic knowledge competence" among the largest number of citizens. The victor in that contest would be well positioned to lead the design of the global knowledge infrastructure being produced by the "nexus of forces" of digital disruption. The competition between the USA and China to lead the design of the next great global knowledge infrastructure can be compared to the nineteenth-century "land rushes" the USA used to open land in the Oklahoma Territory to white settlement, and to the first great global knowledge economy "land rush" triggered by the commercialization of the Internet in the late 1990s. The vulnerability of the current international trade law regime to disruption by China's efforts to disseminate its own legal and values culture through global networks and platforms is considered next, and placed within the context of China's distinctively pluralist legal culture. The chapter concludes that it may not be in the self-interest of Western nations to discount too heavily the possibility that China might ultimately prevail in its efforts to preempt the USA from the role of lead designer of the next great global information infrastructure.

II A KNOWLEDGE REVOLUTION MAY TRIGGER A GLOBAL INFORMATION INFRASTRUCTURE LAND RUSH

All your base are belong to us.[16]

Between 1889 and 1895 in what later became the state of Oklahoma, the US General Land Office carried out seven "land rushes" to allocate land to white settlers.[17] Settlers could claim lots of up to 160 acres of land and if they lived on the land and

[15] E Tse, *China's Disruptors: How Alibaba, Xiaomi, Tencent, and Other Companies Are Changing the Rules of Business* (New York, Portfolio, 2015).

[16] Internet meme derived from the English subtitle on the Zero Wing video arcade game produced in Japan in 1991. J Benner, "When Gamer Humor Attacks" (*WIRED*, 23 February 2001), https://perma.cc/6BZF-VTLE.

[17] See "The Encyclopedia of Oklahoma History and Culture," https://perma.cc/Q2HN-A5PW.

farmed it, they could acquire title to it after five years. For a variety of reasons, including endless litigation between "boomers" who claimed land after the official start of the land run and "sooners" who had snuck in before the official start, the process was never repeated in any other American territory following the settlement of Oklahoma. But the general idea of a "land rush" or "land run" remains seared into American cultural memory and provides an apt metaphor for the emerging superpower contest to lead the development of the next great global knowledge architecture.

The first great global knowledge infrastructure competition reminiscent of an Oklahoma land rush began in the early 1990s as network engineers began to reject the International Organization for Standardization (ISO) Open Systems Interconnection (OSI) model for a comprehensive global information architecture in favor of the much simpler TCP/IP (transmission control protocol/internet protocol) standard that defines the Internet.[18] The US Department of Defense's Advanced Research Projects Agency (ARPA) had begun testing designs for a "packet-switched" network (i.e., not "circuit-switched" like a telephone network) in 1969. In 1972, the "International Network Working Group" (INWG) was launched by European and American research scientists and network engineers with the mission of developing a global data networking standard to complement global telephone networking standards. The efforts of ARPA and INWG to develop a standard for computer networks proceeded collaboratively for a few years, but bifurcated around 1976. European research scientists and network engineers then helped to launch a broad, collaborative, international effort that turned into the ISO OSI project, while the American research scientists and network engineers worked within ARPA and with support from the US Department of Defense. In 1983, the "Internet" was born when the US Department of Defense began requiring the use of the TCP/IP networking standard within the growing community of academic researchers and defense contractors it was funding. By the early 1990s, the OSI project got bogged down in the effort to build an international consensus in support of a comprehensive framework of standards while the more narrowly scoped TCP/IP project powered ahead with actual adoptions among a growing number of public and private sector users in the USA and around the world.

When the US National Science Foundation turned over maintenance of the "backbone" of the global data network defined by the TCP/IP standard to the private sector in 1995, its Acceptable Use Policy prohibiting commercial use of the Internet was officially terminated, and the global internet commerce "land rush" took off. Because American academics, businesses and government agencies already had a decade or more of experience working with the Internet on the day the Internet land rush started, they enjoyed an enormous competitive advantage over their

[18] AL Russell, "OSI: The Internet That Wasn't" (IEEE Spectrum, 30 July 2013), https://perma.cc/V7EH-635X.

foreign counterparts in countries whose academics, businesses and government agencies had been working on the OSI standards.

Once it was obvious that the American solution would prevail over the multilateral solution developed under the aegis of international standards bodies such as the ISO and the International Telecommunications Union (ITU), other nations have repeatedly, but so far unsuccessfully, attempted to wrest control over the Internet from the USA. When other Western nations began threatening in the 1990s to challenge US control of the Internet, the USA responded in 1998 by establishing the Internet Corporation of Assigned Names and Numbers (ICANN), a California nonprofit corporation, to act as a global, multistakeholder forum within which Internet governance issues could be resolved under the watchful eye of the USA. In 2003 and 2005, the United Nations organized the World Summit on the Information Society in an effort to address digital divide issues and promote inclusive global internet governance strategies. Many critics of the dominance of US interests in global internet governance demanded that authority over the Internet be turned over to the ITU to manage together with the global telephone system, a suggestion the USA flatly rejects whenever it is made. The US response to both summits was to reaffirm its commitment to letting the private sector lead the development of the global information architecture, to retain US control over the "root servers" that provide the foundation for the global domain name system, and to ignore criticism of its influence on governance matters.[19] Because the Internet was not designed to accommodate censorship, countries that do not welcome the influence of American values in their societies – including in Bahrain, China, Iran, Russia, Saudi Arabia, Syria, Turkey and the United Arab Emirates – have been forced to construct and operate their own filtering systems to block their citizens' access to internet content they find objectionable.[20]

The Internet today remains a global network of networks that all make use of TCP/IP communications protocols for interoperability. Global support for the Internet notwithstanding, these controversies are due in part to the positive "network effects" consumers around the world enjoy from using it. A network may be defined as:

> a set of actors or nodes along with a set of ties of a specified type (such as friendship) that link them. The ties interconnect through shared end points to form paths that indirectly link nodes that are not directly tied.[21]

A network effect is one example of a market "externality" (i.e., a cost or benefit not reflected in a product's price). A positive network effect arises when the value to

[19] M Farrell, "How the Rest of the World Feels about U.S. Dominance of the Internet" (*Slate*, 18 November 2016), https://perma.cc/9CJ3-VWNB.

[20] J Clark et al., "The Shifting Landscape of Global Internet Censorship" (2017) Berkman Klein Center for Internet & Society Research Publication, https://perma.cc/B389-87RV.

[21] DS Halgin and SP Borgatti, "On Network Theory" (2011) 22 *Organization Science* 1168, at 1169.

a consumer of a network increases the more other consumers use the same network. The popularity of telephones, fax machines, personal computers and email is due in part to positive network effects.[22] Price competition among producers of interoperable goods and services that make up a network may benefit consumers if a network is defined by open standards rather than closed proprietary solutions.[23]

Economists studying networks and network effects coined the terms "first mover advantage" and "increasing returns to scale" to describe the distinctive features of competition carried out in markets defined by interoperability standards compared to competition in markets for natural resources or for agricultural or industrial products.[24] Because individuals are often not motivated to join new networks until enough other users have joined to create positive network effects, the promoter of a new network often faces a "chicken and egg" problem of how to attract new users before a critical mass of users can be enrolled. The so-called first mover advantage arises once a network has been successfully launched, making its users reluctant to migrate to a new network until it is certain that all other users will also migrate. Users of an existing network may find themselves "locked in" to that network if promoters of a new network cannot persuade enough users to leave the existing network. One way to diminish the risk of lock-in to a single proprietary network service provider is to define networks with "open" interoperability standards. This permits many competing firms to participate in the operation of a network simultaneously without fragmenting the network and diminishing the positive network effects users enjoy while at the same time securing for users the benefits of competition among network service providers.

If the operator of a successful network can also launch a "two-sided market" (also known as a "multisided market" or a "multisided platform") that runs on the network, this may amplify the market power of the operator.[25] A simple model of a multisided platform is a two-sided market where the participation of two very different groups, each subject to very different terms and conditions, sustains the market. Traditional newspaper publishing is an example of a two-sided market with readers being one "side," advertisers being the second "side" and the newspaper publisher acting as the "platform operator." Traditional stock markets such as the New York Stock Exchange can also be thought of as a two-sided market, bringing together companies issuing securities and investors buying securities, with the issuers subsidizing access by investors. Multisided platforms may bring together three or more distinct groups: LinkedIn is a three-sided platform organizing different experiences for individuals, recruiters and advertisers, while Microsoft Windows

22 J Farrell and G Saloner, "Standardization, Compatibility, and Innovation" (1985) 16 *RAND Journal of Economics* 70.

23 ML Katz and C Shapiro, "Network Externalities, Competition, and Compatibility" (1985) 75 *American Economic Review* 424.

24 C Shapiro and H Varian, *Information Rules* (Boston, MA, Harvard Business School Press, 1999).

25 J-C Rochet and J Tirole, "Platform Competition in Two-Sided Markets" (2003) 1 *Journal of the European Economic Association* 990.

operates as a three-sided platform for individuals, equipment manufacturers and third-party software developers.[26] Google's Android mobile ecosystem has many different sides including users, telephone manufacturers, third-party app developers, network carriers and advertisers.[27]

Although two-sided, or multisided, markets exist apart from ICT networks, many of the most successful global information economy enterprises – such as Google, Apple, Facebook, Amazon, Microsoft, Netflix, Airbnb, Uber, Salesforce, eBay, Twitter, Alibaba, Tencent, Baidu and Xiaomi – operate as digital platforms. In order for a multisided market to operate successfully, the platform operator must devise a pricing strategy that maximizes the commitment of both sides to the success of the platform. Newspapers traditionally charged advertisers high prices for access to readers, and used those advertising revenues to subsidize readers. A successful platform pricing strategy normally imposes high prices on the side that is most committed to the success of the platform and uses low or subsidized prices to attract less committed users.

While one way to think about digital platforms is as private marketplaces, they can also be thought of as private regulators or governance systems.[28] Just as territorial sovereigns can tax citizens either for the benefit of the sovereign personally or to defray the cost of providing public goods to citizens, successful digital platform operators may charge one or more groups of users prices fixed high above their production costs either to provide a return to their investors or to subsidize the cost of providing the platform as a public good to members of a different group. This ability of very successful platform operators to charge high prices to some groups of users for long periods of time, combined with the dearth of European digital platforms, has incited European competition regulators to target them for heightened scrutiny and enforcement efforts.[29]

Up to this point, the public-facing efforts of governments to project their authority into the global internet have tended to focus on publishing information for citizens, and providing access to government-to-citizen or government-to-business services rather than trying to establish a public sector multisided platform. However, the economic logic of positive network effects and the capacity of multisided platforms to operate as self-sustaining governance mechanisms could just as easily serve public sector goals as private sector goals. A few countries such as Singapore have begun to operate sophisticated portals for government services that integrate a wide range of public sector services into an accessible dashboard that might one day evolve into

26 A Hagiu, "Strategic Decisions for Multisided Platforms" *MIT Sloan Management Review* 55, no.2 (Winter 2014), https://perma.cc/RBC8-KNXR.

27 M Campbell-Kell et al., "Economic and Business Perspectives on Smartphones as Multi-sided Platforms" (2015) 39 *Telecommunications Policy* 717.

28 JK Winn, "The Secession of the Successful: The Rise of Amazon as Private Global Consumer Protection Regulator" (2016) 58 *Arizona Law Review* 193.

29 N Petit, "European Competition Policy in Digital: What's Next?" (*Competition Policy International*, 4 August 2019), https://perma.cc/ALS5-XL7B.

a public sector multisided platform. The service today known as "National Trade Platform" (NTP) in Singapore was originally launched in 1989 with the goal of reducing barriers to cross-border trade. Singapore's NTP may be among the most mature and successful "platforms" for the delivery of government services in the world, but even the NTP has not yet publicly embraced the "multisided platform" model to expand its reach.

One of the few positive developments to emerge from the generally disappointing conclusion of the World Trade Organization (WTO) Doha Round of negotiations was the Trade Facilitation Agreement (TFA) in 2017.[30] With the TFA, WTO members commit to "the simplification, modernization, and harmonization of export and import processes."[31] Because the primary focus of the WTO TFA is on narrow operational issues such as the creation of national "single window" trade facilitation systems[32] rather than broader economic issues, it might inadvertently serve to accelerate the creation of global digital trade facilitation platforms. The term "single window" in this context might best be understood as referring to a portal or channel through which communications between public and private sector parties might flow more easily. The Singapore NTP trade portal is a good example of such a single window system: it provides importers and exporters with a single point of contact with Singapore regulators.

Once enough national single window systems are up and running, the focus of WTO members will eventually turn to the kind of interoperability issues involved in transforming national systems into a multisided global digital trade facilitation platform. Some WTO members may be able to shift their focus to these interoperability issues before others. In 2019, the Asia Pacific Economic Cooperation (APEC) Committee on Trade and Investment (CTI) benchmarked the efforts of APEC members to adopt interoperable single window systems.[33] The APEC CTI found that Association of Southeast Asian Nations (ASEAN) members and Pacific Alliance members had achieved the highest level of its "capability maturity model" and so could support cross-border interoperability.

Some private sector efforts to launch true multisided trade facilitation platforms have also begun to gain some traction. In 2017, Alibaba and other stakeholders in China partnered with the government of Malaysia to launch the Electronic World Trade Platform (eWTP),[34] and by 2020, Belgium, Ethiopia, Rwanda and Thailand

30 "Global Trade after the Failure of the Doha Round" (*New York Times*, 1 January 2016), https://perma.cc/JAG7-G7C4; Protocol Amending the Marrakesh Agreement Establishing the World Trade Organization, Decision of 27 November 2014, WT/L/940, adopted 28 November 2014; entered into force on 22 February 2017 following the ratification by two-thirds of the WTO membership.

31 World Trade Organization, "World Trade Report 2015" (2015), https://perma.cc/CV54-DR4X, at 34.

32 WTO Trade Facilitation Agreement (TFA), art. 10.

33 APEC Committee on Trade and Investment, "Compendium of Best Practice Technology Solutions for Single Window Interoperability" (2019), https://perma.cc/EJ5D-A9NY.

34 B Jaipragas, "Free Trade for Minnows: How Alibaba Gave Malaysia's E-hub Hopes a Boost" (*South China Morning Post*, 13 November 2017), https://perma.cc/63MH-2PJ4.

as well as the Chinese cities of Hangzhou and Yi Wu were participants.[35] In 2018, the Singapore information technology company vCargo Cloud announced the launch of its CamelONE trade facilitation platform.[36] By 2020, the CamelONE trade facilitation platform was offering logistics and trade finance services through Singapore's NTP with the support of the Monetary Authority of Singapore.

It has not yet become clear which nation or region will be in the best position to seize the "first mover advantage" in the new global knowledge economy land rush triggered by disruptive "nexus of forces" innovations. The USA is unlikely to be deposed as chief architect of the global knowledge architecture merely by the kind of efforts undertaken so far by individual enterprises such as China's Alibaba or Singapore's vCargo Cloud, or regional associations of emerging economies such as ASEAN or the Pacific Alliance to promote the interoperability of national single window projects. By contrast, it is possible the USA could be deposed by a concerted effort by China. The remaining sections of this chapter will examine different factors likely to contribute to the leadership of the global knowledge economy remaining under Western control or coming under China's control.

III THE ROLE OF ARTIFICIAL INTELLIGENCE IN THE NEW LEGAL ORDER OF UNCERTAINTY IN WORLD TRADE LAW

In considering this question, then, we must never forget that it is a constitution we are expounding.[37]

The [European] Community constitutes a new legal order of international law for the benefit of which [European nations] have limited their sovereign rights.[38]

Historical experience has proven that failures in the economic sphere can result in major disorder, and failure in the ideological sphere can result in major disorders as well.[39]

As the trade war between the USA and China erupted in 2018, one pessimistic commentator announced the death of the WTO.[40] By 2020, the dire predicament of the WTO had become obvious to even casual observers.[41] In 2018, President Trump announced he would block the appointment of judges to the WTO Appellate Body, and by 2020 it could no longer accept any new appeals because there were no longer

35 "Electronic World Trade Platform: Public Service Platform," https://perma.cc/9CXW-CQCA.

36 NS Wei, "Riding the Digital Silk Road" (*Business Times Singapore*, 13 March 2018), https://perma.cc/57CS-FD7A.

37 *McCulloch v. Maryland*, 17 U.S. (4 Wheat.) 316 (1819).

38 *Van Gend en Loos v Nederlandse Administratie der Belastingen* (1963) Case 26/62.

39 九号文件: 关于当前意识形态领域的形势和主要任务 [Document No. 9 on the Current Situation and Main Tasks in the Field of Ideology (2013)].

40 E Alden, "Trump, China, and Steel Tariffs: The Day the WTO Died" (Council on Foreign Relations, 9 March 2018), https://perma.cc/XG3N-Z7D4.

41 B Baschuk, "Who Will Lead the WTO and Help It Avoid Collapse?" (*Bloomberg*, 21 May 2020), https://perma.cc/9RCD-L64D.

enough judges left to form new review panels.[42] As the WTO and the legal order it anchors are increasingly hobbled by the indifference or even hostility of some of the very world powers that were once its staunchest defenders, all participants in the world trade system now confront a new legal order of uncertainty. The emerging superpower contest between the USA and China to lead the development of the next great global knowledge architecture will likely be fought out within this terrain of legal uncertainty.

Although the WTO's many detractors do not all agree on what is wrong with it, some of its shortcomings are alleged to include the way intellectual property rights are currently handled, the unequal allocation of costs and benefits of trade liberalization within national economies, and the apparent ability of a few countries such as China to extract disproportionate benefits under the current regime.[43] (The perception that China is uniquely positioned to exploit the current world trade system is, of course, relatively recent, given that Chinese accession in 2001 was conditioned on its agreement to exceptionally onerous concessions.[44]) While some manifestations of the emerging global knowledge economy – such as intellectual property rights or telecommunications – may clearly be governed by the international law regime governing trade, others – such as data flows or the market power of digital platforms – are not. After the Doha Round ended in stalemate and the USA withdrew from negotiations on regional trade agreements such as the Trans-Pacific Partnership Agreement, it is unclear how the WTO system can address any of the most serious criticisms leveled against it or respond to new challenges such as AI.[45]

One commentator has suggested that any new order of international trade law shaped by China's primacy in the global economy will likely retain many features of the old order:

> But even if China's influence has grown, it has no desire to step into America's shoes and provide global leadership . . . China regained its strength by plugging into the rules-based global order that America gifted to the world in 1945. China has no desire to overturn this order. It would be happy to cooperate with America within it.[46]

Given the enormity of the differences between law in China and in Western nations, as China's influence in shaping international trade law and legal institutions

[42] A Swanson, "Trump Cripples W.T.O. as Trade War Rages" (*New York Times*, 8 December 2019), https://perma.cc/7VY9-Y8V3.

[43] J McBride and A Chatzky, "What's Next for the WTO?" (Council on Foreign Relations Backgrounder, 10 December 2019), https://perma.cc/5BZB-M7UL.

[44] Xiaohui Wu, "No Longer Outside, Not Yet Equal: Rethinking China's Membership in the World Trade Organization" (2011) 10 *Chinese Journal of International Law* 227–270.

[45] A Goldfarb and D Trefler, "How Artificial Intelligence Impacts International Trade" (2018), https://perma.cc/W6ZJ-QGUW.

[46] K Mahbubani, "China: Threat or Opportunity?" (*Noema Magazine*, 15 June 2020), https://perma.cc/7XTU-NDTS.

continues to increase, the result is nevertheless also likely to be increased legal uncertainty for Western nations.

Just as the current WTO regime has its strengths and weaknesses, an international trade law regime influenced by Chinese law and legal institutions would also have strengths and weaknesses, although the strengths of such a system might not be readily apparent to China's detractors. This is in part because China has explicitly committed to the pursuit of "rule by law" rather than the "rule of law" as that term is understood among practitioners of public international law.[47] The policies and procedures of the CCP can be understood as a source of law in China somewhat like customary law, although much more authoritative.[48] As constitutional law expert Xu Xianming explained in 2017, "The Communist Party is simultaneously in the law, under the law and above the law."[49] The government of China, including its formal legal institutions, cannot serve as the ultimate repository of political power because the CCP enjoys a special status somewhat like "first among equals."[50] Within this hybrid "political-legal" order, the exercise of judicial power by the courts is protected from interference from other branches of government, social organizations or individuals, but not from the Party.[51]

Compliance with law, whether international or municipal, may be seen as a function of the severity of the consequences for noncompliance combined with the probability of those negative consequences being meted out.[52] If China can succeed in projecting its regulatory culture into global arenas by influencing the design of the next great global knowledge architecture just as the USA did with the Internet, then distinctively Chinese mechanisms for monitoring compliance with law might come to assume a greater role in international trade law. Furthermore, China is in the midst of developing just such a distinctively Chinese framework for monitoring compliance with law: the China social credit system (CSCS).

Under the CSCS, PRC government agencies are permitted to share data on compliance by individuals, companies and social organizations with various laws and regulations, and can place the names of serious offenders and serial scofflaws on blacklists and subject them to various restrictions on their activities. The regulators

47 KN Ng, "Is China a Rule-by-Law Regime?" (2019) 67 *Buffalo Law Review* 793.

48 P Chang, "Diversified Legal Sources of Property Rights and Rules on Their Application" (2014) 4 *Chinese Journal of Law* 114.

49 "徐显明，我的理解是，共产党既在法律之中，也在法律之下，还在法律之上[Xu Xianming: My Understanding Is that the Communist Party Is Within, Below and Above the Law]" (*China Digital Times*, 16 April 2017), https://perma.cc/24A2-TCJW.

50 The idea of "first among equals" (or *primus inter pares*) was a term used in Rome to describe the exercise of power by designated individuals within a system where members of the patrician class shared political power. ME Davies and H Swain, *Aspects of Roman History 82 BC–AD 14: A Source-Based Approach* (London, Routledge, 2010), at 384.

51 L Li, "Political-Legal Order and the Curious Double Character of China's Courts" (2018) 6 *Asian Journal of Law & Society* 19.

52 GS Becker, "Crime and Punishment: An Economic Approach" (1968) 76 *Journal of Political Economy* 169.

using the CSCS to increase the effectiveness of their enforcement efforts include those dealing with taxation, the environment, transportation, food safety and foreign economic cooperation, as well as the execution of court judgments.[53] While in 2018 some commentators were unable to detect a significant role for AI in the CSCS,[54] subsequent commentators have concluded that AI already plays an important role in CSCS.[55] Given the great success enjoyed by AI applications in credit evaluation in the West,[56] and the centrality of AI generally in the Belt and Road Initiative (BRI) and China's domestic economic development programs, it seems safe to assume that the role of AI within the CSCS will increase in the future.

Coverage of the CSCS in Western media often exaggerates its technological sophistication and the degree to which its different elements are integrated, resulting in intense criticism of what is presumed to be its profoundly dystopian nature.[57] What goes by the name CSCS is not a single, monolithic organization but rather a collection of different policies and pilot programs designed to increase the negative consequences of not complying with legal obligations or well-established social norms as well as the positive consequences of conscientious compliance with law and important social norms.[58] Viewed from this perspective, the CSCS can be understood as a collection of government interventions designed to correct some of the "social traps"[59] that plague Chinese society today. Social traps in social domains are analogous to market failures in economic domains, and thus something that carefully targeted government intervention might remedy or at least neutralize.

China has already begun to extend the reach of the CSCS internationally within the BRI framework.[60] If China succeeds in integrating AI into its legal institutions, whether through the expansion of the CSCS or otherwise, as well as in embedding its legal values in a global digital trade facilitation platform, Western nations may find the resulting new global order of international law not merely uncertain but alarming as well. Yet such an evolutionary development is consistent with Western notions of transnational law as contested, dynamic and provisional, continuously

53 J Horsley, "China's Orwellian Social Credit Score Isn't Real" (*Foreign Policy*, 16 November 2018), https://perma.cc/NE45-SLWM.

54 Y-J Chen et al., "'Rule of Trust': The Power and Perils of China's Social Credit Megaproject" (2018) 32 *Columbia Journal of Asian Law* 1.

55 S Feldstein, "The Global Expansion of AI Surveillance" (2019) Carnegie Endowment for World Peace Working Paper, https://perma.cc/5GE5-C57M; S Hoffman, "Engineering Global Consent: The Chinese Communist Party's Data-Driven Power Expansion" (2019) Australian Strategic Policy Institute, Policy Brief Report No. 21, https://perma.cc/8FA3-3UR6.

56 "Explainable AI and the FICO Score" (FICO, 14 November 2018), https://perma.cc/G65N-HFED.

57 See P Dockrill, "China's Chilling 'Social Credit System' Is Straight Out of Dystopian Sci-Fi, and It's Already Switched On" (*Science Alert*, 20 September 2018), https://perma.cc/QFZ9-5V4U.

58 X Dai, "Enforcing Law and Norms for Good Citizens: One View of China's Social Credit System Project" (2020) 63 *Development* 38.

59 J Platt, "Social Traps" (1973) 28 *American Psychologist* 641.

60 "一带一路"国际合作城市信用联盟成立 ['Belt & Road' International Cooperative City Credit Alliance Established]" (*Xinhua*, 10 October 2020), https://perma.cc/7M8S-M3Y8.

emerging partially formed from incomplete resolutions to conflicts arising within and across different legal domains.[61]

Sociologists use the term "institutional isomorphism" to describe a process whereby different organizations come to resemble each other, and recognize coercive, normative or mimetic variations.[62] Coercive isomorphism compels conformity while normative isomorphism involves the dissemination of rules through the work of professionals. Mimetic isomorphism is produced by the voluntary copying of features of an institution that are perceived as beneficial. While China's detractors may believe that Chinese legal institutions and values could never prevail over their Western counterparts except through coercion, normative and mimetic isomorphism may also contribute to reshaping international trade law into something closer to China's idea of law. The work of global standard-setting organizations might contribute to the kind of normative and mimetic isomorphism that could expand the influence of Chinese legal values in international trade arenas. It should come as no surprise therefore that China has recently announced its intention to lead the development of global standards for disruptive "nexus of forces" innovations, including AI.[63]

Legal anthropologists have long recognized that treating law as a distinct and separate sphere apart from other human experience cannot produce an accurate account of legal processes. Legal anthropologists may begin their analysis by noting that legal institutions operate on multiple levels simultaneously and that a plurality of legal institutions interact with social structures outside the law in many different ways.[64] These overlapping domains can be referred to individually as "semi-autonomous social fields"[65] or collectively as "legal pluralism."[66] As Sally Falk Moore explained:

> Though the formal legal institutions may enjoy a near monopoly on the legitimate use of force, they cannot be said to have a monopoly of any kind on the other various forms of effective coercion or effective inducement. It is well established that between the body politic and the individual, there are interposed various smaller organized social fields to which the individual "belongs." These social fields have their own customs and rules and the means of coercing or inducing compliance. They have what Weber called a "legal order."[67]

61 G Shaffer, "Theorizing Transnational Legal Ordering" (2016) 12 *Annual Review of Law & Social Science* 231.

62 PJ Dimaggio and WW Powell, "The Iron Cage Revisited: Institutional Isomorphism and Collective Rationality in Organizational Fields" (1983) 48 *American Sociological Review* 147.

63 N Wilson, "China Standards 2035 and the Plan for World Domination – Don't Believe China's Hype" (Council on Foreign Relations, 3 June 2020), https://perma.cc/H74S-HF2N.

64 L Pospisil, "Legal Levels and Multiplicity of Legal Systems in Human Societies" (1967) 11 *Journal of Conflict Resolution* 2.

65 SF Moore, "Law and Social Change: The Semi-Autonomous Social Field as an Appropriate Subject of Study" (1973) 7 *Law & Society Review* 719.

66 J Griffiths, "Legal Pluralism," in N Smelser (ed.), *International Encyclopedia of the Social & Behavioral Sciences* (Amsterdam, Elsevier, 2001).

67 Moore, note 65 above, at 721.

China's legal system manifests many characteristics of legal pluralism. For example, in 2016, the CCP issued a "Guiding Opinion" declaring that all laws, regulations and public policies should be implemented in a manner that supported appropriate social values, and in 2018 it announced a plan to insure that the core values of socialism are fully incorporated into law.[68] By blurring the boundary between law, politics and morality, China is turning away from the modern notion of morality as a negative domain of unconstrained individual choice and turning toward mobilizing plural sources of law to promote conformity to specific ideas about individual morality. Even if this pluralist model of law is not appealing to China's critics in the West, it may be appealing to many of the nations in the Global South who wish to emulate China's economic miracle and do not consider the Western notion of the rule of law a feasible goal for them to pursue.

While those Western knowledge workers most likely to find their working conditions transformed by the rapid expansion of AI are quick to decry the dangers it poses, more level-headed observers consider its potential social benefits together with its potential social costs.[69] The intransigence with which many lawyers in Western nations have resisted dimensions of digital transformation accepted as routine or even necessary by other citizens of Western nations is noteworthy in this regard, and may reveal more about the epistemic culture of the legal profession in the West than the likely impact of AI on human labor.[70] Given their resistance to using lesser forms of automation of knowledge work, it should come as no surprise that Western trained lawyers are strenuously resisting any move away from bespoke production and distribution of legal services.[71] By contrast, given China's interest in transcending Western notions of the rule of law, it should come as no surprise that China is embracing the automation of legal services more enthusiastically than Western nations.[72] If China advances more quickly than the West in finding ways to automate the delivery of legal services, then the systems it develops might incorporate legal pluralist notions more fully than their Western analogs as a result of normative and mimetic isomorphism.

Leaders of nations in the Global South that have not yet embraced the modern Western ideal of rule of law might find attractive an international trade law regime that is both more compatible with their own pluralist legal systems and provides them increased access to global markets by means of a global digital trade facilitation platform. According to the World Bank, China has lifted 850 million of its citizens

68 D Lin and S Trevaskes, "Creating a Virtuous Leviathan: The Party, Law, and Socialist Core Values" (2019) 6 *Asian Journal of Law and Society* 41, at 42.

69 A Howard and J Borenstein, "The Ugly Truth about Ourselves and Our Robot Creations: The Problem of Bias and Social Inequity" (2018) 24 *Science & Engineering Ethics* 1521.

70 C Brooks et al., "Artificial Intelligence in the Legal Sector: Pressures and Challenges of Transformation" (2020) 13 *Cambridge Journal of Regions, Economy and Society* 135.

71 R Susskind and D Susskind, *The Future of Professions* (Oxford, Oxford University Press, 2016), at 30.

72 Sarah Dai, "Shanghai Judicial Courts Start to Replace Clerks with AI Assistants" (*South China Morning Post*, 1 April 2020), https://perma.cc/A8NV-BQWJ.

out of absolute poverty since Reform and Opening began in 1978.[73] In 2016, in response to the question "Overall, are you satisfied or dissatisfied with the way things are going in our country today?" asked in a survey that the US Pew Research Group carries out annually in China, 86 percent of respondents reported being satisfied.[74] If the nations of the Global South are offered the choice of participating in the conventional Western international trade law regime and a new Sinocentric international trade law regime based on legal pluralism and they conclude they face less risk of regime instability within the Chinese alternative, they might well find the Sinocentric alternative more appealing. If China can draw enough emerging economies into its sphere of influence through its BRI investments, access to CSCS surveillance technologies and more accommodating culture of legal pluralism, that might be enough to tip the balance in China's favor in the competition to lead the design of the next great global information infrastructure.

IV CONCLUSION: WHOEVER RULES THE GLOBAL KNOWLEDGE INFRASTRUCTURE RULES THE WORLD?

Whoever rules the waves, rules the world.[75]

As American baseball player, manager and cultural icon Yogi Berra observed, "It's tough to make predictions, especially about the future." With the next great global knowledge economy land rush just beginning, one of the few conclusions that can safely be drawn is that many Western observers appear to be discounting too severely the possibility of China's ultimate success. If the ambition of China's leaders to regain what they perceive as China's rightful place at the vanguard of human civilization[76] can be realized more quickly by harnessing the Knowledge Revolution, then in light of the pragmatism China's leaders have repeatedly shown since 1978, it is possible that China's leaders will find a way to overcome any anxieties they may feel about AI and push forward. If China expands the scope of its CSCS initiative to its BRI partners in the Global South, and decides to pursue a first mover advantage by launching the first successful global digital trade facilitation platform, then its investments in AI would serve to reinforce its rise to superpower status.

Just as one of the principal foundations of the British Empire was Britain's naval power, China may find a way to use superiority in AI as a foundation for its ascent to

73 World Bank, "China: Overview," https://perma.cc/6YPD-HG6U.

74 R Wike and B Stokes, "Chinese Public Sees More Powerful Role in World, Names U.S. as Top Threat" (Pew Research Center, 5 October 2016), https://perma.cc/J4KF-AK8C (since 2002, the percentage of Chinese reporting to the Pew Research Group they were satisfied has ranged from a low of 48 percent to a high of 91 percent).

75 AT Mahan, *The Influence of Sea Power Upon History: 1660–1783* (Upper Saddle River, NJ, Prentice Hall, 1980).

76 M Schuman, *Superpower Interrupted: The Chinese History of the World* (New York, PublicAffairs, 2020).

superpower primacy in the global economy. In 1960, J. C. R. Licklider foresaw the rise of human–computer symbiosis and suggested it should consist of humans setting the goals of technological innovation while machines carry out routine processes.[77] If implementations of AI focus on complementing human labor rather than replacing it and the result is increased productivity, rising earnings and greater demand for labor,[78] then the ability to secure a global competitive advantage in AI might help to decide which superpower emerges victorious from the current contest between the USA and China. And then it could be said that whoever governs the global knowledge infrastructure governs the global economy.

77 JCR Licklider, "Man-Computer Symbiosis" (1960), https://perma.cc/P4Y3-NQAA.

78 DH Autor, "Why Are There Still So Many Jobs? The History and Future of Workplace Automation" (2015) 29 *Journal of Economic Perspectives* 3.

17

Trade Law Architecture after the Fourth Industrial Revolution

Lisa Toohey

I INTRODUCTION

Technology stands to fundamentally change almost every aspect of human existence, with international trade and the international trade law system being no exception. There are two primary ways in which this change is taking place. The first is the capacity of technology to fuel the creation of new goods and services that can enter the global marketplace and be traded with greater speed and ease than their more physically embodied counterparts. The second is the possibility for technology to facilitate the regulation of international trade in ways that are more efficient, cost-effective, and inclusive.

While a considerable amount of attention is paid to this first change – how technology will impact the nature of what is traded – relatively little attention is paid to the way in which technology might change the modes and methods by which trade regulation is achieved. To the extent that future trade regulation has been considered, questions generally focus on how trade rules will change to adapt to technology, by modifying existing rules and including new disciplines.[1] So far, there has been no examination of how a future World Trade Organization (WTO) might itself take advantage of technology to restructure how it manages trade and fulfils its mandate. That mandate includes serving as a facilitator of trade agreements and market access negotiations, a forum for resolution of trade disputes, and a watchdog for national trade policies.[2]

Therefore, this chapter will examine current predictions about how the 'Fourth Industrial Revolution' will change the nature of trade, and then consider how trade regulation functions currently undertaken by organisations such as the WTO might be undertaken in future. To this end, in Section II the chapter first considers the emergence of a data-driven trade regime, brought about by emergent technologies,

[1] See M Burri, 'How Should the WTO Respond to the Data-Driven Economy?' (2020), https://perma.cc/U5PK-5ABN.

[2] These roles are defined in the Marrakesh Agreement, 15 April 1994, 1867 U.N.T.S. 154, 33 I.L.M. 1144 (1994). See also WTO, 'Four Roles of the WTO', https://perma.cc/4VJ7-YYN6.

particularly artificial intelligence (AI), distributed ledger technologies (DLT, blockchain being a prime example), and the Internet of Things (IoT). In Section III, the chapter will consider how a data-driven trade law architecture might change the way in which the current WTO operates, focusing on issues such as dispute settlement, negotiations, notifications, and monitoring. Section IV concludes.

Before proceeding, it is necessary to stress that this chapter is fundamentally a 'thought experiment' – setting aside current technological limitations for consideration of what capacities are predicted to be available in future; setting aside political realities that limit consensus and structural change in favour of considering what could be possible if political will could be guaranteed; and – although it is an extremely important consideration – setting aside the question of the digital divide between well-resourced and less well-resourced states.[3] While absolutely acknowledging that these are important issues worthy of proper consideration – and that considerations of development deserve primacy in the trade system – they are outside the scope of the present chapter. With freedom from these limitations, it is possible to explore the transformative potential technology could have on a world trade law system for the future, allowing the possibility of future work 'circling back' to examine how all states can be supported to share in the potential benefits of both trade and technology.

II CHANGING GLOBAL TRADE AND THE FOURTH INDUSTRIAL REVOLUTION

The nature of trade has changed dramatically since the days of the General Agreement on Tariffs and Trade (GATT), and even since the creation of the WTO, with modern trade being characterised by an ever-increasing services sector and a very substantial increase in global supply chains, where components of goods, and their final assembly, are produced in multiple countries, and multiple cross-border transactions for a single final item are common.[4] The creation of global value chains was very much facilitated by improvements in technology, initially in transport and logistics, but accelerating dramatically with advances in information and communications technology (ICT).[5]

In 2015, Klaus Schwab, founder of the World Economic Forum, coined the phrase 'Fourth Industrial Revolution' to describe the impact of data-driven technologies that will merge the boundaries between the physical and the digital, the artificial and the biological. Schwab sets out the way in which societies and their

[3] R Azevêdo, 'DG Azevêdo: E-Commerce Needs to Be a Force for Inclusion' (WTO, 3 July 2019), https://perma.cc/JP2J-CLVU.

[4] B Hoekman, 'A 21st Century Trade Agenda: Global Supply Chains and Logistics Services', https://perma.cc/EV5R-N3K3.

[5] R Baldwin, *The Great Convergence: Information Technology and the New Globalization* (Cambridge, MA, Belknap Press of Harvard University Press, 2016). See also A Park et al., 'Supply Chain Perspectives and Issues: A Literature Review' (2013), https://perma.cc/ESK7-MJ82.

economies have been transformed by a successive wave of revolutions. These revolutions were, in order, the change from an agrarian to an industrial society, globalisation, the age of information, and then finally the upcoming Fourth Industrial Revolution. Its hallmark, according to Schwab, will be the seamless melding of technology into every facet of society, making it difficult to distinguish along traditional boundaries the beginning and end of 'technology', with progress taking place on a scale and at a pace not previously experienced.[6]

There is broad consensus that AI, blockchain, the IoT, and 3D printing are the emerging innovations most capable of fundamentally changing the nature of international trade.[7] These technologies will create new or reconceptualised products that can be traded, such as autonomous vehicles, intelligent robots, and nanotechnology-containing products, along with a multitude of services that will come to dominate the global market. This 'new wave' of services and goods will raise fundamental questions for the content of the trade rules, for example the nature of the regulatory division between goods and services,[8] the adequacy of existing trade rules to protect new forms of intellectual property,[9] and questions of trade, privacy, and data protection.

As a result, WTO rules will need to be adapted to incorporate and address new types of products and services, to advance agreement on trade-related aspects of e-commerce, to address rights and obligations in relation to flow of data, and to review agreements such as the GATS to make it adequately technologically neutral.[10] Technological change has also caused new issues for dispute settlement, with the WTO noting that '[a]s international trade increasingly involves both digital products and digital methods of transmission and delivery, the WTO dispute settlement system has increasingly found itself tasked with resolving disputes related to aspects of the digital economy'.[11] An example of the difficult questions that can arise without a clear legal framework for new technologies is *EC – Computer Equipment*, which required determination of whether products such as network cards fell within the European Communities' tariff schedule for 'automatic data-processing equipment'.[12]

6 K Schwab, *The Fourth Industrial Revolution* (London, Penguin Random House, 2017).

7 Global Shapers Community Geneva, 'Trade 2030 and the Fourth Industrial Revolution (4IR): Bringing the Vision and Thoughts of the Youth to the World' (2018), https://perma.cc/M3FG-VT4J.

8 S-Y Peng, 'A New Trade Regime for the Servitization of Manufacturing: Rethinking the Goods-Services Dichotomy' (2020) 54(5) *Journal of World Trade* 669–726. See also P Low, 'Rethinking Services in a Changing World', ICTSD/World Trade Forum Policy Options Paper, https://perma.cc/VFW8-BNZF.

9 See, for example, SA Aaronson, 'Artificial Intelligence Is Trade Policy's New Frontier' (CIGI, 11 January 2018), https://perma.cc/A5UH-NX7K; L Zhang and KK Shang, 'The WTO Disciplines and Trade in Products Powered by Artificial Intelligence: Old Wine and New Wine-Skin?' (2019) 12(1) *Journal of East Asia & International Law*31.

10 RW Staiger, 'On the Implications of Digital Technologies for the Multilateral Trading System' in WTO, *World Trade Report 2018* (2018), https://perma.cc/N7TT-4X4F, at 150.

11 Ibid., at 168. See also Yuka Fukunaga's Chapter 8 in this volume.

12 Appellate Body Report, *European Communities – Customs Classification of Certain Computer Equipment*, WT/DS62/AB/R, WT/DS67/AB/R, WT/DS68/AB/R, 5 June 1998.

The following subsection A explores how technology will continue to challenge and change the international trade system generally, and more specifically in relation to transformational technologies such as AI. However, as this chapter argues, focusing just on how trade patterns will change, or even how the content of trade rules will change, is only part of the bigger picture. Attention also needs to be given to how trade organisations themselves can and must change to adapt to technology.

A *Technology and Trade: What Is Changing?*

In a paper for the World Economic Forum, Christine Lagarde identified a number of ways in which our data-driven world would cause transformations in the nature of trade. She points, firstly, to a huge increase in the proportion of trade in services, and secondly to a new wave of productivity that may see the use of technology such as 3D printing to bring customised manufacturing back to advanced economies, as well as to the possibilities of technology bringing about a more just and inclusive trade system.[13] Part of the transformation to which Lagarde refers is already evident, particularly in relation to storage of data remotely, a concept that was unthinkable even a short time ago. According to the Open Data Institute, cloud storage of data is now used by some 2 billion people globally,[14] making it one of the most widely traded of cross-border services.

While many technologically based innovations are generating change, there are three in particular that experts predict will have the most fundamental impact upon the international trade system – AI, blockchain, and the IoT. The key attributes of each will be examined in turn, focusing on how international trade law currently considers each technology, and then upon how the technology itself might be used to improve trade law architecture.

1 Artificial Intelligence

At the heart of AI is recognition of data patterns and iterative 'learning' from that data – in other words, it is an engagement with data that goes beyond collating information to include building and interpreting rules for the use of that information – and 'reasoning', where rules and data can be used and applied appropriately to reach conclusions. This can take a range of forms, some of which have been around for many years (for example, IBM's Deep Blue or Apple's Siri), and others which are still many decades away. O'Halloran and Nowaczyk offer a five-fold classification of AI that illustrates its broad range of functions:

[13] C Lagarde, 'Here Are 4 Building Blocks for the New Era of Trade which Will Benefit Everyone' (World Economic Forum, 30 May 2018), https://perma.cc/GLL3-9S35.

[14] L Kay, 'What Are the Links between Data Infrastructure and Trade Competitiveness?' (2019), https://perma.cc/6VXA-LYJ2.

1. Rules-based systems that set parameters and conditions to enable scenario testing;
2. Machine learning that applies algorithms to decipher patterns and linkages in the data by continuously updating 'learning' through an iterative process;
3. Neural networks that identify interconnected nodes through multi-layered data to derive meaning;
4. Deep learning that leverages pools of high-dimensional data to identify patterns of patterns; and
5. Pattern recognition that uses tools, such as natural language processing, to classify and interpret data.[15]

One of the most sophisticated examples of usable AI today is Google Duplex, an intelligent assistant that is voice activated and can interact with a human caller at the other end of the line, and make phone calls.[16] Autonomous vehicles are being deployed across the developed world, and AI-enabled diagnostic technologies are being presented as superior to expert humans in the identification of potentially successful embryos for IVF transplants.[17]

Current work at the WTO has primarily highlighted the potential for AI to drive trade efficiencies across manufacturing, transport, and supply chain management – in other words, for efficiencies on the private-party side of the trade equation. This would include, for example, the use of autonomous vehicles throughout much of the logistics process, greatly reducing cost. The WTO's research also makes reference to customs efficiencies, which are an important aspect of trade facilitation. Outside observers tend to focus more on issues such as the exponential growth of trade in data, pointing out that the data aggregation and analytic capacity of AI raises issues of trade in data of a scale never before encountered. 'Big data' is by its nature a cross-border transaction, with applications typically synthesising data gathered, transmitted, and re-transmitted across national borders. Aaronson identifies three themes in trade-focused discussion of AI, which are starting to appear in regional trade agreements:

> Today, trade policy makers in Europe and North America are working to link AI to trade with explicit language in bilateral and regional trade agreements. They hope this union will yield three outputs: the free flow of information across borders to facilitate AI; access to large markets to help train AI systems; and the ability to limit cross-border data flows to protect citizens from potential harm consistent with the exceptions delineated under the General Agreement on Trade in Services. These exceptions allow policy makers to breach the rules governing trade in cross-border data to protect public health, public morals, privacy, national security or

[15] S O'Halloran and N Nowaczyk, 'An Artificial Intelligence Approach to Regulating Systemic Risk' (2019) 2 *Frontiers in Artificial Intelligence* 7, at 8.

[16] See 'Google Duplex: A.I. Assistants Calls Local Businesses to Make Appointments' (YouTube, 8 May 2018), www.youtube.com/watch?v=D5VN56jQMWM.

[17] 'Ivy – Artificial Intelligence in IVF', https://perma.cc/K3XZ-5BSJ.

intellectual property, if such restrictions are necessary and proportionate and do not discriminate among WTO member states.[18]

There is also a focus on the race for AI primacy within the global trade system, noting that different countries have adopted different rules on privacy and use of big data, and that this can operate alongside policies designed to attract research and development (R&D) within their borders.[19]

From a trade architecture perspective, AI offers new and interesting possibilities for better trade regulation, bringing together data insights previously inaccessible because of their complexity, and driven by unprecedented volumes of data on trade flows and transactions across all levels of the supply chain from producer to consumer. This AI capability offers future potential for better dispute avoidance, automatic application of trade rules to cross-border transactions, and possibilities for real-time, dynamic trade measures to protect domestic markets from distorting trade practices. These possibilities are discussed in more detail later.

2 The Internet of Things

The second technology of relevance to trade governance is known as the IoT, a term referring to technology that 'equips everyday objects with identifying, sensing, networking and processing capabilities that allow them to communicate with one another and with other devices via the internet to achieve particular objectives'.[20] The potential uses of the IoT span the entire range of human life and economy – from wearable health devices and automated homes, to smart communities, through to manufacturing, agriculture, and supply chain management. For example, automated sensors on a factory floor can respond to changes in temperature or pressure; machine components can communicate maintenance requirements; and smart devices have transformed agriculture by automatically adjusting pesticide or fertilizer use to actual weather or soil conditions.[21] The data generated from these sensors has a myriad of uses beyond just more efficient production practices, providing information also of relevance for research and policy.

Just as containerization revolutionised maritime trade, so too the IoT has already begun to revolutionise global supply chains and logistics practices, where RFIDs

[18] SA Aaronson, 'Data Minefield? How AI Is Prodding Governments to Rethink Trade in Data' (CIGI, 3 April 2018), https://perma.cc/W7RX-LR3Y.

[19] A Goldfarb and D Trefler, 'AI and International Trade' (2018) National Bureau of Economic Research Working Paper No. 24254; see also P Cihon, 'Standards for AI Governance: International Standards to Enable Global Coordination in AI Research and Development' (2019), https://perma.cc/9XWX-5GLN.

[20] WTO, 'World Trade Report 2018: The Future of World Trade – How Digital Technologies Are Transforming Global Commerce' (2018), https://perma.cc/5CBR-FK7V, at 6.

[21] US Government Accountability Office, 'Internet of Things: Status and Implications of an Increasingly Interconnected World' (2017), https://perma.cc/WFP3-HKXU.

(radio frequency identification devices) can track shipments through the transit process. One example used in the WTO's Future of World Trade Report is shipping company Maersk's use of remote devices in its refrigerated containers to monitor performance and improve predictive maintenance – which in turn can reduce costly claims against it for damaged cargo.[22] Another potential trade benefit of automatically collected data is improved compliance and reduced risk of fraud, as well as more streamlined customs processing, as production and transport data can be correlated to verify the composition, origin, and attributes of goods. This is particularly the case when 'smart tags' can be combined with blockchain technology.

Seamless electronic borders, currently one of the negotiation points of Brexit, envision the use of mechanisms such as RFID chips attached to all goods crossing the border, embedded weighing points under border roads, and facial recognition and video cameras to scan vehicle numberplates.[23] This data can be transmitted directly to central databases and stored in the blockchain. Other government functions can also take advantage of the blockchain, with it providing almost inscrutable records for the purposes of tax collection, customs valuation, and customs clearance. As sensor technologies evolve and diversify, they have the potential to provide data about sanitary and phytosanitary measures, as well as the technical specifications of goods.

3 Distributed Ledger Technologies Such as Blockchain

Blockchain is the term typically used to describe DLT, although more correctly, blockchain is a form of DLT – in the same way that a Granny Smith is a variety of apple, but not all apples are Granny Smiths. The hallmark of DLT is that they are like databases for information storage, except that, as their name suggests, the storage is distributed rather than centralised. This distributed data can be independently verified through the system, rather than relying upon a trusted intermediary to certify the accuracy of the data. As Werbach explains, there are two primary benefits to this distributed ledger approach – the first that transactions can be verified and trusted without the need to trust any particular individual in the transaction – which is of great benefit in a globalised world where trust is difficult to establish. The second benefit is the reduction of transaction costs, as 'the single distributed ledger replaces many private ledgers that must be reconciled for consistency'.[24] The most widely

22 See WTO, note 20 above, at 67.

23 A Nardelli, 'This Leaked Report Reveals the "Technological Solutions" Explored by Liam Fox to Keep the Border in Ireland Open After Brexit' (*Buzzfeed News*, 7 February 2019), www.buzzfeed.com/albertonardelli/leaked-report-irish-border-technology (note that in the context of the Brexit debate, it is generally conceded that the technology would not be viable until approximately 2030); see B Kentish, 'Leaked Memo Warns Hi-Tech Brexit Border Solution "Years Away"' (*Belfast Telegraph*, 18 April 2019), https://perma.cc/M7W9-VEK2.

24 K Werbach, 'Trust, but Verify: Why the Blockchain Needs the Law' (2018) 33(2) *Berkeley Technology Law Journal* 487, at 491.

known example of this technology in action is cryptocurrencies such as Bitcoin, although the potential of the technology goes vastly beyond cryptocurrencies.[25]

In the international trade sphere, blockchain could be used to dramatically enhance current efforts in trade facilitation. This approach is already being tested in the financial services sector as a means of streamlining interbank transactions, and in trade through a partnership called Tradelens between IBM and Maersk, designed to reduce the large administrative expenses associated with the handling of containers.[26] Blockchain replaces paper-based processes, and party-to-party messaging is replaced with centralised, electronic storage of information, which will offer not just economic benefits but also the possibility of secure access to information for parties outside the trade transaction, including governments and international organisations.

Current examples of this technology include pilot initiatives to trace the trade of diamonds, through the TRACR project,[27] and the IBM Foodtrust tool to track the authenticity of seafood and other key food products.[28] Similarly, Clipeum is a European bank joint venture that allows clients a 'corporate vault' in which to store transaction information, and a means of granting and revoking access to that information to financial institutions. Governments too, such as the United Arab Emirates (UAE), are aiming to transform the transactions they undertake, with the UAE expecting to have half of its government's transactions blockchain-based by 2021.[29]

DLT, particularly through the use of smart contracts, complements AI to offer transformative potential to international trade. As the World Customs Organization explains,

> Blockchain organizes data into blocks, which are chained together in an append-only mode. It has the capability to move any kind of data swiftly and securely and, at the same time, make a record of that change, movement, or transaction instantly available, in a trusted and immutable manner, to the participants in a Blockchain network. In addition, the use of 'smart contracts', a set of rules that are written down and executed automatically, enables the avoidance of intermediaries, which act as arbiters of money and information.[30]

This is the approach taken by the UAE, which offers a glimpse of the future of trade. It has partnered with industry to create a one-platform system for licensing and

25 For a contrary view, see E Schuster, 'Cloud Crypto Land' (in press) *Modern Law Review*, https://doi.org/10.1111/1468-2230.12603.

26 'Maersk and IBM Introduce TradeLens Blockchain Shipping Solution' (IBM, 9 August 2018), https://perma.cc/S6NE-D9B6.

27 'Tracr', www.tracr.com.

28 'IBM Food Trust: A New Era for the World's Food Supply', https://perma.cc/9LME-ZAUX.

29 World Economic Forum, 'Inclusive Deployment of Blockchain: Case Studies and Learnings from the United Arab Emirates' (2020), https://perma.cc/8JKD-JFL3.

30 'Blockchain: Unveiling Its Potential for Customs and Trade', https://perma.cc/JUL8-NURR.

registration of traders and the digitisation of shipping and export documentation, including export authorisations and certificates of origin.[31]

The WTO has also studied the ramifications of DLT and blockchain, noting the ability of these technologies to improve transactional efficiencies and reduce administrative costs:

> The intrinsic characteristics of the technology also make it a potentially interesting tool to help implement the WTO Trade Facilitation Agreement (TFA) and to facilitate business-to-government (B2 G) and government-to-government (G2 G) processes at the national level. Blockchain and smart contracts could help administer border procedures and national single windows (a single point of entry through which trade stakeholders can submit documentation and other information to complete customs procedures) in a more efficient, transparent and secure manner, and improve the accuracy of trade data.[32]

While the WTO has invested considerable time in identifying how the object of its regulation will change – namely trade – it has not openly engaged in discussion on how it as an organisation might change or evolve as a result of DLT and blockchain. While the same report notes that a consignment of flowers from one continent to another generates a huge pile of paperwork that will one day be transformed by blockchain, the report does not talk about the WTO adapting its own processes to make trade regulation more efficient. Here too there is potential for the same technology to create seamless, automatised resolution of regulatory issues – including the identification, assessment, and evaluation of trade remedies of safeguards, countervailing duties and antidumping duties.

There is also an opportunity within the WTO to consider the automation and potential convergence of trade data to drive a new approach to rules negotiations, trade policy reviews, accession negotiations, and market access negotiations. Both data and documentation could be automatically generated from smart sensors, with information about customs valuation and product origin generated from data gathered along the supply chain and stored on the blockchain. At this point it becomes possible for government certification processes to take place automatically, with databases granting certifications using automatic decision making. For example, the components of a mobile phone will have been tracked as they enter the country of assembly, with the details of the supply chain being stored in a blockchain. The data trail can be combined with other data sources used to calculate the production cost of the product, a valuation for customs purposes, and used by an importing government to determine applicable tariffs and duties. 'Through [government] participation in the blockchain', Okazaki notes, 'customs would be able to collect the necessary data in an accurate and timely way (all data

[31] World Economic Forum, note 29 above, at 12.

[32] E Ganne, 'Can Blockchain Revolutionize International Trade?' (2018), https://perma.cc/H3JF-RSLL, at IX.

tied to the commodity like seller, buyer, price, quantity, carrier, finance, insurance, status and location of the commodity)'.[33]

III DATA-DRIVEN TRADE LAW ARCHITECTURE

As this chapter has explained, a data-driven world of trade is emerging, and emerging rapidly. Some impacts of these changes are clear, such as the changing nature of trade itself, intensification of the shift from trade in goods towards trade in services and intellectual property, and erosion of their definitional barriers, the need for data regulation that balances competing interests of rights and obligations, and new, complex questions about human rights and trade.[34] For the WTO, these changes necessitate rethinking substantive trade rules and the creation of new rules, advancing its work programme on e-commerce,[35] and working with other organisations such as the United Nations Commission on International Trade Law to ensure that suitable e-commerce regulations are in place. At the same time, states with a particular national interest in technology are advancing digital trade provisions on their own terms through bilateral and regional agreements.[36]

As indicated earlier, there is potential to use the same technologies that will transform trade and trade rules to transform the functions and operations of the WTO. At a time when many are critical of a lack of progress in multilateral trade fora, with some attributing aspects of the problem to the organisation and its mandate rather than the behaviour of its members, it becomes particularly important to consider what might be done better in an organisation.[37]

One part of the puzzle when exploring how the WTO might embrace the possibilities of transformative technologies is to consider where in the trade ecosystem key activities are taking place, and the challenge is how and on what terms an international organisation can engage. As the examples in this chapter have shown, projects such as Tradelens are driven by large, multinational corporations – in this case, IBM and Maersk – to create an open standard platform that has built a 'trade ecosystem', which in its own words is a 'global network of interconnected shipping corridors [that] will link ports and terminals, authorities, ocean carriers, inland

33 Y Okazaki, 'Unveiling the Potential of Blockchain for Customs' (2018) WCO Research Paper No. 45, at 3.

34 See, for example, H Gao, 'Google's China Problem: A Case Study on Trade, Technology and Human Rights under the GATS' (2011) 6 *Asian Journal of WTO and International Health Law and Policy* 347.

35 World Trade Organisation, 'Electronic Commerce', www.wto.org/english/tratop_e/ecom_e/ecom_e.htm. See also Henry Gao's Chapter 15 in this volume.

36 For comprehensive analysis of these agreements, see the TAPED Database, created by Mirra Burri and others: www.unilu.ch/en/faculties/faculty-of-law/professorships/managing-director-internationalisation/research/taped.

37 See, for example, the list presented in J Nakagawa and CB Picker, 'An Introduction to Utopian and Dystopian Post-WTO Regimes and Environments', in MK Lewis et al. (eds), *A Post-WTO International Legal Order: Utopian, Dystopian and Other Scenarios* (Cham, Springer, 2020), at 10.

transportation, 3pls, shippers, and other actors'.[38] While Tradelens already has government bodies as part of its ecosystem, it does not envisage an obvious role for the WTO. Similarly, Boston Consulting Group produced a comprehensive White Paper examining how 'data field interactions' could be optimised to harmonise the flow of information between participants in the trade process. Their mapping of 'players' included five different types of parties – corporates (importers and exporters); banks; facilitators such as insurers and freight forwarders; disruptors such as tech companies; and 'governing bodies', which they specify as including the importing and exporting customs services. This is a very telling 'lens' through which trade is analysed by the commercial sector – in addition to being transaction driven, international organisations do not feature strongly, let alone convey a clear sense of how the WTO fits in.[39] While they identify the importance of standards and interconnection protocols, there is no clear sense of the regulatory role that the WTO and the international community as a whole plays now and could play in future. This type of analysis shows the importance of enhanced effort by the WTO to be involved in these types of conversations, and to consider its own initiatives to generate global platforms.

Therefore, the remainder of this chapter takes up the challenge of considering how the WTO might reconfigure its management of trade, providing an audit of a range of areas in which change – some radical, some less radical – could allow the WTO to better facilitate future trade. Below are ten ideas to illustrate the range of potential changes that could be possible (again, reminding readers of the 'thought experiment' provisos set out in the introduction to this chapter).

1. Better negotiations – and fewer. The complexity of multilateral market access negotiations is due in part to the number of participants and the difficulty of modelling outcomes from different scenarios. AI is capable of producing sophisticated optimisation models to cross-reference market gains and suggest concessions that could be made by WTO members, modelling trade creation and trade deviation to optimise overall trade benefits.[40] Data could be more easily correlated from different private and public sector sources to enhance its reliability, and better model the distributional effects of proposed changes. As member acceptance of use of algorithms increases, it would be possible for members to agree in advance to be bound by algorithmic determinations of market access, and for these to be automatically generated

38 A Jorgensen, 'Tradelens' (27 November 2018), https://perma.cc/MSN6-E3VG.

39 'Digital Innovation in Trade Finance: Have We Reached a Tipping Point?' (2017), https://perma.cc/CYA4-PUYZ, at 9.

40 For example, a computable general equilibrium model is generally recognised to be the most effective methodology for modelling concessions in multiparty negotiations, but is also recognised to be expensive and very time consuming, and require large amounts of data, leading to choices of less satisfactory but less difficult models. See M Bacchetta et al., 'A Practical Guide to Trade Policy Analysis' (2012), https://perma.cc/P3HJ-ET4P, at 8–9.

under the auspices of the WTO with automatic entry into effect. This stands to benefit smaller and more vulnerable states who are negatively impacted by the politicisation of the process.

2. Better data on real-world compliance. The design of the WTO Dispute Settlement System requires a state to take on what is likely to be a grievance of one or more of its private corporate citizens. The political reality is that most failures to comply with WTO rules will not result in dispute unless the breach is substantial and systematic. However, this gives a very distorted picture of real levels of compliance with WTO law across the board – especially on applied tariff rates, quotas, sanitary and phytosanitary measures, and trade remedies. A data-driven trade organisation that is able to harness the 'big data' of international trade derived from business and government sources will gain a much richer picture of adherence to WTO rules, and the transparency will provide incentive for states to ensure more rigorous compliance.
3. Automatic, dynamic, real-time measures. Data will become available more quickly, with a higher level of verifiability and specificity, which has the ability to change how subsidies and safeguard mechanisms are applied and maintained, and provide granular data that can help determine appropriate balances between market protection and market access. This could allow 'real-time' changes to market access when certain conditions are met, and automatic calibration of volumes within agreed ranges, without the direct involvement of member states. Traders and WTO members would have instant, accurate information on subsidies and safeguard mechanisms in operation at any time.
4. More sophisticated technical assistance. Learning has long been a feature of the WTO's outreach activities, but more recently initiatives such as Tradelab have taken advantage of their digital platform to connect developing country governments and non-government organisations with pro-bono advice services offered primarily by trained law students.[41] Technology such as chatbots is already available, and could be used to semi-automate technical advice services to help provide support for developing country officials in locating and interpreting trade law obligations.
5. New outreach activities. The WTO has made an effort to extend its outreach activities to businesses, for example through its joint 'small business champions' programme with the International Chamber of Commerce,[42] the 'ePing' sanitary and phytosanitary and technical barriers to trade alert system,[43] and trader-focused information pages.[44] One of the great promises of technology is its potential to democratise law by narrowing the gap

[41] 'About TradeLab', https://perma.cc/AB4U-Q5RW.

[42] 'Small Business Champions Initiative', https://perma.cc/JL6A-CE6M.

[43] 'ePing', www.epingalert.org/en.

[44] 'The Trade Facilitation Agreement (TFA): What's It About?', https://perma.cc/C67G-MADJ.

between experts and non-experts, facilitating self-help by making knowledge more broadly accessible. This has been a prominent feature of domestic legal systems,[45] but the same logic applies to the international trade law environment as well. This can be made available globally and free, accessible via a mobile phone, and could help developing country exporters identify entry requirements for markets in which they wish to trade. End users could ask questions in natural language, and use question and answer formats to generate documentation to apply for permits and licences. This could reduce or eliminate the need for brokers in trade transactions, ensure better compliance, and generate efficiencies across the supply chain, as well as improving trader engagement with the WTO.

6. Replacement of notification bureaucracy. Notification processes have been a key area of capacity building for the WTO, which notes that the process is burdensome precisely because it is both necessary and important.[46] The notification system is still largely paper driven, with hundreds of notifications required.[47] For example, the Agreement on Import Licensing Procedures obliges members to notify the WTO on the source of import licensing procedures and to lodge copies of those procedures, provide updates, and complete a detailed annual questionnaire. However, there are numerous shortcomings with the current process – the system is slow to document changes, administratively burdensome on states,[48] and does almost nothing to communicate import licensing provisions to those that need to know – traders. WTO notification databases could be designed to dovetail with member governments' blockchain and e-government initiatives, such as those of Dubai, to make this information mostly accessible without the bureaucracy of notification.
7. Better management of contingent measures such as antidumping duties. Retaliatory antidumping is considered to be on the rise[49] and directly undermines the trade system. Disputes such as the zeroing cases further illustrate the challenges of bringing reluctant states into compliance.[50] Centralising

[45] In the domestic context, see L Toohey et al., 'Meeting the Access to Civil Justice Challenge: Digital Inclusion, Algorithmic Justice and Human-Centred Design' (2019) 19 *Macquarie Law Journal* 133.

[46] 'The importance attached by negotiators to this issue explains the very elaborate system of notifications and cross-notifications put in place under the terms of most Agreements. Notifications are a necessary burden, particularly for the administrations and governments of developing countries'. See 'Technical Assistance in Meeting Member's Notification Obligations', https://perma.cc/3HDN-EHKZ.

[47] See, for example, the extensive list in Annex 1 of the Decision on Notification Procedures.

[48] See also 'Technical Cooperation Handbook on Notification Requirements' (2019), https://perma.cc/R84T-PUXM.

[49] RM Feinberg and KM Reynolds, 'The Spread of Antidumping Regimes and the Role of Retaliation in Filings' (2006) 72 *Southern Economic Journal* 877.

[50] The most notable of the zeroing cases included: *United States – Final Dumping Determination on Softwood Lumber from Canada*, WT/DS264/AB/R (31 August 2004); *United States – Laws, Regulations and Methodology for Calculating Dumping Margins (Zeroing)*, WT/DS294/AB/R (18 April 2006); and

control of antidumping duties through the WTO would be feasible through the use of smart contracts and AI. Integrity, transparency, and monitoring could be greatly improved by using a WTO portal for states to initiate antidumping actions. Traders and government would have access to data, but the system would use automated or supported rendering of margin calculations. If data suggested that a product was being dumped in a foreign market, based on trade and sales data, antidumping duties could be automatically attached by use of an algorithm, and antidumping duties remitted to states as part of a fully integrated trade transaction.

8. Rethinking rules. One of the most exciting longer-term possibilities is to create trade measures that can be self-executing in the sense that they do not rely on states to apply or rescind them. For example, the WTO's technology systems would have the capacity to monitor trade flows, prices, and other relevant data, and automatically activate safeguards such as import restrictions based on algorithms, for precisely the duration required to mitigate serious injury. Sunset clauses would operate automatically, and data would be collated from data from the government and private sector.
9. Enhanced support for integrity, human rights, and sustainability. Sustainability data and other credentials can be attached to the blockchain providing information about a product or service, facilitating the communication of this information to consumers, allowing the management of pollution/carbon tax and credit schemes, and helping to minimise tax avoidance and financial fraud. Trade-based money laundering is a greatly increasing category of sophisticated financial crimes that uses physical shipments to launder money, disguising and moving the proceeds of crime on the pretence of legitimate trade in goods. It is considered one of the most difficult to identify, as it relies on techniques such as falsifying the invoiced value of goods, misrepresentation of the nature of goods or services, or misrepresented financial transactions.[51] While consumer demand and government interest may see these schemes evolve from the private sector, the WTO could take the lead or engage in a partnership to roll out a global programme.
10. Small claims arbitration. Online filing and dispute resolution platforms have become an expected part of the justice landscape. It is increasingly commonplace to see the use of AI as part of document management and document review, and supported decision-making tools have been deployed, frequently controversially and poorly, to help judges assess complex phenomena such as the chance of recidivism.[52] The trade law environment contains a particularly

United States – Continued Existence and Application of Zeroing Methodology, WT/DS350/AB/R (4 February 2009).

[51] See S McSkimming, 'Trade-Based Money Laundering: Responding to an Emerging Threat' (2010) 15 (1) *Deakin Law Review* 37.

[52] For discussion of the problematic nature of some algorithms, see Toohey et al., note 45 above.

large number of data-intensive decisions that lend themselves to supported decision-making technology. Certain types of disputes take 'airtime' but involve largely transactional parts of trade that currently take up a lot of time, resources, and political goodwill. With tariffs, antidumping, subsidies, safeguards, rules of origin, and customs valuation largely automated, and with the possibility of significantly streamlining the identification of some breaches of most favoured nation, sanitary and phytosanitary, and technical barriers to trade obligations, we may be able to devote remaining energies to the truly complex issues of the interaction between trade and human concerns such as human rights, public health, and sustainability. As technology advances, a small claims arbitration jurisdiction could be created to offer traders a single portal for resolution of these issues. Notwithstanding the significant challenges of creating algorithms that are transparent and just,[53] arbitration could be undertaken by AI or by human arbitrators supported with smart databases.

IV CONCLUSION

It may seem like fanciful thinking to imagine a world in which all parties and stakeholders in an international transaction – traders, exporting government, importing government, and international organisations – automatically collate, verify, and apply relevant trade laws to a transaction without the need for much human intervention. However, the foundations for such a system already exist and are evolving rapidly. This chapter has sought to come to terms with the dramatic changes to trade presented by technology – to trade itself, to trade transactions, to trade rules, and to a reconceptualised role for an international trade organisation.

It is worth emphasising what was stated at the outset – that the challenges of equity and political engagement are real, and may seem insurmountable. To translate these ideas into reality would require political willpower that surely seems unrealistic at this time. However, given the speed with which private enterprise is creating platforms, change may come sooner than we expect, with governments able to see the advantages of efficiency that integrated systems can bring. In that sense, change is imminent regardless of the preferences of WTO members or the organisation itself.

Technology of the type outlined in this chapter presents a fork in the road for the WTO (or a future trade organisation) by recalibrating its relationship with member states and the types of action perceived by states as part of their sovereignty – such as the calculation of antidumping duties. It also has the potential to recalibrate the

53 See ME Kaminski, 'Understanding Transparency in Algorithmic Accountability', in W Barfield (ed.), *Cambridge Handbook of the Law of Algorithms* (Cambridge, Cambridge University Press, 2020), at 121–138.

relationship of individuals with international law by offering more direct mechanisms for engagement and dispute resolution.

At the same time, much work is needed to better understand the range of technological changes that are possible, and to build nuanced and considered responses. This chapter has sought to provide a modest contribution to that effort.